MICHIGAN'S GERMAN HERITAGE

John Andrew Russell's

HISTORY
of the
GERMAN INFLUENCE
in the
MAKING OF MICHIGAN

Edited by *Don Heinrich Tolzmann*

HERITAGE BOOKS
2011

HERITAGE BOOKS
AN IMPRINT OF HERITAGE BOOKS, INC.

Books, CDs, and more—Worldwide

For our listing of thousands of titles see our website
at
www.HeritageBooks.com

A Facsimile Reprint
Published 2011 by
HERITAGE BOOKS, INC.
Publishing Division
100 Railroad Ave. #104
Westminster, Maryland 21157

Copyright © 1994 Don Heinrich Tolzmann

— Publisher's Notice —
In reprints such as this, it is often not possible to remove blemishes from the original. We feel the contents of this book warrant its reissue despite these blemishes and hope you will agree and read it with pleasure.

International Standard Book Numbers
Paperbound: 978-0-7884-0153-4
Clothbound: 978-0-7884-8976-1

Preface

Today, German-Americans in Michigan amount to 29%, or 2.7 million of the state's total population of 9.2 million, according to the 1990 U.S. Census, thereby making it the largest ethnic group there. (1)

Clearly, such a large group has impacted on all aspects of life in Michigan, and it would be difficult to imagine what the state would be like without the important ingredient of the German element. (2) In every field of human endeavor, a major role has been played by German-Americans.

It is no understatement, but rather a simple fact, that if you do not understand the role German-Americans have played in the history and development of Michigan, then you cannot and will never understand the state. (3) Another way to put it, is that any history which does not include, or provide adequate coverage of one-third of the state's population, is clearly incorrect and incomplete.

The fact that German-Americans have been, however, largely excluded and ignored for much of the twentieth century is a direct result of the anti-

German hysteria of the two world wars, which obscured the role German-Americans have played in American history. (4) Only since the celebration of the American Bicentennial in 1976 has there been an upswing of interest in according German-Americans their appropriate place in the annals of American history. (5)

Russell's history, originally published in 1927, provides a comprehensive survey of Michigan's German heritage. (6) It contain a great deal of local and county history, as well as biographical and institutional history. It also contains valuable bibliographical references for the study of the German element of Michigan, which will be of use for further research in the area. (7)

Since the first publication of this volume in 1927, much has transpired in German-American history, however, this work should provide the basic foundation for any study and research dealing with Michigan's German heritage.

Notes

1. See U.S. Bureau of the Census, **1990 Census of Population Supplementary Reports: Detailed Ancestry for States.** (Washington, D.C.: Government Printing Office, 1992).

2. For a general survey of German-American history, see LaVern J. Rippley, **The German-Americans.** (Boston: Twayne, 1976). For a recent briefer survey, see Willi Paul Adams, **The German-Americans: An Ethnic Experience.** Translated and Adapted by LaVern J. Rippley and Eberhard Reichmann. (Indianapolis: Max Kade German-American Center, Indiana University-Purdue University at Indianapolis, 1993).

3. For an overview of German-American historical writing, see Don Heinrich Tolzmann, "German-American Studies, 1492-1992 and Beyond," in: Don Heinrich Tolzmann, ed., **Germany and America, 1450-1700: Julius Friedrich Sachse's History of the German Role in the Discovery, Exploration, and Settlement of the New World.** (Bowie, MD: Heritage Books, Inc., 1991), pp. 16-28.

4. Regarding the Anti-German Hysteria, see Frederick Luebke, **Bonds of Loyalty: German-**

Americans and World War I. (DeKalb, Ill.: Northern Illinois University Pr., 1974).

5. For a survey of recent German-American history, see Don Heinrich Tolzmann, German-Americana: Selected Essays. (forthcoming volume).

6. Russell's volume appeared under the following title: The Germanic Influence in the Making of Michigan. (Detroit: Universit of Detroit, 1927).

7. For further references to works dealing with Michigan German-American history, see Don Heinrich Tolzmann, German-Americana: A Bibliography. (Metuchen, NJ: Scarecrow Pr., 1975), pp 41-42; Don Heinrich Tolzmann, Catalog of the German-Americana Collection, University of Cincinnati. (München: Saur, 1990), Vol. 1, pp. 275-76; Arthur R. Schultz, German-American Relations and German Culture in America: A Subject Bibliography, 1941-1980. (Millwood, NY: Kraus, 1984), pp. 886-889; and Karl J.R. Arndt, The German Language Press of the Americas: Volume I: History and Bibliography, 1732-1968: United States of America. (München: Verlag Dokumentation, 1976), pp. 209-220.

FOREWORD

This piece of writing has no high purpose, in the sense in which that term is interpreted by people who conceive that all their acts shall be inspired by very great motives.

It is rather a modest contribution to community good nature and understanding, the making of which has grown out of the writer's observations of an unhappy state of mind existing among many friends of a life-time who are fellow-citizens of his own state.

The World War left many wrong impressions. Not the least of these was that new, and in some cases unamiable relationships, had been established, as one of its results, between some elements of our composite population, which had done their full share toward the national upbuilding, and other groups and classes who had made similar contributions.

One of these elements is the German-American population which, though it had no responsibility for initiating the conflict now happily ended, gives evidence, from time to time, of a state of embarrassment based on a mistaken belief that their own and their ancestor's shares in the making of the American Republic and its states are unappreciated.

These contributions, in the case of the group in question, have been very great. Many of them are practically unknown to the members of the group themselves, because they have been rendered by very modest people, in some cases; or outside the better known activities of some others; or in special fields, again; or in times which are now so remote that they have become a part of history, rather than the more striking of the yesterdays.

In no part of the United States have these influences for goodness, culture and progress been more important than in Michigan. This study of them has been confined to that state, largely because its boundaries are the limit of the writer's knowledge on most subjects; and largely, too, because the deeds wrought by German-Americans in Michigan make enough of a text for one writing. If the recollection of these deeds and transactions should prove interesting as to Michigan, that fact may become an incentive to other students to uncover and publish the details of similar activities of the same group in other American sovereignties. In truth, there are plenty of them for separate treatment.

So, this book is deliberately planned to be almost provincial in its scope, and to be "cozy", rather than consequential or important. Incidentally, its writer has no blood-brotherhood with those whom he discusses; but he is none the less appreciative of their contributions to the greatness of the state of which he is an inheritor in common.

That is why "The Germanic Influence in the Making of Michigan" came to be written. Perhaps it may serve its very humble purpose of making some people feel proud of themselves and their ancestors for their part in the common work, and their neighbors surprised that they can claim so much.

The writer owes his obligations to his friends, Mr. Lewis E. Rowley, of Lansing, Mr. Henry A. I. Andries and Mr. Carl E. Schmidt, of Detroit, for verifications of his memories on some points, and the procurement of more exact information on many others.

J. A. R.

Detroit, March, 1927.

CONTENTS

FOREWORD

CHAPTER I.   THE EARLY GERMAN SETTLE-
MENTS IN AMERICA   17
Some Early Arrivals—The Settlement of Germantown—Furore for Emigration—The New York Settlement—Rough Doings about Land—The Pennsylvania Settlement—The New Jersey Settlement—Maryland and Virginia—The Carolinas and Georgia—Germans in New England—Basis of the Foundations—Distribution of the Early Comers.

CHAPTER II   THE COLONIAL PERIOD OF THE NORTHWEST   32
The Causes of the Various Migrations—A German Governor of Canada—A German Military Commander—The Period of Henri Bouquet—An Early-Day Social Event—The Cost of British Possessions—Haldimand's Solicitude About Rum—The Two Schiffleins—An Ancient Land Scandal—Other Germans of the Period.

CHAPTER III THE POST COLONIAL PERIOD   49
The First Germans in Michigan—Some Important Land-Holdings—The Earliest Post-Colonial Immigrants.

CHAPTER IV   THE STATE'S INVITATION TO IMMIGRANTS   56
The "Auswanderer Wegweiser"—The Prices of Land—The Period of Achievement.

CHAPTER V   THE GROWTH OF THE GERMANIC POPULATION OF MICHIGAN   61
The Territorial Origins—Twentieth Century Changes.

v

CHAPTER VI	THE EARLY "AUSWANDERER." The Unimpressive Beginnings — The Processes of Distribution — Organization of the Scott Guard.	66
CHAPTER VII	VARIOUS COUNTY SETTLEMENTS. The Washtenaw Germans—The Wayne County Settlers—German-Americans from the East — The Southern Michigan Settlement — The Settlement in Genesee — The Settlement in Allegan—The Oakland County Pioneers — The Shiawassee Pioneers — The Oakland County Beginnings — The Pioneers of Macomb — Some Early Land-holders — The Settlers in St. Clair.	72
CHAPTER VIII	THE SETTLERS OF WASHTENAW AND SAGINAW. The Beginnings at Ann Arbor—The Pioneers of Saginaw and Bay—Settlements in Other Counties—Upper Peninsula Pioneers.	89
CHAPTER IX	THE DEFENSE OF TERRITORY, STATE AND NATION No Race Delinquent—The Revolutionary and Pioneer Period—Revolutionary Heroes of the Blood-The War of 1812—The Black Hawk War—The Mexican War.	98
CHAPTER X	THE CIVIL WAR General Poe's Commendation of Colonel Schneider — The Sixth Michigan Volunteers — Mexican War Veterans' Return to Service — German-Americans in Every Regiment — General George Alexander Custer — The Compliment of a Loser — Colonel Michael Shoemaker — Some Striking Instances.	110
CHAPTER XI	THE WAR WITH SPAIN The Beginnings of an Adjutant-General—A Soldier Who Became a Mayor—The Thirty-Third Michigan — The Thirty-Fourth Michigan — The Thirty-Fifth Michigan — The Roster of the Dead.	122
CHAPTER XII	THE WORLD WAR National Basis of Recruiting—General Crowder's Compliment — Percentage of German-American Recruits.	135

CHAPTER XIII	THE ACKNOWLEDGEMENTS OF BRAVERY 　　The Congressional Medal of Honor — The Distinguished Service Cross — The French Cross of War.	142
CHAPTER XIV	THE CONTRIBUTIONS TO LEARNING	148
CHAPTER XV	THE UNIVERSITY OF MICHIGAN 　　The Early Regents—Faculty Members of German Training—American Teachers—A Contribution to Agriculture—Group of German-Trained Americans—A Great Professor of Law — The Originator of Ward Instruction—The Pioneer in Forestry — Sons of Carlsruhe, Munich and Leipsig — Men from Bonn, Strasburg and Berlin — A German Authority on Old English—A Group of German-Named Professors.	151
CHAPTER XVI	THE MICHIGAN AGRICULTURAL COLLEGE 　　Notable Accession of German Names.	169
CHAPTER XVII	THE MICHIGAN SCHOOL OF MINES 　　A Great Teacher of Chemistry.	173
CHAPTER XVIII	THE UNIVERSITY OF DETROIT 　　Four German-American Pioneer Teachers—A Group of Peripatetic Teachers.	175
CHAPTER XIX	THE DENOMINATIONAL COLLEGES	180
CHAPTER XX	CONTRIBUTIONS TO PRIMARY AND SECONDARY EDUCATION 　　English Taught from the Start—Teaching before School-Houses—The Lutheran and Catholic Teachers—The Christian Brothers—Modest Pioneer Pedagogues — Scholars of High Standing—Communities of Teaching Sisters.	182
CHAPTER XXI	THE GERMAN-AMERICAN SEMINARY	192

| CHAPTER XXII | THE CONTRIBUTIONS TO SCIENCE | 196 |

Indian Etymology and Grammar —The Compiler of the Geological Survey — The Work of Raphael Pumpelly—The Developer of the Copper Mines—The Work of General Weitzel — A Coterie of Geniuses — The Father of Reforestration—The Founder of Detroit Observatory—A Great Naval Astronomer—Colonel Shoemaker's Collection of Maps—A German Map-Maker of 1720—Charles Frederick Wappenhans.

| CHAPTER XXIII | THE CONTRIBUTIONS TO ART | 213 |

The Religious Paintings—The Public Collections — The German-American Painters— German-American Sculpture — Julius Theodore Melchers—Famous Artist Sons of Michigan.

| CHAPTER XXIV | THE CONTRIBUTIONS TO MUSIC | 223 |

The First Formal Concert—The Advent of Wilhelm Yunck—The Little German Bands—The German-Trained Music Masters.

| CHAPTER XXV | FAECKEL - TRAEGER | 230 |

The Bearers of the Lights—Distribution of Michigan German Scholars — Two Famous Engineers.

| CHAPTER XXVI | THE RELIGIOUS LEADERS | 237 |

The Catholic Dioceses—Pioneer Catholic Missionaries.

| CHAPTER XXVII | PASTOR LOEHE, OF NEUEDETTELSAU | 243 |

The Foresight of Pastor Schmid—Antedated the '48 Movement —Other German Protestant Pastors—The Early Jewish Rabbinate.

| CHAPTER XXVIII | THE FIELD OF BENEVOLENCE | 253 |

The Deaf-Mute Institute.

| CHAPTER XXIX | THE PROFESSION OF MEDICINE | 257 |

Dr. Anthon's Service at Detroit — Dr. Herman Melchior Eberts — Other Pioneer Physicians — The First Operator for Strabismus — Dr. Peter Klein — Dr. Herman Kiefer — Dr. Brumme and Dr. Carstens — Dr. Edward Dorsch — Dr. Michael

	Carl Theodore Plessner — Dr. John Flinterman and Dr. Spranger — The Discoverer of Podophyllin—The Early Work Horse Doctors — Pioneer Work.	
CHAPTER XXX	THE PROFESSION OF LAW George Morell — The Abels — John Van Armin — Otto Kirchner — Franz Christian Kuhn — Edwin F. Uhl — Early German-American Advocates.	275
CHAPTER XXXI	THE PROFESSION OF ENGINEERING The Early Surveyors — A Descendant of Muhlenburg — A Developer of Hydro-Electric Power.	281
CHAPTER XXXII	THE PROFESSION OF ARCHITECTURE William Himpel — Frederick Spier and William C. Rohns — Albert Kahn — Louis Kamper — Emil Lorch.	286
CHAPTER XXXIII	THE PROFESSION OF JOURNALISM Carl Schurz — Robert Reitzel — The German Language Press — August Marxhausen — Engelbert Andries.	291
CHAPTER XXXIV	THE CONTRIBUTIONS TO COMMERCE AND INDUSTRY John Jacob Astor — Importance of His Business — A Group of Mid-Century Business Men — Colonel Frank J. Hecker — German Adaptability to Industry — Many Industrial Pioneers — Up-State Industrial Founders — The Development of New Industries — Adventures in Scientific Industry — Western Michigan Industrial Pioneers — Beginners of Motor Industry.	300
CHAPTER XXXV	PARTICIPATIONS IN BANKING The Savings Bank Founders — The Career of Edward Kanter—Other German-American Bankers.	318
CHAPTER XXXVI	THE DEVELOPMENT OF NATURAL RESOURCES Germans Who Prospered in Mining — The First Copper Mill.	322

CHAPTER XXXVII	THE GERMAN-JEWISH BUSINESS MEN	328
	The Brothers Rothschild — The Brothers Butzel — Emil Solomon Heineman — Simon Heavenrich — Julius Houseman — Louis Blitz — Jacob Seligman — The Brothers Schloss — The Jewish Pack-Peddlers.	
CHAPTER XXXVIII	EXPERIMENTS IN COMMUNITY LIFE	336
	The Frankenmuth Colony — Community Virtues — Some Other Communities — Dr. Schetterly's Experiment — "King" James J. Strang.	
CHAPTER XXXIX	PERSISTENCE IN INDUSTRIES AND PROFESSIONS	343
CHAPTER XL	GERMANIC NAMES IN OFFICIAL LIFE	347
	State Officials of German Lineage — Regents of the University — German-American Senators — German-American Representatives — Representation in the Electoral College — Representation in Congress.	
CHAPTER XLI	THE GEOGRAPHICAL IMPRESS OF THE RACES	358
	Beginnings of Modern Place Names — The Impress of German Settlement.	
CHAPTER XLII	SOME "FIRST" PEOPLE AND THINGS	362
	EPILOGUE	365
	BIBLIOGRAPHY	367
APPENDIX A	THE GERMAN-AMERICAN OFFICERS OF THE CIVIL WAR	375
APPENDIX B	THE GERMAN-AMERICAN DEAD OF THE WORLD WAR	393

THE GERMANIC INFLUENCE
IN
THE MAKING OF MICHIGAN

THE GERMANIC INFLUENCE
IN
THE MAKING OF MICHIGAN

CHAPTER I
THE FIRST GERMAN SETTLEMENTS IN AMERICA

Some Early Arrivals—The Settlement of Germantown—Furore for Emigration—The New York Settlement—Rough Doings about Land —The Pennsylvania Settlement—The New Jersey Settlement—Maryland and Virginia—The Carolinas and Georgia—Germans in New England—Basis of the Foundations — Distribution of the Early Comers.

Without indulgence in intensive detail, it is worth recording that the Germanic race had an important part in the early settlement of the territory that later came under the dominion of the United States. Professor Albert Bernhard Faust, of Cornell University, in his monumental work on "The German Element in the United States", claims that Martin Behaim, a native of Nueremburg, who has some shadowy claim to having seen the coasts of Brazil before Columbus discovered America, was at least an eminent cosmographer, a maker of globes and a personal friend of Columbus and Magellan. Martin Waldseemueller, who was a Catholic Canon of Freisburg from 1480 onward, suggested the naming of the new continent after Vespuccius in his "Carta Marina" of 1516.

It is claimed that there were Germans in the Alsatian and Hessian Protestant groups who were in the Huguenot settlement of Port Royal, South Carolina, in 1562; as there were some others in the settlement of Jamestown in Virginia, in 1607, where such names as Unger, Keffer and Switzar were current in the earliest days.

The first Governor of New Netherland, Peter Minnuet, or Minnewit, was a native of Wessel, in the Rhineland, and Jacob Leisler, the first popular Governor of New York, was a native of Frankfort-on-Main, who came to New York in 1660. Leisler had some strong principles of liberty in his make-up. He was a "No-Popery" man in his day, and when fined by Gov. Andros for participation in the movement, he went to prison rather than pay a fine. He had a stormy career as Governor, led a revolution, and wound up on the scaffold in 1691, his heirs being attainted; a judgment which was later reversed by the English law lords, with a sort of apology to Leisler's memory for his unjust condemnation and execution, a purely formal proceeding which did not alter the facts for poor Leisler.

The Swedish colonial promotion on the banks of the Delaware of 1638, had as Governor from 1642 to 1653, John Printy von Buchan, a German soldier-adventurer who was with Gustavus Adolphus in the Thirty Years War.

Some Early Arrivals

Dr. Hans Kierstede, a Magdeburger, was a practicing physician in New Amsterdam in 1638, and married a daughter of Anneke Jans, the owner of the famous Manhattan Island farm that has kept, until the present day, a host of supposed heirs under contribution to the lawyers in attempts to recover their title.

John Lederer explored Virginia and North and South

Carolina in 1669-79, writing out the story of his travels in Latin.

A Wurtemburger named Heinz was the first German in Texas, according to Father Hennepin, being a member of La Salle's expedition.

Religious refugees from the Palatinate, who settled at Germantown, in Pennsylvania in 1683, were to a large extent directed by Francis Daniel Pastorius, of Frankfort-on-Main, who organized and held one share in the Frankfort Company, which bought 25,000 acres from William Penn for 500 English pounds, shares of 5,000 acres each being also taken by Jacob Van de Walle, Kasper Merian, William Neberfeldt and Daniel Behagel, all of Frankfort.

A group from Kriegsheim bought 18,000 acres more from William Penn, and settled it with families bearing such characteristic names as Arets, Kunders, Tisen, Luchen and Schumacher. The Germantown pioneers had among them people of the names of Wertmuller, Dilbeck, Backer and Schumacher.

The Settlement of Germantown

Pastorius was the first burgomaster of Germantown. He devised a court seal, with the motto "Vinum, Linum et Textrinum", which he himself turned into German as "Der Wein, der Lein und der Webeschein," or, in effect, Vine-growing, Flax-culture and Weaving. He made an ordinance against undue indulgence, limiting his burghers to a gill of rum and a quart of beer a day, being not quite a prohibitionist nor yet a friend of excess. His authority was superseded in 1700 by that of Falckner, Keplius and Jawert. Keplius was a mystic, who believed in bodily transfiguration into heaven, as did his contemporaries, Koster, Falckner, Seelig and Matthai. They were all disappointed in their religious expectations, dying normally in their beds like the good gentlemen that they were, and being laid away by their posterity.

The Germantown settlement and its neighbors were augmented by the wars and by the activities of the ship-owners who then had, as in later days, their agents seeking passengers to the New World. They published in Europe glowing descriptions of the possibilities of life in the Carolinas and Pennsylvania to increase the volume of American-bound travel.

A Furore for Emigration

There was a furore for emigration to America in that day, leading to counter-propaganda in the old country. There were many hardships of the sea. The migration was promoted by greedy ship-owners and masters, eager for the profits to be derived from the emigrants whom their agents excited to go across seas from Germany and other European countries. The temptation of the sailing masters to overload their ships and oppress their passengers was based upon the speculative character of the traffic. People with short funds were induced to make the American adventure, and to pay for their passages were sold into service by the masters on their arrival in the New World for varying periods. For, strange as it may seem, there was need of agricultural labor in America in that day.

There were tremendous mortalities on the trips. Gottleib Mittelberger tells of a shipload of 340 emigrants, who were battered by the storms off the coast of Ireland, starved and wrecked, so that only 21 of them arrived at Philadelphia; while Pastor Kunze tells of "a ship bearing 1,500 Germans, of whom 1,100 died at sea." The capacity of the sailing vessels of the period makes one doubt the accuracy of these figures, but the situation was probably bad enough.

With all the hardships enough survived to make the beginning of a great racial strain which had its influence in the making of the North American colonies and the later American Republic. Even the system of sale into virtual slavery for periods of from one to five years was turned into economic account. Those who had no funds on embarkation could have come over no other way. Many of those who had means carefully concealed the fact, accepted sales into service for their passage money, took advantage of the servitude to learn the language, customs and agricultural methods of the country, and upon the expiration of their periods of redemption, so-called, invested their secreted funds in land.

The New York Settlement

In 1708, through the encouragement of Queen Anne, of England, Joshua von Kocherthal, of Frankfort-on-Main, led an emigration to America, by way of England. His group had in it names like Faber, Gulch, Weigand, Webber, Plettel, Lorenz, Volk and Schuneman, the owners of which were young and middle-aged tradesmen. They were first naturalized as English subjects and then sent out to New York, where they made their settlement on the Hudson and named it Newburg, which is its name yet. The territory surrounding Newburg was generally described as the "German Patent."

The great pioneer German immigration to America occurred in 1709 and 1710. Religious and political persecution was rife in the Palatinate and thousand of natives of this territory made their way through Rotterdam to England. There were 13,000 of them in London as the winter of 1709 approached, most of them dependent upon charity. They made a problem for the Lords of Trade, who solved it mathematically.

A tenth of them, being Catholics, were shipped back home. Five hundred were peddled out to the employment of the Bedford fishermen, who then controlled the Newfoundland fisheries. Thirty-five hundred more were planted in Munster, in Ireland, where they intermarried with the Irish and became "Hibernis Hibernior ipsis." Of the remainder 600 were sent to the Carolinas under Graffenried and

Michel, who were from Berne, in Switzerland, and who founded New Berne in what is modern North Carolina. The pick and flower of them, some 4,000, were reserved for the colony of New York. They sailed from England late in 1709, in ten ships, crowded like cattle, with the new Governor of the Colony, Robert Hunter, as their official chaperon. Hunter says that 1,700 of the 4,000 died at sea of ship fever, or after their arrival on what is now Governor's Island. One ship, the Herbert, was lost off Long Island.

Hunter had a scheme to plant them "up-state" in New York, as would be said nowadays, sending them to the pine woods, to produce tar and turpentine for the British navy, and save its sovereign owners the indignity of having to buy these supplies from the Russians and Swedes. The scheme didn't turn out well, partly because the Governor did not know much about such enterprises, partly because the Palatine immigrants were unskilled at the work, and partly because there were disputes about the land titles.

One thing led to another, the immigrants dispersing themselves through the valleys of the Mohawk and Schoharie rivers, and founding their villages of Rhinebeck, Germantown, Mittleburg, Hartmansdorff, Brunnendorff, Gerlachsdorff, Kneiskerndorff, Weisersdorff and others of similar designations. Though many of the foundation names have passed away, there are yet, in the valleys of the Schoharie and the Mohawk, Middleburg, the Bernes — New, East, West and South, — New Poltz, Rhinebeck, Sloatsburg, New Blenheim, Lawyersville, — Anglicized from Lauersville — and plenty of other places whose names betoken the race of their founders.

Rough Doings About Land

There were rough doings about the occupancy of land in that day and place, as in every early settlement, and battles royal against them who tried to put the sturdy Pala-

tines off the lands whose titles began with purchases from
Indians, Gov. Hunter's permits and other colors of titles of
more or less distinctness. Sheriff Adams, of Albany, came to
their territory once to put some of them off lands claimed
by the Seven Partners of Albany — to whom Hunter had
given some form of title — but the Sheriff went home minus
an eye and with two cracked ribs, part of his homeward
journey being astride a rail, his palanquin-bearers being the
women of the colony.

It was rough going in those days for the Germans of
the Schoharie and Mohawk valleys, as it probably was for
everybody else in those times under the best of conditions;
but the Palatine colony reduced the lands to cultivation, and
their progeny scattered over Eastern New York, producing
many a good man and woman for the colony and the state
later established. Among them was John Peter Zenger, who
made the first legal battle for the liberty of the press in
America in 1735, the judgment in his case becoming a prece-
dent for the English Parliament when, in 1792, it framed the
Fox Libel Act for Great Britain. William C. Borick, a descendant of these settlers, was Governor of New York from
1843 to 1845.

The Pennsylvania Settlement

From 1710 to 1727 some 8,000 Germans entered the port
of Philadelphia each year. Mennonites from the German
cantons bought 10,000 acres in present Lancaster County,
and got along well with the Quakers, whose religious beliefs
were similar to their own, and with the Indians, who were
encumbered with no religious beliefs at all. Then nearly
all the Dunkards there were in Germany came from Westphalia to Berks County. The Schwenkfelders, who were a
Silesian sect, settled in Montgomery County. As time passed
the Lutherans, Reformed and Moravian, came to swell
the German population of Pennsylvania, developing outstanding leaders such as Heinrich Muhlenberg, Michael Schlat-

ter, Zinzendorff, and Spangenberg. Not many Catholics were in these immigrations. Out of 65,000 Germans in Pennsylvania in 1760, there were but 900 Catholics, most of them at Philadelphia, Lancaster and Goshenhoppen. By the time of the Revolution there were nearly 90,000 of the race in Pennsylvania, nearly all farmers, the remainder the servitors of an agricultural population.

The Settlement in New Jersey

The Atlantic coast was America in those days. Naturally settlements established in Pennsylvania and New York grew along the seaboard. This was true of those of the Germans no less than of the other races then inhabiting the present territory of the United States. They were in New Jersey as early as 1707, settled in what is now Morris County, spread into Somerset, Bergen and Essex Counties, recorded their baptisms as early as 1710, and by 1762 had more then 300 family names set down in church records which have survived.

These Jersey Germans bred a good race. When the revolution came about Pastor Gilbert Ammeling, of Amwell, sold all his property and loaned the five thousand pounds which he received for it to the Continental Congress. He lost the receipt and never got it back. The British Government did him the honor of putting a price on his head during the Revolution. Gen. Frederick Frelinghuysen, Revolutionary soldier, member of the Continental Congress and of the Convention of 1787, was a grandson of Reverend Theodore J. Frelinghuysen, born at Lingen, in East Friesland. Johann Peter Rockefeller, who "came from Germany about 1733 and died in 1793," was an ancestor of John D. Rockefeller, of Standard Oil fame, who had the quotation just given inscribed on a monument which he erected near Flemington, in 1906, on ground which his ancestor had dedicated as a grave yard. Pastor Caspar Wack, of Morris county, who lived through the Revolution, survived that conflict long enough to become the chaplain of an American regiment in the war of 1812. Moravians settled at Hope, in Warren county.

Muhlenburg, the Pennsylvania patriot, one Sunday at the beginning of the Revolution started his sermon in his clerical gown, preached fervent religion from his text for a while, then drifted into patriotism, and with the exclamation, "As there is a time to pray, so, too, there is a time to fight," threw off his pastor's attire and revealed himself clothed in the uniform of an American officer. He gave as good an account of himself in the pursuits of war as he had in the ways of peace.

Settlements in Maryland and Virginia

Cornelius Comegys and August Herman were in Maryland in 1660. Martin Faulkner settled a farm in Anne Arundel county in 1680. In 1730 D. Barnetz established Baltimore's first brewery, and in 1759 Andrew Steiger was the city's first public meat dealer. The first board of aldermen of Baltimore, on its incorporation as a city in 1796, had Engelhardt Yeiser, Peter Hoffman and George Lendenberger as three of its seven members. Washington's purchasing agent in the Revolution, Jacob Kuhlbord, was a Baltimore German, and Veit, a Baltimore merchant, was the host of the Continental Congress when it fled from Philadelphia to the Maryland metropolis. The Congress continued its sessions, interrupted at Philadelphia, in Veit's hall at Baltimore.

Weekhart Liebering, whose family name became Anglicised into Levering, lived to be 109, had great-grand children who were in the Revolution, and a descendant, Joshua Levering, who was the candidate of the Prohibitionists for President in 1896. The ancestors of President Mayer, of the Baltimore & Ohio Railroad, came over from Wurtemburg in 1752. John Frederick Amelung, from Bremen, established a glass factory near Frederick, made the first hollow glassware in America, devised decanters, punch-bowls and glasses, presented "two capacious goblets" to General Washington, and his factory was referred to by the first President in his correspondence with Mr. Jefferson.

Virginia German settlements began in 1714 with 12 families. They were Westphalian iron-workers, from Muesen and nearby places in the old country, and made charcoal iron for Governor Spottiswoode. Many more groups of people from the old country followed these, settling lands sold them by the earlier owners of great tracts, or by their compatriots who had purchased portions of the original grants and were thrifty enough to make an honest dollar by reselling them to the new arrivals of their race.

Robert Harper, said to have been German born, founded Harper's Ferry. Henry Kagey, Dunker minister, of New Market, a Swiss German, had a great-grand-son, John Henry Kagi, who was John Brown's secretary of war. Bishop Spanggenburg, of the United Brethren, in 1748, preached in both German and English as far inland as the present territory of West Virginia. The Germans of Virginia went into the uplands because they could own and till their own lands. This procedure kept them apart from slaves and slavery. They liked neither.

Settlements in the Carolinas and Georgia

The first settlement of the Carolinas, in 1710, was a land speculation. Baron Christ Graffenried, of Bern, a Swiss, had a partnership with Louis Michel, another Swiss, in the acquisition of a hundred thousand acres at a ha'penny an acre and sixpence a year rental per hundred acres. They brought out six hundred and fifty Palatines, and sold them the lands. Part of the settlers were the victims of an Indian massacre in their second year of residence, and all of them were cheated out of their titles by the two land-jobbers, whose creditors took their property. This didn't discourage more Germans from coming to the Carolinas. A few had settled James Island in Charleston Harbor in 1674, and a second migration of Salzburgers came in 1734. On the Savannah River John Peter

IN THE MAKING OF MICHIGAN 27

Purry, from Neufchatel, had been operating a colonization scheme since 1731. The British Government paid him 400 pounds sterling for every group of 100 able-bodied colonists he delivered on the Carolina plantations. He grew rich on the traffic. Queen Anne's government allotted a district 100 miles west of Charleston to German immigrants. It was named Saxe-Gotha. Actually it was settled by Rhinelanders and Wurtemburgers. Charleston became a centre for distributing Germans through the South.

Strangely, it was not Carolina Germans who colonized Georgia, the neighbor colony. There was a good deal of real estate operating in those days, even as there is now; though with this difference, that the land was much cheaper than it is today. The English Kings usually set up their gentlemen friends with a charter to colonize in America, sometimes with a partnership in the new venture for their Majesties, sometimes in requital of old domestic debts, often with both considerations. Their Majesties were gay gentlemen, and it cost them a good deal to live, so that they were not averse to turning a profit of any sum from a groat to a guinea, or a thousand of either.

King George II, in 1732, gave one of these grants to a group of twenty-one of his gentlemen friends, the acreage allotted being in the Georgia colony, and among the specially designated classes of acceptable settlers, besides the English, were the Scotch Highlanders and the German Salzburgers, many of whom were Waldensians in religion and had been exiled by the Catholic Count Archbishop of Salzburg, so that there was little controvery about their going to the Georgia colony. One place was as good as another. In almost every case they were led by pastors of their respective variations of belief, some of the religious divisions in doctrine being scarcely perceptible, yet sufficient to sort out one group from another. Their descendants, with names wondrously Anglicised, survive in Georgia.

One of these royal charters brought Germans into New England. It was another case of land speculation. Jonathan Waldo, a Pomeranian, was in Boston before 1700 as the agent of a Hamburg house. His son, born in Boston, partially educated at Harvard, finished his schooling in Germany, became a Hanoverian soldier under the Elector who became George I. of England, and followed the king to London. There he made friendships which later on gave him influence enough to be instrumental in straightening out the title to the Muscongas Patent, in the present state of Maine. He got half the area of the grant for a fee, and proceeded to exploit it for settlers in truly modern style.

Germans in New England

He had a book printed at Speyer in 1791 with the imposing title of "Kurtze-Beschreibung deren Landtschafft Massachusetts Bay, in New England. Absonderlich des Landstrichs an der Breyton Bay, so dem Koeniglichen Britischen Obersten, Samuel Waldo, Erbherrn des Breyton Bay, Zugehoerig, Sampt denen Hauptbedingungen nach Welchen, sich fremde Protestanten daselbst ansiedeln moegen." He brought out forty families from Brunswick and Saxony in 1740, who were supplemented by one hundred and sixty more in 1742. They were illy supplied with funds, badly supported by Waldo, and had rough experiences with the Maine winters and rougher ones with the Indians, who all but destroyed them in 1746.

Another settlement made by Joseph Crell, a Franconian, who had published a German newspaper in Philadelphia, was based upon a grant of two townships in present western Massachusetts and Vermont and two in Maine, for settlement by German Protestants. Crell or Crellius, as his name was Latinised, was an astute colonist and had trafficked in immigrants at Philadelphia. Crell's land scheme failed, and his colonists, both in Maine and Massachusetts, fared badly.

IN THE MAKING OF MICHIGAN

By and large, the early German immigration to America was based upon three overruling conditions, the differences of religion and consequent persecutions in the homeland; the greed of the ship-owners to gain passage money from Europe to the new continent, and the operation of speculative ventures in land under more or less honest representations and conditions, mostly less. But where there was so early and so widespread a sowing of seed, there was bound to be a crop, and the German immigration of the eighteenth century gave a good account of itself. Its participants settled on agricultural lands, established themselves in modest business and industrial ventures and became rooted to the soil and sympathetic with the aspirations of their neighbors.

As a rule they were thrifty, and as an economic consequence, they were accumulative of capital—so that they were almost always, from the earliest times, able to contribute to early and simple joint-stock enterprises, such as flouring mills and tanneries—but for the most part their wealth took the form of land and cash money. Their land-holdings, made available in fee in a manner not possible under either the economics or the land laws of the Fatherland, rooted them to the soil by ties closer than those of any of the French peasants—whose virtue in this respect was apostrophized in a later day by Emile Zola.

Having fled from persecution abroad they were naturally averse to even its semblance in their newly-found homes, so that one finds that when conditions began to ripen for the American Revolution, the Germans were almost wholly of the Revolutionary party. There were exceptional Tories, but these were few. Indeed for twenty or thirty years before the Revolutionary War the British authorities who controlled the American land-jobbing seemed to have sensed the dangers of planting more of these liberty-loving foreigners in the older colonies and diverted the newer streams of Germans to Nova Scotia and New Brunswick, a process in which they were ably assisted by a newer breed of shipping-masters, still anxious for the profits of the 'cross-the-ocean traffic.

Distribution of Early Comers

The descendants of these early German people scattered all over the country. The genealogies are full of their mixtures with other bloods and their pioneering into newer portions of the still New World. A typical example of these penetrations, chose without invidious distinction, is to be found in the ancestry of a member of the Sixty-Ninth Congress.

The pioneer settler of the Shenandoah Valley of Virginia, Baron John Hite, who migrated to America from Strasbourg, Alsace, in the early part of the eighteenth century, bringing with him a large number of Alsatian Huguenots to lands lying between the Blue Ridge and the Alleghany mountains, has a descendant in the person of Representative Walter F. Lineberger, of California.

Representative Lineberger has a background of six generations of pioneer forebears in America, beginning with John Leyenberger, who arrived at the port of Philadelphia on August 26, 1735, on the English ship "Billander Oliver," having emigrated from the village of Wittelsheim, near Mulhouse, Upper Alsace. This pioneer soon migrated to the section of the Shenandoah Valley where Strasburg, Va., now stands. He finally acquired from Lord Fairfax 1,100 acres of land on the Little Hawk's Bill Creek, near what is now Page County, Va., under a deed dated September 19, 1749. Prior to the Revolution, John Leyenberger's son, Peter, migrated to Lincoln County, in western North Carolina, and in 1835, Peter's son, David, migrated to Tennessee. In the "gold rush" of 1849, John Lineberger, son of David, and grandfather of the present Congressman, went to California in a sailing vessel around Cape Horn, and helped to lay the early foundations of that State. He voted for John C. Fremont for President in the California election in 1856.

These are the high-lights of the earlier immigrations of the Germans, imperfectly sketched and without detail, because they have little to do with the principal theme of this writing, which is the more modern settlement of Germanic people in the Middle West of the United States, and particularly in the State of Michigan; and they are only presented to account for the beginning of the settlement of these people in America, and the back-ground which they furnished for accessions to its population from identical sources.

CHAPTER II

THE COLONIAL PERIOD OF THE NORTHWEST

The Causes of the Various Migrations—A German Governor of Canada — A German Military Commander — The Period of Henri Bouquet—An Early-Day Social Event—The Cost of British Possessions — Haldimand's Solicitude About Rum—The Two Schiffleins—An Ancient Land Scandal—Other Germans of the Period.

The Germanic element entered rather more than it is usually credited with doing into the early history of the Middle West of North America, of which Michigan has come to be an important province. Historically the territory of the Great Lakes basin was explored and settled by the French, who, by the time they became settlers within its area, looked to Montreal and Quebec as their origins, rather than to Paris, having become more French-Canadian than French-European.

As the territory became known, and to be considered worth fighting for and having for its economic and colonial values, the British came into it for trade purposes of territorial dominion. Their continuous state of conflict with the French and the Indians has no pertinence to this study further than it explains the early injection of people of various extractions into the body of the early settlers.

From the beginnings most of these people were French and English. Some more of them were Irish and Scotch. A notable number were Germans. The appearance of these last was due to the operation of other causes than influenced the coming of the others, causes which were peculiar to the people and somewhat unconnected with each other. This explains why there have been three or four distinct historical arrivals of peoples of German blood in Michigan. Even outside the operation of these causes, a proportion of the state's early population, derived from this racial strain, is accounted for by the presence of the mere wanderer, who belongs to every race and who has gone to every place. These reasons classify as follow:

Causes of Various Migrations

First, the presence in the British colonial armies, prior to the American War of the Revolution, of German soldiers of the type that were hired from their princes or were isolated adventurers of that period. And into this group must be allocated those who, having been British soldiers in that war, were later patriated in Western Canada, and found their way across the present national boundary;

Second, the migration, westward, of persons of German blood and descent already in the United States, their racial strain derived from earlier Germanic settlements in the eastern part of the country. These people were quite as distinctively German as if they had come directly from abroad, being the results of purely German environments in their New York and Pennsylvania village homes. A great many of them have been claimed as Dutch, partly from the suggestion contained in their family names, partly from the early practice of classifying all Germans as "Dutch," in the vernacular;

Third, the settlement in the United States, largely in Michigan and Wisconsin, of families of devout German peasants, who came out, quite long before the Revolution of 1848, as participants in missionary enterprises undertaken among the Indians, and whose motive in settlement was purely religious and had nothing to do with the political movement which occurred after their departure from the homelands; and

Fourth, a condition which may merge into the foregoing, being the supply of migrants provided, perforce, by the Revolution of 1848; the practice of the German emigrant of that period being along the line of seeking out his new home where his "landsman" had already pioneered the way, and of looking to the favorable economic opportunities, in agriculture, industrial employment and commerce, which had disclosed themselves to the pioneer Germans of the missionary period.

This segregation of the origins of present day German-Americans in Michigan will help to account for the length of time during which German-American names have occupied places in Michigan history and the diversity of locations in which they have appeared from time to time.

A German Governor of Canada

The territory which is now the state of Michigan has experienced a variety of rulership. Mr. Charles Moore has phrased this control aptly by describing it as having been "Under Three Flags." The first of these ensigns bore the lilies of France, and from 1603 to 1760 there was a line of French governors, with Chauvin and Peter Francis, the Marquis of Vaudreil, respectively, the Alpha and Omega of this sequence of rulers. The Cross of St. George began to fly over Michigan in 1760 and continued to hold legally until long after the war of the American Colonies for their independence had ended.

There were eleven British Governors during this period. The one who ruled longest and during the most critical times was Sir Frederick Haldimand, Governor-General of Canada from 1778 to 1784, including parts of Michigan, as far west as Wisconsin, and down through Ohio and Indiana to the Ohio river.

Haldimand was one of a pair of German military men who, following the custom of the times, had gone into the employ of the British Kings. Through assignment to duty in America and most definitely to Canada, they came to exercise a great deal of authority and influence over what is now the territory of Michigan. Haldimand's companion-in-arms was Henry Bouquet. Both were born in Switzerland, Bouquet of a French father and a German mother, Haldimand of German parents on both sides. They were personal friends from boyhood, and their histories run parallel through many years of their respective lives. They were both types of the professional soldiers of the period in which they lived.

A German Military Commander

Henri Bouquet was born at Rolle, Switzerland, in 1719, of a French father and a German mother. He died at Pensacola, Florida, in 1766. He first entered the Dutch service, then that of the King of Sardinia, where he met up with General Haldimand. The two of them joined up with the British army in 1756. Bouquet came out to America in the following year. In 1758 he operated against Fort Duquesne. He was naturalized as a British subject in Canada in 1762. In 1763 he was in command at Philadelphia. In 1764 he led an expedition against the Ohio Indians. His headquarters were in Montreal from 1760 onward, after the cession of Canada to the British by the French, and he directed operations as far northwest as Mackinaw and westward to St. Joseph. This field of activity brought the officers at Detroit under his jurisdiction. Copies of his military papers, as well as those of Haldimand, are in the possession of the Michigan Historical Society.

Frederick Haldimand was born at Neufchatel, in Switzerland, in 1718, and he died at Yverdun, in his native land, in 1791. He took service as a young man in the Sardinian army and then served in the Prussian army for a period, beginning in 1754. In 1756 he was hired by the English King and for a time was an adviser of the British military authorities. He was sent to America in 1757, was at Ticonderoga, Oswego and Montreal and in Florida before 1767, and in 1778 he succeeded Gen. Sir Guy Carleton as Governor-General of Canada. He held office until November, 1784.

Haldimand was made Governor-General not so much for government as for military leadership. In time he had on his hands the problem of disposing of those of the Hessian troops whom the British had hired from their princes for service in the Revolutionary war, and who, after its ending, were not content either to settle in the United States or go back to Hesse; and he had a great deal to do with the settlement of the American Tories, or United Empire Loyalists, in the Province of Upper Canada, now Ontario.

Hessian Patriation in Canada

As to the Hessians there was a bit of governmental commerce in settling them in Canada, because the contract with the Landgraf of Hesse under which they were leased out to the British, contained a clause which provided for a payment of ten pounds sterling for each man who was not returned, unless he was personally willing to stay in America. The patriation in Canada of those who did not wish to remain in the new dominion of the United States was, therefore, a process in which British administrative economy and good colonization methods were combined.

Haldimand was not a particularly lovable character. He ruled with a strong hand and was not averse to the use of savage warfare against civilized white people. There was a general tendency on the part of the British to make the most of their German settlers in the Canadian plantation. This was Haldimand's policy, and that the policy was not abandoned is evident from Lord Dorchester's proclamation, after Haldimand's time, erecting four Provinces in Upper Canada, for court and registration purposes, and naming them Hesse, Nassau, Mecklenburg and Lunenberg. Michigan fell into Hesse, and that was its legal designation until the British evacuation in 1796.

Haldimand's colonists did not all stay by him in Ontario. Quite a number were attracted across the border and settled. Bouquet's military authority over Michigan, exercised from his headquarters at Montreal, began in 1760. He had German-born soldiers in his service, so from his time onward, names of Germanic aspect begin to appear in the history of the state. Among these was a family named Hambach, Henry and William of whom were in Detroit as early as 1761, while a third, Jacob D. Hambach, was as far west as St. Joseph in the following year. They were all in the fur trade, a traffic concerning which William Hambach sent Gen. Bouquet some information in a letter of June 27, 1761. In the following month Bouquet got another letter, this one from Henry Hambach, begging him to allow a quantity of rum to be sent out to him from Montreal, "for to sell it to the inhabitants at this place."

The Period of Henri Bouquet

In August, 1761, it appears from Bouquet's correspondence that Ensign Schlosser was sent on from Niagara to Detroit. Schlosser was heard from with some regularity thereafter. In the month after his arrival at Detroit he was joined, under orders from Bouquet, by Lieut. Elias Meyer, who had been at Sandusky and who brought with him Ensign Henry Carl Pauli. While in Detroit, this duty, which was temporary, Meyer experienced the high cost of living of the period, about which he later complained to Bouquet. He had to pay three "ecus" per dozen for fresh eggs, an "ecu" being an old French money value equal to an English crown, or five shillings.

About this same time, Capt. Campbell, a British officer, induced Sergeant Steiner, whose time had expired, to stay in Detroit another year. Meantime, Andrew Hirschman was in a company under Campbell's authority at Sandusky. Captain Etherington, who was also stationed at Detroit, reported on September 1, 1762, that the time of two of his soldiers, Jacob Lamplan and George Peighthal, had expired, and Jacob and George were sent back to Montreal to go back to Hesse or to be induced to remain in Canada.

There were annoying events during Bouquet's time, which go to show that there is really very little that is new under the sun. In 1762 it was quite necessary that communication be kept up with Mackinaw, entailing transport by water. On September 24, 1762, Lieut. Jehu Hay wrote to Gen. Bouquet that "there is not enough water in Lake St. Claire to carry the vessels through to Lake Huron," and that "the sand-bars now run away out into the lake," a condition not wholly different from that charged to be the result of the construction of the Chicago canal in a much later period.

An Early Social Incident

Hambach's plea to Bouquet to send out some rum to Detroit "for to sell it to inhabitants of this place," seems to have been answered in the affirmative. In October, 1762, Capt. Campbell, before referred to, was on military duty as far afield as St. Joseph and had Ensign Schlosser as part of his company. An incident occurred while he was there which may lead one to the conclusion that Capt. Campbell must be set down among that class of gentlemen who did not carry their liquor handily. There was a bit of a party in the wilds at which Capt. Campbell got into a condition which required Ensign Schlosser to restrain him. Evidently, to head off the results of a complaint and to give Gen. Bouquet the inside of the matter before it came to him officially from Campbell, Hambach sent a letter to the Commander-in-Chief from Fort St. Joseph, October 14, 1762, advising him that, at the recent social event, Mr. Schlosser had been obliged to "control" Capt. Campbell, "while he was in liquor recently," relating naively that "the gentleman gets what you would call merry, and then being in absolute mastery, it gets into his head." All of which goes to show that the world hasn't changed a great deal in the last century and a half at least.

In the latter part of 1762, Capt. Gladwin, the same who had some interesting experiences with Chief Pontiac, reported that among the men discharged from the First Battalion of the Royal American Regiment were Henry Johannes, Jacob Schmorrenberger and Peter Harliman, whose time had expired. As their names do not appear in later records of the place, the presumption is that they were returned to Montreal and thence to Europe. In 1764 Ensigns Prosser and Pauli, of whom we have heard before, wrote to Bouquet from Detroit asking for promotion. They had to write a second time to remind him, this time asking to be reimbursed for losses in the service, Prosser's claim being eighty pounds and Pauli's seventy pounds. At the time of this correspondence, Diedrich Brehm was a Lieutenant in the King's employ at Detroit. After a short tour of duty there he wrote to Bouquet asking to be permitted to leave the service. He was evidently coaxed to stay, as he appears later in the service of Gen. Haldimand, his cognomen being occasionally Anglicised from "Dietrich" into "David."

The Cost of British Possession

Haldimand, too, had many German born and descended officers and soldiers in his military establishment. He rather favored them himself. His aide-de-camp and confidential inspector was Diedrich Brehm, by this time a Captain, whom he sent up to Detroit on many occasions to keep an eye on both the military and the financial administration. One was pretty closely knit to the other. It cost the British a pretty penny to hold on to the territory which is now Michigan, and as the drafts were all drawn on the Governor-General, Haldimand had much cause for complaint. He was a rather conscientious auditor. Great expense figures shocked him. He was a voluminous letter writer, and a deal of his correspondence with the commandants at Detroit and Mackinac had reference to the excessive cost of maintenance of the military establishment.

At that, English money was called for in pretty substantial sums. Haldimand's criticisms were not always effective. No sooner had he, in 1780, chided Colonel De Peyster, in charge of Detroit, for sending him a draft for 64,035 pounds, saying that "the frequency of these amazing demands is a matter of very serious concern to me," than he had another draft the next half year from the same source for 44,962 pounds. Counsels of economy meant very little, whether they proceeded from Haldimand or not.

The unregenerate modern, who is not carried away with tales of ancient virtue, would be inclined to assume that where there was so much opportunity there was a good deal of "graft."

There was a lot of money spent about the Michigan settlements during General Haldimand's administration. The British government was a sort of a "sucker" for everybody who chose to draw on it. During 1788, drafts for 79,195 pounds sterling; in 1779 for 128,709 pounds; in 1780 for 118,-701 pounds; in 1781 for 133,922 pounds, and in 1782 for 48,-295 pounds were paid at Quebec by Haldimand to various persons in authority in Detroit. Beside these items, 294,000 pounds were drawn from the Michilimackinac post during Haldimand's control.

This makes a total of 806,822 sterling pounds for military expenses at Detroit and Mackinac during four years. This was better than 4,000,000 dollars directly spent at two frontier posts in that period, besides other expenditures payable at headquarters and overhead costs. Haldimand's papers make it clear that about 10,000,000 dollars were spent in his time to hold the west, of which Michigan was a part.

Besides his apparently justifiable complaints about the spending of money, Haldimand had two other idiosyncrasies which are revealed in his correspondence. George MacDougal had squatted on Hog Island, in the Detroit river, now Belle Isle Park of the city of Detroit. Haldimand insisted on retaining the island as a common for the use of the Crown and the garrison and inhabitants of Detroit. Haldimand thought the island should be devoted to raising food for the garrison at Detroit, which at that time was being victualled from Niagara. He was constantly writing to the local commandant to clear off the usurpers of title. Finally Major De Peyster made a dicker with Mrs. MacDougal to pay her 334 pounds for the improvements on the Island. On the occasion of announcing the happy termination of negotiations to the Governor-General, Major De Peyster slipped him another draft for 14,714 pounds for expenses, this one almost under the guns of Haldimand's most recent remonstrance against extravagant spending.

Haldimand's Solicitude About Rum

Haldimand's other care was the morals of the Indians. While he had no niceties about using them in warfare against the whites, he was anxious to keep them fit, and was strongly averse to their use of rum. In July, 1779, he wrote to Captain Lernoult, at Detroit, chiding him about the amount of rum that had been consumed at Detroit in the preceding year. The quantity seems to have been 17,520 gallons. Considering that there were only about 1,200 people in and around the post that year there was hardly a rum famine. The next year Haldimand wrote to De Peyster at Detroit, telling him to withhold rum from the Indians, and stating that he desired it kept from them "because of the pernicious effects it has upon their warriors and young men and the poverty and disease it brings upon their families." So that, all in all, General Haldimand had qualifications which would have graced a later age.

He was a bit of a diplomat at that. Under the Treaty of Nov. 30, 1782, the British were to have evacuated the western territories of the United States. General Washington, with a letter from Hudson, N. Y., July 12, 1783, to General Haldimand, sent Baron Steuben to receive possession of the posts and fortresses of the northwest frontier, stating that "as a foreigner, and an officer of rank I beg leave to recommend Baron Steuben to your post, and as a gentleman you will find him in every way worthy of your civilities." This letter had to do with the forts at Detroit and Mackinac, among others.

At Sorel, August 11, 1783, Baron Steuben having received a verbal answer from Haldimand, asked him to put his final answer in writing and impressed upon Haldimand that the Articles of Peace were definitive, and stated that he demanded a safe conduct and liberty of visiting the possessions within the United States then occupied by the British. General Haldimand replied to Washington, saying "that the strict observance of my duty and the rules of war leave me no alternative but to refuse to comply with your requests until I shall be authorized to receive them."

At all events Haldimand's position must have been acceptable as the best he could do, and a week later Baron Steuben thanked him in writing for his courtesies and went back home. The British did not get out of the territory until 1796.

Some Early Colonial Period Germans

During the years that passed from 1761 to 1796 there were Germans coming into and going out of what is now Michigan territory with the authority of the British control. Some had been there earlier and were established.

Under Jay's Treaty British subjects might remain within the American borders if they saw fit, but must declare their intentions with reference to their nationality. Among those at Detroit who retained their British citizenship were Jonathan Schifflein, George Jacob Rudhart, William Hands, Conrad Showalter and Joseph Gruenist.

There had been a good deal of trading in the Mackinac and Sault Ste. Marie territory very early. In 1786 among the traders in this area were Lawrence Ermatinger, Adam Lymburner, one Rangman, and a Jewish trader named Ezekiel Solomons. The last named went up to Mackinac in 1777 with a passport from the military authorities at Quebec, which, said the letter of transmissal, "was granted him in consideration of his creditors." Solomons finally went as far north as the Nipigon river, on the north shore of Lake Superior. John George Zanelius was a trader at the same time at Mackinac. There was a Sergeant Hartman in the British force at Mackinac in 1782.

Francis Diehl's name was on the roll of the Indian department at Detroit in 1783, as reported to Haldimand. He was a smith at the Shawnee Town and Melchior Becker was a rifle-cutter. They got twelve pounds apiece per year for pay. When a census was made of the Loyalists of Detroit in 1784 by Lieut. Jehu Hay, he listed William Paulding, Jacob Rassy, Jacob Quant and Peter Schunck. Two years before that Col. De Peyster, in arranging for a shipment of American prisoners to Niagara wrote, as his opinion, that "I suppose it is not intended that the families mostly German, who have taken oaths and are settled on farms, should be included."

The Two Schiffleins

Of the group who cut a figure in these times and who were of German extraction two were outstanding in the records of the day, and, as star differeth from star in glory, one of the two outshone the other. They were the two Schiffleins, Jacob and Jonathan. They were brothers, of Hessian origin. They were among those of the group who were patriated in Upper Canada after the Revolution. They had one trait in common. That was acquisitiveness. Neither seems to have failed to get what he wanted for failure of asking for it. Jacob Schifflein was appointed, June, 1777, a First Lieutenant of the Detroit Volunteers, accompanied General Hamilton to Vincennes, where he was made a prisoner

and was sent to Williamsburg, in Virginia, whence he escaped.
He got to New York and Quebec in 1780. On Oct. 28, 1780, he
was sent from Quebec to Detroit. In 1783 he asked General Haldimand for some extra pay for his services and hardships, and during the year he got 180 pounds and some shillings and pence in requital. In October of the same year
he got a grant of land from the Huron and Ottawa Indians,
seven miles square, on the Canadian side of the river, opposite the lower end of Bois Blanc Island and near the present
Amherstburg.

Jonathan Schifflein had similar military experiences
with the British. In a memorial made August 20, 1790, to
Lord Guy Dorchester, Governor-General of Canada, he recited
that "in 1777, being ever-ready to support the unity of the
empire and the rights of the Crown over her rebel subjects,"
he went on an expedition under General Hamilton against the
fort at Vincennes and he would like to get an extra half pay
for it. He collected. He was eager for the ownership of
land. In August, 1787, he had Capt. Alexander McKee certify
that he had served in several expeditions carried on
from Detroit against the enemy's frontiers. This certificate
turned up in a claim for added compensation. In 1793 he asked
the Committee of the Council for a grant of 700 acres on the
Detroit river. He got it, and it was subsequently confirmed
to him by the land commissioners as Private Claim No. 113,
in Ecorse, Wayne County. His name appears on a multitude
of pay-rolls and expense accounts.

An Ancient Land Scandal

Under the treaty of November, 1794, the British agreed
to give up the western forts, including those in Michigan, on
or before a given date in 1796. During this interval Schifflein
was exceedingly busy. Together with Jacobus Visgar, an
Albany man of Dutch extraction, and some other associates
he was busy at procuring grants of land from the Indians

covering the area from the Cuyahoga river, in Ohio, across the middle of Michigan to Saginaw Bay.

There was formality or informality about these cessions, as best suited the purpose of Schifflein. A good deal of rum appears to have been used as a lubricant for the negotiations with the Indians. These transfers turned up promptly in a curious transaction.

Upon the conclusion of Wayne's treaty, Eben Allen and Charles Whitney, of Vermont, and Robert Randall, of Philadelphia, entered into a contract with Jonathan Schifflein, John Askin, Sr., Wm. Robertson, John Askin, Jr., David Robertson, Robert Jones, and Richard Patterson, all of Detroit, but who acknowledged British subjection, to obtain from the Congress of the United States, by purchase, the title of all the land within the limits of the Lower Peninsula of Michigan not already appropriated. This land had an area then estimated at from eighteen to twenty million acres and the sale was to be based on the understanding that the grantees would extinguish the Indian title.

A stock company of forty-one shares was formed. Five shares went to the Detroit partners, a full share going to Schifflein. Twelve shares went to the Philadelphia and Vermont men, who were to furnish for them 500,000 dollars of capital, with liability for an assessment of as much more, if that amount of capital were found necessary for the completion of the project. Twenty-four shares were to be divided among members of the Congress for their votes. The Philadelphia men enlisted the adherence of some of the southern members of the Congress, and sought to interest Daniel Buck and Theodore Sedgeman, Representatives from Vermont.

Robert Randall claimed that he had a majority of voters pledged to a favorable vote in the Senate in December, 1795, and lacked only three votes in the House. The Vermont men told about the scheme to President Washington and on December 28, 1795, it was exposed in the House of Representatives. As a result there was an investigation and a scandal that compared favorably with those relating to the Credit Mobilier and Teapot Dome subjects in later congressional history. There were admissions of interest in the scheme, but the scandal died out with no punishment of the participants.

Meantime Schifflein and his Detroit associates were quite busy in obtaining grants from the Indians. For instance, in July, 1795, a special council was held with certain Chippewa, Ottawa and Pottawatamie chiefs, in the neighborhood of present Owosso, in which deeds were given by the Indians to lands covering fourteen present counties of the state for twenty-five pounds sterling. When the scheme went to pieces, the operators still had their Indian colors of title, and these they sold in 1797 for 200,000 pounds New York currency, the equivalent of half a million dollars. Shortly thereafter Schifflein retired from the scene of his frontier operations and took up his home in western New York.

There was no special racial turpitude discoverable in this transaction. Schifflein had good Yankee, Irish and Scotch associates in his enterprise, and the operation and its morals were both characteristic of a period of adventure and speculation. Their likes are to be found in much of the early real estate history of the country.

Germans of the British Period

There were other Germans in the territory during these latest years of British occupation. A group of discharged loyalists asked for grants of land in the District of Hesse in 1791. Among them were Jacob Quandt, William Menninger, Leonard Schalch, Jacob Klawater and Jacob Rudhardt. Their names suggest their origin. Israel Ruland, born on Long Island in 1757, of German descent, came to Detroit in 1772 and bound himself to Garret Graeverat for forty pounds, to serve until he should come of age. He was arrested for American sympathies in 1779. Ten years later he was a silversmith in Detroit. On the pay-roll of His Majesty's shipyard in Detroit, from December 29, 1777, to April 24, 1778, was the name of Jacob Bogard, a German carpenter. He got twelve pounds a month.

When the British finally got out of the western forts the District of Hesse became Wayne County, of the Northwest Territory. The British carried away with them four volumes of the records of deeds at Detroit, three of which were recovered a century later through the courtesy of the government of the Dominion of Canada. The fourth was recently located.

There were many sequels of the occupation which indicated the presence of Germans. William Treigehen applied to the British to compensate him for losses sustained in the Mackinac country. Just before the evacuation, Gother Mann, commandant of the Royal Engineers, asked to have Bois Blanc Island, in the Detroit river, retained by the Crown for military purposes. Capt. Frederick August Schalch, of the Royal Artillery, was located at Detroit just before evacuation. Lieutenant Jacob Radenhorst was a British officer at Mackinac at the same time. William Claus, who was Deputy Superintendent General of the Indian affairs, moved off to Fort George, where he held office as late as 1825.

Nor were the military occupations the only sources of German settlement in the present territory of Michigan. The British, despite the American victory in the War of the Revolution and the treaties made at its close, were pretty hopeful of retaining dominion over the Great West, from Canada to Florida, and hoped to conquer Louisiana, which stretched from the Gulf of Mexico up into the Oregon country. One incident of these campaigns was a sortie made in 1780 by Capt. Henry Bird, an English army officer, with a force of 150 white men and a thousand savages. Among his whites were Simon Girty, Matthew Elliott and Alexander McKee, experts in the art of inciting Indians to war upon the Americans, and men whose names will ever be odious in the history of warfare. This expedition was directed against Ohio and Kentucky. Among the prisoners taken, at Ruddle's Station, in Kentucky, were Leonard Kratz and his wife Mary. Kratz was born at Teutonhofen, near Frankfort-on Main, in 1756, and in 1776 was brought to America as one of the Hessian troops hired out to King George. He was captured at Saratoga, imprisoned for a while in Virginia, set free, and made his way into Kentucky, where he married. On their capture by the English and Indians man and wife were given as slaves to different Indian masters, and brought to Detroit in different convoys. Mrs. Kratz's baby was killed en route. They were reunited at Detroit, where they lived some years, finally being established at Amherstburg, Ont., where Kratz died in 1829.

These were the high lights of the British period of dominion over Michigan, showing the presence of Germans in its present area, drawn thither by one reason or another. For the purposes of this history it is sufficient to show they were in the territory.

CHAPTER III

THE POST-COLONIAL PERIOD

The First Germans in Michigan—Some Important Land-Holdings—The Earliest Post-Colonial Immigrants.

The colonial period of the history of Michigan ended in 1796. Up to that time the present area of the state had, as has been shown, a sprinkling of people of German blood in its sparse population, these having been drawn thereto by various exigencies of adventure, trade or military occupation. With the beginning of the control of the United States there came a parting of the ways. People of all kinds who were then located, including those of German blood, made choice of their sovereignty, as was provided for in the treaty of peace, and many who were loyal to the British Crown withdrew from the territory altogether. Those who remained took on a new status, that of American citizens, among them a proportion of those of German origin.

There were quite a number of these, so many as to be noticeable in a small population. Dr. Herman Melchior Eberts, who had been in the settlement since 1791, became Sheriff of Wayne county. He started a set of books on his dues from his patients, beginning with the first day of 1796. The entries show that he had several people of German names among them. Incidentally these records survive. In 1796 he attended Thomas Schmidt, who was the proprietor of a tavern, Martin Frappe and John Noethe. In 1779 Maria Faser was his patient. In 1800 Anthony Roth was the beneficiary of his ministrations. In 1802 Francis Becker, and in 1803 John Fisher, and in 1806 William Koester appear to have been given opportunities to profit by his physic, while in 1812 Paul Ramte was among his patients.

At this period of the world's history the Germanic people were not much tempted to roam afar from their homeland. The conditions in the Germanic Kingdoms were not unprosperous and the temptations to stray were not strong. There had been an earlier American immigration from Germany, but its sources and its destinations were confined to definite places on the seaboard and others not far inland, and it was now history. There were among the Germans, as among every other race, a minority who were affected by the wanderlust, and who, as sailors, or traders, or preachers of the Gospel, went far afield. Their percentage was small as compared to the mass. So that it was not until the religious disquietude of 1820 onward and the political disturbances of the late '40's of the nineteenth century that any great mass emigration of the Germans to the Midlands of North America took place.

Before that there had been some stray Germans in Michigan, as there had been some stray Irishmen, an Italian or two or three, and a few representatives of some other breeds. For that matter the stray Germans were in Michigan as early as any of the rest. The first of these, and the first recorded German inhabitant of the present area of Michigan, was Michael Yax. He appears to have been a settler in the Pennsylvania colony at Germantown, when he started in 1747 to the Point Coupee colony of Germans in Mississippi, who had been settled there in John Law's "Mississippi Bubble" colonization scheme of 1716 and thereafter. He was taken a prisoner by the Indians on the way, by a band of Ottawas from Detroit, probably at some point in Kentucky, into which the Detroit Indians made forays from time to time. They brought him to the fort at Detroit, together with his wife and his child, and they were ransomed by M. de Longuiel,

IN THE MAKING OF MICHIGAN 51

Commandant of the Strait, where Yax settled down to farming, was given a settlement of three arpents width on the North Shore, and was later "grub-staked" with an outfit of agricultural implements, some domestic animals, some ammunition and some food. This was in 1751. His wife, Catherine Herkinee, was originally a Lutheran, but in 1755, she joined the Roman Catholic faith by a solemn profession, the history of which Pere Simple Bouquet set down at much length in the baptismal register of St. Anne's Church. This record establishes the racial identity of Yax and his wife as "both of German origin." She had eleven children. Mrs. Yax died in 1789 and Michael Yax himself in 1793. They were both buried from St. Anne's. The family settled in Grosse Pointe, some of them drifted into present Macomb county, in the neighborhood of Chesterfield, and their posterity are still numbered among the population of Detroit and its vicinity.

To Yax and his wife is definitely assignable the distinction of being the first German-born man and woman in a Michigan settlement, Yax himself as the first Roman Catholic German and his wife as the first Lutheran, until her union with her husband's religious communion.

Dr. Anthon, of whom we will see more later, was a surgeon at the fort of Detroit under Gen. Haldimand's tenure of military authority, as early as 1764. Joseph Moore, a Philadelphia Quaker who came out to attend an Indian treaty at Sandusky in 1793, came to Detroit. In his Journal he tells of having stopped over at River Rouge in a tavern of Jacob Troxler, "a Dutchman." He gives Troxler a good name as an inn-keeper.

There were a few officers of German names with the British toward the latter end of their occupation of Detroit and Mackinaw. Lieut. Edward Henn, of the Sixth Regiment, and Capt. F. A. Schalch, of the Royal Artillery, were on a board of survey which condemned six guns at Detroit in 1795. In 1796, the Little Otter, an Indian chief in the employ of the British as a warrior, delivered Henry Darias, "a German soldier who served under Gen. Burgoyne" to Thomas Duggan, clerk of the Indian Department. Darias had evidently deserted the British side and been apprehended.

Some Important Land Holdings

When the Land Commissioners came to confirm the titles to the private claims under the provisions of the treaty which extinguished the British title in Michigan, they appear from the records contained in American State Papers to have been somewhat exacting in their requirements of testimony regarding the continued, hostile, open and notorious ownership of the various claimants. Quite naturally these were mostly persons of French blood, and these confirmations of title, made from 1807 onward, were nearly all based on claims of occupancy and ownership running back twenty and thirty years anterior to the dates of confirmation. Despite the dominance of French claimants, there were even then some names which showed unmistakable German origin.

For instance, Private Claim No. 69, on the Rouge River, in Dearborn township, later a part of the home estate of Mr. Henry Ford, was confirmed to the widow and heirs of Gottfried Corbus in 1807, while Private Claim No. 40, in Fordson, was confirmed to John Steinback in the same year; Private Claim No. 93 in Dearborn, to George Hoffman in 1808, and Private Claim No. 113 in Ecorse in 1808 to Jonathan Schifflein. The last mentioned has already been identified in these pages.

One of the private claims was confirmed to Michael Yax, or Yacks, the spelling of whose name varies in different documents, and a son of the Michael Yax who was the first German in Michigan. He had Private Claim 387, in Grosse Pointe, confirmed to him in 1808, while Pierre Yax, another son, got Private Claim 344, in Grosse Pointe, in the same year; Simon Yacks, Private Claim 458, also in Grosse Pointe, in 1808; and John Yax, Private Claim 306 in 1808.

IN THE MAKING OF MICHIGAN 53

Then there was Colonel John Francis Hamtramck, whose tombstone in Mt. Elliott Cemetery, Detroit, indicates that he was "the friend of the immortal Washington" and that his fellow-officers provided for the elaborately inscribed marker which is still preserved over his remains. The origin of John Francis Hamtramck, whose name is linked with the local geography of Wayne County, has been variously related. Actually he was born in Quebec, of German parents from Trier. He gave a good account of himself in his generation, was considered a good soldier by Gen. Anthony Wayne, and was sent to Michigan to take over, in the name of the American government, the command of Detroit, upon its relinquishment by the British after the close of the war of 1812. Hamtramck died at the age of 42, and his son, John Francis Hamtramck, Jr., was in the war with Mexico and in 1848 was Governor of Saltillo.

In other parts of Michigan there were some early Germans. Martin Heydenburk was a school teacher at Mackinac in 1822. His grandfather was a German, one of the Hessian troops sent out to assist the British in the Revolutionary War, who took the first opportunity to desert them as soon as he discovered the rights of the controversy. He hated England so intensely that he conducted some annual derisive rite on the anniversary of his desertion, consisting, some say, of a vigorous stamping on the British ensign. His grandson, Martin, remained at Mackinac for nine years, later settling in the neighborhood of White Pigeon, and being identified with religious activities all his life.

The Early Post-Colonial Immigrants

General Cutcheon and Mr. Henry M. Utley, in "Michigan as Province, Territory and State", say that "as early as 1825 Conrad Bessinger came to Ann Arbor. So far as it is possible to trace, the next German settler did not arrive until 1829. In 1834 the rush for land was on and people were coming to Michigan in such droves that it was almost impossible to house and feed them comfortably. These were New York and New England immigrants who were looking to better their conditions by making homes for themselves in a new and fertile country where land was cheap. In 1833 more public land was sold in Michigan than in all the preceeding years from 1821 to 1833 put together. With this swelling tide of immigration there were doubtless many people of foreign birth, who, arriving in the country, were swept into the westward advancing column."

The first German Evangelical congregation in Michigan was organized in 1833. Its house of worship was built about two miles west of the present site of Ann Arbor Court House and was dedicated in December of the same year. The whole cost of the building was $265.32. This church was in charge of Pastor Frederick Schmid, who was sent as a missionary to the state by the Basle Evangelical Missionary Society. German congregations were founded in 1833 in Detroit and Monroe. They were administered by Pastor Schmid and others.

A Roman Catholic missionary, writing of this period, gives his testimony of the situation in the following language:

"Real German life, as it is found in American states, one can find in Michigan only in three places, for in all other places our people are too scattered to form congregations that might support a German preacher.

"(1) In Detroit, there are two large German congregations, the stronger being Catholic, and having built a church; the other, also having a church of its own, being Protestant (the Reverend Mr. Schade). The members of the two congregations live in harmony with one another, and never allow their religious differences to interfere with their social intercourse. At marriages and baptisms they are never concerned about which preacher they should choose, but that they should have a good time in the German fashion. A large number of Germans remain in the city only so long as to earn money enough to buy land outside and establish farms.

"(2) The second German colony, and the most prosperous, is that near Ann Arbor. The Germans there came largely from Wurtemburg, and are under the Protestant preacher, the Reverend Mr. Schmid. Their grain and cattle are unsurpassed in Michigan.

"(3) The third German colony is that on the Grand River, in the neighborhood of Lyons, Ionia county, under the Reverend Mr. Kopp, from Westphalia. The colony is called Westphalia."

CHAPTER IV

THE STATE'S INVITATION TO IMMIGRANTS

The "Auswanderer Wegweiser" — The Prices of Land — The Period of Achievement.

The mission movement had dotted the lower part of the state with many German settlements. Pastor Schmid had started several such places. The Loehe-trained pastors, of whom more is told later on, had done much toward colonization in other sections, principally in the Saginaw valley and the country eastward to Lake Huron. Pastor Schwartz alone founded colonies and churches at Forestville, Port Sanilac, Argyle, Port Crescent, Bingham and Siegel in the 45 years of his service. The other leading early settlements were in Monroe, Washtenaw and Macomb. There were a good many Germans in Wayne. Their industry and thrift as farmers had made a good impression on their fellow-citizens.

Epaphroditus Ransom, of Kalamazoo county, became Governor in 1848. He was a man of much learning and foresight. He had been for twelve years previous to his governorship a Judge of the Supreme Court. He was a Vermont man, where his preceptor in the law was Peter R. Taft, of Townsend, grandfather of President Taft. He was a progressive agriculturist and stock breeder. He induced the Legislature of 1848 to pass legislation favorable to immigration and the purchase of state lands by newcomers. Under the hat, the state really needed the proceeds of the land sales for its treasury. He appointed Edward Hughes Thompson, of Flint, Commissioner of Immigration. The German-American element of the population of Michigan may well look upon Mr. Thompson as their foster-father in citizenship. Spending part of his time in New York and part in Stuttgardt, Germany, he directed what the state's official papers describe as "a stream of valuable emigrants to the state."

The Auswanderer Wegweiser

He began his work in 1849 by publishing very extensively, at state expense, a pamphlet, "Auswanderer Wegweiser nach dem Staate Michigan." This was the formal invitation of the state to the German prospects for immigration. Read in the light of today's economics of Michigan it is an interesting picture of the basis of state hopes as painted nearly 80 years ago.

To begin with, very little is said of the Upper Peninsula. The map of desirable land for settlers is colored to attract attention to Sanilac, Tuscola, Genesee, Saginaw, Shiawassee, Midland and Gratiot counties. The railroads shown extended from Detroit to Niles, from Monroe to Hillsdale, from Adrian to Toledo and from Detroit to Pontiac. The present city of Grand Rapids is not marked upon it. Saginaw is marked, but not Lower Saginaw, or Bay City. Mackinaw and Sault Ste. Marie are the only Upper Peninsula cities named. The river system is shown with much accuracy. The text bears upon the extent of lake commerce, the imports and exports of the state, and the production of the various staples.

Not more stress could be laid upon the excellence of the modern road system than was then laid upon the "magnificent" system of wagon roads, which included one dirt highway from Detroit westward, another from Detroit to Fort Gratiot, still another from Detroit to Saginaw, with Pontiac and Flint on the way. The remainder of the roads were mere plains trails. The township and sectional survey system is set down with exactness. The characteristics of the soils, whether of clay, sand or loam, are set up. Above all, there is a rhapsody about the German settlements already made and the religious attentions given their inhabitants by Pastors Craemer, Sievers and Graebner. The names of these pioneer German Lutheran missionaries were used to charm many a group of their race into the new country.

The Prices of Land

One's money went quite a distance in buying land in those days. The highest price was the "ten shilling land," that which was sold by the state at a dollar and a quarter an acre. Some more could be gotten as low as 90 cents an acre. As a matter of fact, state warrants were at a discount, could be used to pay for land, and by ingenious financing through their use land could be gotten as cheaply as 75 cents an acre.

It made some difference what kind of German and other European money one had with which to do his land-buying. The Hamburg bank mark was worth 35 cents. The reichsthaler of Prussia and North Germany was worth 69 cents, but the reichsthaler of Bremen went for 78 3-4 cents. Prussian gulden were worth 22 3-4 cents, but the Basle gulden exchanged for 41 cents. The livre of Neufchatel had a value of 26 1-2 cents. The Saxon reichsthaler had an equal value with that from Prussia, but the Rhenish reichsthaler was worth but 60 3-4 cents. Austrian gulden had a value of 48 1-2 cents.

So the invitation ran on in words of pride and hopefulness about Michigan, purposefully made attractive to its German readers, bidding them gather their bank marks and their reichsthalers, their gulden and their livres together, come to Michigan and settle its lands. When they arrived at Detroit, if they needed guidance and direction, they were to ask their way of the late Mr. Chauncy Hurlbut, the kindly old pioneer merchant, who, dying without kin, made the children who play in the Detroit Waterworks Park his heirs. The truth of this information was carefully certified by the Mayor of the City of New York, the President of the German Society thereof, and the President of the Swiss Welfare Society, of the same city, and was relayed to the public through the German press with such success that within a year 2,800 Wurtemburgers came to America, most of them to Michigan.

Mr. Thompson's propaganda had an odd and a lasting effect in Germany. Some of his travels led him into other parts of the country, where he impressed the resourcefulness of America in general and Michigan in particular upon financiers and capitalists. The reaction from this educational process was discovered some years later when William Walton Murphy, of Jonesville, became Consul-General of the United States at Frankfort-on-Main, just after the beginning of the American civil war, and was able to place the early issues of war bonds of the United States with the Frankfort bankers at a time that their acceptance as a promising investment was being refused in the English money market.

From this time onward German immigration came into Michigan in great volume. It was accelerated by various causes. One was the correspondence with the mission colonies and the scattered Auswanderer, who were doing well and were enthusiastic about their new home-land. Another was the actual necessity of the "Forty-Eighters" finding a new and safe abiding place where conditions fitted in with their ideas of democracy. Not the least, again, was the commercial side of the traffic as it affected the fortunes of the steamship lines operators, who promoted the immigration actively, as their forbears had done two centuries before. Incidentally the first through steamship ticket from Hamburg to Michigan was sold as early as 1841, by the late Richard R. Elliott, of Detroit.

How this immigration accumulated Germans in Michigan and had its effect on the eventual composition of its people is best read from the story told of the figures of population given in the records of the federal census.

The Works of the Newcomers

From this time forward the influence of the Germanic immigrants to Michigan must be traced by their works. They had given up an old allegiance and taken upon themselves a new one. They came to participate in and enjoy the liberties of a free country, in one of its most promising sovereignties. They came to apply the parable of Stephen Decatur, "My country, may she be ever right, but right or wrong, my country." Hence, there fell to them the duty of defense of the new fatherland, when it needed defense, and in this respect the mass immigration of the '40's and '50's had a good pattern already set for them by the few of their blood and race who had already preceded them into Michigan. They brought with them skill in peculiar trades and craftsmanships, to be fitted into the economics of a newer country than that which they had left, and to be made their contributions to the economic common good. They brought certain cultivated attainments and aspirations, to be freely given and adapted to the growing civilization with which they were joining as a part and a factor; these being mostly in the line of educational wealth and potential contributions therefrom, as well as refinements in music and other arts to which no American group, and particularly none in Michigan, had, prior to their advent, the opportunity to give much attention, largely because of the hardships incident to the foundation period.

Therefore, from this time forward one must measure the Germanic influence in the making of Michigan by what it did for the state along the various lines of endeavor hereinbefore indicated; and the further developments of this study of the subject will be confined to these topics, considered as broadly or as intimately as may be necessary for a distinctness which is not meant to be encyclopedic.

CHAPTER V

THE GROWTH OF THE GERMANIC POPULATION OF MICHIGAN

The Territorial Origins—Twentieth Century Changes.

The United States Census of 1830 was, as we look upon such economic data nowadays, a modest and rather useless compilation for any purpose outside its primary one of providing the information upon which representation in the Congress should be based. The same was true of the Census of 1840. Neither of these collections of facts about the population took account of native-born or foreign, let alone the interesting facts of origins by place or race. The Census of 1850 was an improvement. The question of negro slavery was becoming important and a deal of attention was given to the figures concerning the number of white males and females, and the number of black slaves and black freemen, both men and women. For the first time some attention was paid to the respective conditions of native-born and foreign-born.

There were 397,654 people in the whole state in 1850. Of these there were 42,756 in Wayne county and 28,567 in Washtenaw county, which were in that year the most populous counties of the state. The foreign-born of all extractions in the state in 1850 numbered 30,678 men and 23,915 women. No segregation into their origins was officially made.

In 1860 the direction of the census extended the scope

of its inquiries to the gathering of information relative to the birthplaces of the residents of the United States. That year there were found 749,113 people of all kinds in Michigan. Of these 38,787 were Germans by birth, or approximately 5.2 per cent. Of these, again, 16,409 were described simply as of German birth, with no reference to their territorial extractions. Of the remainder, 660 were Austrians who were grouped with the Germans. Then there were 2,522 from Baden; 1,525 from Hesse; 214 from Nassau; 9,635 from Prussia and 4,275 from Wurtemburg.

Territorial Origins

In the Census of 1870 there was more exactness in the inquiry as to the territorial origins of the German-born who were counted that year in Michigan. The total population of the state had grown in a decade to 1,184,059. Of that total the residents, citizens and alien, of German birth, numbered 64,143, nearly 5.4 per cent of the whole. By this time, however, there had come up more than a full generation of native-born Americans, whose fathers and mothers were immigrants from the German States, and an estimate has been made that this native generation, living when the census of 1870 was taken, numbered, at the very least, an additional 98,000 souls. At any rate, of the foreign-born included in the enumeration, there were 4,437 from Baden; 6,164 from Bavaria; 86 from Brunswick; 160 from Hamburg; 1,234 from Hanover; 2,935 from Hesse; 5 from Luebeck; 5,202 from Mecklenburg; 228 from Nassau; 54 from Oldenburg; 28,600 from Prussia; 1813 from Saxony; 82 from Weimar; 8,658 from Wurtemburg; and 4,416 who were registered, generally as "German." The largest accessions during this decade, shown by the better distribution of "Germans" into their various territorial origins, were from Baden, Bavaria, Mecklenburg, Prussia and Wurtemburg.

Between 1870 and 1880 the term "German" had come to have a distinctive national significance and it is not surprising that in the Census of 1880 a great proportion of those recorded as foreign-born were set down as "German," rather than credited to the smaller states which constituted the Empire. The total population of Michigan in 1880 was 1,636,937. Of these 88,525 were native-born German people, this time again 5.4 per cent of the total, showing that the immigrant additions to the population of the state continued to be not only proportional to its accessions from all other sources, but were sufficient to repair the losses by death and removal from the state which occurred during the decade. By this time, also, two full generations of the posterity of the earlier accessions had come up, amounting, by an empirical estimate, to approximately 141,000 persons of native birth and German blood, in addition to 88,525 who were born abroad.

The federal Census of 1890, seemingly, had as its keynote the provision of figures upon which to base several economic theories connected with the labor movement, and outside the figures on these topics the statistical usefulness of the work is limited. By the time of its taking, "Germany" had become a common source of origin for the foreign-born who came from that country, and the earlier political subdivisions were neglected. The number of foreign-born in Michigan in 1890 was 543,880, out of a total population of 2,093,889. Of this more than half million foreign-born, the Germans were 135,509, the Austrians 3,639 and those from Luxemburg 279. They began to have a more distinctive distribution over the state. The greatest group, 43,356, were in Wayne county; the next largest, 9,855, in Saginaw county; while there were in Macomb 4,463; Berrien 3,491; Huron 3,119; Kent 4,270; Lenawee 2,375; Monroe 3,009; St. Clair 3,725 and Washtenaw 4,102.

It will be noted that by 1890, after a period of 40 years of active entry of Germans into Michigan, resulting to some extent from the state's own invitations to immigrants, the percentage substantially increased, rising to 6.46 per cent of the total. Meantime the fecundity of the race was asserting itself to the extent that, of white persons of foreign ancestry, from one or both parents, in the state at the time the census of 1890 was taken, there were 316,757 creditable to such German antecedents. This greater figure includes the lesser one of 135,509 of actual foreign-born given hereinbefore, and must not be added to it. It does show that in 1890, of the entire population of Michigan 10.35 per cent were either of actual German birth or were of German origins in the generation just preceding.

By 1900 the state had grown to have a population of 2,420,982 souls. Despite the increase, the total of foreign-born had experienced a falling off, both in its total and in its percentage relation. The total number of all kinds of foreign-born people in the state in that year was 541,653, compared with 543,880 ten years before. The total number of foreign-born creditable to German sources was 125,074, while 20,218 Poles were credited to that race. although they were born in territory under German dominion, and 6,049 Austrians were in the state.

No accurate statistics of American parentage with definite foreign origins were provided this year, except that the total number of residents of Michigan in 1900 who were of foreign parentage, one or both, was 357,629, a gain over the figures for 1890, as the result of two causes. One of these was the fecundity of the races, which the German-Americans enjoyed in common with all the other strains, the other that the second generation from the pioneers was farther along in the period of its formation.

Twentieth Century Changes

The greatest changes in the population of the state occurred between 1900 and 1920. By 1910 the population of Michigan had increased to 2,810,172, of whom 660,000 were foreign-born. During the next decade the state's population went up to 3,668,412, of whom 729,292 were foreign-born. Of these 86,047 were of German birth, while about 410,000 of the total population, including these, appear to have been of Germanic origin, either through birth or descent from one or both German parents. Applying some empirical rules of growth, none of which are absolute, it is calculated that in 1920 the population of Michigan included about 670,000 people of German blood, either actually foreign born, the descendants of one or both German parents, or natives who were the descendants of German grandparents through native-born parents.

From this point onward, through the operation of restrictive immigration laws, the absolute cessation of German immigration from 1914 to 1918, and the dying off of the foreign-born stock, the number of persons of German birth must be expected to fall off, while the number of those of near or remote Germanic origin will continue to grow at a percentage quite equal to the growth of the total population of the state.

Of the foreign-born Germans still resident in the state in 1920, 37,745 were in Wayne County; 5,300 in Saginaw; 2,900 in Kent; 2,420 in Macomb, and 2,079 in Bay, accounting for nearly 50 per cent of the total in these five counties.

Of the total population of the state in 1920, 18.3 percent may be calculated to have been of immediate or remote German origin.

CHAPTER VI

THE EARLY "AUSWANDERERS"

The Unimpressive Beginnings—The Processes of Distribution — Organization of the Scott Guard.

To appreciate the processes of settlement of Michigan by the various contributions to its population one must follow the history of the gateways into the territory which now composes its area. The earliest gateway was by that of the St. Lawrence River and the lakes. By that route came the French explorers, the British conquerors and the few Germans who are recorded in the Colonial period. That was the highway of the fur trade. The second was the Ohio gateway, the westerly end of trails beginning at Pittsburgh and leading to Marietta, and thence by the foot of Lake Erie into Eastern Michigan, or along the Cumberland pike and from it northward into what is now Southern and Western Michigan. This was a route rendered fairly safe from Indian assailants, and through it, in wagon trains or on horseback, eastern and southeastern Americans found their way to the Old Northwest. The east, as has been shown herein, had many early Germanic settlements, and of its emigrants to the Northwest the German-Americans formed a considerable percentage. This accounts for the early prevalence of people of this breed in Southern Michigan to the west of Detroit.

The third gateway was the Erie Canal. New York was the great port of entry for European immigration, and the Erie Canal and the Great Lakes furnished a ready access to the new country where lands were cheap and futures promising. This route, even when the railroads got as far west as Buffalo and a rail and lake journey from the Atlantic became available, was most commonly used by the immigrating millions who came into the United States from 1845 to 1890. A due proportion of Germans traversed it, like the rest.

An understanding of these gateways gives the key to the presence of people of German blood in Michigan during several eras and their distribution into various sections. It has already been shown that a few came through the Laurentian gateway. Those who were early and scattered settlers in Southern Michigan were second and third-growth products from the earlier Germanic settlements from New York, New Jersey and Pennsylvania and from as far as Maryland and Virginia. The group who came out to form peasant missions and the refugees from the consequences of the '48 Revolution came by way of the Erie Canal. In the cases of both these latter classifications, the city of Detroit constituted the sieve which separated those who were determined to be agriculturists from those to whom the blandishments of cities were attractive.

The Unimpressive Beginnings

Most of the early Germans whose settlement in Michigan was not derived from the patriation in Canada located in and around Detroit. In 1827 thirty-nine foreigners, not naturalized, were residents of Detroit, the majority of them Germans. These were added to by accessions detailed farther along in this record. In 1833 they had become numerous enough to form separate religious congregations.

Even while there were quite a few Germans in Michigan in the earlier decades of the nineteenth century, their contemporaries did not seem to be impressed by their presence. The late Mr. Robert E. Roberts, who, as a pioneer of the early city, made many contributions to its written history, discussed the early population of Detroit in a letter which appeared in the Detroit Free Press, May 8, 1877. Writing of a period fifty years before that date, he said that in 1827 there was but one German in all Michigan, General John E. Schwartz. This, of course, was not so, but it indicates the small impression which the Germans who were present made upon native fellow citizens.

Levi Bishop, the author of the epic poem, "Teuchsa Grondie," in which the traditional Indian history of the city of Detroit is told, when speaking of the period around 1837, said that the population of Michigan at that time included, besides the Americans and the French, "some English, some Germans and a few from Hungary." Incidentally, Mr. Bishop, who came into the state from Buffalo about the year of which he was talking, referred to the French who had been in Michigan two hundred years ahead of him as "foreigners"; showing that some modern solecisms are not so modern after all.

The Processes of Distribution

In 1802 the tax lists for Detroit showed Michael Yax, John B. Yax, Simon Yax and Peter Yax among the land-holders in the district, their lands being in the present Macomb County area, in the neighborhood of Chesterfield, and some in present Grosse Pointe. In what was then called Sargent township, now part of Macomb County, Joseph Blein was also rated as a land-holder at the same time. Christian Clemens, the founder of Mt. Clemens, was on the St. Clair township list. A Mr. Everts, colloquially described as "a Dutchman," was located at Frederick, on the Clinton River in 1812.

When B. F. H. Witherell took the territorial census for the district of Detroit in 1827, the city had a population of 2,152, and among the names of the residents appeared those of Julius Eldred, Wilhelm Firehaudt, John Steinback, John Streit, John Kremer and Peter Yax.

There were some German immigrants who came to Michigan in the '30's. Michigan was then mostly Detroit. Peter Machris, from the boundary of Lorraine, came to Detroit in

1832, and lived on the site of the present Wayne County courthouse. Then he bought some land within the present Detroit city limits on the Gratiot road for $1.25 per acre that is worth $25,000 an acre at this writing. Peter was a laborer for Gen. Larned for a while and then became a shoe dealer. John Bour, an Alsatian shoemaker, came in the same year as Machris. That was the year that John Maladon came to Detroit. John Schmittdiel was also in Detroit in 1832. The following year Andreas Huber, a carpenter from Baden, arrived. He married Schmittdiel's daughter.

In 1833 thirty-three families, largely Bavarians, named Seideff, Jung, Claus, Michael, Hommel and Speicht, and eight families from Neustadt, in Kur-Hessen, came to the city. The Neustadt families were those of Wilhelm Gies, Joseph Gies, John Groll, Henry Vidior, Henry Diegel, Henry Reichenbach, and Anton Stadler. The Greusel family came in the same year. So did George Weber and his brother-in-law, Kallenbach, from Hesse-Darmstadt. Weber's wife had come with her father, Joseph Laible, the year before. Conrad Seek was the city's leading tailor in that time. He had been wiped out by the fire of 1805, but seems to have survived as a practitioner of sartorial art.

In the same year, came John Weitzel, Diedrich Borneman and George F. Seitz, from Baden. Seitz, brought his two sons, John H. Seitz and Fred Seitz, who cut an important figure later as bankers and real estate operators. They owned most of the present site of the Buhl Building, in down-town Detroit, were forever speculating, and almost constantly on the ragged edge financially, as the result of taking on too much investment. In 1834 Anton F. Barlage came with his father, mother and sisters. All but Anton died of the cholera after a two weeks residence. A group of Alsatians came in 1835, including the Moehling and the Steinmetz families and Henry Miller. David Bernard Eggeman came from Switzerland. These were Catholics. A goodly group of German Protestants were their contemporaries.

Among them were David Stricker, August Kunze, John Heiss, and families named Plank, Kaiser, Immel, Seefreid, Bauer, Neff, Gohl, Heimsch, Waechterhaeuser, George, Metz, Eisenach, Graf, Betzer, Stauch, Beste, Herbst, Schneider, Amrhein, Kies, Wolf and Miesel. It was from these that Pastor Schmid got his first Lutheran congregation. Peter Miller, who came about this time, "Schwartz E. Peter" or "Black Peter," as he was called, became treasurer of Wayne County in a later day. In 1837 Dr. Brockhauser arrived. So did William Presser, whose two step-sons, Peter and William Fischer, were among the leading early jewelers of Detroit, remaining in business for more than fifty years.

Organization of the Scott Guard

In 1841 there was a good deal of popular favor for Gen. Winfield Scott who had carried on the Black Hawk War and was destined to have enduring fame come to him in the war with Mexico. So when the First Battalion of the Frontier Guard was organized it was called the Scott Guard. Among its organizers were John V. Ruehle, Nicholas Greusel, Fritz Kaufman, John Greusel, Fred Ruehle, Joseph Koehler, Jacob Gies, William Barie, Lorenz Behr, Joseph Gies, Joseph Henkel, Anthony Katus, Frank Martz, Michael Martz, Anton Millius, Michael Winterhalter, J. Wagner, Conrad Ling and Paul Gies. The Brothers Orth were the Guard's musicians. The Guard's uniforms were made by Henry Keeler, a tailor who had come from Hesse-Darmstadt, the year before, and who was so proud of his creations that he paraded through the streets on Sundays after church hours attired in his own uniform.

By 1845 the Detroit City Directory, containing 2,800 names, showed 250 of German appearance. John H. Gies was a potter and Joseph Jelsch a tanner. Dr. Lemke was city physician and the only German public official. He had professional contemporaries in Dr. Ege and Dr. Brockhauser. Anton Pulte, destined to become a great jobber, was a young

IN THE MAKING OF MICHIGAN

grocer. During this year a group of Westphalians came in. Among them was Frank Brueggeman, a grocer, who sold beer. He has the distinction of being the person who introduced beer glasses with handles. He had a fellow tradesman, Michael Laubacher, an Alsatian, for a neighbor the same year. Laubacher helped erect the first Catholic Cathedral of Detroit and St. Mary's Church for the German Catholics. He bought twelve acres of land, now part of Mt. Elliott cemetery in Detroit, for $180. Today its land value, if realizable, would be a million dollars.

The emigrant who came in that year who made the best record was John V. Ruehle, a twenty-year-old baker from Baden, whose brother Frederick and his father, mother and sisters were with him. John V. Ruehle became an early alderman, was in the Legislature in 1844, got his Majorship in the Mexican War, was a member of the city water board in 1859 and started off again into the Civil War when he was forty-nine years old.

CHAPTER VII

VARIOUS COUNTY SETTLEMENTS

The Washtenaw Germans — The Wayne County Settlers — German Americans from the East—The Southern Michigan Settlement—The Settlement in Genesee—The Settlement in Allegan—The Oakland County Pioneers—The Shiawassee Pioneers—The Oakland County Beginnings—The Pioneers of Macomb—Some Early Land-holders —The Settlers in St. Clair.

The Washtenaw county colony of Germans seems to have attracted a good deal of contemporary and historical attention. John George Kohl, a German traveller, who wrote about them in 1855, recalled that "the first were some few who came from the villages near Stuttgart about 1830. It was just the time when Michigan was lauded to the skies, just as twelve years later, it wás Iowa, Wisconsin and Minnesota. The early settlers helped to build the city of Ann Arbor, and wrote home about their prosperity. The word was passed from village to village; first a dozen men, then a dozen families, crossed the ocean until five to six thousand Swabians had settled around Ann Arbor (1855). The native speculators bought up the land near the prosperous settlers, but the increased price of land did not stop the purchasers; for the Swabians kept on extending their farms. Detroit's German newspaper, already in existence toward the end of the '40's, did not prosper greatly until the large German immigration of the '50's was added to the Michigan population."

IN THE MAKING OF MICHIGAN 73

The really important immigrations of Germans into Michigan and the ones which made an impress upon the state were those which occurred from 1830 to the '70's. These were occasioned by two causes. The first was a religious movement, detailed farther on, for the evangelization of the American Indians, or at least some of them. The other was the revolutionary movement of 1848-1849 in the homeland. That effort proving fruitless, thousands of young Germans of breeding, brains and education conceived that a future of liberty, consistent with their ideals, in the fatherland was hopeless. Most of these came to America as the most likely place in which to realize their purposes. Incidentally, not a few others went to South America, as did many Irish emigrants from their home land during the same period. This fact accounts for the earliest Celtic and German plantations in Colombia, Peru, Chile and Argentina.

One of the consequences of these two moving causes effective in the distribution of people of the old country over the world, was the incorporation into the population of Michigan of a Germanic constituent that was not only large but far-reaching in its influence.

The Wayne County Settlers

The modern German settlement of the real "auswanderer" in Michigan was from two sources, migrations from earlier German-American settled localities and immigration from the old country. The former of these contributions began as early as 1825; the later in 1830 or thereabouts. The former constituted a rather steady flow of new residents; the latter was spasmodic and irregular for some years, until it began to be furthered by the action of the state government in the direction of inducing a Germanic immigration by the use of what would nowadays be called propaganda.

Between these two basic conditions of settlement, the third and fourth decades of the nineteenth century brought a good many of the race into the state. The earliest came through the Ohio gateway; the later through the Erie Canal and the Lakes. They spread over many of the counties, largely those in the three southern tiers from east to west. The reasons for these locations were apparent. That was the direction into which led the highways of the period.

In Wayne County Peter and Henry Fralick were pioneers of Plymouth in 1825, coming from Pennsylvania, where the family name of their ancestor was Froehlich. Peter Korte was in Greenfield in 1837, John Horger in 1839, and Jacob Esper in 1843. All were direct from Prussia. In Grosse Pointe Michael Greiner settled in 1831, and John Caspar Salter in 1836. Jacob Fox was in Dearborn in 1847. Jacob and John Slinger, Pennsylvania "Dutchmen," were in Huron in 1834, John Arnheim came direct from Germany to Livonia in 1832, and John C. Baur to the same township in 1836. Frank Noeker, a Westphalian, got into Hamtramck in 1846. Charles Kamerer got into Nankin in 1839, direct from over-seas. In Plymouth the Amblers and the Bradners were Wayne County New Yorkers among the pioneers. Jacob Humbert and Christ Hoffsteller, Alsatians, arrived in Redford in 1832. Frederick Rieden was settled in Springwells in 1843 and Michael Rieden in 1845. John Conrad was one of the organizers of Brownstown. He was the great-grandson of Michael Conrad, of Gross Weiss, on the Rhine. John Conrad came to Michigan through Pennsylvania and New York. His son, Charles Frederick, was an important developer of mineral and timber resources in the Upper Peninsula. Frederick Moring was in Taylor in 1852. Ecorse, originally settled by French, got Martin Sweitzer in 1850, John Frank in 1852 and Jacob Heintzen in 1854. All were German born. The Blanck family were in Hamtramck in 1852.

In 1857 Louis Campau became reminiscent before the Michigan Historical Society at Detroit, and while discussing prisoners taken by the Indians during the War of the Revolution and who remained in Michigan, spoke of Henry Cottrell, an American "Dutchman," whose residence was near Cottrell-ville, on the St. Clair River. "He was," said Mr. Campau, "one of the prisoners referred to. He was an extensive farmer, a whole-souled 'Dutchman', highly respected. He died about 1815."

German-Americans from the East

The Yerkes family got into the town of Plymouth in 1826, when Joseph Yerkes, who was born in Pennsylvania in 1769, took up land from the government. The family were descended from Harmon Yerkes, a Hanoverian who settled in Eastern Pennsylvania and whose son Anthony was the father of Stephen Yerkes, whose son Joseph settled in Plymouth. Later on one of Joseph Yerkes' neighbors, as neighboring went then, was Henry Houk, a Steuben county, N. Y., German descendant, who was born in 1797, got into what is now Northville in 1833, and cast his first vote for Andrew Jackson.

Jacob Cornell, a Poughkeepsie, N. Y., German scion, got into Livingstone County in 1834. Henry Scheyrz, a pioneer of Ingham, born in Germany in 1819, got into the state when he was 22, and John Herman, from Darmstadt, got into Lansing in 1872.

In Calhoun county the first Methodist Sunday School class was organized in Battle Creek in 1836. John Wentz and his wife were members. The Free Will Baptists organized a church at Homer in the same year and Homer Jacob and Clarissa Rosencrantz were members of it. All of them were from Schoharie county, New York.

Jacob Crager, born in Wayne county, N. Y., in 1819, of a German parentage, came into Bainbridge town, of Berrien county, in 1844.

Cass County's earliest German seems to have been Charles Haney, who came direct from Baden, in 1831, and who was a peddler and a clock repairer. Louis Rheinhard, descended from a Hessian soldier who had settled in Virginia, got a farm on Baldwin's Prairie, in 1828 or 1829. George and Catherine Steck came to Porter township, of the same county, directly from Germany, in 1849.

Clinton County's earliest German-American family was that of John Swegles, Jr., who came out from Steuben County, N. Y., in 1840. Swegles was one of the founders of St. Johns, which was laid out as soon as the Detroit & Milwaukee railroad route was surveyed in 1853. Morris Fedewa, the pioneer of the great Catholic settlement which centered about Westphalia, came from abroad in 1842, when he was 30 years old. He settled in Dallas township first. Peter Ulrich, who was German born, got into Dallas in 1845. In 1849 Peter Schnack came out from Tompkins county, N. Y., and with him a nephew named Hulse. Peter Petsch, Prussian born, settled in Westphalia in 1854. Martin Maier, Wurtemburger, brought his family and his father-in-law, Jacob Landerberger, into Watertown in 1854. The first Saxon to arrive was Christopher Jacobs, who went into Riley township in 1857. Jacob Brown, who later became an important merchant in Detroit, was a pack peddler through Clinton county in the earliest '50's. He traded his goods for furs.

Eaton county had an early sprinkling of Germans. Sylvanus Hunsiker, an Onandaga Co., N. Y., German-American, located in Bellevue Township in 1833, and Bernhard Bader, German born, took up land from the government in the same township in the next year. The Daniel Hager family, from Somerset Co., Pennsylvania, settled near Vermontville, in 1836. They were described by contemporary Yankees as "of the solid type of Germans." Christopher Brum, who was also born in Germany in 1813, settled in Vinton township in 1846. John Locker, of the same nativity, settled in Benton township in 1852. Samuel Waltensdorf, also German born, settled in the county in 1854.

The Southern Michigan Settlement

Sons of Gottfried Corbus, he who settled on Private Claim 69, in Dearborn, long before, moved out to Allen's, in Hillsdale county, in 1829, where Richard Corbus died. Joseph, his brother, settled in Gerard township, and lived there until 1876. Christopher Baer got into Prairie Ronde the same year. In Hillsdale city David Bechard, a Hamburger, appeared as a roving peddler in the '40's, and became a settled dry goods dealer in 1850.

Christian Prussia established a tannery in Jackson in 1830. It lasted only two years. At the end of that year Christian was on the tax rolls for $10 worth of real estate. The year after Prussia arrived Samuel Klein opened a cabinet shop, otherwise a furniture making shop, in Jackson. In 1835 Tunis Vrooman arrived in the city from Middleburg, N. Y. He was of half German descent, as was his wife, Hannah Kineske, whom he had married at Carlisle, N. Y.

As early as 1837 Jacob Colclazer, who was the first librarian of the University of Michigan, preached at Kalamazoo. Frederick William Curtenius, later Mexican war veteran and Adjutant-General of the state, was a trustee of Kalamazoo College in 1833. Elder Henry Limbocker founded the Methodist Church in Kalamazoo in 1841 and that at Eckford a year later. In 1852, Sylvester Fredenburg, descendant of the Hudson river colony of Germans, came out from Columbia county, N. Y., and helped organize Wakeshma township. Samuel Dierstein, who originated in Genesee Co., N. Y., was the early settler of the Otter Lake portion of Lapeer County.

John J. Schnol, Pennsylvania German of a family two generations in America, took up some land a mile west of Clinton, in Lenawee county, in 1826. Franz Heinrich Hagerman made the first opening in Seneca township in 1833, putting up a log cabin near Morenci. In 1834 he bought a section of land in Medina township. Adam Siebring followed him into the same town in the succeeding year, and two years later Adam took up new land in Ogden township. Wilhelm Rafel was in Lenawee town in 1840. Arnold Smeltzer started farming in Macomb township in 1842, and Henry Smith, from Uschendorff, Bavaria, did the same in 1857. He built the mill at Tecumseh.

St. Joseph county had some early settlers of the race. In 1833 Philip H. Hoffman had a home in Three Rivers. In 1834 a man named Schnable, who had come out from Philadelphia, built a mill and power dam at the same place. Aaron Habenbach, a Birks county, Penn., German, came to Constantine in 1835. In 1836 one Lantz built a tavern at Three Rivers. Joseph Henry Kreischer settled at Lockport in 1837. In 1838 the itinerant minister, John Irkenbach, supplied the Methodist church at St. Joseph. Among the settlers of 40 years before that date who were remembered at the annual meeting of the county pioneer society in 1887 were Heinrich and Peter Beltenbender, Louis and Joseph Wachterhauser, and Lorenz Schellhaus.

In Tuscola county Jacob Alber, born in Germany, took up a farm in Juanita township in 1849. John Strohwaer, a Darmstadt man, got into Aylmer township in 1852. He was a private in the Eighth Michigan Infantry in the civil war. George Schmidt, who was born at Kissingen-on-Main, in 1827, settled at Vassar in 1850. Nicholas Lausen got to Caro in the same year.

In 1837 Richard Fishbach started a cobbler's shop at Howell. Jacob Skillbeck succeeded him in his business. Egbert Albright, a Pennsylvanian, had a grist mill at Hartland, in Livingstone county, in the early '30's. Ferdinand Weller, who came from Asch, in Austria, in 1856, settled at Howell and learned the printing trade. He became a prosperous newspaper man in Muskegon later on. He was a leading Democrat of his period.

The Settlement in Genesee

The first white people to appear in the neighborhood of Flint, were two pioneer French missionaries and a French trader named Boilieu. The fourth was Jacob Smith, a native of Quebec of immediate German ancestry. He got into what is now Genesee county and built a trading house in 1819. He had his post on the Grand Traverse of the Flint River. He was a Captain in the American army in the war of 1812. He was known to the Indians as "Wah-be-sins," "the Young Swan." He assimilated his habits and ways of living to those of the Indians, wore their dress, talked their language and was their friend.

When General Cass came to make a treaty with them at Saginaw for the extinction of their title, the chiefs were all in opposition until Smith's influence was invoked. When Gen. Cass agreed to having eleven sections, or 7,040 acres, of Indian land go to Smith in requital for the Indians' debts and their love and affection for him, the negotiations for the treaty went on very smoothly. Smith owed Louis Campau some money, and as was usual at such negotiations, Louis was present to collect his account out of what his debtors might get. Smith had a stock of goods which Campau sought to get in settlement, but as the Indians at the treaty had a good deal of money and Smith wanted to turn his goods into cash, he got the Indians to hold out until his goods were sold and he might pay directly in cash. Campau had to wait and lost one profit. Smith married an Indian woman and had children. His 7,040 acres of land caused a deal of litigation, but the title was confirmed in his heirs. He led a life of great hardship, dying all but alone in Flint in 1825, a faithful Indian giving him the last attentions.

Joseph and Adam Carl Kline, born of German parents in the Mohawk Valley, settled in Grand Blanc in 1833. Jacob Dodder, a New Jersey German, began farming in Linden in 1835.

The Settlement in Allegan

Allegan county's early settlers, in the 1830's, included many eastern men of German descent, from Pennsylvania and New York. A historian writing in 1878, said that "in 1835 there was quite an infusion of Germans." Among them were Jacob Bruner, John W. Steininger, and Fred Muma, who eventually took high rank as farmers, and pioneer families bearing the names of Rossman, Ammerman, Johannes and Stegeman, the latter group largely from Rochester. Edward Johannes settled near Saugatuck in 1834. The Ammermans built a saw mill on Dumont Creek. In the '40's Christopher Arndt settled in Dow township, Catherine Burkhardt in Hopkins, Johannes Tripp in Laketown and Henry Maentz and Henry Sprann in Monterey. In 1837 the Methodist church in Allegan county had John Irkenback as its presiding elder.

As a matter of fact, the German immigrants antedated the Hollanders in Allegan county. Among the very oldest settlers were Jacob Arndt, who settled in Dow township; Fred Schraeder, who took up government land in Leighton township, and Henry Mauetz, who settled in Monterey in the early '40's, of the nineteenth century. Peter Beisel had been ahead of them in Athens township, settling in 1831; as was Henry Eberstine, who came direct from the old country and walked most of the way from New York to locate on Goguac Prairie in 1834.

In that year the hotel at Marshall was run by a man named Vandenburg, who was called a "Dutchman" and who may have been Dutch or German. "Deacon" Betterle, of German descent from middle New York, took up land on Goguac Prairie in 1836, and Jeremiah Hardenburg, a Victory, N. Y., son of German ancestors, brought his wife, Polly Haden, out with him to Burlington township in 1837. At that time another New York "Dutchman", as he was called, William Michael, was settled on Goguac Prairie, and acquired a reputation as a local singer. His grandfather, Moorhaus, himself German born, lived with Michael and fiddled for the barn-dances of 1837 on a violin which he had bought in Montreal in 1800, and which was made in 1600 by Jacob Steiner, a violin maker of Innsbruck, in the Tyrol, who had learned his trade at Cremona.

Peter Mann, who was of German lineage, settled in Gerard township, of Branch county in 1839, coming from Schoharie county, N. Y. James Godfrey Corbus, whose father had settled in Dearborn, went to Bronson in 1832. In 1836, Conrad Reep was supervisor of the poor in Quincy township. He was a Pennsylvanian. A year earlier than that Alexander Odren took his wife, who had been Elizabeth Steinbeck, and who was born in Detroit in 1795, to a farm in California township. Charlotte Hildebrand was in Algansee township in 1840. Thomas Heisrodt, out of Orleans county, N. Y., settled in Ovid town, in 1856.

There were some early arrivals of people of German blood and nativity in Calhoun county. About the first to impress himself was Claus Inselman, who was an umbrella mender in Marshall in 1835, and who drove the stage from Marshall to Kalamazoo. Peter Kocker, Pennsylvania born, came to Marshall in 1837. Although he was 48 years old when the civil war began he went into it as a private soldier. In 1838 Solomon Plattner was elected supervisor of the town of Fredonia, and the next year John Fredenburg, an Albany man of German extraction, who had some knowledge of surveying, began laying out lands in the town. He himself settled at Lyon Lake. Christian and Polly Bochman came out from Northampton county, Pennsylvania, and settled in Marengo in 1844. Peter Krenerich came out from Bavaria, where he was born in 1824, and settled in Sheridan township in 1850.

The Calhoun county Germans were pronouncedly anti-slavery. A. D. Van Buren, a local chronicler, tells about Conrad Eberstein, who was an "old" settler of Battle Creek in 1856, participating in an anti-slavery meeting in Battle Creek, where he denounced Buchanan roundly in a marked German accent.

In the fall of 1818, Jacob Eilett, a New York state "Dutchman," looked over land at Silver Lake, in Oakland county, with a view to location. It didn't suit him and he passed on. The next year Michael Kempf bought land in Troy township. Stephen Rossman, a Middleburg, N. Y., German of three generations in the county, settled at Oxford in 1823. John Hagerman, Pennsylvanian of the same descent, settled in Bloomfield in 1833. Michael Bloomberg from Clavernack, N. Y., got into Southfield in 1836. William Reid, who was born in Germany, settled in Milford in 1840. Capt. Parke tells that when he went to Pontiac from Detroit in 1821 there was a family by the name of Kaiser settled on the Saginaw turnpike, now Woodward avenue, between Royal Oak and Pontiac.

The Oakland County Pioneers

At the west end of the county, in Novi township, Rudolph Sebring, a New York state German, set up a wagon shop at Novi Corners in 1828. Incidentally some of this man's blacksmithing was done for Erastus Ingersoll, one of his neighbors, who invented the first mowing machine, which he patented in 1827, and which he continued to improve, with Sebring's assistance. Among Ingersoll's posterity was the manufacturer of the Ingersoll cheap watch. Joseph Eddy immigrated into Novi in 1828 from the Hudson river county, talking in such broken German-English that his neighbors couldn't understand him. Joseph was evidently a devotee of the open spaces, where the strong men come from. He had left the valley of the Hudson because its population was too congested to suit him, and he was not long at Novi until the increasing settlement made him begin complaining of Oakland county, which was getting too many "frame haeusen" to agree with his ideas.

Daniel Fangboner, Warren county, N. J., descendant of an early German settlement, settled two miles east of Rochester in 1831.

IN THE MAKING OF MICHIGAN 83

The earliest German settler of Shiawassee county was Frederick Frieseke, who came to Owosso in 1834. He had been a Prussian soldier under Blucher at Waterloo. He lived to be 90 years old, dying at Owosso in 1883. One of his descendants, born in Shiawassee county, is a famous painter. Elizabeth Gould, who came with her husband to Shiawassee town in 1838, was born at Ray Hill, Penn., in the house of her grandfather, Householder, a wealthy German of that place. Otto Brandt, born in Hagenau, Germany, in 1819, settled near Owosso in 1847. He married Rachel Spenkenberl, daughter of a neighboring farmer in 1851. George Stichler moved into Woodhull township in 1854. About the same time Joseph Bellheimer came from Brock's Gap, Va. He was descended from a Wittenberg family that had come into Pennsylvania in 1700. Father Peter Godez, a Hungarian, organized a Catholic parish at Woodhull, in Shiawassee, in 1847. His almost all-German congregation built a log church. Jacob Eberle, Baden born, ran a hotel in Owosso in 1853.

The St. Joseph Pioneers

Christian Betzing, Frederic Bent, George Argus, John Falkstein, John Dobbreton, Louisa Hellwig, Margaret Humell, Sophia Klett, Henry Lohrman, John N. Luthardt, Dora Margenruth, Rachel Mandorff and Conrad Schmidt, were among the early settlers of St. Joseph county. They were all born in Germany, and came in from 1835 to 1850. The early population of the county also included Pennsylvanians and New Yorkers of German ancestry with such names as Bittenbender, Broman, Casper, Hackman, Hackenberg, Haybarger, Hoffman, Hoch, Klein, Schaeffer, Reifschneider, Roming and Sigler.

Barry county had some early German settlers. Jacob Traut came out from Pennsylvania and settled there in 1834. Four years later at the first election in Johnstown, Solomon Gettman was elected constable. He came out from Pennsylvania. By 1850 there was quite a sprinkling of Eastern Germans in the country. Woodland Center's Methodist Sunday School class included John and Laura Dillenbeck, and Pine Lake class had in it four Lindermans, Thomas, Elizabeth, Margaret and Adeline.

The Pioneers of Macomb

The first important German settlement in Macomb county was that of the Moravians, leaders of whom, having been disturbed in their mission at Sandusky during the War of the Revolution and its sequences, were arrested by the British as disloyal to them and brought to Detroit. The charges against them were made by the savage allies of the British, were later retracted, and the British commandant suggested their settlement near the Clinton river, in the neighborhood of the present Mt. Clemens. On July 29, 1782, the Missionaries Zeisberger, Jungman, Edwards and Jung with the wives of Zeisman and Jungman, and nineteen male and female Indian adherents, founded a settlement called New Guadenhutten, in the present town of Clinton, two miles west of Mt. Clemens. The community built a street of block houses, were joined by the Missionaries Weygand and Schebosch from Bethlehem, in Pennsylvania, and gathered enough adherents to number fifty-three persons in their community. Among these was Richard Connor, an Irishman who had been captured by the Indians and who had become attached to their mission in Ohio, later rejoining that at New Guadenhutten. When it became apparent that their lands were to be opened up for settlement they were bought off by the British for two hundred dollars and went back to Ohio. Their settlement had no appreciable influence, other than to form the basis for Richard Connor's claim to the sites which they abandoned, which were later confirmed to him as Private Land Claims Nos. 137 and 138.

Zeisberger's observations during his four years stay in the Detroit district confirm the early presence of Germans in the territory. In 1782 "a German soldier asked to borrow a book from us," he says in one part of his "Journal"; and when, in 1794, he re-located at the mouth of the River Thames, on the Canadian side of Lake St. Clair, he met "seven Baptist Germans from Detroit."

The original important German American settler of Macomb county was Christian Clemens, for whom Mt. Clemens city is named. He was born in Pennsylvania in 1768, came to Detroit in 1795 and settled on the site of Mt. Clemens in 1798, dying there in 1844. He was a descendant of the early settlers of Pennsylvania, was distinctively German in his manners and tastes, and retained a noticeable German accent until his death. In 1830 Robert Weltz, New Jersey son of German parents, came to Detroit, but passed on to Mt. Clemens after a few months.

A few Germans were among those who took up land from the government in Macomb county in the 1830's. They began to come in early in this period and there were many whose residence in Michigan antedated the '48 movement in the home country.

Some Early Landholders

In Warren township, of Macomb, land was taken up from the government in 1833 and 1834 by Christian Keiser, Henry Gies, John Groll, George Jacob Stauch, Frederick Guth and John Eggert. In the same year Jacob Sommers, Jr., took up land in Sterling. A little later a group of German immigrant farmers established themselves at Waldenburg village. Peter Yax had been in Chesterfield as early as 1796. Abraham Burkholder was clearing his land in Lenox in 1833, and the same year Stephen Goetchius was a resident of Romeo.

Michael Crissman, one of the pioneers of Romeo in 1833, was a New Jersey man, son of John Crissman, a German soldier on the American side of the War of the Revolution. Joseph Weller, of exactly the same kind of ancestry, settled in

Chesterfield in 1831. Peter D. Lerich, grandson of a Buck's
county, Penn., revolutionary soldier, and son of a Warren
county, N. J., soldier of the war of 1812, settled in Utica
about 1836. Christian Gerlach was a schoolmaster in Erin
township in 1834 and Gottfried See a settler. Charles and
Wilhelmina Rein had a farm in Erin in 1844. John Hartsig,
a German Swiss, came to Michigan in 1828, and settled in
Warren township in 1835. He was a driver on the old Utica
& Detroit horse railroad, which preceded steam transportation.

Ludwig Weskowski was an engineer in Macomb County in 1838, directing the work on the Clinton and Kalamazoo
Canal. Traugott Lungerhausen, who came to America from
Prussia in 1833, after spending some of the intervening years
on the first canal at St. Mary's Falls, got into Mt. Clemens
in 1854. Charles Schank got into Brucetown in 1842. He
was a Monroe county, N. Y., descendant of the first plantations in America. Amandus Holmich, a Prussian, settled in
Warren in 1851. George L. Volkening, from Menden, in
Germany, was in Macombtown in 1848. John Freidhoff, a
Bavarian, was in Erin in 1848. William Donner had a farm
near Romeo in 1852. John Wolf came from Sarentin, Germany, to Clinton in 1854. Nicholas Ameis, from Bremen,
came to Erin in 1858. George B. Bertz, from Hesse-
Darmstadt, got into Chesterfield in 1855. John Peter Miller, German born, settled in Warren in 1842 and Charles
Schank, a Monroe county, N. Y., man, came to Michigan in
1848 and settled in Macomb town in 1850. Anthony Henk,
a Prussian, owned a large farm near the Wayne county
line in 1845.

The decades of '50's and the '60's brought many
Germans directly into Macomb County. Their numbers are
reflected in the census figures given in another chapter. They
were practically all agriculturalists, though some were trained for business abroad. John Kuhn, who came to America
later, and to Mt. Clemens in 1874, had been, for instance,

trained in the Seligman banking house at Frankfort-on-Main. His son, Franz C. Kuhn, became a Justice of the Supreme Court of the State.

Early Germans in St. Clair

Henry Cottrell, of the St. Clair river territory, and from whom many of the name are descended, was born in Schenectady, N. Y., in 1774, of German ancestors named Hoover. On their way west the boy was taken a prisoner by the Indians, brought to St. Clair and adopted by the Cottrell family in 1784. Curiously this family's name was then spelled Kottrell. Charles Flugel, who was a drummer for the Thirteenth Infantry, at Niagara, in the war of 1812, settled in Port Huron in 1837. John Balthaser Mulithner, a Bavarian born in 1823, became a farmer in the county in 1852. Nicholas Wonderlich, an Austrian, was 34 years old, when he settled on a farm near St. Clair, about the same time.

"Aunt Emily" Ward, the sister of Eber Brock Ward, the great developer of Michigan marine and railroad interests, and a pioneer of steel making in the United States, lived in St. Clair for a long time. She was a woman of charitable impulses. It is related that she mothered and brought up two "German orphans" of her neighborhood, Theobold and Christian Otgen. The former became a Congressman from Milwaukee and the latter the manager of the Bayview Rolling Mills, on the north shore of Lake Michigan out of Chicago.

St. Clair county's first Germans were undoubtedly the Harsens, Jacob and Bernardus, who were of Hessian blood, who purchased lands from the Indians, on the mainland, before 1797, and obtained a title to the swampland of Harsen's Island which formed the basis for some interesting land-title litigation a long time later. Jacob's first tenancy was under an Indian deed for 999 years, and was for a consideration of $50. In 1835 the Rev. Henry Gehrine, said to have been of eastern German-American ancestry, was Methodist pastor at St. Clair. The Harsens were Lutherans but were of his flock. John Netter, from Coblenz, an old country employe of the family of Carl Schurz, got into St. Clair county and took up land in 1849. John Asman, born in Germany in 1827, became a merchant in Port Huron in 1853. Hon. John Miller, a pioneer of St. Clair county, and the son of Pennsylvania Germans, came from Buffalo in 1842. Among the pioneers of St. Clair county were names such as Duengle, Schunk, Schoenfield, Winkle, Uppleger, Marth, Crouse, Westrick, Hartline, Buehler, Guldenstein, Zermer, Beckman, Hoffman, Raddike, Feske and Pluddeman. Most of these people lived to a great age.

CHAPTER VIII

THE SETTLERS OF WASHTENAW AND SAGINAW

The Beginnings at Ann Arbor—The Pioneers of Saginaw and Bay—Settlements in Other Counties—Upper Penninsula Pioneers.

The German settlement of Washtenaw, was one of the earliest made in Michigan. The honors of pioneering are fairly divisible between two early arrivals. One of these was Conrad Bessinger, a baker from Mannheim, in Baden, who arrived at Ann Arbor, September 18, 1825. A month or two earlier, Daniel Frederick Allmendinger, took up land in Lodi township from the government. Miss Rominger, a local historian, says that Frederick Schilling arrived in the same town in 1829.

A group of Wurtemburgers had settled in Ann Arbor by 1830. They were all Lutherans and wished pastoral service, so Henry Mann wrote to the Mission House at Basle, in Switzerland, for a missionary. It sent Frederick Schmid, who had just completed his theological studies and who arrived in Ann Arbor August 20, 1833. By this time the settlement was composed of 34 families, all from Wurtemburg, and in that year they organized the first German parish in Michigan, locating their house of worship a mile and a half west of Ann Arbor on a very bad trail, which is now "M-17" of the state road system. In this congregation there were pioneer families of the county, including such names as Mann, Mack, Fritz, Allmendinger, and others, the posterity of whom have given a good account of themselves in the later history of the state, as appears in other divisions of this work. The nucleus of the colony attracted other Germans from the old country, most of them of the agricultural type, who took up land in the various townships, the balance of them locating at Ann Arbor or on the bad highway on which the church was located, which was by this time an important trail into the country farther west.

There was a good deal of neighboring between this and other early German communities in Michigan, particularly that at Monroe, where Pastor Schmid served in his ministerial capacity contemporaneously with his service at Ann Arbor. In addition thereto Pastor Schmid had much enthusiasm for the conversion of the Indians, and he made many journeys over long distances into what was then the wilderness of the state, on such religious errands. He had a very practical eye for agricultural lands, and for timbered areas, so that his returns from these journeys were eagerly awaited for the tales which he told of the fine territory which awaited the industry of the settler.

This accounts for the stray emigrations from the Ann Arbor colony into the present territories of Jackson, Livingstone, Ingham and even Gratiot and Saginaw. For instance, New Salem, in the "Thumb" district, was settled by a group of young farmer adventurers from Scio, in Washtenaw, and as is related on other pages, the fertility of the present Frankenmuth neighborhood was spied out early enough by Pastor Schmid to have him make it the objective of Pastor Craemer and his colony when they came into Michigan in the middle '40's.

Without going into intensive detail, the success of this first plantation may be deduced from the fact that by 1850, when Washtenaw had 28,576 inhabitants, more than 4,000 of them were of German birth, a figure which persisted through later immigrations, until the census of 1850 recorded 4,102 German born residents of the county.

Pastor Schmid survived until 1883, was proud of his part in this material development of the state, and could, as his earthly career came to an end, say of it with all truthfulness, in the words of the Roman elder, "Omnis quid vidi, et quorum pars magna fui," all of it had he seen, and of some of it had he been the greater part.

Other Washtenaw Pioneers

There were other Washtenaw settlers whose coming was not wholly related to the original pioneering. Christian Heydlauff married Anna Wagner in Wurtemberg in 1831, and the two of them came to Michigan in 1837, settling in Freedom township. Michael Haminiski, a German, purchased land in Ypsilanti town in 1824. In 1825 Cornelius Ousterhaut, whom some claim as a German, and some as a Hollander, had one of the nine houses in Ann Arbor. Rev. John A. Bauman, pioneer Protestant missionary of that period held service in his house that year. Cornelius Semmons, of Ulster Co., N. Y., and of German descent, went to Washtenaw in 1832, settling in Webster town. Three years later he moved over to Jackson county, taking up a farm in Blackman. Anthony S. Schwarthout, born in Seneca Co., N. Y., of German ancestry two generations back, located in Ypsilanti in 1826. He served both in the Pottawattomie and Black Hawk Wars and when the latter was over, he moved to Saginaw County in 1835. Henry Kimmel lived five miles northeast of Ypsilanti in 1830.

Jacob Ambruster settled in Scio in 1832. The first marriage in Sharon was in 1832, Lorenz Keiff marrying a Miss Palmer. In this same year, Clement Loveder, an English-born farmer of German ancestry, was situated on the Willow Run, east of Ypsilanti, and in 1836, Henry Stumpenhausen was his neighbor near Ypsilanti. Wilhelm Kanause got into Washtenaw County in 1830, but does not appear to have become a settler.

In 1825 John Laury, of Pennsylvania, "Dutch" descent

on his mother's side, moved into Washtenaw, settling near
Manchester. In 1840 his mother, Hanna Laury, who lived
with him, was described as a fluent German speaker.
  In 1836 the Basle Mission House sent John Henry Schwab
to be an assistant to Pastor Schmid. The names of the
pioneers by this time were Mann, Schmitt, Gross, Fritz,
Hornung, Paul, Kempf, Wagner, Stottsteiner, Kern, Beck,
Laubengayer, Nietheimmer, Almendinger, Schumacher,
Schleicher, and Steiner.
  The additions to the colony were fairly steady. Jacob Haas
settled in Lima in 1835. John George Scheiver, who was one
of five brothers who were all named John, but with different middle names, came in 1836. Conrad Krapp, from
Hesse, arrived in the same year. Christian Eberbach, who
came in 1838, had already been educated in Stuttgart as an
apothecary. Some of them lived a long time in the county,
John Keider, born in Germany, and an early settler, died
in Dexter in 1887, aged 108. Nobody knew how long he had
lived in Washtenaw. Henry, Conrad and Gilbert Roe, pioneers of Lansing, were born in Amena, Dutchess County,
N. Y., coming to Michigan in 1831. They located first in
Washtenaw, where they were pioneers of Sharon.

Pioneers of Saginaw and Bay

  Saginaw and Bay county got their greatest contributions of Germans as the results of the Lutheran missionary
foundations in the early '40's and the influx of revolutionary
exiles in the later years of the same decade. Albert Miller,
who was a voluminous writer on the history of the Saginaw Valley, says that in 1848 very many Germans had made
homes in the Saginaw Valley, they all had some money and
"in commencing their homes, were compelled to spend some
of it among the farmers." Mr. Miller said that by preference
they selected land in swales and swamps which had been neglected by the early settlers, and by clearing and draining
these lands they made a rich farming country. This is on-

ly true in part. The original German selections were of both up-land and meadow.

E. L. Wentz, from Binghampton, N. Y., who claimed German ancestry, arrived in Saginaw May 13, 1837, and lived there for some time. He was an early timber prospector. During an election in 1838, the canvassing board had to make a trip from Saginaw to Bay City.. On their way they stopped at the log house of Joseph Holtslander, at the present Carrollton. Charles Siefert, who had been in the Prussian army, got to Saginaw in 1844. There was then complaint of the district being malarial. Siefert was apparently immune. He lived out his ninety-fourth year. John G. Hemmeter, a pioneer of Saginaw City, helped him prove the injustice of the charge of insalubrity against the territory. He lived to be 92, dying in 1901. Rudolph Schacker was the neighbor of both of these from 1847 onward. He was Saginaw's first cabinet maker. John D. Edelman, an eighteen-year old Bavarian lad, settled in Bloomfield township in 1847, and started to clear a farm. Being of an industrious turn he took and executed the contract for clearing the timber off Genesee Avenue, Saginaw's present main street. Nicholas Smelzer, who became a merchant, arrived in Saginaw in 1849. Bernard Hack, a Rhinelander, settled in Bloomfield town in 1849. The next year William Landskroener, from Westphalia, became his neighbor. The latter was only an 18-year old boy when he arrived. Adolph Kirchner got into Tittabawassee town in 1850, directly from Germany, and started farming. William Roeser and his wife were his fellow townsmen the same year, coming from Rudolphsbath in Germany. Gustavus A. Riegel, from Stettin, got into Saginaw city in 1850, as the direct result of the immigration arguments of Dr. Plessner, who wrote State Immigration Commissioner Thompson's "Auswanderer Wegweiser" referred to on other pages. Riegel joined a Missouri regiment in the civil war, and "fought mit Siegel."

The same literature brought Otto Roeser and Frederick Dieckman into Saginaw. Roeser had graduated from the University of Halle in 1846, as a law student, and was admitted to the court in his native land. He landed in Saginaw in 1850. Diechmann was from Hovestadt, in Westphalia, had been educated as a surveyor, and was government surveyor of highways and non-commissioned officer of the Prussian army, when the revolution of '48 broke out. He promptly became captain of a company of insurgents, was self-exiled, and landed in Cheboygan in 1848 and in Saginaw in 1849.

In the same year Saginaw added John Sederick and Herman Romeike, both Prussians of middle age, who became farmers. Charles Peters, old country born, was 32 when he went into Buena Vista in 1852. Gottlieb Lange opened a Saginaw hotel in 1852, and John Koeplinger, Bavarian 16-year old, became a clerk in 1853 and had a store of his own at 20. John M. Hiesrodt, who was out of a Columbia county, N. Y., family, settled in Saginaw township in 1854. Though he was 41 years old when the civil war broke out, he went into the service and landed up for a spell in Libby Prison. Gottlieb Rudolph Bruske, from Silesia, arrived in 1854. He became a story writer of some reputation in later life.

Men of Good Education

Three of the best educated of the earlier accessions to Saginaw county's rapidly growing German colony, not excepting the clergymen, were Otto Roeser, Emil Anneke and Dr. Michael C. T. Plessner. Some account of the last named will be found in another portion of this writing, where he is classified with his fellow professionals. Anneke was born at Dortmund, in Prussia, in 1823. He took his mathematics, science and law at the University of Berlin. He was a revolutionist in 1848, and escaped to America, where from 1848 to 1854 he was a reporter on the New York State Zeitung. In 1855 he edited a German paper at Detroit. He was elected Auditor General of the state in 1862, and in

1866 practiced law in Grand Rapids. Later he established himself at East Saginaw. His grand-son was in the Spanish-American war.

Otto Roeser was also a Prussian from Halle. He studied theology in the University of his native city, but turned to the law in 1846 and graduated therein. The revolution also had an influence in his change of residence to a new continent. He landed in Saginaw in 1850, became a farmer and was a minor public official of much usefulness to his neighbors.

In Bay county there were in 1850 three recorded Germans, living in Lower Saginaw, now Bay City. They were Conrad Hage, Philip Simon and Christopher Heintzman. These were outside the missionary communities. They must have gotten company early for the grand jury list of Bay County for 1859 shows Charles Heinzman, Fred Keisler, Albert Wedthoff and Michael Winterhalter among the jurors.

Settlements in Other Counties

John Van Geisen, old country born, settled in Ionia county in 1844. By 1859 there were enough Germans in and about Ionia to start a German Evangelical church.

In 1835 Father Viscoszky, who spoke German, conducted the first Catholic service, in Muskegon. The same year William Lasley, a New Jersey descendant of the early German settlement, came as a boy of 17 to Muskegon. He had been a year in Michigan before that. In 1847 Frank Jung, born at Trier, in Germany, reached Muskegon. The next year August Plumhoff, who was born in Hanover, settled in Ravenna township, in the same county. In 1850 Julius Bosksche, F. John Hetz, Frederick Drexelius and Kiester Werner settled in Muskegon, having been led by Nicholas Kempff, who arrived in the previous year.

Kent had a few early Germans. Charles Schaefer, born near Wilkes-Barre, Penn., settled in Walker town in 1853, but three years later moved off to Mecosta county, of which he was also a pioneer. William Koch came in 1853, Julius Houseman, Bavarian, later a merchant and Member of Congress, came in the same year. Christopher Kusterer was also of this period of entry. He started a brewery, which three generations of his family managed. About this same period Nicholas Schumacher, from German Flats, N. Y., and George Schroeder from Dannebrock, in Germany, arrived. Nicholas Geik, Bavarian born in 1821, landed in Michigan in 1844, and settled in Gaines township in 1854.

Ingham had some early German settlers. Frederick Yeiter, a German born, settled near Lansing in 1847. Henry Lederer from Baden, settled in Lansing in 1851, as did Philip G. Strong, a 24-year old wagonmaker from Lorraine. Henry Ferle, a Hesse-Darmstadt man, was twenty-one when he settled there in 1854. Frederick Alton, a middle-aged cooper from Wittenberg, was thirteen years in other parts of the United States before he got there in 1857.

In Grand Traverse county from 1839 and 1840, Peter Grenshky was interpreter for Henry R. Schoolcraft. He was a half-breed, said to have had a German father. In 1841 Lewis Miller, son of a German father from Waterloo, Ontario, came into the county, with "Deacon" Joseph Dove, who is said to have been of German ancestry as well.

Charles S. Linkletter was the historian of Benzie county. His parents came into Almira township in 1862, from Steuben county, N. Y. He says that nearly all who came into the county in 1863 were from the same place and of German racial origin.

Among the pioneers of Kalkaska county were Fred Lantzer and Carl Seeling, of the town of Orange. They came in the middle '60's and were born in Germany.

Early Upper Peninsula Germans

In the upper peninsula there were many early Germans, outside those noted in the mining industry on other pages hereof. In 1852, when the first term of court was held at

IN THE MAKING OF MICHIGAN 97

Marquette, George Ruhlein and Louis Schweitzer were petit jurors. An early graduate of the 1846 literary class of the University was Savillon S. Schoff. He made his way into early mining in the northland. In 1855 Henry Bade, Sr., William Heckerman and Henry Seiman, cleared the first farms at the Birch Creek settlement in Menominee county. This was about the earliest agricultural development in the county.

So in the early days in every section of Michigan that bears in distance from the rest any correspondence to the Biblical distances from Bersheba to Dan, or that which is measured from Greenland's icy mountains to India's coral strands, Germans and German-Americans came into the state to participate in the inheritance which, both naturally and officially, it promised to these who would bring brains, order and industry to the task of subduing a new country to the purposes of agriculture, commerce and industry. The greatest influx was in response to the widespread invitation which was the deliberate official action of the state, undertaken in 1848, and actually carried out in the following year.

CHAPTER IX

THE DEFENSE OF TERRITORY, STATE AND NATION

No Race Delinquent—The Revolutionary and Pioneer Period—Revolutionary Heroes of the Blood—The War of 1812—The Black Hawk War—The Mexican War.

Michigan's participations in the warfare of the nation have been frequent and intense. The present territory of the State was, in the first days of its acquaintance with Europeans, an area that was coveted for dominion and profit. Both France and England desired it, to serve the purposes of the crude notions of colonial advantage that existed for each of them in the earliest days. Neither nation had as its motives in colonization the high-minded purposes that have crept into history through the expressions of the altruistic writers, who interpret such activities subjectively, and who have pleated many rhetorical wreaths to encircle the brows of rulers and statesmen who were really very human and very sordid.

The North American continent, as a field for colonial exploitation, meant to the French and the English opportunities for engagement in the fur trade, as a public interest, and the division of the lands and the trade opportunities of the new territory among the king's favorites and his creditors, as a private one. As a matter of consequence there were many European political rivalries over the opportunities for money-making in the area of which Michigan was a part.

Toward the middle of the eighteenth century there were contests between the British, who ruled what is now the territory of the United States, and the French, who ruled what is now the Dominion of Canada. These culminated in the acquisition of control by the British in 1760 and the transfer of dominion over Canada, which carried with it the sovereignty of what is now Michigan. This rule lasted until the tardy evacuation by the British after the War of the Revolution, a cession of authority that was delayed, under one dishonest pretext or another, until 1796. Later on, in the War of 1812, between Great Britain and the United States, growing out of English trespasses upon the freedom of the high seas, which the United States rightfully claimed for its mariners, the fortunes of war once more put the territory of Michigan under British control for a short period.

Still later the young Republic of the United States had its own troubles. There were wars with the Western Indians, for which forces had necessarily to be drawn from such frontier settlements as Michigan. The conflict with Mexico called for more military support for the flag of the nation. The civil war between the people of the South and the North over the issue of slavery next ensued and had to be fought out. Three and thirty years after its close the destruction of the U. S. S. Maine in Havana harbor constituted a reason for war with Spain. Before the twentieth century was well into its 'teens the World War was precipitated, and into it, by a succession of unfortunate events, the United States was drawn.

No Race Delinquent

These various excursions of the United States to the field of Mars called out, successively, lesser or greater numbers of her men to defend the honor and the claims of the nation. In the long look over the history of these events it can be honestly said that no element of the country's population, taken by and large, was delinquent in its duty; and this statement applies alike to native born, foreign-born and alien-descended; and even to those denizens of the country who had not yet been endowed with her citizenship when her interests were endangered. The exceptions of any kind or at any time were so few that they are negligible. So that while there has been a healthy competition by various groups and classes for credit for participation in these various emergencies the claimants have usually been actuated by the motive of appearing "primus inter pares" rather than by a desire to seem super-virtuous. In the adventures into warfare, the German-American citizens of the United States, and of Michigan in particular, have taken their proportional part, and some of them even shared in the earlier forays and defenses which are a part of the history of the pioneer period.

The ensuing recitals of names and deeds occur in these pages, not for the purpose of presenting the participating group as animated by a higher patriotism than its fellow-citizens, but rather to show that it has not been laggard.

Revolutionary and Pioneer Period

The later years of the eighteenth and the earlier years of the nineteenth century show a good deal of sporadic settlement of Germans in Michigan's present territory. Some of these settlers are cited in other pages in connection with land settlements and the like. Eventually the names of some of the men of this period found their way on to the rolls of the United States and the State's military forces.

This was particularly noticeable in the War of the Revolution, the War of 1812, and later in the Black Hawk War. The first of these conflicts was not waged in the territory of which Michigan became a part, though perusal of the history of some of its sequels carries the student somewhat into the area. Practically all of the War of Independence period was included in the years of Gen. Haldimand's administration as Governor-General of Canada, which has already been recited, and in which few Germans participated on either side in Michigan, because there were comparatively few in the territory. The second of these two conflicts brought into prominence Col. John Francis Hamtramck, a Revolutionary soldier of German descent, born in Quebec in 1757. His parents were natives of the Diocese of Trier in Germany. He went over to Northern New York when he was twenty, and became, in 1777, a Captain of the Fifth New York Regiment in the Revolution, serving in the national army continuously. He commanded the left wing of General Wayne's army at Miami in 1794. He was the first United States Commandant at Detroit and its dependencies when the government got control of the west after the surrender of General Hull and the return of control to the United States. He died at Detroit, and is buried in Mt. Elliott Cemetery, in that city. Hamtramck was but forty-five years of age when he died. He was originally buried in the old French Catholic cemetery in Detroit, but his remains were later removed and re-interred in the newer Mt. Elliott cemetery, where their resting place is still marked by the grave-stone placed over them on their original burial. The character of Col. Hamtramck cannot be better described than in the words which may still be read on the face of this slab, and which are as follows:

> SACRED TO THE MEMORY OF JOHN FRANCIS HAMTRAMCK, ESQ., COLONEL.. OF.. THE.. FIRST.. UNITED STATES REGIMENT OF INFANTRY AND COMMANDANT OF DETROIT AND ITS DEPENDENCIES. HE DEPARTED THIS LIFE ON THE 11TH OF APRIL, 1803, AGED 45 YEARS, 7 MONTHS AND 28 DAYS. TRUE PATRIOTISM, AND ZEALOUS ATTACHMENT TO NATIONAL LIBERTY, JOINED TO A LAUDIBLE AMBITION LED HIM INTO MILITARY SERVICE AT AN EARLY PERIOD OF HIS LIFE. HE WAS A SOLDIER EVEN BEFORE HE WAS A MAN. HE WAS AN ACTIVE PARTICIPATOR IN ALL THE DANGERS, DIFFICULTIES AND HONORS OF THE REVOLUTIONARY WAR; AND HIS HEROISM AND UNIFORM GOOD CONDUCT PROCURED HIM THE ATTENTION AND PERSONAL THANKS OF THE IMMORTAL WASHINGTON. THE UNITED STATES HAS LOST A VALUABLE OFFICER AND A GOOD CITIZEN, AND SOCIETY AN USEFUL AND PLEASANT MEMBER; TO HIS FAMILY THE LOSS IS INCALCULABLE AND HIS FRIENDS WILL NEVER FORGET THE MEMORY OF HAMTRAMCK. THIS HUMBLE MONUMENT IS PLACED OVER HIS REMAINS BY THE OFFICERS WHO HAD

THE HONOR TO SERVE UNDER HIS COMMAND, A SMALL BUT GRATEFUL TRIBUTE TO HIS MERIT AND HIS WORTH.

His son, John Francis Hamtramck, Jr., was in the army in 1813 to 1822, was a Colonel later in the Mexican War, and in 1848 was Governor of Saltillo, in Mexico.

Revolutionary Heroes of the Blood

There were no soldiers of the Revolution of German blood from Michigan. There are records of a few people of German birth or extraction in and around Detroit, who were suspected of sympathy with the American cause and were imprisoned. These instances were necessarily few, by reason of the limited number of Germans present in the area of the state.

There were a few German-Americans among the Revolutionary soldiers who later came out to Michigan. One was Derick or Dietrich Hulick, descendant of the primitive German settlement in New Jersey, who served in Col. Frelingheysen's New Jersey Regiment in 1777, and the year after in Capt. Joachim Gulich's company. He saw service in the War of 1812. He came to Michigan in 1839, and is buried at Lakeville, in Oakland county. Martin Du Bois, who was born at New Paltz, N. Y., in 1764, was in Col. Wessenfel's Ulster County, N. Y., regiment in 1777. He is claimed as both of French and German ancestry, some tracing him to a German ancestry from the French Hugenots, who settled in Germany on Frederick's invitation to come across the border, enjoy religious liberty and pay their taxes without complaint. He came out to Michigan in 1854, and is buried at Leslie, in Jackson county.

John Peter Frank, who joined a colonial regiment in 1776 and served with Washington, came out to Michigan in 1832 and settled at Lake Odessa. The Lord favored him with twin daughters when he was 78 years of age.

William Pangborn, one of the Mohawk Valley German progeny, was born in 1742. He served under Washington, was in the Fourth New York Regiment in the Continental line, and later in the War of 1812. He came out to Michigan early enough to be on the pension list in 1821. Pangborn lived to be 110 and is buried at Ionia.

George Sorter, who was of Pennsylvania German ancestry, born in 1756, came out to Michigan and settled at Raisinville, near Monroe. He served through the entire Revolutionary War.

Aaron Brinck, a New York soldier of the Continental army, came to Michigan and was on the pension roll from Wayne county from 1822 to 1833, getting $60 a year for six years and $96 the rest of the time. He drew in all $2,100 in pension money.

Henry Cremer, who was in the Twenty-Ninth Infantry in the War of 1812, was put on the pension roll in Wayne county in 1816 and died in 1830.

Louis Jacobs, a private of the Michigan Volunteers, was on the Wayne county section of the pension roll from 1823 to 1832, getting $4 a month most of the time.

Frederick Miller, a Fifth U. S. Infantryman, from Albany, was on the roll in Michigan for a year before his death, which occured in 1820.

Henry Meyers, another Wayne county pensioner, was in the Albany company of the Sixth New York Volunteers in the Revolution.

Adam Overrocker, who was born in 1760, was in the Continental line as a member of the Albany company of the Fourth New York regiment. He came out to Washtenaw county, where he was put on the revolutionary pension roll in 1833, when he was 73 years old. He got $80 a year for three years.

Jacob Rattenhauer, whose pension payments were transferred from New York to Wayne county, Michigan, in 1830, was one of the earliest pensioners of the Revolutionary War. He was put on the roll at $5 a month in 1789 and later raised to $8 a month. He drew $3,345 in all for pension money.

In Col. Proctor's army in the battle of French Town, on the River Raisin, two soldiers named John Spackman and John Troester were wounded, Jan. 22, 1813.

The War of 1812

The War of 1812 brought another German warrior into Michigan. This was John E. Schwartz, whose name appears in much of the early territorial history. John E. Schwartz was born in Vienna and spoke German. He was in Gen. Wayne's army in the Indian campaigns, and settled in Michigan after his arrival in Detroit as a member of one of Wayne's expeditions. He was an exceedingly active citizen, who dealt in furs, was town auctioneer in 1829, sat in the second Convention of Assent when Michigan got into the union, was the first Adjutant-General of the state and founded the village of Schwartzburg, on the Rouge River, halfway between Dearborn and Plymouth. Two of his sons were educated in St. Philip Neri College, the pioneer Catholic higher school of Detroit, which was started in 1834, and discontinued in 1840.

There were men of German family names in Gen. Wayne's force which was located in Detroit in 1797. His orderly book contains a general order for August 4 of that year detailing Lieut. Kramer for duty at the garrison until further notice. He was in charge of the guard on August 11 and was on court martial duty for several days thereafter. One of his orders during his first week of activity detailed Privates Jacob Casterlein, James Scrimger and John M. Krezer to dig ditches for the sewerage of the post.

The Black Hawk War

The Black Hawk War occured in 1832. Chief Black Hawk and his Indians had killed settlers in Wisconsin, were threatening the settlements in Illinois, and there were fears that he would attack the foundation at Chicago. The federal government asked for four companies of 100 men each from Michigan. It turned out to be not very much of a war, but the martial spirit ran high toward it as a military adventure, with some intensification from the possibilities of each participant getting 160 acres of land as a sort of bonus. The troops were gathered in various parts of the state, some of them assembled at what is now Fort Wayne, at Detroit, and others along the line of the Detroit and Chicago turnpike. They marched to Chicago. There were various bivouacs on the way, the principal one at Niles. Of the brigade officers under General John R. Williams, the commander of the Michigan Brigade, was John J. Ulman, serving as Quarter-master, a German-descended man who later helped survey that part of Wayne County which is now Wisconsin.

The state had a few scattered German settlers then, young men as a rule, and they entered into the service from motives both of duty and adventure. Peter Beisel, Jr., and Jesse Baum were in Capt. Anderson's Company from White Pigeon. Joseph Meyers and Stephen Ackle were in Capt. Daniel's Company. Peter Gall, Abel Custer, and William Ruland were in Col. Humphrey's force from Monroe. George William Hoffman and August Tietsort were in Col. Houston's force. In Capt. Goth's Company from Blissfield, Michael Kregger was first sergeant. Johannes Engel and Hiram Jacobs reported at Niles from Sturgis Prairie. John Van Armin, a Kalamazoo lawyer, was in the forces. Martin Bernhardt was one of the men in the Branch-Hillsdale county company. Saul Fenstermacher, of Jackson, was in the force which encamped near Blackmar's tavern at Jackson. Peter H. Adamy, who died in 1862, had the real military record of all the Michigan German-Americans in this war. His grandfather was a German-born citizen of Montgomery county, N. Y., and saw service in the War of the Revolution. Peter enlisted and served in the War of 1812 and in the Black Hawk War in 1832, settling later on in Monroe county.

Josiah Rosencrantz, a Mohawk Valley, N. Y., German who lived at Nisbett's Corners, near Battle Creek, was in one of the Black Hawk war companies. His son, Mortimer R. Rosencrantz, was later appointed to a cadetship in West Point, gained honor in the army, and planted the colors of his regiment on Chapultapec, in the Mexican War.

So far as long service or experiences of danger were concerned the Black Hawk war turned out to be a good deal of a joke. Its participants got some lands or scrip for their allotments after their return to civil life and everybody was satisfied.

The Mexican War

Compared with other conflicts in which the nation has been engaged since its creation, the War with Mexico was not a great adventure. The Texans had declared their independence in 1835, seceding from the Republic of Mexico formed under the Constitution of 1835, which set up a union of states not unlike that of the United States, Texas and Coahuila being united as one of the constituent states. There had been an American settlement in the State since 1821, under a contract between the Mexican government and Moses Austin, of Connecticut, who undertok to settle three hundred American families in exchange for a grant of land as large as some empires. When Gen. Barragan became Dictator in 1835 he undertook to degrade the states, theretofore sovereign after the American model, into departments of the federal government. The Texans revolted, set up their own government under Gen. Sam Houston, a Tennessee man, and were attacked by Gen. Santa Anna, who had succeeded Barragan as dictator. Then came the massacre of the Alamo in 1835, the defeat and capture of Santa Anna at San Jacinto, and the Mexican General's consent to Texan independence while he was a prisoner, a condition which undoubtedly assisted in making him see the logic of the situation. Later on Texas, now with a hundred thousand Americans in its population, sought and secured admission to the American union as a state.

Mexico's sovereignty then took in the present areas of the United States that are known as New Mexico, Arizona and California, and, generally everything west of the Rocky Mountains up to the forty-second parallel of latitude, beyond which pretensions under the Treaty of Ryswick, claims founded on the Bull of Pope Alexander VI. of 1493, the discovery of the Pacific by Balboa in 1513 and De Soto's claims of discovery, and some actual settlements left a controversy about dominion that was finally settled in 1846 by the Ashburton Treaty. This left the California territory a desirable accession to the United States, which the Democrats, under President Polk, favored, while the Whigs, led by Henry Clay, opposed it.

Polk's election, the admission of Texas to the American Union and the evident purpose to acquire California started the Mexicans on the enterprise of trying to recover Texas, and they mobilized on the Rio Grande. They got severe defeats at Palo Alto and Resaca de la Palma early in 1846, but, being gluttons for punishment, prepared to come back for more.

On May 11, 1846, the American Congress, Democrats and Whigs being now united, declared that a state of war with Mexico existed, put $10,000,000 at the President's disposal and authorized him to call for 50,000 volunteers. Two days afterwards he called for infantrymen from Michigan for the regular army and a mounted company of dragoons. The infantry company and the dragoons were assembled, the body of the latter composed of men all over six feet tall, and were ready for transportation in the spring of 1847 when another call, this time for a full regiment of infantry, was made upon Michigan. This was the First Volunteer Regiment. Col. Thomas B. W. Stockton was its Colonel. John V. Ruehle, the Baden baker who had come to Detroit in 1832 and helped found the Scott Guard in 1841, was its Major. It had ten companies. Frederick William Curtenius was Captain of the "A" Company, he being a Kalamazoo man who was afterwards Adjutant-General of the state. Grove A. Buel, with a Saxon ancestry, was Captain of the "B" Company. Nicholas Greusel, Jr., was Captain of the "D" Company. His family had come from Bavaria in 1833. John Wittenmeyer was Captain of the "F" Company, he being one of the Scott Guard privates from Detroit. John Van Armin, a Kalamazoo lawyer who was of mixed Dutch and German ancestry, and who was a great Democratic orator of his day, was Captain of the "I" Company. Curtenius's, Buel's, Greusel's and Wittenmeyer's companies got away in December, 1847, and went into action. When the rest of them started, peace had been declared, but that was not known in the North. There was no telegraphic service then.

The Fifteenth United States Infantry, in active service in the War with Mexico, had three companies from Michigan in its make-up. While in service Eugene Van de Vanter, of mixed Dutch and German ancestry, became Captain of the "A" Company, and Isaac De Graff Toll, of Monroe County, of the same racial mixture, Captain of the "E" Company. Capt. Toll's great-great grand-father, a Mohawk County, New York, German settler, was killed at Beachdale, New York, in 1748, in the Mohawk Indian wars. Of the personnel of the companies that went out, the Scott Guard outfit from Detroit was nearly all German and one company from Monroe was of mixed German and French origins. Francis Flanders, a lumber mill worker of German descent, from Fawn River, in St. Joseph County, was the regimental drum-major. George H. Nickar, from the same neighborhood, died at Puebla, and Abraham Bers, at Perote, while Richard Corbus, of Niles, was wounded at Coyacan. Michael Winterhalter, of Detroit, whose son later became a Rear Admiral of the Navy, and Capt. Mortimer Rosencranz, son of an early German settler of Calhoun county, and who planted the flag of his regiment on Chapultepac, were both in service. John Francis Hamtramck, Jr., son of Col. Hamtramck, who took over control of Detroit in 1813, became Governor of Saltillo, pending the conclusion of peace. Frank W. Kurner, of Jackson, went through the conflict and lived long enough thereafter to go through the Civil War.

For its enormous results to the nation, the Mexican War was not a great conflict. It was almost over when it started. Michigan's participation in it cost the state but $17,000.

CHAPTER X

THE CIVIL WAR

General Poe's Commendation of Colonel Schneider—The Sixth Michigan Volunteers—Mexican War Veterans' Return to Service—German-Americans in Every Regiment—General George Alexander Custer—The Compliment of a Loser—Colonel Michael Shoemaker Some Striking Instances.

The State of Michigan furnished 90,747 men to the Union Army from the beginning of the civil war to its end. Of these 21,517 were native born sons of Michigan, and enough more to make a total of 67,468 were natives of the United States. Canada and the rest of British North America provided 8,886. The remainder, 14,393, were of European birth. Of these, 3,761 were born in England, 3,929 in Ireland, and 4,872 were natives of Germany. The largest foreign group approaching any of these was the Scotch, who made up 763 of the soldiers from Michigan.

The German-born were far from all the soldiers of Michigan in the Civil War who were of German blood. The German group, having been comparatively recent arrivals from a scene of revolution in the homeland, were devoted to the profession of arms and for some years before the outbreak of the American Civil War the younger men had organized themselves into "Guards" and other designations of military societies.

Thus it was that the First Michigan Infantry, recruited for the three months that the optimists of the period thought would be sufficient to conquer the rebellious Southerners, had as its "E" Company the Steuben Guard, of Ann Arbor, with William F. Roth, of that city as its Captain, and George F. Mogk, of the same city, as its First Lieutenant. Capt. Roth was mustered out in the succeeding August, but Lieut. Mogk, continued in the service in the First Infantry, became a captain on the day of the battle of Bull Run, was made a prisoner and exchanged, and was mustered out at the end of 1864. The "F" Company of this earliest regiment was the Michigan Hussars, of Detroit, with Bernhard Mauch as its First Lieutenant, and Joseph P. Sanger as Second Lieutenant. Mauch was wounded and captured by the enemy at Bull Run in 1861 and died of his wounds while a prisoner. Sanger re-enlisted in the First U. S. Artillery after his three months enlistment, made a First Lieutenancy therein in 1861, and was breveted Captain and Major successively for bravery. He continued in the regular service and was a Captain therein in 1875.

The Second Michigan Infantry's organization followed fast upon that of the First. The "A" Company of this organization was the Scott Guard of Detroit, with Louis Dillman, Captain; John V. Ruehle, Jr., First Lieutenant and Gustave Kast, Second Lieutenant. The "E" Company which was organized at Niles, had Robert Breitschneider, of that city, as its Captain and was the regimental color company. Capt. Dillman became a Major in the second year of the war and a Lieutenant-Colonel in July, 1862. He served until July, 1863, and was in command of the regiment at the siege of Yorkton, at Fair Oaks and at Malvern Hill. Ruehle was the son of a Mexican war veteran, who was himself a Lieutenant Colonel of the Sixteenth Infantry in the Civil War. The younger Ruehle became a Captain in his first year and served until April 19, 1864. Lieut. Kast became a Captain of the Sixteenth Infantry. Breitschneider became a Captain of the Twelfth Infantry.

Major Dillman received the personal commendation

of Brig. Gen. "Phil" Kearney, in a memorandum addressed to him during the Battle of Fair Oaks, in which Kearney said, "You have added new laurels to your past distinction and shall have full credit for these days."

Poe's Commendation of Col. Schneider

During the war Frederick Schneider, of Lansing, who had entered the service as an enlisted man, was promoted until he became Lieutenant Colonel of his regiment and finally Colonel, to date from March 18, 1865. General Orlando M. Poe wrote of him and his service; "Where is the regular who was more regular than Frederick Schneider when he rode at the head of the regiment at the close of the war in Washington, at the Grand Review. He fitly represented the valor and sacrifice of the old Second Michigan Regiment of Volunteers."

John Lincoln Clem, an Ohio German-American boy from Newark, whose mother's name was Mary Weber, tried to enlist in the Second Michigan Infantry in 1861, but was rejected on account of his youth. He finally enlisted as a drummer boy in 1862, and went through the war. In 1870 President Grant appointed him to the regular army, in which he became Major-General. He was Chief Quartermaster of the Department of the West from 1911 to 1915.

Frank Zoellner, of Detroit, who was Sergeant Major of the regiment, achieved a lieutenancy in the early part of 1863, was wounded at Knoxville in the latter part of the year, and died of his wounds. John J. Busch, of Saginaw, who joined the troops as a commissary sergeant, made a lieutenancy and was killed in action before Petersburg in July, 1864. August Goebel, of Detroit, was a Scott Guard man, was a Regimental Adjutant in July, 1861, and was made First Lieutenant and Captain the following year. He resigned in 1863.

War in retrospect, has its humors as well as its tragedies. One of the former is found in the certification by

IN THE MAKING OF MICHIGAN

Adjutant Goebel, of Battalion Order No. 1257, of the Regiment in July, 1861, announcing that "each Company will be entitled to three casks of Lager Beer and Fifty Bologna Sausages every Sunday Morning."

Anna Etherage, a young woman of Detroit, described as being "of German descent," volunteered as a nurse at the outbreak of the war, with this regiment and was presented with the "Kearney badge" by the famous general whose name it bore.

The Third Michigan Infantry was organized almost as soon as the Second. Among its officers were Lieut. Frederick Schriver, Capt. Adolph Birkenstock, Lieut. Max Von Kraut and Lieut. Felix Zolly, all of Grand Rapids. Schriver was wounded in action at Groveton, Va., Von Kraut lasted a year and retired from disability, and Zolly made a first lieutenancy and fell out from the same cause.

The Fourth, Fifth and Sixth Michigan Infantry Regiments were organized by Gov. Blair, at state expense, in the face of advice to the contrary given by Simon Cameron, Secretary of War. The "H" Company of the Fourth was from Jonesville, with Moses A. Funke as its Captain. He served a year. The "E" Company of the Fifth was commanded by Augustus Zanier, of Port Huron, and the "K" Company, which was from Saginaw, had Henry Miller as Captain, and Alexander Alberti and Hugo Wesener, as its First and Second Lieutenants respectively. Miller served into 1863, Alberti made a captaincy and served to the end of 1864, and Wesener lasted a year in service.

The Sixth Michigan Volunteers

The Sixth Michigan had Frederick W. Curtenius as its Colonel. He had been in the Mexican war, was the Adjutant-General of the State prior to the outbreak of the war, and his successor, Gen. John Robertson, said that "to the efforts of Col. F. W. Curtenius, of Kalamazoo, then Adjutant General, the State was more indebted for whatever efficiency was found in the Militia at the out-break of the war, than to the meager and limited provisions of law." In this regiment Lieut. Charles Heine was an officer of the "E" Company.

John P. Eberhard, of Burr Oak, was a Lieutenant in the "K" Company of the Seventh Michigan. He was killed in action at Antietam in 1862. Jacob Maus, of Hastings, was a Lieutenant of the "F" Company of the Eighth Michigan. He stood out through a year of the war. Charles H. Richman, of Saginaw, was a Lieutenant of the "A" Company of the Tenth Michigan. He served through the entire war. Benjamin Riesdorf, of Monroe, was a Lieutenant of the "I" Company of the Eleventh Michigan. He was mustered out in the July following the fall of Richmond.

Niles was the rendezvous of the Twelfth Michigan. Its Surgeon was Dr. George L. Brunschweiler, of Eagle Harbor, and the "E" Company Captain was Henry Gephart, of Niles. Dr. Brunschweiler lasted a year in the service, and Gephart served for about the same time.

Bernard Vosburg, of Galesburg, was Captain of the "A" Company of the Thirteenth Michigan. He resigned after a year's service.

The Fourteenth Michigan went into service with Joseph Schefnicher, of Saginaw, and John C. Line, of East Saginaw, as the Lieutenants of the "A" Company; Caspar Ernst, of Nunica, as Lieutenant of the "F" Company; and Charles B. Rose, of Westphalia, as Lieutenant. Ernst became a Major and was mustered out in 1865. Lind became a Captain and died during the war. Rose died of disease in Mississippi in the second year of the war.

Mexican Veterans' Return to Service

The Sixteenth Michigan had John V. Ruehle, Sr., of Detroit, as its Lieutenant Colonel on organization. Ruehle was a middle-aged man when he went into the service, having been in the American army in the Mexican war. He retired in 1862, and returned to Detroit, where he was a leader in the patriotic movements.

Jacob Webber, of Lansing, was a Lieutenant of the "G" Company of this regiment, and Gustavus Kast, of Detroit, who was in the First Michigan at the outbreak of the war, was Captain of the "H" Company. Webber served a couple of years and Kast had two years of service in all.

William Winegar, of Grass Lake, was a Lieutenant of the "F" Company of the Seventeenth Michigan, and John Goldsmith, of Jackson, Captain. Christian Roth, of Jackson, was a Lieutenant of the "G" Company. Winegar became a Captain and served until he was retired for disability. Roth served through the entire war and was breveted a Lieutenant Colonel at the close of the war for "special service during the confinement, trial and execution of conspirators." He was in charge of the guards of the Surratt group who were implicated with John Wilkes Booth in the killing of Lincoln.

The Twentieth Michigan had Peter Kauffman, of Charlotte, as a Lieutenant of its "G" Company. The Twenty-First had Herman Baroth, of Ionia, as Captain of its "K" Company. Kauffman and Baroth were in service a year.

Joseph Goetz, of Mt. Clemens, was Captain, and Augustus Czizek, of the same place, Lieutenant of the "G" Company of the Twenty-second Michigan. Henry Braidenback, of Lexington, was Lieutenant of the "F" Company. Czizek served a year, Goetz was discharged for disability at the close of the conflict and Braidenback became a Captain and was mustered out in 1864.

Frederick Augustus Buhl, whose ancestors were from Saxony, was a Lieutenant of "B" Company, of the Twenty-Fourth Michigan. He went over to the First Cavalry and was made a Captain. He died of wounds received in action in 1864.

Jacob Ewalt and Edwin F. Kimmel, of Berrien Springs, were the Lieutenants of "C" Company of the Twenty-Fifth

Michigan. Ewalt became a Captain and served until he was discharged for disability in 1864. Kimmel served almost to the end of the war.

German-Americans in Every Regiment

The Twenty-Seventh Michigan had Frederick Myers, of Houghton, as a Lieutenant of "C" Company and Paul Gies, of Detroit, as a Lieutenant of "E" Company. Myers became a major, was wounded in the battle of the Wilderness and discharged for disability at the close of the war. Most of these regiments were recruited from the fairly well settled rural districts of the cities of the States. Yet there were exceptions to this rule. The northwestern shore of the Lower Peninsula was rather sparsely settled when the war began, yet in August, 1862, Lieut. Jacob Siebert, of Manistee, recruited the "Lake Shore Tigers" in Manistee and Grand Traverse counties, for the Civil War. Among his recruits were Charles E. Lehman and Jacob P. Hans. Later on Jacob Berger, Ferdinand Cord, Philip Egler and Martin Wachall, left from that country for the war. They got into various regiments.

The Thirtieth Michigan was composed of colored soldiers with white officers. One of these was Edward Dubendorf, of Coldwater, who was a Lieutenant of Company "I".

Battery B, of the First Michigan Light Artillery, had Albert F. R. Arndt, as its First Lieutenant near Griswold, Georgia, in 1864. This command's casualties included those to Corporal Frederick Beninghoff, and Private Charles Baughman, each of whom lost a leg; and Private John Endlich and Jacob Wolf, who were seriously wounded. Battery "K" had as its Captain John C. Scheutz, and as its Lieutenants Adolph Schill and Christopher Hupert, all of Detroit. The Commander of the Fourteenth Battery was Capt. Charles Heine, of Marshall.

The Fifth Cavalry had in its "G" Company, John Zunderman, of Essex, as a Lieutenant. The Sixth had as

IN THE MAKING OF MICHIGAN 117

Lieutenants Peter Cramer, of Woodland, and Charles Bolza, of Grand Rapids. The latter was killed at Gettysburg, where the Michigan Cavalry Brigade was commanded by Gen. George A. Custer, later of Monroe and of German ancestry.

A list of all the officers of German blood who served with Michigan regiments during the civil war is given in an appendix hereto. Obviously the listing of all the private soldiers of the same blood would be voluminous and inexpedient.

General George Alexander Custer

Two outstanding figures in the history of the civil war were men whose names were linked with Michigan regimental activities, and who were of German extraction. One of these was Gen. George Alexander Custer; the other was Col. Michael Shoemaker. Both were of remote, rather than immediate German ancestry. Both were of families with a military record.

Gen. Custer was the grandson of Michael Koester, a Hessian officer on the British side in the Revolution, who was with the Hanau regiment which, incidentally, was the one with which Dr. Herman Eberts, the first Sheriff of Wayne County, came out as surgeon. Michael Koester was taken a prisoner by the Americans in 1778, was paroled, and settled in Pennsylvania, going over to Maryland later on. His son, born in Maryland, moved to Ohio, from which state the future general was appointed to the United States Military Academy. During Custer's Academy term the elder Custer moved to Monroe, in Michigan, which was Capt. Custer's home thereafter.

Custer reported into service the day after the first battle of Bull Run. He was on Kearney's staff and later on that of Gen. McClellan, for whom he had a regard which amounted to adoration. He wanted the command of the Seventh Michigan Cavalry, but Gov. Blair would not give it to him. Later, after Gen. Meade had made him a Brigadier-General, he was in command of the Michigan Cavalry Brigade, the Seventh included, when but twenty-four years old. He was the romantic cavalryman of the war, youthful, daring, successful and handsome. His broad white hat and yellow curls made him a shining mark. Charles Moore, in "The Days of Fife and Drum," gives this description of his characteristic daring in the final campaigns of the Civil war:

"In the Shenandoah Valley on the beautiful eighth of October, 1864, Custer, a division commander now, rode out in front of his lines in full view of the enemy. His yellow hair once more flowed over his shoulders. A broad sailor collar, a streaming scarlet tie, and a velvet jacket, well nigh covered with gold braid, made him a dazzling spectacle as he gracefully doffed his sombrero to salute his gallant foe. The attention was meant for Rosser, who had been Custer's class-mate and rival at West Point.

"'You see that officer?' said Rosser to one of his staff. 'That's Custer, the Yanks are so proud of, and I intend to give him the best whipping today he ever got. See if I don't.'

"The words were no sooner out of his mouth than Custer, at the head of the Third Division, was bearing down on him. Rosser's artillery helped him drive back the Michigan boys, till the Union guns in turn broke the force of the enemy's onslaught. Then there was a fair battle. Rosser vainly tried to meet Custer's sabers with powder, his men turned and fled and for twenty-six miles to Mount Jackson there was a clear track for what came to be known as the 'Woodstock Races'.

"So General Custer came to be a Major-General, and by way of celebrating, in February of 1865, he followed Early from Staunton to Waynesboro, seventeen miles, through mud and rain and whipped him and Rosser unmercifully. Appomattox found Custer, next to Sheridan, the most brilliant cavalry officer of the army, and the Confederate General Kershaw asked the privilege of surrendering his sword to him as 'one of the best cavalry officers this or any other country ever produced.'

"On the final review at Washington, when Custer's unruly horse bore him indecorously past the reviewing stand, the excited multitude, fearing for the life of a soldier whom rebel bullets could not harm, gave a tremendous shout of joy as the General, his horse calmed, rode gravely back to pass the stand a second time and to receive the garlands of flowers prepared for the conquerors of peace."

Little wonder that this picturesque soldier, who later lost his life in the Battle of the Little Big Horn, with the Sioux Indians, was, on the occasion of the celebration of the Semi-Centennial of the State, June 15, 1886, apostrophised by Chief Justice Cooley in these words:

"That mighty man of war, George A. Custer, a lion in battle and a child by the fireside; how the mountain passes of Virginia thundered beneath the tramp of his horsemen as he hurled them upon the enemy, striking never a light or dallying blow and winning never a barren victory."

Colonel Michael Shoemaker

Michael Shoemaker was a native of German Flats, Herkimer County, in the Mohawk Valley, of New York. His grand-uncle was Gen. Nicholas Herkimer, who was mortally wounded at Oriskany in the campaign that led up to Saratoga and the surrender of Burgoyne's army. His father, Robert Shoemaker, was a Captain in the war of 1812. His maternal grandfather, Michael Meyers, was a Judge. His maternal grandmother was Catharine Herter. Shoemaker was in Detroit in 1835, went farther west, became a contractor and had a share of the work on the Illinois and Michigan Canal. He settled in Jackson in 1842, became a State Senator, and was Collector of the Port of Detroit in 1856. He was a Union Democrat, and in January, 1862, was commissioned Colonel of the Thirteenth Michigan Infantry. This regiment was raised by ex-Senator Stuart of Kalamazoo, who, like Colonel Shoemaker, was a staunch Democrat, but the condition of whose health forbade his assuming active duties and the command of the regiment was accepted by Shoemaker. His regiment served in the Shiloh and Corinth campaigns under Gen. Garfield, was transferred to the Army of the Cumberland at Nashville, and during the operation in Tennessee he was captured, sent to Libby Prison, exchanged, and was back with his regiment at Murphysboro, where at the cost of a third of his force, it turned the tide of battle. His son's death and his wife's illness withdrew him from the army in 1863, and he devoted a great deal of the remainder of his days to public service. In 1876 he was again sent to the Senate, where he was the author of the laws providing for the closing of saloons and prohibiting the sale of liquor on election days, and providing for close accounting of county finances.

Distinctions in the Civil War

Dr. Henry F. Lyster, a gallant Irishman and a great Michigan surgeon later on, was surgeon of the Second Michigan Infantry in the Civil war. He records that on July 18, 1861, he attended the first Michigan soldier wounded in the war. He was Matthias Wollenweber, a Private of Company "A". Three days later Dr. Lyster made the first amputation suffered by a Michigan soldier. This was at Bull Run and its subject was Frederick Waustinberg, of the same company. Waustinberg lost his left arm.

There have been some striking German family contributions to American warfare. Four brothers, Elias; John, Jacob and David Reigle, New York born and descended from German sources, enjoyed a reunion at Clare in 1926. All four had seen service in New York regiments in the Civil War. One of them had transferred to the Twenty-Ninth

Michigan Infantry. A half-brother, Henry Reigle, served in the Spanish-American war from Michigan.

On the first call for Volunteers George Welz, of Detroit, enlisted in the First Michigan Engineers. His three sons, Jacob, George and Philip Welz, followed him into service. This was the entire man-power of his family, leaving the wife and mother of the family, Wilhelmina Welz, alone at home. When some commiserating neighbor sought to console Mother Welz over her desolation and to convey that her sacrifice was too great for one woman to be called upon to bear, she replied:

"Some mother's sons must save the Republic; why not mine?"

Her patriotic parable was graven on her tombstone in Elmwood cemetery, in Detroit, by her soldier sons. One of her sons and her nephews participated in the Spanish-American war a quarter of a century later.

The veterans of the Civil War made Col. Louis Kanitz, of Michigan, a German war veteran, their State Department Commander in 1894.

CHAPTER XI

THE WAR WITH SPAIN

The Beginnings of an Adjutant-General—A Soldier Who Became a Mayor—The Thirty-Third Michigan—The Thirty-Fourth Michigan—The Roster of the Dead.

On April 23, 1898, President McKinley issued a proclamation calling for 125,000 volunteers to engage in the war with Spain. Michigan's quota was 4,104, to compose four regiments of infantry. The Michigan National Guard was reorganized by assigning the Second Independent Battalion to the First Infantry, the First Independent Battalion to the Second Infantry, and accepting eight companies from various parts of the state to fill out the Third and Fifth Infantry regiments.

These regiments were renumbered in series with the Michigan organizations supplied to the national government in the civil war, whose enumeration had gone as high as the Thirtieth, becoming respectively the Thirty-First, Thirty-Second, Thirty-Third, Thirty-Fourth and Thirty-Fifth Regiments of Michigan Volunteer Infantry.

The Michigan Naval Reserve, 11 officers and 270 men, was also put at the disposal of the Federal Government.

As these regiments went to the war Fred Shubel, Jr., of Lansing, was Lieutenant Colonel of the Thirty-First Infantry; Lieut. Charles H. Rule, of Jackson was Regimental Quartermaster; Lieut. Frederick L. Abel, of Detroit was

IN THE MAKING OF MICHIGAN 123

Adjutant, and Charles A. Burmaster, of Detroit, was bandmaster. The "A" Company had among its officers Martin L. Belser, as Second Lieutenant; John W. Haarer, as a sergeant; William L. Walz, Edward O. Schairer, and Ernest Bethke, corporals, Louis A. Krauss as artificer, and Albert Allmendinger as wagoner. These soldiers were all from Ann Arbor. Among the privates of this company were Oscar F. Burkhardt, Waldo B. Bach, Henry H. Heitman, Charles F. Juttner, Gustave M. Meyer, Andrew Maulbetsch, Adolph G. Andres, Herman J. Ennis, John H. Gutekunst, William L. Kimmel, George T. and Edward W. Hoelzle, Albert Kline, Fred Von Walthausen, Gustave H. Sodt, Lee Stumpenhausen, Otto Schwemen, Arthur Wistrand, Max Wittlinger and Theophilus Weinman, all of Ann Arbor.

The "B" Company of this regiment had Frank Freitag as its quartermaster sergeant, Charles C. Burger as a sergeant and Edwin Spies as musician. Among its privates were Charles F. Bohn, John Beyer, Henry J. Dietz, George R. Erlacher, Henry J. Griewalm, Charles A. Gussenbauer, Charles P. Hoeft, James H. Inglehardt, Herman W. Kramer, Charles F. Laage, Herman D. Meyer, John Beyer, Ernest Meyers, Fred W. Matthes, Joseph C. Seaboldt, T. Xury Swick, Albert O. Schultz, and John M. Vogt. These men were from Adrian.

The "C" Company had in it Privates Edward H. Grossman, John Kraut, Frank Pagel, Lewis F. Holtz, Charles W. Herman, William C. Marx, Edward A. Uphaus, George D. Schaffer, John Senger, and Gus Nuertheuer. These men were mostly from Tecumseh and Manchester.

The "D" Company was largely from Jackson and Lansing. Its' list of privates included such names as those of John C. Freitag, Clarence S. Linderman, Florenz Breitmeyer, George J. Stadelman, Frank Stadelman and Christian Schneirle.

The "E" Company had John C. Durst, as First Lieutenant; Walter J. Hasse and Frank P. Dunnebacke as corporals, and Walter C. Hoffman as musician. The company roster had on it the names of Henry Behrendt, later United States Marshal for the Eastern District of Michigan; Fred W. Baumgras, Ralph S. Finckelstein, Otto M. Eichels, Frank J. Eckenfels, Paul Lepke, Nicholas Moers, Jacob J. Zeeb, and Karl A. Zimmerer. Most of these were from Lansing.

Company "F" was composed of men from Mason and its vicinity. On its list of privates were Fred Bortle, Frank H. Emmer, Harry Flintz, William Kunkleman, Wilbur Raum, and Frank H. Stallknecht.

Andrew Stoll was first sergeant of the "G" Company, and among those who stepped to his orders were Philip J. Becker, Charles H. Hyzer, George Richel, Jacob Vokach, Otto Von Rener, Paul Ziegler, and John Kolb. These were nearly all Washtenaw men.

Company "I" was from Detroit. Lewis Thal was a sergeant and Edward W. Bruchner corporal. It was full of Atkinsons, Bourkes and Shaughnessys, but they had among their companions-in-arms Aloysius Bailer, Bert Derindinger, Frank Diedrich, Willis Hauser, Rudolph Peschke, Willibrod Therrien, George P. Welz, Reinard Hundriesser, and Edward P. Woleben.

Beginnings of an Adjutant-General

The "K" Company had William H. Sink for its Captain; Louis P. Muffatt for quarter-master sergeant; Henry W. Busch for a sergeant; William Kress as a corporal; David Cohen as musician, Joseph Mathiel for artificer and Edwin J. Wuest as its wagoner. On the "buddy" list were the names of Louis A. Andrich, Adolph Dittmar, William H. Forester, Frederick W. Frede, Max H. Jabusch, Emil Kuhn, Paul A. Kraft, William Veth, Arthur Zerbe, Alexander A. Kosack, Charles Meiers, John W. Shafer, and Edward Schlitz. These men were all from Detroit.

The "L" Company was from Detroit and Wayne County. The present Adjutant-General, John S. Bersey, made his bow

IN THE MAKING OF MICHIGAN 125

to Mars with this Company as its First Lieutenant. Among his associates were Frederick J. Perren, sergeant; Starr Voght and Conrad Orth, corporals; and Privates Stephen E. Bohn, Maurice M. Butzel, Gustav Baumgart, Frederick W. Cron, Charles J. Gerbert, Peter Gehrke, John Freck, Walter J. Kerschner, Harry Kramer, Frederick Ryff, John E. Stetzer, Arthur P. Schroeder, William E. Schmild, Carl Scherff, Julius Weiss and William R. Wobrock.

The "M" Company was a group of French and German-Americans from Monroe. Their ancestral races about divided the company honors and John M. Gutman was Captain; George J. Schmid, Second Lieutenant; Otto E. Reisig, first sergeant; Gustave A. Ferner, quarter-master sergeant; August C. Verboren, William J. Luft and Fred J. Schultz, sergeants; Gustave F. Marx, musician, and Adam F. Cron, artificer. On the roll call were the names of George E. Armbruster, Austin Bruckner, Fred T. Axt, Leonard Buerlein, Carl A. Cruner, Laurence Graessle, Alexander T. Deinzer, Louis A. Kline, Anthony A. Kopke, Charles Korf, Otto H. Kring, Hugo A. Meinicke, Otto H. Ohr, Ernest W. Ott, Harry Schultz, William J. Steffes, Arthur F. Wagner, George Waltz, Joseph Weigel, Louis Wilhelm and Joseph and Gustave Zeller.

The Thirty-Second Michigan had an Irish-American Colonel, McGurrin; a Major of the same breed, Reynolds, and a Chaplain likewise bred, the Reverend Francis C. Kelley, now the Catholic Bishop of Oklahoma. But it had a German-American Major, too. in William B. Kalmbach, of Grand Rapids, and its principal musician was Mendelsohn Marrin, of the same city. As a matter of geography it was not recruited from a section of the state into which much early German-American settlement had penetrated. Notwithstanding, the race was tolerably well represented. In the ranks of its "A" Company were Martin C. Stohanak, George M. Magel, Andrew E. Nackhauer and William D. Veilhaber. The "B" Company had in its files Frank H. Englehardt, William J. Gessler, John P. Fetz, Fred W. Mohnke, Henry F. Nyjoff, William H. Richter, Arthur R. Siegel and Albert A. Vogel. The "C" Company's list of privates included Herman Behrens, Henry Burgdorff, Fred G. Bremer, Theodore Gehring, Oscar P. Lienau, Gus L. Stein, Henry D. Schultz and William F. Stohrer. It had Harry Krum and Carl Baumer, as sergeants and Henry Fletter as a musician. The "D" Company, largely from Battle Creek, included among its fighting men Walter H. Buechner, Louis F. Kress, William Schmid, Charles F. Schneiffer and Louis F. Werstein. The "E" Company had Oswald W. Fiebig, of Grand Rapids as Second Lieutenant; Bernard P. Snitseler as quarter-master sergeant, and Arthur Ansorge, Paul L. Bischoff, Frank A. G. Feltzer, Louis H. Gunther, Charles Gephert, Alexander A. Leishman, Adolph Maier, William C. Meyer, Edward J. Mohrhardt, Theodore E. Stein and Edward L. Wagner among its private soldiers. The "F" Company, which was largely from Grand Haven and its neighborhood, had William Sleutel as quartermaster sergeant, William J. Michael as a sergeant, Thomas Zeldenrust, Frank C. Behm and Herman C. Kohloff as corporals, and William C. Kreft as artificer. Among its private soldiers were Edward S. Deuser, Albert Foerster, Frank R. Grunst, John H. Pippel, George J. Slager, Ralph C. Yeager and Herman Woltman. The "G" Company was almost wholly a Grand Rapids outfit. Walter K. Schmidt was its First Lieutenant, William A. Ansorge a sergeant, and Henry M. Warber its wagoner. The privates included Armin W. Brand, Frederick W. Forstman, Frederick Kuemmerle, Edmund J. Maretz, William J. Pulte, Philip W. Seipp, Carl A. Stauffer, Frank A. Stauffer, Claude Sintz and Anton F. Seif. The "H" Company had William C. Ergenzinger, as a sergeant and Edward C. Ansorge as artificer. Among its privates of evident German-American descent were Carl P. Bessmer, Henry A. Grebel, Charles O. Gunther, Ernest C. Huling, George H. Jacobs, George B. Kulp, Jr., Frank L. Kampf, A. Schulte, Albert G.

Landauer, Charles F. Prange, Frederick Reus, Frank A. Schuman, Karl L. Solosth, and Leonard Sweiger.

A Soldier Who Became a Mayor

The "I" Company was from Detroit. Louis F. Hart was the Captain; Leonard G. Eber, Second Lieutenant; Edward Stickle and Frederick Bahr, corporals; Frank A. Meyfarth, quartermaster-sergeant; Conrad Dietle and John P. Heinle sergeants, and William J. Allman and William R. Jacob, corporals, and Charles Wallaster a musician. The files included John W. Smith, later Mayor of Detroit; Gus J. Andres, George L. Buchman, James A. Boeberitz, Frederick Barschell, Louis H. Funk, Herman A. E. Glied, Gustave Herwarth, Charles Hippler, Otto Hoffman, Joseph Japes, Herman Kaps, William Kramer, Frederick Kube, Otto Klein, Charles E. Manske, Edward Michels, Louis Martz, William Menchinger, Anthony Michenfelder. Joseph Neff, Otto Nieding, Albert Pauli, Gottlieb F. Rommel, Paul Rusch, Charles Seizer, Paul Schultz, John Schmitt, Heiman Stork, Otto Schmidt, Fred R. and Edward Schmalzreidt, Anthony Schnieder, Louis Zurck, Otto Wandrie, Frank E. Weiland and Frederick Waltz.

The "K" Company had George L. Winkler as Second Lieutenant, Edward A. Stricker as sergeant, and Ernest W. Nichlin and Julian J. Steyskal as musicians. The files included John A. Bockheim, Otto Cezek, Charles Diehl, Gustave Fromberg, Frank C. Gies, Oscar Gorenflo, Frederick Hoffer, Emil E. Jost, Titus J. Kaiser, Anthony Kubitzky, Lewis W. Kunze, Albert Mahler, Herbert Mueller, John Schwern, Emil A. Sterns, Joseph E. Schulte, Martin J. Treichler, Claudius H. Von Essen, and Charles H. Weber.

The "L" Company was Capt. Henry B. Lothrop's Company from Detroit. The quartermaster-sergeant was Ernest C. Kast and Louis M. Hefner was a sergeant. The list of privates included Edward A. Bruger, Linnaeus P. Burgner, Robert Brockman, Albert J. Brandt, Peter Dusbieber, Paul

G. Duerr, Frank S. Geppert, Peter Henningsen, Frank H. Hillebrand, Moses A. Hart, Louis K. Kirschner, Matthew A. and August P. L. Krausman, Charles F. Lueber, Frederick Maier, Bernard Schroeder, Walter R. Wagner and William E. Valentine. The "M" Company was Captain Considine's Company and was the historic successor of the famous Irish-American militia company, the Montgomery Rifles. But when it went into the Spanish-American war it had William Korte and Anthony O. Steyskal as corporals, and among its "high privates" John Behrens, Alexander Dunneback, William Heimbuch, Gregory Krein, August F. Kunz, James H. Kenslar, Herman Methner, George Schlagenhuff, William Schmidt, Walter C. Schmeck, Charles A. Schultheis, Joseph A. Wolf, and Anthony Wagner to keep company with their Irish-American fellow-heroes.

The Thirty-Third Michigan

The Thirty-Third Michigan Volunteer Infantry had Frederick J. Schmidt, of Saginaw, as its Lieutenant-Colonel on organization. Paul M. Roth of Owosso was its Major; Oscar W. Achard of Saginaw, its Quartermaster; William F. Fiesel of Saginaw, its sergeant-major and Frank Heric, of Bay City, its chief musician. The "A" Company had Heinrich M. Gangus as its first sergeant. Most of its men were from Flint and the neighborhood. Among them were Bert Friedenburg, Albert J. Hauser, Martin Skall, William J. Weldman and Henry W. Ziegel. The "E" Company largely from Alpena, had Jacob Emmick as a sergeant. Its files had in them Frank J. Behring, Carl Beyer, Frederick Denner, Fred Dorr, Paul P. Dehring, Harry D. Geiger, Otto F. Grimm, Charles Hartig, Jr., John Muschal, Christian A. Oppenborn, Nicholas Schmitz, Albert Peppler and George C. Widner.

The "C" Company was a Bay City crowd. William N. Schultz and Henry H. Hoffman were sergeants; Frank Koth and George T. Whaler, corporals; Walter Kurzrock a musician and Emil Gelinas artificer. The soldiermen of the company included Edward A. Fladung, John M. Goepfert, Frederick A. Haut, John Karpus, Louis C. Knack, Florenze Lutzke, William Metzger, Frederick Meyers, Charles Mueller, Andrew G. Noback, Gustav G. Reinhardt, John Riegle, Henry H. Schroeder and Charles L. Walk.

The "D" Company was mostly from Saginaw. Ferdinand F. W. Giesel was Captain; Frank Arndt and Peter Crist, sergeants, and Charles F. Doering, musician. William H. Auger, August A. Bucholz, William R. Brandt, Rudolph Endert, Charles J. Ewald, Fred C. Eggert, Louis W. Fessler, Charles A. Genske, Emil O. Hartig, Ernest C. Inglehardt, John Kalkbrenner, Richard G. G. Krause, Frederick J. Mayer, Max H. Pansler, Charles H. Pagel, Julius A. Schieb, Charles Schweinshaupt, Edward J. Schneider, Gustav Wagner, John A. Stadtlander, Edward L. Zentz, George W. Zeigen and Albert C. Zoeller were among the enlisted men.

The "E" Company had George H. Stolz, of Saginaw, as its Second Lieutenant; Edward Hahn as a corporal, and among its privates were Frank Burmeister, Ernest F. Brunner, Theodore Dicksheidt, William Dietsch, Frederick Harmes, Frank Heike, Joseph Hasler, Fred G. Leser, Charles F. Peters, Robert O. Reschke, Gottfried Ross, Charles J. Sonnenburg, Fred Schroeder, Fred M. Schindehitte, George F. Trautz, Joseph J. Wolf, Louis Waterstrandt and William Waack. The "F" Company was a Port Huron outfit. Among its soldiers were Adolph E. Dreyer, Wm. G. Halfman, Albert Hartenstein, Jacob M. Kromenaker, Robert H. Krenkel, George L. Maurer and Rudolph Papst. The "G" Company was a Shiawassee county organization. August Sneider was its quartermaster and Albert Frieseke was a corporal. Among the "buck privates" were George Haupt, Fred Kamm and Henry Rubelman.

The "H" Company was from Cheboygan way. William F. Meisel was one of its sergeants and Edward A. Geyer and William F. Beyer were its musicians. The files included Otto Bohn, Eugene A. Geyer, Wm. J. Heinzel, Johan Hangartner, Charles J. Heffting, Walter H. Hein, Charles F. Koschig, Frank Neymeier, Frank J. Schwartz, and William Wizeler. The "I" Company came from Benton Harbor. George E. Schairer was a sergeant, Louis H. Foeltzer a corporal, and Roscoe Roeder a musician. Among their company mates were Charles Loeffler, Charles E. R. Krueger, Charles H. Lederer, Fred Murchel, Louis Ruppert, William E., Thomas G., and Elmo Swem, John A. Schairer, Charles Wibschardt, Will W. Wertzberger and Fred C. Zeigler. The "K" Company was a Three Rivers crowd. Among its members were Albert Benfer, Daniel J. Everhardt, August C. Greenberg, Samuel E. Gembling, Albert Greenberg, Wm. C. Hartman, Fred L. Kaiser, Frederick A. Kramb, Charles O. Romig, Eugene Spangler, Otis D. Weinber, and Edward W. Wortinger.

The "L" Company had Carl A. Wagner, of Port Huron as its Captain and Herman A. Tiefenthal as a musician. The files had in them Charles H. Beier, Custer Borst, Robert G. Hosler, Maurice M. Lang, Ferdinand Sebright and Frederick Upell. The "M" Company had Theodore F. Bornman as an artificer, Daniel W. Smith as quartermaster sergeant, and Herman Schmidt as wagoner. Smith was later a candidate for Mayor of Detroit. The privates' roll had on it Frederick W. Baier, James R. Bayer, Frederick C. H. Beyer, Andrew Bloetscher, George E. Bleil, August Ehrenfreid, David Goldman, Chas. H. Groth, Adolph J. Milbrandt, Edward L. Mundt, Lewis F. Pagel, Henry Pheiffer, John G. Paulin, William A. Schmidt, Jacob A. Speier, Carl G. Trebein and George J. Veth.

The Thirty-Fourth Michigan

The Thirty-Fourth Michigan Volunteer Infantry had John P. Peterman, of Allouez, as its Colonel, and Julius M. Wilhelm as Assistant Surgeon. The "A" Company had Ernest L. Hesse as its quartermaster sergeant, and on its roll were Leonard Bruner, Charles E. Harger, John P. Hindermeier, Fred Grohn, Herman Reitzman and Frank Raub, The "B" Company had Otto Kettner, Charles H. Lehr, August Otin, Henry F. Schudlike, James Schuster, Herman Schultz, Matthew C. Welbes, William J. Wenzel, and Frederick J. Wolff. The "C" Company had on its roll John Stoepple, Oliver C. Stauffer, Peter Borgman, James Brandt, William Bluhm, John Essenburg, Frank P. Foegen, G. Hibner, George V. Hibner, Frank A. Hohenstein, Walter H. Krebs and Henry Mohr. The "D" Company had Julius H. Fliege as Captain, William H. Thielman as First Lieutenant, Charles Koppelman as first sergeant, Henry Kaufman as a corporal, and among its private members Peter C. Doering, Laurence C. Distel, Augustus H. Gansser, William A. Gertz, Edward Grimmeke, Martin Messner, John F. Mueller, John Messner, John E. Moen, William Schenk, Adam Schick, Jacob M. Wagner, and William Weis.

The "E" Company was an Iron Mountain outfit. In its membership were Paul Altman, Joseph H. Burg, Rudolph J. Conrad, Charles Marx, Emil Marsch, Henry B. Schwelenbach and Charles H. Wicke. The "F" Company was from Houghton and its neighborhood. Rudolph J. Haas was its Second Lieutenant, Carl Christ Rath its quartermaster sergeant, and Henry L. Breitman, Albert Haas, Robert H. Kehl, Elmer A. Otto, John T. Plessman, Edward A. Perlenbach, August G. Schlaack and Charles C. Tabbert among its privates. The "G" Company, drawn from Sault Ste. Marie, had in it Paul Besner, Conrad Hehman, John A. Steinten and Walter Wirth. The "H" Company's membership included Frank A. Hoffman, Julius Bentzen, John A. Grils, Aldrich Grils, Richard Koppe, Earnest F. Greger, Richard Lasch, Emil W. C. Lasch, George Mayer, Walter E. Ritz, Edward W. Wanzer, Fred W. Wegner and Urban Zimmerman. The "I" Company had on it the names of Leonard P. Gemund, George M. and Ernest S. Greenwalt, Laurence Hauselman, Adolph

Kordt, Stephen H. Otto, Fred W. Rummler, John Retterstoff, and Herman G. Jahnke.

The "K" Company had Claude R. Sweitzer, August Brinkert, William Breitzman, Anthony Britz, August J. Jorn, Nicholas M. Lenz, John W. Lennebacher, Theodore J. F. Oehmke, August J. Schwark, John L. Schwark, and William A. Stillmeyer. The "L" Company's membership included James A. Leisen, Charles Grunert, Frank H. Gigler, Henry Koester, Jr., Walter Peters, Henry Renken, Joseph Schroeter, Gustav Schultz and Steven Valentine. The "M" Company's list included William J. Breithaupt, Robert F. Herkner, Charles E. Kipplinger, Emil Nerlinger and Andrew Sieder.

The Thirty-Fifth Michigan

The Thirty-Fifth Michigan Volunteer Infantry had, as its Major Harry H. Bandholtz, who later achieved distinction in the regular army; as its Quartermaster Sergeant, John J. Dunneback, and as a hospital steward, Albert H. Eber. The "A" Company had Joseph L. Kraemer as its First Lieutenant, Alphonse Balck as its Second Lieutenant, Charles E. Krohn as a corporal and Albert G. Weidensee as a musician. Kramer later became a famous newspaper illustrator. Balck was later a Detroit newspaperman of standing. Among the privates were William R. Briese, Joseph Kautenberg, Carl O. Mord, Henry K. Meyer, Henry Neuman, Eldert Neinhouse, Joseph P. Moeller, Frederick Schmieding and Fred M. Staal. The "B" Company's musician was Christ Rosen, and among his "buddies" were Frank Amstutz, Louis A. Ellinger, James Kuhns, and Peter Sherrick. Two of the "C" Company's corporals were George Schlee and William M. Bache, and in the list of privates were John Fischer, Herman Kreger, Moses Stahle, John A. Ruefli, and Charles Woerfel.

"D" Company had Sylvester S. Zeluff as its First Lieutenant, Conrad F. Herzog, Andrew Maurer, and Carl W. Schaffer as corporals, and in the files Albert Brochman, Herman F. Brochman, Christ W. Libstaff, William J. H. Mueller, William G. Reichert, Benjamin Schupp, John Schrader, Theodore J. Schrader, Henry Steffens, John R. Stroub, John Strech, Edward Traub, Collie O. Waltz and Fred W. Werner. "E" Company's corporals included Charles Kerns, Henry Schust, Adolph Vasser and Carl P. Lunning, and the files Henry C. Bremer, Ernest J. Henrich, Fred Pobanz and Charles C. Zeim. "F" Company's roster had on it the names of Charles L. Ahnert, William Begeman, Walter J. Brant, Charles J. Burger, Thomas Blashak, Bernard R. Freda, Edward G. Groth, Arnold A. Letherer, Richard Lietz, Herman J. Markhoff, Magnus Meier, Bernhard Meiss, William A. Ranspach, August Schultz, Hugo Steinhauser, William H. P. Wenner and Oscar E. Wollensack.

The "G" Company's list had on it Walter S. Derendinger, Charles H. Deneke, John Burkenstock, William S. Boger, Frederick Harben and William F. Schlachter. The "H" Company had Paul W. Swartz as its quartermaster sergeant, George F. Sommer and Frank Conrad as corporals, and Aaron Rosenthal as a musician. The ranks included Conrad Enders, Guy Rosenkrans, and Zopher Yoder. The "I" Company's list included William F. Behrend, Henry T. John, Frank Bebel, Joseph Schiffender, and Edward Swadling. The "K" Company had in its membership Jack Conrad, Charles W. Deiner, Charles G. Glasser, Nicholas C. Hoey, Alfred H. Holsenburg, Isidor Lang, Louis F. Werner, John Zanger and Edward K. Zimmer.

The "L" Company's Captain was William G. Fleishauer, and George H. Sipper was a corporal. Among the privates were Gustave H. Breternitz, Charles Edinger, Charles H. Kimpel, Robert F. Klein, Frederick C. Reimold, Albert Mostetter, and William R. Wolpert. The "M" Company had William F. Freyer, Albert Josman, Albert Schlusler, George Schram, Gustave F. Schlusler, Charles H. Schuck, Carl Promenschenkel, Theodore E. Schwink, John J. Moeller and August E. Winterstein.

During the progress of the war Martin Belser was commissioned First Lieutenant of Company "A" of the Thirty-First Regiment, George G. Schmid was made First Lieutenant of Company "M", John W. Haarer was made Second Lieutenant of Company "M" and Albert Hartenstein became Second Lieutenant of Company "L" of the Thirty-Third Regiment during the conflict.

The Michigan Naval Reserve, which manned the U. S. S. Yosemite in Cuban waters during the Spanish-American war, had in its complement of men Landsmen J. C. Ammerman, P. A. Bonjoff, J. Grieshaber, Jr., A. J. Janke, A. H. Kessler, H. Hess, F. E. Reschke, W. A. Stecker, J. P. Scheib, Walter E. Welz and C. H. Widman; Seamen T. A. Becker, E. T. Bernart, C. F. Heyerman, V. E. Schwan. H. S. Siebel, W. M. Lanback, E. E. Anneke, E. H. Wetzel, and L. C. Wurzer; Fireman F. E. Bellman, F. A. Eckert, H. D. Schnebner, W. M. Schulte, G. Tausenfreund, A. C. Myers, J. Meyers, A. Ruhl, and in other capacities, A. L. Beck, F. C. Hecker, A. E. Ibershoff, E. A. Engle, R. G. Kirchner, F. C. Massnich and G. F. Rich.

The Roster of the Dead

The dead of these five regiments in the Spanish war included twenty-eight men of traceable or apparent German ancestry. These men were: Captain John Gusman; Musician C. N. Etzkorn; Privates William J. Weidman, Frederick Demner, Charles A. Genske, Max H. Pansler, Frederick Hams, Charles F. Koschig, Edward A. Flading, Samuel E. Gemberling, Albert Grunburg, George Lind, John Essenberg, Albert G. Meyers, Peter P. Haan, Frank J. Muck, Martin Messner, Frank H. Ott, Frank A. Hoffman, Adolph Kordt, Stephen H. Otto, Albert Benhke, Henry Koester, Jr., Henry K. Meyer, Lewis Mangold, Herman Kreger. Frank Conrad and Theodore Shadegg.

They sleep with their fellow-heroes of other bloods and breeds, beside whom they fought the battles of their common country.

CHAPTER XII

THE WORLD WAR

National Basis of Recruiting—General Crowder's Compliment—Percentage of German-American Recruits.

The World War, which began in 1914, had been in progress nearly three years before the United States were drawn into it. As a military conflict it stands unparalleled in history from the fact that, with few exceptions, every civilized state in the world had some part in it. The British people were not only represented by forces drawn from their own "tight little islands," but by colonial troops enlisted in their dominions in Canada, Africa and Australia. The French people, in addition to levies from their own population, drew for man power on Africa and Asia. While there was a free sea the Germans drew some reinforcements from their colonies, and had as allies the forces of Austria-Hungary and Bulgaria. Russia, originally attached to the Allies, experienced a change of attitude, and finally became the victim of internal disturbances which made valueless her external assistance on either side of the conflict.

During the first three years of the World War, and while the United States were not involved therein, the sympathies of German-Americans were quite generally with the Fatherland. This made the realignment of sentiment a rather difficult mental and emotional operation for them when the United States were drawn into the conflict and declared war against the Imperial German Government. The change in sympathy was, however, no more difficult for them than for many thousands of Americans who had not, up to that time, become convinced that all the right lay on one side of the controversy.

The entrance of the United States into the war set up a condition where sympathy with the national enemy was no longer tenable on the part of American citizens, whether German or other. The sympathy, therefore, had to give way to national loyalty, though this sentiment could not and did not exclude regret that things had to be as they were. For the first time in that period of the country's history which covered the German settlements therein, people of that blood who were recently or anciently established in the country were confronted with the duty of carrying on warfare with their own kind of people, some of them so close as to be within the nearer degrees of kindred. The ordeal, at the best, tore heartstrings. It was met honestly and bravely.

The World War was, in the organization for its conduct, a different kind of war from those which had preceded it, and in which the United States were a belligerent. In the earlier wars the national armies were composed of state regimental organizations, were of state origin and bore their enumerations until the end of the conflict. The same was true of the Spanish-American War.

National Basis of Recruiting

In the World War the recruiting and assignment of forces was on a national basis from the outset. The enlistment and selection of soldiers, their assignment to various arms of the service, their disposition at home and abroad, the replacement of wounded or exhausted troops with a fresh human supply, and the recording of the personnel were all matters of national concern, rather than state affairs, as they had been in the earlier conflicts referred to.

There was, therefore, no opportunity for local or racial enthusiasms to exploit themselves so conspicuously in the national service as they had done in earlier wars. It was "dot-and-carry-one" for Americans of every type and extraction. There was neither incitement nor place for Irish Brigades or Iron Regiments. The human supply was organized into lettered companies, these in turn into numbered regiments, these again into enumerated brigades, and the brigades into divisions and armies.

That was the modernization of warfare which makes it more difficult to trace the participation of any specific kind of Americans in the organized armies of the nation, as has been done in the cases of its earlier adventures on the field of Mars.

Under the organization of the American forces for the World War there were proportionally just as many participants, under the law of averages, of each class, color, lineage or extraction composing the whole population, as there were persons of each of these classifications fit for war service in the whole population.

As there were, at the time of taking the 1920 census, approximately 18.3 per cent of the people of the whole state of German birth or antecedents in Michigan, it must be assumed that the same percentage of people of this blood, whether foreign-born, first generation native-born, or descended from earlier generations of settlers, was included in the Michigan contribution to the National Army.

The total number of persons of military age registered in Michigan during the World War, by the Selective Service, was 873,383. Of these 211,105 were aliens of various extractions, or 24.17 per cent of the whole. Of these aliens, again, 10,675 were German males between the ages of 18 and 45, and 4,200 more were German males between the ages of 14 and 18. The percentage of German alienage, or persons who had not yet undertaken naturalization in the United States, then resident in Michigan was, therefore, 1.1 per cent of all those subject to military duty, within the American limit of age, and 1.8 per cent, if those are included who were between the ages of 14 and 45. These figures of German alienage, compared with the average alien representation of 24.17 per cent in the various registrations, show how much more closely the German immigration into the state had been followed by the processess of naturalization and assumption of citizenship than was the case with other and newer racial contributions to the citizenship of the state.

General Crowder's Compliment

These German aliens, moreover, stood in a class by themselves. They were ineligible to reception into the National Army because of their technical "enemy alien" status. They were involved by this condition through no blame of their own. It was the result of the operation of law. This phase of the situation is discussed by Provost Marshal General Crowder, in his Second Report on the Operations of the Selective Service System, as follows:

"As the exclusion from the service of aliens was demanded by international law, by public policy and by the effective operation of our forces, local boards were strictly charged with the duty of exempting every one of them from the draft."

The State of Michigan sent into the armed forces of the United States, from April 2, 1917, to Oct. 31, 1918, a total of 142,397 men, of whom 32,403 entered by enlistment in the Army; 96,480 were inducted through the operation of the Selective Service Act; 11,463 enlisted in the Navy, and 2,051 enlisted in the Marine Corps. Applying the percentage relation of persons of German birth and descent in Michigan at the beginning of American participation in the World War, namely 18.3, the German-American contribution to these increments to the armed forces of the nation from Michigan as a source, numbered approximately 26,048.

To the unskilled these figures may seem large. The application of the law of averages becomes justified when they are compared with other figures which bear a relation to them. One set of these is the comparison between Michigan's increment to the armed forces of the United States in

IN THE MAKING OF MICHIGAN 139

the Civil War and the comparative increment in the World War. There were 749,113 people in Michigan at the beginning of the Civil War and 1,184,059 in 1870. If the growth in the intervening decade was even, the population of the state at the end of the Civil War was 966,586, indicating an average population for the period 1861-1865 of 857,848. This population contributed soldiers to the Unicn Army numbering 90,747, or 11 per cent of the average population. In 1910 the states's population had risen to 2,810,172, which by 1917 had grown to 3,410,940, assuming an even growth during the first seven years of the decade. This population was called upon to furnish 142,397 men to the World War, or 4.2 per cent of its mass, a very much lower percentage than that required in the Civil War.

Since the Civil War there had been a marked influx of Germans into the state, these figures being shown in another chapter of this work; and there had been the natural accretion of three generations from the primary stock, besides the result of inter-marriages with other stocks. The calculations made elsewhere herein show that in 1910 there were 410,000 people of German blood in Michigan, including 86,047 of actual German birth. This figure had grown to 670,000 in 1920, indicating in 1917 a German-extraction population of about 576,000, from which the claim that Michigan's contribution to the National Army in the World War included 26,000 men of German ancestry is shown to be not far wide of the mark.

Percentage of German Recruits

The amalgamation of the product of the German-American stock with the total population of the whole state leaves few typically Germanic groups through which the proportion of Michigan's German-American contribution to the World War can be definitely traced. That it was at least up to the average of all other contributions seems certain from the fact that, where traceable, it appears to have been above the average. The few Germanic groups which are still distinctly identifiable are those which are assembled into the religious organizations, notably those of the Lutheran church. Many of the congregations of persons of this belief have compiled statistics which are illuminating. For instance, Trinity Evangelical Church of Detroit, with 881 communicants, sent 53 men to the war, or 6 per cent of its group membership; Immanuel Congregation of the same city, sent 55 out of its 860 members, or 6.4 per cent; Stephanus, with 1,000 members, sent 117 men, or 11.7 per cent; St. John's, with 1200 members, sent 100 men or 8.33 per cent; Bethel, with 400 members, sent 36, or 9 per cent; Messiah, with 1,000, sent 57, or 5.6 per cent; Immanuel, of Bay City, with 800 members, sent 49, or 6 per cent; St. Johns, of the same city, with 500 members, sent 30, or 6 per cent; Zion, of Bay City, with 200 members, sent 30, or 15 per cent; St. Lorenz, of Frankenmuth, with 1,500 members, sent 62, or 4.1 per cent; Trinity, of Monroe, with 500 members, sent 36, or 7.2 per cent; and many others in much the same proportion.

From the distinctively German memberships of this church organization in Southeastern Michigan, 1,418 young men were enrolled in the National Army, of whom 32 paid the supreme sacrifice.

The records of American participation in the World War have not yet been sufficiently analyzed to give much information as to the race-stocks of its participants. How well the German-American served is attested by the number who received the honors of war in the form of testimonials of their bravery. The names of a great many of these are given in an ensuing chapter. What their government thought about their service is recorded in the Second Report of Provost Marshal General Crowder on the Operations of the Selective Service System, in which he says:

"A final word must be added on behalf of those registrants of German stock who loyally stood by the American flag. There were thousands of them. A natural distrust at first attended them in public opinion; and the notorious intrigues of the German Government to secure their support have perhaps left in the public mind an emphasis on that feature. It is, therefore, worth while here to place on record the reassuring experience of the local boards, an experience which should preserve equally in our memory the other side of the picture. How large and loyal a share of genuine support was given to the draft by families of this race stock may be illustrated by typical letters from local boards."

CHAPTER XIII

THE ACKNOWLEDGEMENTS OF BRAVERY

The Congressional Medal of Honor—The Distinguished Service Cross—The French Cross of War.

The Congressional Medal of Honor, conferred upon soldiers of the Republic by special Act of Congress for conspicuous gallantry in action, is the highest encomium which the United States Government confers upon its defenders. Of the millions of men who have served in the nation's armies about three thousand have received the Congressional Medal. Of these, only four received two medals, and of these two were men from Michigan. One of these was of German ancestry, being Thomas W. Custer, Second Lieutenant, Company B, Sixth Michigan Cavalry, brother of Gen. George A. Custer. The Custers were originally Ohio people with a German ancestry two generations back. General Custer once said of him, "If you want to know my opinion of Tom, I can only say that I think he should be the General and I the Captain."

Of the other Michigan men who received the Medal of Honor, Frederick Alber, a Manchester man, who was a 24-year old private in Company A. of the Seventeenth Michigan Infantry, got his for rescuing a Lieutenant of his regiment who had been captured by three of the enemy. Peter Syke and Frederick Ballen, were Adrian men, who joined Captain William H. Ward's infantry company, organized in their home city. There being no vacancies in a Michigan regiment, the company offered its services to the Governor of Ohio, who accepted it as Company B of the Forty-Seventh Ohio infantry.

IN THE MAKING OF MICHIGAN   143

Ballen was given the Medal of Honor for heroic action at Vicksburg in 1863. John Hack, another Adrian man of the same company, was given the Medal for participation in the same action at the same place. He was an eighteen-year old when he won his distinction. Joseph B. Kamp, another eighteen-year older, who was similiary honored, was from Whitmore Lake, in Washtenaw. He was first sergeant of Company D, Fifth Michigan infantry, and he won his honor by capturing the regimental flag of the Thirty-First North Carolina Regiment, of the Confederate Army, at the Battle of the Wilderness in 1864. Another member of the same company and regiment, John W. Menter, of Superior, in Washtenaw, got his Medal of Honor for capturing the flag of another Confederate regiment. Conrad Noll was an Ann Arbor man, a member of Company D of the Twentieth Michigan Infantry. At Spotsylvania, in 1864, when the regimental color-bearer was shot, he seized the standard and fought his way out, though the enemy was on left flank and rear. He got the Medal for his action.

The Distinguished Service Cross

When the World War was in progress, provision was made for the recognition of valor among the soldiers of the Republic by provision for conferring the Distinguished Service Cross for exceptional instances. Among the Michigan men who were given the Distinguished Service Cross during and at the close of that conflict, as verified by the Michigan Historical Commission, were Captain Oscar L. Buck, of the 165th Infantry, 42nd Division, who came from Detroit; First Lieutenant Leo J. Crum, of the Medical Corps, attached to the 126th Division, who was a Kalamazoo man; Ben Cone, of Detroit, corporal of Company I, Sixth Regiment, U. S. Marine Corps, whose honor was posthumous; Theodore T. Gariepy, of Detroit, who was a corporal of Company C, 125th Infantry; Raymond Genicke, of Detroit, a private of Company H, 128th Infantry; Clement A. Grobbel, of Warren, a corporal in Company K, 339th Infantry, who won his honor for heroism in Russia; Dick Heydenburk, of Wayland, private Company D, Third Machine Gun Battalion, and a descendant of the Heydenburks of the Revolution; William C. Holtzgrebe, of Escanaba, private Company K, 125th Infantry; Albert L. J. Ihrke, of Mayville, private Company B, 47th Infantry; Chester C. Kromer, of Grand Rapids, corporal Company K, 128th Infantry; Alfred H. Kuhlman, of Rogers City, private 116th Ambulance Company, 104th Sanitary Train; Frank S. Marek, of Grand Rapids, corporal Company M, 126th Infantry, 32nd Division; Harry J. Ollrich, of Mt. Clemens, private of Company E, 125th Infantry, who lost his life and was honored after his death; Hubert C. Paul, of Detroit, private, 337th Ambulance Company, which was attached to the 339th Infantry in service in Russia; Herman Plauman, of Detroit, private Company H, 128th Infantry; George H. Pohl, of Mt. Clemens, corporal Company G, 126th Infantry; Paul W. Redeker, of Manistique, corporal Company M, 125th Infantry; Charles Schmitz, private Company I, 9th Infantry, 2nd Division, who came from Saginaw; Barnard A. Schultheis, of Flint, private Machine Gun Company, 125th Regiment; Fred M. Schultz, of Bay City, corporal Company M, 16th Infantry; George F. Schultz, of New Buffalo, private Company E, 16th Infantry; Theodore H. Sieloff, of Detroit, corporal Company I, 339th Infantry; Rudolph Socha, of Detroit, private Battery D, 119th Field Artillery; Fred C. Stein, of Atlanta, corporal Company F, 125th Infantry; Floyd W. Steinhilber, of Highland Park, First Lieutenant, 354th Infantry; Victor Stier, of Detroit, private Company A, 339th Infantry, who lost his life in the war; John Teichler, of Menominee, sergeant Company I, 125th Infantry, who was also killed; William F. Weine, First Lieutenant, 125th Infantry, an Alpena man, who was another victim; Bernard Weiner, sergeant, 43rd Company, 5th Regiment, U. S. M. C., from Detroit, who died in service; Walter H. Wiechman, of Detroit, corporal Company D, 103rd Infantry; Archie M. Zavitz, Freeport, sergeant Company I,

IN THE MAKING OF MICHIGAN

126th Infantry and Clarence H. Zech, Detroit, private, 337th Ambulance Corps, 339th Infantry.

The Distinguished Service Medal was conferred on Brig. Gen. Harry H. Bandholtz, originally from Constantine, and Edward G. Heckel, Colonel, 125th Infantry, from Detroit.

The Navy Cross was conferred on Lieutenant Carl V. Essery, from Detroit; Lieut. Walter Seibert, of Marlette; Rear Admiral Albert G. Winterhalter, who was born in Detroit, and George Henry Knaepple, chief machinist's mate, of Detroit.

The French Cross of War

The French Cross of War was conferred on Earl .L. Adelsperger, of Detroit, sergeant, Company C, 125th Regiment; Brig. Gen. Harry H. Bandholtz, of Constantine, who also received the Cross of the French Legion of Honor; Ernest Malcolm Bantz, of Detroit, sergeant 17th Company, 5th Regiment U. S. M. C.; Harold G. Barthel, of Detroit, Company K, 339th Infantry (Russia); Frank A. Bauman, of Traverse City; Harry Beuker, Central Lake, sergeant, Company H, 125th Infantry; Ernest Bluhm, of Muskegon Heights, private, 1st Ammunition Company, 2nd Division; Anton C. Cron, Lieutenant Colonel 104th Infantry, who was appointed to the army from Michigan; Theodore J. Beschner, of Monroe, Second Lieutenant "M" Company, 23rd Infantry; John L. Depner, of Waldron, private Company M. 166th Infantry, 42nd Division; Henry Faessler, of Pontiac, sergeant Battery D., 17th Field Artillery, 2nd Division; Oscar Falk, of Menominee, Captain, Company F, 125th Regiment, 32nd Division; Theodore T. Gariepy, of Detroit, sergeant Company C, 125th Regiment, 32nd Division; Raymond Genicke, of Detroit, private Company H, 128th Infantry, 32nd Regiment; William C. Giffels of St. Johns, First Lieutenant, 310th Engineers, 85th Division (Russia); George F. Goebel, of Jackson, Second Lieutenant, 142nd Infantry, 36th Division; Charles A. Hebner, of Detroit, sergeant Company M, 339th Infantry in Russian Service; Edward Hein, of Lansing,

146 THE GERMANIC INFLUENCE

private 331st Supply Q. M. C.; Raymond James Hess, of Homer, private 45th Company, 5th Regiment U. S. M. C.; Dick Heydenberk, of Wayland, private Company D, 3rd Machine Gun Section; William D. Hoeltzel, of Battle Creek, Ammunition Service, Sec. 600; Bernard C. Holdorf, of Bessemer, master engineer, 107th Engineers; William E. Holtzgrebe, of Escanaba, private, Company K, 125th Infantry; Milo R. Hulliberger, Freeport, Second Lieutenant, 141st Infantry, 36th Division; Albert L. J. Ihrke, of Mayville, Second Lieutenant, 141st Infantry, 36th Division; Fred W. Kalbrenner, of Detroit, private Company L, 125th Infantry, 32nd Division; Theodore F. Kessler, of Escanaba, Captain, Ordinance Dept., Service of Supply; Otto C. Ketelhut, of Detroit, sergeant, Company C, 61st Infantry, 5th Division; Adelbert Kratz, of Chesaning, sergeant Company A, 310th Engineers, 85th Division, (Russia); Simon Junst, of Grand Rapids, private Company B, 1st Gas Regiment; Raymond Link, of Detroit, sergeant Company C, 120th M. G. B., 32nd Division; John C. Mehl, of Big Rapids, First Lieutenant, 146th Infantry, 37th Division; Walter W. Meier, of Dundee, private Company K, 128th Infantry, 32nd Division; Rudolph Minch, of Detroit, Private 18th Company, 5th Regiment U. S. M. C.; Frank Neider, of Detroit, private, 43rd Company, 5th Regiment, U. S. M. C.; W. J. Niederpruem, of Detroit, Captain, Headquarters 32nd Division; Harry J. Ollrich, 125th Infantry, 32nd Division; Theo. W. Pautsch, of Detroit, sergeant, Company C, 339th Infantry, 85th Division (Russia); Herman Plauman, of Detroit, sergeant, Company C., 339th Infantry, 85th Division (Russia); Paul M. Radtke, of Manistee, private, Company C, 1st Brigade Battery, 2nd Division; Carl John Rittinger, of Lowell, First Lieutenant, Signal Corps, General Headquarters; Peter P. Rost, of Calumet, private Company B, 107th Engineers, 32nd Division; Oscar C. Rummler, of Belding, corporal Company B, First Field Signal Battery, 32nd Division; Albert Sauller, of Manistique, private 97th Company, 6th Regiment, U. S. M. C.; Arthur Schaap, of Holland, private Company H, 126th Infantry, 32nd

IN THE MAKING OF MICHIGAN

Division; William B. Scheffer, of Port Huron. sergeant Company L, 125th Infantry, 32nd Division; Harold M. Schmidt, of Saginaw, private Company I, 9th Infantry, 22nd Division; Keith H. Schroder, of Battle Creek, private, section 601, Ambulance Service; Bernard A. Schultheis, of Flint, private, Machine Gun Company, 125th Infantry, 32nd Division; Fred M. Schultz, of Bay City, corporal, Company M, 16th Infantry, 1st Division; George F. Schultz, of New Buffalo, private Company E, 16th Infantry, 1st Division; John Shutter, of Kalamazoo, corporal, Company H, 23rd Infantry, 2nd Division; Joseph F. Seewacker, of Detroit, sergeant, 18th Company, 5th Regiment U. S. M. C., 2nd Division; Frank Sochel, of Detroit, private 47th Company, 5th Regiment U. S. M. C.; Walter A. Springstein, of Detroit, private, Headquarters Company, 339th Infantry, 85th Division, (Russia); Fred C. Stein, of Atlanta, corporal Company F, 125th Infantry, 32nd Division; Joseph Steyskal, of Detroit, corporal Company K, 339th Infantry, 85th, Division (Russia); Christian G. Stillmeyer, of Calumet, mechanic Company G, 125th Infantry, 32nd Division; Ann Straub, of Detroit, nurse; John Teichler, of Menominee, sergeant, Company L, 125th Infantry, 32nd Division; William F. Weine, Alpena, First Lieutenant, 125th Infantry, 32nd Division; Carl G. Wencke, of Battle Creek, Captain 601st Army Service; Walter H. Wiechman, of Detroit, corporal, Company D, 103rd Infantry, 26th Division; Berthold H. A. Wilken, of Detroit, private 43rd Company, 5th Regiment, U. S. M. C.; Theodore J. Zech, of Detroit, private Company M, 339th Infantry, 85th Division (Russia); and William Zielke, of Detroit, private Company G, 23rd Infantry, 2nd Division.

Colonel Heinrich A. Pickert, of Detroit, who went through the entire war, following his participation in the Mexican Border encampments just prior to it, was given the honor of a special citation for valor by General Pershing.

CHAPTER XIV

THE CONTRIBUTIONS TO LEARNING

In no department of human activity has the Germanic influence in the making of Michigan been more distinctive than in the field of education. While not by any means exclusive, this influence has been very extensive. There were reasons for this condition. Even before German men and women began to come into Michigan in the numbers which made them and their descendants a very respectable percentage of the population, the influence of the race on education was effective within the state. There was no public school system until Michigan was well into the '30's of the nineteenth century. America students had been going to Germany for education as early as 1810. Madame de Stael's "Germany", printed in London in 1813, gave a broader view of Germanic culture than had previously obtained in the United States.
When M. Victor Cousin's "Report on the State of Public Instruction in Prussia," in 1831, was made to the French Ministry of Education, and after it had been translated, four years later, by Sarah Austin and published in New York, popular education in the United States was only in the making. The "Prussian system" came to be a phrase describing a plan of education based upon freedom of access to schools operated at public expense, with state supervision, and with three gradations of scholastic teaching, those of the common school, the high school or academy and the University This system was opposed to the earlier ecclesiastical and private systems.

When the making of the Michigan Constitution of 1835 was in process the "Prussian system" was practically incorporated into that fundamental law, through the activity of Isaac E. Crary and Rev. John D. Pierce, who were familiar with the Cousin report. Professor Hinsdale says, in his "History of the University of Michigan," commenting on the provisions for a school system contained in the basic law as it was first written:

"In effect all the Prussian ideas are here; primary schools, secondary schools and a university; public taxation and state supervision."

That was the initial Germanic influence upon education in Michigan, and a very important one because it determined the form of public scholastic organization. Since that time it has become the basis of organization of the private systems as well.

Contributions to Primary Education

But the system did not come all at once. Meantime private schools were maintained, operated both by laymen and church organizations. The Germans were coming in, largely in colonies; largely, too, in groups which had their several religious leaders. Of the latter groups, the division, again, was into Roman Catholic and Evangelical Lutheran bodies. These organized themselves into congregations, and, in so many cases that it was the rule, each of them strove to give the youth of their respective groups an education to fit them for contact with the world, and also a training in their respective religious beliefs. The parochial school system, therefore, furnished the newly-arriving German imigrants an outlet for their educational enthusiasms.

But this was not the only contribution. There were two other classifications of influence which began very early and have continued to the present time. German scholars, born abroad and educated in their home lands, found their way even so far afield as Michigan. They offered their talent for application to educational effort, in their new homeland. Meantime, American and other students proceeded to Germany to its famous and competent institutions, either for general courses or for the study of specific subjects, returning to America equipped for the dissemination of human learning, after they had either gained their original stores or augmented them in the halls of the German seats of culture.

CHAPTER XV

THE UNIVERSITY OF MICHIGAN

The Early Regents—Faculty Members of German Training—American Teachers—A Contribution to Agriculture—Group of German-Trained Americans—A Great Professor of Law—The Originator of Ward Instruction—The Pioneer in Forestry—Sons of Carlsruhe, Munich and Leipsig—Men from Bonn, Strasburg and Berlin—A German Authority on Old English—A Group of German-Named Professors.

One of the most striking instances of this transmission of learning from the masters of one continent to the students of another is afforded by the history of the University of Michigan. In its very beginning the process commenced and it continues until the present time.

Under the first organization of the University the Regents were appointed. Of the earliest group John Fredenrich Porter, a regent of 1837, who was born at Albany in 1806, was of German antecedents and tutorship. He was, in addition to being a Regent, one of the representatives of the state in the disposal of the Michigan Central Railroad to a private corporation in 1846. Michael Hoffman, another Regent of the same year, was a New York man, a descendant of the early German immigration which settled about Herkimer and Clifton. Isaac Edwin Crary, a Regent in 1837, was the man who had, with "Father" Pierce, studdied Cousin's "Report on the State of Education in Prussia," and who was the leading factor in incorporating the "Prussian system" into the Constitution of 1837. Rev. George Duffield, the first of his name to come into Michigan, and a University of Pennsylvania man, had a paternal ancestry reaching into Antrim, in Ireland; but his mother was Faithful Schleirmacher, of an early German family of Strassburg, Pennsylvania. He was a Regent from 1839 to 1848.

Rev. Martin Kundig, a Regent appointed in 1841, was a Catholic priest from the German canton of Schwys, in Switzerland, born 1805, and arriving in Detroit in 1833. He had made extensive literary, classical and scientific studies at colleges in Einsiedeln and Lucerne, and finished his studies in Rome. He is described by Prof. Hinsdale as a "very punctual and efficient member of the Board." Incidentally, he is the only citizen of his faith who was ever a member of the Board of Regents, either by appointment or election.

Rev. John Guest Atterbury, who was appointed a Regent in 1848, had been taught by German professors in Yale. His son is the present President of the Pennsylvania Railroad. Regent Jonas H. McGowan, who was a U. of M. man himself, had a Scotch father and a German mother, Susanna Hartzell. Regent James Shearer, (1846-1848) who was a great deal of a builder and architect, had a remote Germanic ancestry. His father came from Antrim, in Ireland, where his father's father in turn had taken to wife a full-blooded German girl. Regent George L. Maltz (1877-1880) had a German father and mother, who lived in Detroit within the memories of people still alive. Regent Lyman D. Norris (1883) had spent some time in 1851 and 1852 at Heidelberg, taking a course in the civil law to qualify himself for dealing with cases involving French and Spanish land grants.

Regent Hermann Kiefer, born in Sulzburg, Baden, in 1825, was a student of the Gymnasia of Mannheim, Freiburg and Karlsruhe, and studied medicine at Vienna, Freiburg, Heidelberg and Prague, taking his doctor's license before the state examiners of Karlsruhe. During his thirteen years of service as Regent (1889-1902) he "was chairman of the committee on the Department of Medicine and Surgery and did important service in the building up and strengthening of that department." So reads the record. Following his retirement from the regency he was made Professor Emeritus of the Practice of Medicine. Regent Levi Lewis Barbour, (1892-1898) studied in Germany for a considerable period after his graduation from Michigan in 1865.

Faculty Members of German Training

The more important usefulness in education at the University of Michigan was that of the faculty members of German birth, extraction or training, who have ornamented the lists of its professors. Some of them were very great men. The beginning of these contacts occured in 1853, when President Tappan went abroad to purchase the equipment for the Observatory of the University, funds for which had recently been provided by the citizens of Detroit. He got into Germany in his travels and came into contact with the astronomer Encke, and the philosopher von Humboldt. He was also seeking a Professor of Astronomy and a Director for the Observatory. Encke recommended a young student of the science who was his assistant at Berlin Observatory. The nominee was modest and unwilling to come to America, so Louis Agassiz and von Humboldt added their urgings to those of Dr. Tappan and Encke.

The result was that Franz Friedrich Brunnow, born in Berlin in 1821; Doctor of Philosophy of the University of Berlin, 1843; Director of the Observatory of Bilk, near Dusseldorf, 1847; gold medalist of the Amsterdam Academy of Science, 1849, for his essay on De Vico's Comet; writer of Spherical Astronomy, 1851, which was translated into French, English, Russian, Italian and Spanish; and successor to Galle as first assistant at the Observatory of Berlin, accepted the Directorship of Detroit Observatory and the Professorship of Astronomy at Michigan. He made his institution widely known, edited a journal, "Astronomical Notices," giving results of his work, and published several scientific papers and works. Among his assistants in 1861 was Orlando B. Wheeler, born in Lodi, Washtenaw County, who made a great name for himself later in the Army. Dr. Brunnow married President Tappan's daughter, and when the President retired in 1863, he and Dr. Brunnow returned to Europe. In 1865 the scientist was made Astronomer Royal of Ireland, succeeding Sir William Rowan Hamilton, the bearer of one of the most brilliant names known to astronomical science.

Professor Abram Sager, born at Bethlehem, N. Y., in 1810, of mixed Dutch and German ancestry, became chief of the Botanical and Zoological Department of the Michigan Geological Survey as early as 1837. His catalogue of the fauna and of the flora of Michigan, completed in 1839, is of the specimens which laid the foundation of the zoological collection of the University's Museum; as his private herbarium, consisting of 1,200 species and 12,000 specimens, which he presented, was one of the greatest gifts of flora of the state. Professor Sager was Professor of Botany and Zoology, 1842-1850; when he turned over to the Medical School, being Professor of Obstetrics, Diseases of Women and Children, Botany and Zoology, 1850-54; of Physiology, added to the foregoing, 1854-1855; of Obstetrics and Physiology, 1855-1860; and of Obstetrics and Diseases of Women and Children, 1860-1875.

American Teachers Taught in Germany

Louis Fasquelle, who came to the Professorship of Modern Languages and Literature in 1846, was a Frenchman, from Calais, and a University of Paris man. He studied German and Germanic literature in Germany before coming to America.

James Robinson Boise, who taught Greek at Michigan, from 1852 to 1868, was a Brown University man of 1840, and its Professor of Greek from 1845 to 1852. He came to Michigan in that year, but before coming, refreshed and im-

proved his knowledge by a year of study spent between the
University of Halle and the University of Bonn. In 1868
the University of Tubingen conferred its honorary Doctorate
of Philosophy upon him.

Andrew Dickson White, who became President of Cornell University in 1867, had been a Professor of History in
Michigan from 1857. He was a Yale man, who had done much
post-graduate work in Germany, to which country he returned
in 1879 as Minister of the United States.

James Craig Watson, famous as Professor of Astronomy,
succeeding Dr. Brunnow, got his Master's degree in 1859
after two years personal instruction by Dr. Brunnow. He
received the honorary degree of Doctor of Philosophy from
the University of Leipsig in 1870.

Edward Payson Evans, instructor in Modern Languages
at Michigan (1862-70) had travelled and studied in Germany
before he began his service at Ann Arbor, to which city he
retired. He was a Michigan graduate of 1854. His later work
was almost wholly in German.

Martin Luther D'Ooge, Professor of Greek at Michigan,
from 1867, was Dutch born and Michigan educated. Upon
his appointment to a full professorship in 1870, he took two
years for study at the Universities of Berlin and Leipsig,
making his Doctorate of Philosophy at Leipsig in 1872, and
returning to Michigan with his wider store of knowledge to
take his place in her faculty.

George Sylvester Morris, thorough-bred New Englander,
and Dartmouth man, who had been a Greek instructor at his
Alma Mater, was brought out to Michigan in 1870 to be a
language professor, remaining until 1879; returning in 1881
as Professor of Ethics, History of Philosophy and Logic,
which position he held until his death in 1889. While at Michigan he translated from the German Ueberweg's History of
Philosophy, and wrote treatises on Kant's Critique of Pure
Reason, Hegel's Philosophy of the State and collateral subjects.

Eugene Woldemar Hilgard, born at Zweibrucken, Bavaria. 1833, was brought to America by his family in 1835, and raised in Belleville, Illinois. When he grew up he returned to Germany, for study at the Royal Mining School, Freiburg, and at Zurich and Heidelberg. The latter institution made him a Doctor of Philosophy in 1853. Two years later he was State Geologist of Mississippi, serving until 1857, when he went to the Smithsonian Institute at Washington as chemist in charge of its laboratory. He returned in 1858 to his Mississippi work and in 1873 was called to Michigan as Professor of Mineralogy, Geology, Zoology and Botany. He remained at Michigan two years, going to the University of California. Michigan gave him its honorary Doctorate of Laws in 1887. In 1894 he was granted the Leipsig medal for advances in agricultural science by the Royal Bavarian Academy of Sciences, and in 1903 Heidelberg gave him a diploma reconferring his Doctorate of Philosophy, granted fifty years before.

A Contributor to Agriculture

Dr. Hilgard has done inestimable service to the agricultural interests of the United States in soil surveys and original suggestions of chemical applications for fertilization, which were first applied to cotton culture in Mississippi and later adapted to many crops of the colder north. Originally an agnostic, Dr. Hilgard became a Roman Catholic while in Washington.

There was a very considerable group of outstanding Michigan professors and instructors who received their original or supplementary training in German schools.

William Henry Pettee, whose Massachusetts ancestry went back to 1685, was Professor of Mining Engineering at Michigan from 1875 to 1904. He got his training from 1866 to 1869 at the Mining School of Freiburg, in Saxony.

Charles Kasson Weed, Professor of Physics in 1877-1885, was a lineal descendant of Adam Karsen, a German pioneer of Connecticut. He himself was a Massachusetts "Tech" man, supplementing his studies by two years work in 1875-76, at the University of Berlin and the Gewerbeschule of that city.

Edward Loraine Walker, Michigan born, and Michigan graduated, taught the classics from 1871 onward until his death in 1898. In 1874 he went abroad, spending nearly all of a three years absence at Leipsig, where the University gave him his Doctorate in Philosophy in 1877.

Elisha Jones, Professor of Latin and Greek at various times from 1870 to 1888, took three years from 1872 onward to improve himself in his specialties abroad, spending the time at Leipsig and Bonn.

Albert H. Pattengill, a Michigan graduate who was a Greek professor from 1869 to 1906, spent the year 1878 in study in German universities. Henry Sewall, who came to Michigan in 1881 as Professor of Physiology, remaining until 1889, did the same thing during 1879 and 1880. Prof. Wooster Woodruff Beaman translated Dedekind's "Essays on the Theory of Numbers" from the German and was a member of the Deutsche Mathematike Vereinigung.

Henry Lorenz Obetz, appointed Professor of Surgery and Clinical Surgery in the Homeopathic Medical College in 1883, holding until 1895, was of Ohio birth, the grandson of an immigrant German on the paternal side, and the son of a German-born mother, she a native of Stuttgart.

Calvin Brainard Cady, who taught music at the University from 1880 to 1888, spent two and a half years, 1872-74, studying his art at Leipsig.

Hugo Emil Rudolph Arndt, who was Professor of Materia Medica in the Homeopathic Medical College, was a native born German, who was educated in the Gymnasium of Kuestrin and later in Berlin. James Craven Wood, Professor of Obstetrics and Diseases of Women in the same school from 1885 until 1895, was of German descent on his mother's side, she being Jane Kunkle. He himself was born in Ohio.

William Ralph Angler, Ohio man, son of William Angler and Mary Hartman, was instructor in Law in 1907, and became an Assistant Professor in 1912. He has also served at Leland Stanford and Columbia.

A Great Professor of Law

One of the great law professors of the University, as well as one of the great lawyers of Michigan, Otto Kirchner, taught in the Law School in 1885-86 and again in 1893-1906, in which latter year he became non-resident Lecturer on Legal Ethics. Mr. Kirchner was a native of Frankfort-on-Oder, who came to the United States as a child, made his way through the law by study with practitioners, and became Attorney-General of Michigan in 1877, holding office for two terms.

Volney Morgan Spalding, a New Yorker and a Michigan graduate of 1873, was called to the University as a Professor of Botany and Zoology, holding from 1876 to 1904. His training included a course in plant physiology at the University of Jena, and two years, 1893-1894, at the University at Leipsig, which gave him the degree of Doctor of Philosophy in 1894.

The same University was the scene of the post-graduate work of Calvin Thomas, a Lapeer county man who graduated at Michigan in 1874, and spent parts of 1877 and 1878 in the study of philology, and who served Michigan as Professor of Modern Languages, Professor of Germanic and Sanscrit, and Professor of Germanic Languages and Literature from 1878 to 1896, when he was called to Columbia University to teach the same subjects. Professor Thomas prepared a German grammar, wrote a Life of Schiller and made the first complete English translation of both parts of "Faust," with English introductions and notes, based on studies carried on in Goethe's private library at Weimar.

Paul Casper Freer, who was lecturer on General Chemistry and later full professor thereof and Director of the Labora-

IN THE MAKING OF MICHIGAN 159

tory of General Chemistry from 1889 to 1904, was the son of a mother of Wurtemburg ancestry, the family name being Gatter. Graduating in medicine at Chicago in 1882 he spent the next five years abroad specializing in chemistry, with physics and mineralogy as minor subjects. He was given his Doctor's degree at the University of Munich. Frederick George Novy, one of the great chemistry and bacteriology teachers of Michigan, got his B. S., from that school in 1886, his Doctorate of Science in 1890, and his Doctorate of Medicine in 1891. He studied at Prague in 1894 and was a student under Professor Dr. Koch in Germany in 1898.

John Jacob Abel, an Ohio man by birth, the son of parents of immediate German descent, a Ph. B., of Michigan in 1883, spent two years thereafter at Leipsig, a year and a half at Strassburg, a year each at Berne and Vienna, and took the lectures at Berlin, Heidelberg and Wurzburg. In 1881 Heidelberg gave him its Doctorate in Medicine. He was Lecturer and Professor of Materia Medica and Therapeutics, 1891-1893, going on to Johns-Hopkins University.

The Originator of Ward Instruction

George Dock, Pennsylvania born and of German ancestry, his mother's family name having been Bombach, studied in Germany from 1885 to 1887 and in 1891 began his long career at Michigan in the Department of Medicine and Surgery. He is credited with the organization of laboratory methods for teaching clinical branches, the establishment of a diagnostic clinic in internal medicine and the application of the system of ward teaching.

Jacob Ellsworth Reighard, Professor of Zoology and Morphology, beginning with 1896 and continuing for many years, was the son of an Indiana physician of German descent. He took a leave from Michigan in 1894-5 to study his specialties abroad, largely at German universities.

James Rowland Angell, son of Michigan's President of longest service and greatest fame, and who is now himself

President of Yale University, studied at Berlin and Halle in 1893, and at Vienna and Leipsig in 1894.

James Alexander Craig, a Canadian by birth and a graduate of McGill, studied divinity and got his degree from Yale in 1883. He spent the next three years at the University of Leipsig, which gave him his Doctorate in Philosophy in 1886. In 1892 he went again to Europe to study, part of the time in the British Museum, but most of it at the University of Berlin, devoting himself to Arabic and Aramaic. Michigan called him to the Professorship of Oriental Languages, and later to Semitic Languages and Hellenistic Greek, in 1893. He has written many works on Oriental subjects, and is a member of the Vorderasiatische Gesellschaft, of Berlin, a society devoted to the pursuit of Oriental literature and problems.

George Allison Hench, Pennsylvanian descended on his father's side from Johannes Hench, a seventeenth century German settler in Pennsylvania, came to Michigan in 1890 as Instructor in German, gradually being advanced to a full professorship. He was a Johns Hopkins man, who did postgraduate work in Berlin in 1887, and spent part of 1888 working an old High-German manuscripts in the Imperial Library of Vienna. His library of Germanic philology is one of the treasures of the University.

Willy Alonzo Dewey, Professor of Materia Medica in the Homeopathic Medical School, spent the years 1883 and 1884 as a post-graduate student at Vienna.

George Hempl, part Slavic, part German — his mother was a Hoentzsche—was a Michigan arts graduate of 1879. He taught in Michigan schools, became instructor in German at Johns Hopkins in 1884 and, from 1886 to 1889 studied at Gottingen, Tubingen, Strassburg, Jena and Berlin. Jena gave him his Doctor's degree in Philosophy in 1889, and he was at once called to Michigan as Professor of English. He went to Leland Stanford in 1907.

Arthur Graves Canfield, a Vermont man, a Williams College A. B., of 1878 and A. M., of 1882, spent the intervening years studying philology in Berlin, Leipsig, and Gottingen. He became Professor of Romance Languages at Michigan in 1900.

Max Winkler, Austrian born, graduated from Harvard in 1889, and in 1890 was made an Instructor in German in Michigan, growing into the Professorship of German Language and Literature in 1902. He spent the years 1892 and 1893 at Berlin. He has been a voluminous writer on German classical literature, particularly the productions of Goethe and Schiller.

Allen Sisson Whitney, a Mt. Clemens man by birth, and by paternity back to William the Conqueror, but whose maternal great-grandfather came to America from Germany, taught school in various Michigan cities before he was called to Michigan as a Professor of Pedagogy. He spent parts of 1895 and 1896 at Jena and Leipsig.

The Pioneer in Forestry

Filibert Roth was another of the very great professors of the University of Michigan. He was born at Wilhemsdorf, Wurtemburg, had his common school training in his native land, was brought to America as a youth, and graduated from Michigan as Bachelor of Science in 1890. He spent his early life in the study of forestry problems and from 1903 to his death in 1925 was Professor of Forestry. His career is referred to in greater detail in another part of this writing. Suffice it to say here that he was one of the best beloved professors of Michigan.

Emil Lorch, head of the College of Architecture, was Detroit born in 1870, studied at Massachusetts "Tech," Harvard and Paris. He was an instructor in the Detroit Museum of Art from 1895 to 1898. His father, Gabriel Lorch, German born, came to Detroit in 1864 and was one of the promoters of German music in his home city.

Gotthelf Carl Huber was born in East India, where his

parents, the Rev. John Huber and his wife, who was Barbara Weber, were missionaries. Their son became a Doctor of Medicine at Michigan in 1887. In 1891-2 he was a student at the University of Berlin, and later, in 1895, he spent a season at the University of Prague. His teaching has been in anatomy and histology. He translated the "Textbook of Histology" of Bohn and Davidoff, and has been a voluminous contributor to "Anatomischer Anzeiger" and "Archiv Fur Microskopieche Anatomie."

John William Scholl, a Michigan A. B., of 1901, has been Professor of German since 1902. Ernest Peter Kukle, a Hanoverian, taught English and Rhetoric from 1908 to 1912.

Aldred Scott Warthin, Indiana born, and whose mother, Eliza Margaret Weist, was of an old Pennsylvania German family, has also been engaged in the teaching of pathology since 1891. He is the translator of Ziegler's "General Pathology."

Egbert Theodore Loeffler, a native of Saginaw and of German parentage, began as an engineer and then took up dentistry. In 1903 he was made Professor of Dental Therapeutics at the University, which was his Alma Mater in his studies for both professions.

Aaron G. Schull, whose mother was a Ryman, and who himself is a Michigan man, has been Professor of Zoology since 1921. His brother, Charles Albert Schull, is Professor of Plant Physiology at the University of Chicago.

Sons of Karlsruhe, Munich and Leipzig

Albert Zivet, Professor of Mathematics from 1888, was born in Breslau, Germany. He was of mixed German and Polish ancestry. His education attainments were gained at a German gymnasium, later at Warsaw and Moscow, and finally at the Polytechnic School of Karlsruhe, where he graduated as a civil engineer in 1880.

Moses Gomberg, Instructor and Professor in Organic Chemistry since 1888, worked at the University until 1896, when he went abroad for further study at Munich and Heidelberg, returning to Michigan as an instructor. He is a member of the Deutsche Chemische Gesellschaft, in addition to several other learned societies.

George Washington Patterson, New Yorker and Scotch-Irish, has been engaged in the teaching of electrical engineering at Michigan since 1889. In 1888-89 he spent his time at the University of Munich, which made him a Doctor of Philosophy in 1899.

Frederick Charles Newcome was a native of Flint and has taught botany at Michigan since 1890. In 1892-3 he attended the University of Leipsig, which gave him his Doctorate in Philosophy in 1893, after which he returned to his service at Michigan.

Theodore Wesley Koch, Pennsylvania, Librarian of the University in 1901 and assistant before that, was the son of William Jefferson Koch and Wilhelmina Boch, descended from the earliest German settlement in the Keystone State.

Walter Robert Parker, Marine City man by birth, graduate of the University of Pennsylvania and Spanish war naval ensign, who became Clinical Professor of Ophthalmology in 1904, had ahead of that experience a training in the eye clinics of Vienna.

Dr. R. Bishop Canfield, who began his service at Michigan as Clinical Professor of Otology, Rhinology and Laryngology in 1904, was a Michigan graduate in Arts and Medicine, who spent parts of 1901 and 1902, in preparation for his life work, as Assistant Surgeon and Clinic Chief in Jansen's Clinic, at the University of Frederick William, Berlin.

Calvin Henry Kauffman, Assistant Professor of Botany since 1908, was a Harvard man of 1896, and a Cornell man of 1902.

Claude Halstead Van Tyne, Michigan born and History Professor since 1904, spent 1896, 1897 and 1898 at Heidelberg and Paris. Joseph Horace Drake, who became Lecturer on Roman Law in 1900, was at Jena and Munich for two years following 1890. Edson Read Sunderland, law instructor and professor since 1901, had a year in the University of Berlin after his graduation in arts at Michigan in 1897. Alfred Henry Lloyd, New Jersey man by birth, was a Walker Fellow in Philosophy from Harvard in 1889. Under the maintenance of his fellowship he spent the next two years at Gottingen, Berlin and Heidelberg, and 1901-2 he spent another year at the last named University. In 1906 he became Associate Professor of Nerval Pathology at Michigan.

Moritz Levi, Professor of French since 1890, was born at Waldeck, Germany, and received his preparatory education in the common schools of his native land.

Men from Bonn, Strassburg and Berlin

Walter Dennison, Saline man by birth, and Instructor and Professor of Latin from 1897 onward, had spent the three years prior to his call to Michigan at the University of Bonn.

Earl Wilbur Dow, of partial German descent on the maternal side, and a teacher of history beginning with 1892, spent the summers of 1894 and 1897 at the University of Leipsig.

George Rebec, Tuscola county man by birth and instructor in English at the University in 1891-3, gave up his place in the latter year to take up graduate study at the University of Strassburg. On his return he taught philosophy at Michigan.

Edward David Jones, economist, and in the faculty of the University of Michigan from 1901, had as part of his earlier training two years at Halle and Berlin.

Julius Otto Schlotterbeck was born in the shadow of the University and was its graduate in pharmacy. His father and mother, Herman William Schlotterbeck and Rosina Christina Kempf, were German born. He first gave instruction in pharmacognosy, from 1892 to 1895. In that and succeeding years he attended the University of Berne, which made him a Doctor of Philosophy.

Alviso Burdett Stevens, Livingstone county man, graduate of Michigan in pharmacy in 1875, put a commercial career behind him in 1886 to become a teacher of his art. He spent 1903 to 1905 abroad, as a student of the University of Berne, which gave him a Doctorate in Philosophy in 1905. Mr. Stevens spent the rest of his life in University work.

John Robert Effinger, descendant of Capt. John Ignatius von Effinger, a German revolutionary soldier of the Shenandoah Valley, began his work with the University as an instructor in French in 1892. He is now Dean of the School of Arts.

A German Authority on Old English

Thomas Johann Casjen Diechhoff was a Hanoverian by birth, a graduate of Michigan in 1892, immediately after that an Instructor in German, and later a Professor. He spent 1897-8-9 as a student at the University of Leipsig, which gave him its Doctorate in Philosophy in 1899. He returned to the University as an Assistant Professor of German. He is an authority on Old English, and the American editor (1902) of an edition of Leipsig's "Nathan der Weise."

Edward Henry Kraus, New Yorker, whose father was German and his mother, Rosa Kocher, German Swiss, spent 1899-1901 at Munich, which made him a Doctor of Philosophy in 1901. He was called to Michigan in 1904 as Assistant Professor of Mineralogy.

Among the assistant professors Theodore John Wramplemeier (Chemistry, 1881-1886) was a student at Strassburg and Zurich in 1883 and 1884. Both his parents were born in Germany and he in Cincinnati. DeWitt Bristol Brace, (Physics, 1885-86) a New Yorker by birth, was a Doctor of Philosophy of Berlin, of 1885, where he was taught for two years by Helmholtz and Kirchoff, owners of two names that stand out in the earlier years of investigation into electricity. Charles Mills Gayley (Latin and Rhetoric, 1880-1889) the brilliant young Irishman who wrote the University Song, "Yellow and Blue," did his post-graduate work in 1886-7 at Giessen and Halle. Frank Nelson Cole (Mathematics, 1887-1895) put in four years 1882-86 as a student at Leipsig and Gottingen. Carl William Belser (German, French, Hebrew, 1889-1893) of German parentage, made his studies in 1877-8-9 at the University of Leipsig.

Frank Casper Wagner (Engineering 1890-) was an Ann Arbor man, a scion of the Wagner and Miller families which were among the early German settlers George Herbert Mead (Philosophy, 1891-1894) was a native of Lunden, Schleswig-Holstein, and got his early education at Lunden and Husum, in his native country. Benjamin Parsons Bourland, (French, 1892-1901) was a student of the Latin College of Neuchatel, and the Royal Gymnasium of Wiesbaden before he entered Ann Arbor High School. Karl Eugene Guthe (Physics, 1893-1903) was a Hanoverian, educated at Marburg, Strassburg and Berlin, and a Doctor of Philosophy of Marburg. Herbert Spencer Jennings (Zoology, 1899-1901) was a Harvard man who as the holder of a fellowship spent 1896-7 as a student at the University of Jena. Henry Arthur Sanders, (Latin 1893-1902) was a Doctor of Philosophy of Munich in 1897. Dr. Thomas Benton Cooley (Hygiene 1898-1905) son of the famous Chief Justice of the State, spent 1900 and 1901 in Germany studying the diseases of children. William Henry Watt (Greek, Latin, Modern Languages 1895) preceded his work in the University with a year at Berlin and Bonn. Alfred Holmes White, (Chemistry 1897-) spent 1896 at the Federal Polytechnicum of Zurich, under Professor Lunge, a famous German technologist. Arthur Lyon Cross, "State o'Mainer," who harked back on his mother's side to the Dochendorffs who settled at Pemaquid, in Maine, in the early 1700's, and who was made Instructor in History in 1899, spent 1899 at Berlin and Freiburg. Johann Augustus Charles Hildner, who became an Instructor in German in 1891, took leave in 1897-8-9 to study at Leipsig, where he was made a Doctor of Philosophy. He returned to the University in 1899. Prof.

Hildner is another of the descendants of the original German settlement of Washtenaw County, in which the University is located.

George Augustus Hulett (Chemistry 1899-1905) of English-Scotch descent himself, was a Princeton man who went abroad from 1892 to 1898, spending much of the time at Leipsig, where he became a Doctor of Philosophy in 1898. Clarence Linton Meader (Latin, 1893-   ) himself of partial German ancestry, studied at Bonn in 1893 and went back to Munich in 1898.

A Group of German-Named Professors

At the celebration of the 75th anniversary of the founding of the University there were in its faculties, Professors, instructors and teachers bearing the names of Huff, Reighard, Winkler, Novy, Roth, Hubert, Loeffler, Gomberg, Koch, Lorch, Levi, Schlotterbeck, Kraus, Tuthe, Strauss, Effinger, Diekoff, Hildner, Boucke, Running, Wagner, Glaser, Eggern, Kraunzlein, Dieterle, Hegner, Emsweiler, Brumm, Kauffman, Breitenbach, Schmitz, Thurnau, Zimmerschied, Hauhardt, Huhl, Kemperman, Kristal, Behrens, Kollig, Fey, Gingreich, Grunwald, Georg, Klingmann, Wuist, Schlichting, Ernst, Lussky, Obetz, Bauer, Klatte, Reye, Baer, Hess, Schere and Wahr.

There were and are others on the faculties and teaching staffs of the University of Michigan and its various schools who have conveyed Germanic culture to the students of the institution either through the influences of their ancestry and training, or in the case of the American-born, through the results of their studies at German seats of educational culture. These who have been mentioned are the historic and the seasoned ones. Indeed, the contribution through American-born teachers who received their post-graduate instruction in the German universities is very striking, as their number must be to those who do not investigate and who have not gotten into the salutary habit of thinking twice. Nor was this beneficent influence confined to the greatest school of learning in the state, its University. It was exerted along other lines and through other channels, as we shall see.

Michigan's University has profited much by the collections of German-American scholars. In 1870 the Hon. Philo Parsons, of Detroit, purchased and presented the library of Prof. C. H. Rau, of Heidelberg, which was rich in works on political economy. In 1925 Dr. Walter Koelz, of the University, brought out of the McMillan Polar Expedition 1,500 bird skins and much new information regarding the habits of birds and their seasonal colorations. In 1883 Mr. J. H. Hagerman, of Colorado Springs, presented his collection of history and political science to the School. Many valuable gifts were made by Dr. Edward Dorsch, of Monroe. The Goethe library of the University is the gift of a group of German-American citizens of Michigan. The Morris, Walter and Hench working libraries, the latter a mine of information on the Germanic languages, were presented to the University by the families of these professors.

CHAPTER XVI

THE MICHIGAN AGRICULTURAL COLLEGE

A German-American Pioneer of Agricultural Education — Notable Group of Germanic Names in the Faculty.

In the organization and growth of the Michigan Agricultural College, German-American citizens and teachers have had an important and an honorable part. The control of this school, on its organization, was in the hands of the State Board of Agriculture. Abraham C. Prutzman, of Three Rivers, was a member of the first board, and he continued to serve until 1873. He had been elected a State Senator in 1872, and this rendered him ineligible for re-appointment to the Board of Agriculture. Mr. Prutzman was born of German parents in Columbus, Pennsylvania, and settled in Three Rivers in 1835. He was one of the pioneer merchants in his part of the state, and later was a leader in civic and cultural enterprises. He was deeply interested in the spread of scientific information regarding farming, and was an early and influential supporter of the movement to establish a State Agricultural College.

Peter H. Felker was an early Professor of History and Gardening. Louis Knapper served as Superintendent of Horticulture from 1880 until 1891. In 1882 Frederick Singelinger was assistant foreman of the farm and J. W. Swartz was engineer. Harrison B. Mohn was foreman of the wood shop in 1893, and the following year Frederick H. Hillman was appointed Instructor in Zoology. Ernest G. Lodeman was Instructor in German and French in 1888, and Louis Bregger and Max Wagener were assistant florists. In 1890 Frank J. Niswander was an Instructor in Zoology, William J. Meyers Instructor in Mathematics, and Walter D. Groesbeck Assistant Secretary. The following year Prof. Herman Klock Vedder entered the Engineering Department and remained with it for thirty-two years. Henry Thurtell became Assistant Professor of Mathematics in 1890, and three years later Charles L. Weil was made Professor of Mechanical Engineering. Ernest Wittlock was foreman of the farm in 1896. In 1896-7 Lieut. Harry H. Bandholz, later a Major-General, was Professor of Military Science and Tactics. In 1900-1901 Hugo Diemer, since become famous as one of the greatest industrial engineers of the country, was Assistant Professor of Mechanical Engineering.

In 1902 John Michel was Instructor in Dairying, and Arthur E. Kocher an Instructor in Agriculture.

Notable Accession of German Names

It was not until 1911 that a notable accession of Germanic names occurred in the roster of College instructors. In that year Wylie Brodbeck Wendt became Assistant Professor of Civil Engineering; Jesse Jeremiah Myers, Professor of Zoology; Gotthilf Fischer, Assistant Professor of German; Ernest Elmer Beighle, Instructor in Mathematics; Otto Rahn, Assistant Professor of Bacteriology; Louise Freyhofer, Instructor of Music; Walter Simon Bittner, Instructor in English and German; Frederick Whelphley Bentzen, Instructor in Chemistry; Stephen Vincent Klem, Instructor in Forestry; Carl Kiefer, Instructor in Mathematics; Leo Ransom Himmelberger, Instructor in Bacteriology; Martin George Feuerhak, Instructor in Mathematics; Andrew Peter Krentel, foreman of the pattern shop; Louise Rademacher, Assistant Instructor in Bacteriology; Karl Ernest Hopphau, Instructor in Mathematics; Joseph Carl Bock, Instructor in Chemistry; Edward Joseph Kunze, Assistant Professor in Mechanical Engineering; Carl Edward Newlander, Instructor in Dairy Husbandry; Lieut. Anton Caeser Cron, Professor of Military Science; Franz Herman Hendrick Von Suchtelin, Instructor in Bacteriology; Herman Henzel, Instructor in English and German; Ernest Roller, Instructor in Physics; George Henry Von Tungeln, Instructor in English; and Anton Scheel Rosing, Assistant Professor in Civil Engineering.

In 1913-14, Linda Louise Himmelein became Instructor in Domestic Art; Louise Rademacher, Assistant in Bacteriology; Walter L. Kulp, Instructor in Bacteriology; Francis Lee Schneider, Instructor in English, and Walter August Reinhert, Instructor in Mathematics.

In 1917-18, Herbert August Gehring became Assistant Professor of Mechanical Engineering; Mabel Louise Leffler, Instructor in Piano; Percy Barnet Wiltberger, Instructor in Entomology; James Blood Hasselman, Instructor in English; Henry Lantz Publow, Instructor in Chemistry; Cecile Van Steenberg, Assistant Professor of Domestic Art; Charles Theodore Bruner, Instructor in Mathematics; Robert Menzel Lautner, Instructor in Horticulture; Ethel Philips Van Wagener, Instructor in Domestic Science; Frank Lawrence Abel, Director of the Band and Glee Club; Emil Conrad Volz, Instructor in Horticulture; Friederika Margretha Heyl, Social Director; Jacob Austin Eicher, foreman of the foundry; Paul Gerhardt Andres, Assistant Professor of Mechanical Engineering; Arnold Scheele, Assistant Professor of Drawing and Design; Herman Carl Lange, Instructor in Drawing; Walter Gotlob Hildor, Instructor in the forge shop; Percy Barnet Wiltberger, Instructor in Entomology; Calvin Jennings Overmeyer, Instructor in Chemistry; Minerva Fouts, Instructor in the Household Arts; William Douglas Meltzler, Instructor of Dairy Manufacturing, and Florence Amelia Stoll, assistant in Domestic Art.

In 1921-22, Wilbur Herman Thies became Instructor in Physics; Louis Gustav Gentner, Instructor in Entomology; Gertrude Louenback, Instructor in Phyical Education; Marion Louise Grettenberger, assistant in Chemistry, and Otto Herman Freideman, Instructor in Bacteriology.

In 1923-24 Josephine Rena Fogle was made Assistant Professor of Home Economics; Royal Stewart Steiner, Assistant Professor of Economics; Sylvia Irene Borgman, Instructor in Home Economics; George Arnold Getman, Instructor in Farm Mechanics; Chester Ferdinand Kuhn, Instructor in English; Carl Curt Dethoff, assistant in Soils; Delbert Swartz, assistant in Botany; J. Conrad Kremer, assistant in the Vocational School; Winnifred Sarah Gettering, Associate Professor of Home Economics; Leory Stewart Folz, Assistant Professor of Electrical Engineering; Godfrey Leonard Alvin Ruehle, Assistant Professor of Bacteriology; Floyd Earl Fogle, Assistant in Agricultural Engineering; John Adendorf, Assistant Professor of Mechanical Engineering; Mary Etta Schellenberger, Instructor in Home Economics; Albert Carl Weimar, Associate Professor of Dairy Manufacturing; Josephine Howard Plattenberg, Instructor in Home Economics; and Herbert William Schmidt, Instructor in Chemistry.

CHAPTER XVII

THE MICHIGAN SCHOOL OF MINES

Dr. George Gottlob Moldhenke's Work—A Great Teacher of Chemistry who Served for Twenty Years.

The Michigan School of Mines was established in 1886. That year John D. Hoffman was Instructor in Mathematics and Drawing. He was rather pridefully described as having "graduated from German schools." In 1889 Dr. Richard George Gottlob Moldhenke was made Professor of Mechanical Engineering and Drawing. In 1890 Dr. H. F. Keller became Professor of Chemistry. He was a graduate of Pennsylvania and had taken his Doctor's degree at Strasburg.

Among the others of actual or apparent German ancestry who have taught at the School of Mines during its existence were Louis Martin Hardenburg, Emil Arthur Franke, Henry Max Goetsch and Gustave Fernekes, in Chemistry and Metallurgy; George Luther Christensen and John Philip Furbeck, in Mechanical Engineering; Carl J. Jauch, Herman Rumple, Carl Henry Knaebel, Ralph B. Wagner, Adolph Nicholas Wold, George P. Schubert, and Alfred Herman Menche, in Civil and Mining Engineering; George Frauheier Stammler, Roy Edward Margenau, Herman Roth Eberle and Nicholas Hubert Manderfield in Metallurgy; Homer A. Guck in English and Technical Writing; George Wass, in Pattern making; and Martin Gerhard Sateren, Charles Edmund Haigle, Robert Rex Seeker, and Albert Sokey in Mathematics.

Among the special lecturers have been William Henry Schacht, General Manager of the Copper Range Company; Albert Edward Peterman, of Calumet, and Albert Mendelsohn, Superintendent of the Baltic Mine.

A Great Teacher of Chemistry

One of the greatest teachers in this school, and, for that matter in the State's educational history, was George Augustus Koenig, born at Willstaedt, Baden, in 1834, and Professor of Chemistry at the Michigan College of Mines from 1892 until his death in 1913. During the first ten years of this period he was also Professor of Metallurgy. Dr. Koenig was a Mechanical Engineer of the Polytechnikum of Karlsruhe, a Master of Arts and Doctor of Philosophy of Heidelburg, a student of the University of Berlin, and a student of the School of Mines at Freiburg. He came to America in 1868, and began his teaching career in Chemistry, Mineralogy and Geology in the University of Pennsylvania in 1872, continuing for twenty years at that institution. During his twenty years at Michigan he rarely missed a class or a lecture and he gave up his work only two Sundays before he died. Besides his teaching, he accomplished much in the field of investigation. He was the first to discover diamonds in meteoric iron. He produced artificial crystals of copper arsenides, some of which have not yet been found in nature. He identified thirteen new species of minerals. He invented processes for the chlorination of gold and silver ores, and for the separation of vanadium from some of its ores, besides devising an assay furnace without a muffle. He was the author of "The Chemistry of Metals." Physically an enormous man, a hard task master for both himself and his students, he was one of the best beloved teachers in the history of the College of Mines; the friend of the students and a constant participant in their recreations.

CHAPTER XVIII

THE UNIVERSITY OF DETROIT

Four German-American Pioneer Teachers—A Group of Peripatetic Instructors—Men who Taught for Love of Teaching.

The University of Detroit had as its forerunner before its erection into a University an institution which was modestly called Detroit College. It was organized in 1877, and has since that time enrolled nearly 30,000 students, having latterly attained, as a University, an attendance approaching 3,000 students annually. Its graduates in Arts, Law, Engineering and Commerce and Finance exceed 3,000 in number. It was founded by the Roman Catholic Fathers of the Society of Jesus, more commonly known as the Jesuits.

Its beginnings were small. Bishop Caspar Henry Borgess, who was a native of Oldenburg, and who ruled the Roman Catholic diocese of Detroit from 1870 until 1888, recognized the need of collegiate training in the state's metropolis, there being neither public nor private educational supply of collegiate grade at the time. He, therefore, extended some necessary aid to the Jesuits, enabling them to make a modest educational foundation.

A faculty of five men composed the primary organization. They undertook their work upon the fees provided by eighty students, whose tuition was forty dollars per year each. Some even of this number were taught gratuitously. The income available in the first year was about $3,000, and it was many years before it grew to be as much as $10,000 The conduct of the school would have been impossible were not its teaching force recruited from a body of men who, without recompense, devoted their lives to higher education.

Four Pioneer German-American Teachers

The first President was the Right Reverend John Baptist Miege, former Bishop of Leavenworth, who after a long missionary career extending from the Red River of Arkansas to the farthest reaches of the Missouri, voluntarily laid off his mitre and went back to the work of a school-master. He was a man of varied and profound learning. His four associates in the first faculty in 1877 were German-Americans, two of them, Fathers Erley and Real, in holy orders, and two others, Joseph Francis Xavier Grimmelsman and Augustine M. Effinger, being on their way to the priesthood. Father Erley was of an old Virginia family of the name of Ehrlich, who were said to have been Lutherans, and his affiliation with the Jesuits is claimed to have caused a family estrangement. Father Grimmelsman was a Cincinnati man of immediate German parentage, was trained at Louvain, and in time became the Provincial Superior of his order in the Missouri province, and still later, President of Marquette University, in Milwaukee, which he built up into an important school. Father Grimmelsman was the first American who did the "grand act" in Rome, that being an offering on the part of the scholars of the various Catholic religious orders, to discuss all the questions in an extensive range of physical and metaphysical science, he representing the Jesuit order.

In the second year of their work they were reinforced by Professors Michael F. Speich and Joseph F. Weber. In 1880 additions to the faculty came in the persons of Professors Joseph H. Meuffels and George A. Hoeffer and Father Aloysius F. Bosche. Professor Meuffels was advanced to the priesthood and has been for twenty-five years past at St. John's college, in British Honduras. Rev. John Peter Frieden, a Luxembourger, came in 1882, and with him Fathers Henry

IN THE MAKING OF MICHIGAN 177

Moeller and Augustin K. Mayer. In 1884, Professor Bernard J. Otting, later President of St. Louis University, after a training in Spain, and Father Michael Eicher came into the faculty, as some of the others passed to duty in other colleges in the jurisdiction of the Missouri Province of the order. In 1886 Father Herman Meiners joined the faculty.

A Group of Peripatetic Teachers

The discipline of the Jesuit order is of a military character, and its application results in the transfer of its men from an original post of duty to a new one at intervals of from three to six years. In its educational work, as a consequence, its teaching members pass from one to another of the institutions under its direction. For this reason its scholastic, or unordained members who are in preparation for the priesthood, may be assigned to an educational institution, serve a period, then be recalled for further study and go back, from time to time, for new periods of duty at the various colleges, This explanation is given to account for the fact that the lifelong careers in education are rarely devoted to any single school by these men, though there are recurrent assignments to the same institution in many cases. One result is that the teaching members are given a broad, rather than a provincial view of life and education. Another is that the desire to acquire local reputations is withdrawn from the catalogue of their temptations.

In the ensuing list of professors and instructors it must be remembered that those who compose it were not the only teachers of the institution under observation, but were the German-American members of the faculties.

Among the men of German birth or extraction who have been Presidents of the University and its antecedent college was Father John P. Frieden, who was a Luxemburger, one of the great exponents of the scholastic philosophy, and a wonderful teacher of pure mathematics. After his tour of duty in Michigan, Father Frieden was sent to the Pacific coast to

Americanize the government of his Society, which had, in the Pacific-American states, remained under the direction of the Italian superiorship from the close of the Mexican war. Earlier he became the Provincial Superior of the Jesuits in the Missouri Province, and President of St. Louis University. The next German-American President at Detroit was Father Henry A. Schapman, a St. Louis man, whose excellences lay in the direction of philosophy and literature, and who continued in office from 1893 to 1897. From 1902 until 1906, the President was Father Louis Kellinger, Kentucky born man, with a strong side for English literature.

Teachers of German Lineage

From the time of the founders onward, among the professors of this school there have been, in the mathematical sciences, including astronomy, Fathers Herman Meiners, Charles J. Leib, George Worpenberg, John W. Kuhlman, Ferdinand Moeller, Joseph F. Rigge, John E. Knipscheer, Frederick A. Gosiger, Francis J. Gerst, Aloys F. Heitkamp, John B. Froebes, Otto J. Moorman, and Aloysius J. Bockhorst. In Chemistry and the physical sciences the teachers, some in holy orders and some not, were Professors Francis Berberich, Adolph J. Kuhlman, Vincent A. Fusz, Michael J. Gruenthamer, Frederick A. Gosiger, John B. Kremer, John B. Froebes, and Hugo F. Schloctemeyer. The teachers of philosophy in the history of the University include in their number Professors Martin M. Harts, Henry W. Otting, Francis A. Preuss and Francis Heierman. Professors who taught languages and literature had among them John A. Gonser, Bernard J. Otting, later President of St. Louis University; Augustine K. Meyer, John B. Kokenge, J. Rheinhardt Rosswinkel, Henry G. Huerman, John Otten, George Augustine Hoeffer, Albert Muntsch, Joseph H. Dickhaus, William M. Hoffend, Christopher J. Kohne, Charles Roemer, Otto Kuhnmuench, Anthony F. Geyser, Anthony A. Honeck, Joseph L. Kemper and Augustine J.

Ruffing. Several of these men were Professors of Germanic language and literature. Fathers Froebes and Kremer and Father Joseph Wilczewski, a Wisconsin man whose family was from German Poland, were the mathematical and scientific backbone of the School of Engineering when it was added to the University organization.

Many laymen of German birth or extraction have taught in or directed the various schools and departments. John P. Weissenhagen, Detroit born man, who became a Judge of the Court of First Instance in the Philippines, was the first director of the Foreign Trade School, Prof. Samuel J. Hoexter, a Stevens Institute man of immediate German ancestry, being his successor.

Incidentally, in this school's announcements there recently appeared an offer to instruct whomsoever applied in the Swahili language, the key to the East African dialects, the instructor offered therefor being the Reverend Ferdinand Kreutkampf, a missionary who had learned the tongue in its habitat.

Many others than those named, both clergy and laymen, of German birth or descent, have been members of the Arts, Engineering, Law and Economic faculties of this University. The list given takes in the pioneers. As most of this labor is voluntarily performed, the lay professors being volunteers and the clerical professors subject to change of location, the periods of service are shorter than in the cases of schools whose teaching staffs are wholly drawn from people who make their art a life-time profession. The proportion of German-Americans among these generous teachers maintains itself in spite of the periodicity of change.

CHAPTER XIX

THE DENOMINATIONAL COLLEGES

The Career of Dr. August Frederick Bruske — Many German-American Teachers in These Schools.

One of the most helpful contributors to educational foundations in Michigan was the Rev. August Frederick Bruske, for twenty-one years President of Alma College. He was born in Prussia in 1846. His family emigrated to the United States when he was nine years old. They bought a farm in Nankin township, of Wayne county. He enlisted in the civil war as soon as he was of acceptable age and served with the Twenty-Fourth Michigan Infantry until the end of the war. Educated at Adrian College and Drew Seminary, he entered the ministry as pastor of the First Congregational Church at Charlotte. His next pastorate was at Saginaw and lasted fourteen years. This pastorate he left to assume the Presidency of Alma College, the foundation of which was based upon a resolution he himself proposed before the synod of the Presbyterian Church of Michigan. He was President of the College for twenty-one years. He took it as a small educational institution with a hundred students and an endowment fund of $150,000, and left it as one of the state's leading sects of culture, endowed to the extent of $500,000, and with a student body of six hundred.

During his educational work he took the cause of the college before every Presbyterian church in Michigan, soliciting endowments and students. As a commencement day speaker he addressed fully one hundred graduating classes at various times. He died at Ypsilanti in 1920.

So far as the authorities of Albion College can discover that institution has had but three professors or instructors of German birth, descent or University education. These were Doctor Frederick Lutz, Miss Selma S. Koenig and Prof. John Zedler. The last mentioned was born in Essen in 1864 and got his A. B., from Albion in 1903 and his A. M., from Michigan in 1908. From 1903 to 1919 he was on the faculty of Albion, going from there to Clark University at Atlanta, and thence to Tennessee.

Hope College at Holland, as befitted its foundation and its religious connections, has been largely served by men and women of Dutch extraction and Reformed Church connections. But its faculties show that an occasional teacher of German birth or training has served its students during its history. The six who comprise the list were Professor S. O. Mast, A. B., Ph. D.; Peter J. Schlosser, Ph. M.; Edward Elias, A. M., Ph. D; Ludwig H. Eyme, Bruno Meincke, A. M. Ph. D; and Freda Heitland, A. M. Miss Heitland is the only one of these in service at the date of this writing.

Adrian College has had eleven persons who have served in its faculty who were German born, of German descent or Germanic education. Five of these were in the Department of Music, four in the Department of Language and one in Philosophy. Their names are Arthur S. Williams, W. Conrad Koenig, Bernard H. Rupp, J. Overholser, Wilbert Ferguson, Lily Shiler Bowerfind, August Reichart, Thomas F. Rinehart, Philip Steinhauser, D. S. Stephens and Dr. Koss, who is referred to in another portion of this book.

Joseph Wm. Mauch, was elected President of Hillsdale College in 1902. Frank B. Myer, A. B., was Professor of Latin and Literature there the same year. George H. Reiker was its professor of Greek and Latin from 1876 until 1882.

CHAPTER XX

CONTRIBUTIONS TO PRIMARY AND SECONDARY EDUCATION

English Taught from the Start—Teaching before School-Houses— The Lutheran and Catholic Teachers—The Christian Brothers — Modest Pioneer Pedagogues—Scholars of High Standing — Communities of Teaching Sisters.

Primary education in Michigan was a plant of slow growth in the early days. The school law, in the beginning, provided that every town which had so many inhabitants should maintain a primary school for so many months in the year. But many towns did not have so many inhabitants, and many others did not maintain schools, and it was a hard matter to get teachers. As a consequence, the beginnings of school history, especially in the earlier years, are to be found in the operation of private schools rather than of public ones. These schools were, to a large extent, founded by organizations of religious people, for the double reason that such was about the only way that schooling could be provided for the oncoming generation, and that the system of private instruction carried with it the opportunity to instruct the younger ones in the religious beliefs of their parents.

There was still another reason which was economic. The scarcity of teachers and the cost of their services, when they were obtainable, was a burden which was alleviated when the work could be done by the church pastor.

So it came about, in some sections of the state, particularly those in which the German Lutherans and Roman Catholics were settled, that the private and church school became the earliest purveyor of elementary learning. As a matter of fact, there is scarcely a record of a German Lutheran colony establishing itself without starting a school as soon as it provided itself with a pastor.

English Taught from the Beginning

These schools had one characteristic that is striking at this late day. From the outset these new citizens sensed the fact that English was to be the common language of the nation, and that, as soon as possible, it must be taught in these schools, whatever the immediate necessity might be of giving instruction in the German language. Thus Pastor Craemer, who was the pioneer of Frankenmuth in 1845, had a school in operation in 1846, in which he himself taught English, having learned it in England before he began his ministerial studies in Bavaria. That this teaching was not amateur may be drawn from the fact that Pastor Cremer was a man of sufficiently high training to be called, four years later, to a College Professorship.

In Saginaw Ottmar Cloeter established a private school under religious auspices as early as 1849, and taught it for eight years. His successor, John A. Huegli, was a man of good general culture, who continued the teaching as well as the pastoral office. In Hermansau John Christ Winterstein conducted a school as early as 1865, later going to North Saginaw and still later to Amelith, in Bay county. Christian Volz was a pastor who founded a parochial school in West Saginaw as early as 1854. John Henry Philip Graebner arrived in America in 1847. The following year he had a school organized at Frankentrost, for the children of twenty-two families. Ferdinand Sievers, who was in college in Hanover in 1846, had "my few school children" under instruction in Frankenlust two years later, before he built his log church. Pastor Deindorfer taught a class in Frankenhilf in 1851, in the home of a family named Ammon, before he had either church or school house. Pastor Julius Erberdt was one of the earliest school masters of Saginaw, wielding the birch, if that was then the magisterial emblem, in 1851. Pastor Sievers spared two days a week from Frankenlust in 1851 to teach classes in Bay City. In 1852 Pastor Eberhardt was doing most of the teaching that was being done in Lower Saginaw, now Bay City. In 1858 Pastor Bruckner taught school at Applegate.

Teaching Before School Houses

In 1846 Johann Adam Schuetz and his wife donated an acre in Erin Town, of Macomb County, for a church and school, and John Frederick Winkler began teaching at once in private homes. Pastor Graebner built a school there in 1858. H. G. Neuchterlein was the first teacher. He got $150 a year. From 1855 to 1856 Pastor Rauschert conducted a primary school alone at Waldenburg, in Macomb county, and his successor, Pastor Freidrich Bocling, was teacher as well as preacher for thirty-three years thereafter. At Richmond, in St. Clair county, Pastor F. W. M. Arendt, who had come from Canada, was teacher in 1872.

In the "Thumb" section of the state teaching began in 1845 with an Indian school at Sebewaing, which Pastors John J. Auch and Simon Dumser taught. In 1853 a school-house site was donated by the German settlers, whose families then were Bock, Schilling, Mullerweiss, Roehle, Aub, Gruehnbeck and Beck. In 1853 Frederick Nuffer began teaching a second school at New Salem, near Sebewaing. There was teaching at Ruth and Port Hope in Huron county from 1868 onward. William Schwartz, fresh from college, established schools in Huron and Sanilac counties, from 1872. Pastor J. N. Hahn started a school in 1876 at Brookfield, in Huron county, in a log shack. Bingham Township, also in Huron, had school teaching in 1886. In 1858 Pastor F. Eppling established a school in Hadley township, of Lapeer county.

In 1854 the teacher of Trinity congregation in Detroit was

Pastor Herman Fick. a German university man who found time to write poetry and compose scientific works, which found their way back into the old country. Earlier than that, in 1845, Pastor Hattstaet had a school in operation at Monroe. John Solomon Simon was his teacher. The same year he organized a school at Raisinville for the children of settlers John Roden, George Finzel, Christian Seib, John George Schoenemsgruber and the Herbsts and Statlers. In 1847 he started a school at Adrian.

These men were followed in the scholastic foundations by others for whom they had smoothed the path. Of the abilities of the pioneer teachers this much must be said, that they were all the products of the Gymnasium and Realschule in their home country, these having the qualifications of the American high school. Some of them were university men. All had the training of the theological seminary, which usually added the humanities to the apologetics. Their successors have been, as a rule, graduates of the pedagogical schools and seminaries of their church, the standards of which are on an even plane with those of their contemporaries. These pioneer teachers practically worked for their keep, the emoluments from their ministerial and pedagogical duties being but a hard living for themselves and their families. Their place in the educational foundations of Michigan is an honorable one, carved in sacrifice and industry.

The early recognition of the necessity of a training in English by Pastor Graebner at Frankenmuth was followed by similar acceptance of conditions in the rest of these foundations. Indeed there is a tradition, from the early days, of an itinerant Irish schoolmaster who was peddled around in the Saginaw Valley, spending a day at one school, being delivered to another overnight, and repeating his round each week, his day a week at each school being spent upon instruction in English.

He is said to have been a curious example, with a pronounced Irish "brogue," teaching German children, "English as she is spoke."

The Lutheran and Catholic Teachers

At the time of this writing practically all of these schools are seats of instruction in the vernacular, the ancestral tongue being taught for cultural purposes and for the imparting of religious doctrine.

The Lutheran Germans of the last mid-century and the twenty-five years succeeding it were not alone in making educational provision for their young people. Like them the Roman Catholics were also imbued with the idea of combining religious instruction with that concerning lay subjects and their parish schools were early established for the double purpose of providing secular education and the giving of religious training supplementing the pulpit and parochial work of their pastors. The economic burden was quite as heavy on them as upon the Lutherans. They developed groups of teaching men and women, devoted by religious vows to the duty of education, without expectation of material reward for their efforts. The efforts of these teachers, most of whom were well trained and many of whom were excellent, resulted in a valuable contribution to the educational fabric of the state, supplementing the state system while it was in the making, and continuing through extension and betterment, to be an important private occupation of the teaching field in Michigan. These brotherhoods and sisterhoods had a considerable number of German-born and German-American men and women among those who were attracted to their membership.

The German Christian Brothers

One of the earliest groups of trained teachers in Detroit were the Brothers of the Christian Schools, a Roman Catholic organization of pious men, not in holy orders, who take vows to devote their lives to teaching, and who are celibates, living in communities. Though this organization is historically of French origin, it has drawn to its membership men of all nationalities, among them many of German birth and ancestry. The educational standards may be judged from the suggestion that two of its members, Brother Azarias and Brother Potamian, stand in the highest ranks of American pedagogues.

These religious teachers, on entering upon their lives of devotion to education, give up their family names and are known outside their legal relations as citizens, by assumed names, thereby practically indicating their renunciation of earthly ties and vanities. They came to Detroit in the early 50's of the nineteenth century, at a time when the state of education, both public and private, was very low, and attached themselves first to the French church of St. Anne, later to the churches of St. Peter and Paul and Holy Trinity, and later still, to the German parish of St. Mary. In time they founded St. Joseph's Commercial College, an educational institution of high standing.

In the Detroit community a great number of these teachers from the very beginning, were men of German birth. The family names of two of the earliest are lost. These were Brother Adelbert, who was from Heissdorf, in Luxembourg, and who went from Detroit to continue his work in India, and Brother Amian, from Niederziessen, in Prussia, who left Detroit to take up his work in the New York Protectory for boys, where he died.

The Modest Pioneer Pedagogues

Others of these early teachers were Brother Phineas, whose family name was Franz Kieffer, and who was from Freimersheim, in Darmstadt; Brother Hugh, who was Valentine Russ, from Baden; Brother Luke, who was Matthias Becker, from Eyll, in Germany; another Brother Luke, who was Nicholas Lauer, from Prussia, and who was the author of a widely published hymnal; Brother Finan, who was Valentine Goos, from Baden, and who came to Detroit in 1863; Brother Cartagh, another Baden man, who was Adam Matthaus, and who came in 1864 and taught for forty-two years thereafter in various schools; Brother Ammian, who was Anton Joseph Schmidt, and who began teaching in Detroit in 1866; Brother Pirmian, who was Frederich Muller, from Hanover, and Brother Amien, who was Robert M. Arends, from Radersvorwald, Prussia, the latter two coming in 1868. In 1870 there came Brother Firmilian, who was Joseph Giezen, and Brother Frogensus, who was Paul Bauck, both from Baden, in Switzerland; and Brother Herbert Virgil, who was Lucas Lembeck, from Prussia. In 1871 the additions to the community were Brother Almerian, who was Jacob Witmer, from Kilwangen, Switzerland; Brother Andrew, who was Henry Pelz, from Buchkelte, in Hanover, and Brother Imbert Victorinus, who was Joseph Vogt, from Aulendorf, in Westphalia. In 1872 Brother Leodicius, who was John Hermeling, from Westphalia, came to the Detroit community. The year 1873 brought another Brother Amian, who was Henry Joseph Kimpel, a Darmstadt man. Brother Junian Peter, from Ockenheim, Germany, and who was Philip Metzler, came in 1874, and having taught for some years and been transferred to another foundation of his brotherhood came back to Detroit for a second period. The same was true of Brother Felan, who was Sebastian Kemper, a Wurtemburg man, who taught intermittently in Detroit from 1875 to 1910. Emilian Camber, a German Swiss, who was called Brother Anselm, came in 1875, and Brother Alfred, who was Leopold Schwab, from Baden in 1875. Brother Hermenegild, who was Casimir Wasserman, from St. Gothard, came in 1880, and Brother Elisian, who was Lorenz Witmer, in the same year. Brother Baldomer Geoffrey, who was Bernard Muller, from Wurtemburg, came in 1875, and was for a very long time a teacher in Detroit. Brother Amelian, who was Joseph Ferners, a Bavarian, came in 1884, and Brother Concordius, who was a Westphalian whose lay name was Albert Steffens, came in the following year.

Later accessions to this teaching faculty included John Diefenbach, from Nassau, Brother Damian; Fridolin Mather, from Bavaria, Brother Amos Michael; Henry Hollenberg, from Hanover, Brother Boniface; Philip Parr, from Bavaria, Brother Wilban; August Stahl, from Prussia, Brother Azedan; Paul Hoffman, from West Prussia, Brother Conrad Ernest; and Wilhelm Vogt, from Westphalia, Brother Besas Adolph.

Scholars of High Standing

Among these men were some scholars of the highest standing. Brother Junian Peter, for instance, was a master of several languages and was an earnest botanist, giving his spare time to the study of the native flora of Michigan, to some of which he called the attention of local chemists as foundations for their materia medica. Brother Elisian, who taught in Detroit for thirty-six years, was an expert as an elementary educationalist, and had a peculiar "way" with him for charming youngsters to whom curricula and disciplines were odious. Brother Amulivin, back in 1894, sensed the coming industrial importnace of Detroit, and founded the St. Joseph Commercial College as a school in which his young men should receive advanced education for commercial life. He shaped the course of the school in its formative period and graduated its first class.

It must not be inferred that this community of educators, who still conduct their institution, was exclusively German in membership. On the contrary, other members thereof were of French, Irish, Danish and pioneer American extractions. As a commentary on the usefulness of humble lives, the community numbered in its membership three modest German brethen, Brother Eucarius, who was Peter Brunold, from the Austrian Tyrol; Brother Jonas, who was Philip Miller, from Thalheim, in Prussia; and Brother Gelinas Clovis, who was Matthias Schneider, from Wurtemburg. These men, not so highly educated, devoted their entire lives to house service and cooking so that their more learned brethren might impart instruction to youth.

The Communities of Teaching Nuns

A very important influence in the private educational history of Michigan was exerted in the early days by the Roman Catholic sisterhoods of religious women who devoted their lives to teaching. The earliest of these organizations, of which there have come to be several, living according to different religious rules and under a variety of authorizations, was the Sisters of the Immaculate Heart of Mary, whose foundation at Monroe dates back to 1845, and whose membership has from that time included many women of German birth and extraction. It is noteworthy that among the pioneers of this foundation were Miss Teresa Maxis and Miss Anna Schaaf, daughters of Maryland German families, who were induced to enter upon their life-work by the Rev. Egidius Smulders, a Redemptorist missionary, of German birth, who spent many, including the latter years of his life, in service in Michigan.

An early contemporary religious society of the same character was the Sisters of Notre Dame, who founded and still serve a large number of German Catholic parochial schools in the state. This foundation originated at Milwaukee and spread into Michigan, the guiding spirit from 1847 onward having been the Reverend Mother Carolina, who, born in Paris in 1824, was the daughter of Johann George Friess, a Bavarian officer in the Napoleonic wars. Mother Carolina gave much personal direction to these foundations in Michigan. When she came to Detroit in 1852 to found St. Mary's School, she had only money enough to pay her railroad fare, and on her arrival had not a penny to pay for a coach or omnibus ride to the site of her new foundation. She relates in her memoir that on the way from the railroad station she met Bishop Lefevre, who greeted her kindly, and said, "Sister, you should have taken a coach to your destination. May God bless you." Commenting on the incident she humorously stated that, at the time, she would willingly have exchanged the Episcopal blessing for twenty-five cents with which to have taken the good Bishop's advice.

CHAPTER XXI

THE GERMAN-AMERICAN SEMINARY

Intended for a National Educational Institution—The Work of Florenz Krecke—Edward Feldner's Career.

Various other private and community teaching enterprises mark the primary educational history of Michigan, many of them very useful and many conducted, in whole or in part, by German-Americans. One of the most ambitious of these was the German-American Seminary, which was founded in Detroit in 1864 and was exclusively Germanic. It was originally planned to be a national institution, but can hardly be said to have attained that degree of importance, but it was a very good school, in spite of that.

A considerable number of German-Americans who had achieved national importance and standing were members of the Republican National Convention of 1864 which nominated Mr. Lincoln for his second term of the Presidency.

These men were highly informed by the spirit of patriotism and conceived the idea of a national educational institution whose purpose should be the training of a group of teachers, of German antecedents or birth, specially educated in the history and motives of the American system of government, and who would inculcate this knowledge into the minds of the youthful German-Americans in the United States. These men were mostly those who had participated in the Revolution of 1848, then fresh in their memories, and were devotees of the democratic idea of government, and opponents of the monarchical idea, some of them to the limit of fanaticism. Their idea of a national institution took root, and in casting about for a location for their institute they selected Detroit.

Florenz Krecke

There was already in that city a foundation, the German-American Seminary, under the direction of a profound scholar, Florenz Krecke. He was then a man in middle life, who had been teaching in the United States for more than ten years. Prof. Krecke was a native of Leina, in Lippe-Detmold, where he was born in 1820. His father was a minister of the Lutheran church, and Florenz Krecke graduated from the University of Jena, in theology. About the time of his graduation his father died and his pastorate was offered to his son. This the latter declined, unless he were permitted to omit, in his preaching, the interpretation of certain doctrines of the church to which he could not give his intellectual adherence. This being out of the question, he became a teacher in his native land, continuing in the profession until he came to America in 1854. He settled in Brooklyn, where for two years he was a private tutor in Greek and Latin. In 1856 he was called to the German-American Seminary, of Detroit. He accepted the call, came to Detroit and there married Amelia Marxhausen, sister of the leading Detroit German journalist of the period, and settled down to a strenuous life of teaching.

Although the idea of a national pedagogical seminary was promoted, it never matured. The state made a grant of 25,000 acres of the "swamp land" of the period, which usually turned out to be pine forests, to the purposes of the institution, but it was never selected and the grant lapsed. In these days it would be intrepreted that there was no legislative authority to make a public donation to a private institution, but this question was never raised.

The German-American Seminary therefore remained a

local, rather than a national school of learning, largely dominated by Prof. Krecke, who continued to teach until the middle '70's when he retired. He had several good men of the teaching profession associated with him. Between them all they taught many young German-Americans of the school's period. John Henry Carstens, afterwards a nationally famous surgeon; Otto Kirchner, later an eminent lawyer, and Carl Eugene Schmidt, a leading manufacturer of leather, were among these. The sons of William E. Quinby, the New England born editor of the Detroit Free Press, were among their pupils.

Prof. Krecke was a really great Latin, Greek, English and German scholar, his genius being literary rather than mathematical and scientific. In later days he has been credited with being ultra-materialistic in his philosophic and theological views, but this does not seem to be borne out by the testimony of his family. They describe him as having had a strict and formal moral code, based upon responsibility to a Deity; but coupled with a belief that, in the face of the conflicting views about religious interpretations, the young should not have the peculiar doctrinal views of parents enforced upon them, but should rather be allowed to select their own connections after arriving at maturity.

Prof. Krecke, after his retirement from the profession of teaching, served as a Police Justice of Detroit, in the place of Justice Boynton, who had become a newspaper editor. He died at Detroit in 1895.

Edward Feldner

With Florenz Krecke, there was associated another teacher of quality, Edward Feldner, Saxon born in 1817 and trained in the Friedrichstadt Seminar in Dresden. He began life as a teacher in a young ladies' school, soon became prominent in the liberal movement and was sent to the Landtag in 1848. He was in the revolutionary movement, its failure sending him as an exile from his country, first to Switzerland and finally to New York, where he arrived in 1849. The intervening years, until 1863, were spent in educational work in the Metropolis and in Hoboken and Bloomfield, N. J. In 1863 he became connected with the German American Seminary, where his work brought him into such prominence that in 1870 he was chosen President of the National German-American Teachers' Association. Prof. Feldner's excellences were along linguistic lines. He wrote a "Little German Grammar" in 1855, which was the first text-book of the kind published in the United States and had a most extended use in the German-American schools. He died in Detroit in 1874.

There were earlier teachers of historic private schools other than religious in the pioneer life of the state, and among them a share of German-Americans. In 1826 Peter F. Brakeman taught school in Algonac. His grandparents were from Hesse-Darmstadt. In 1834 the Rt. Rev. Frederick Rese, Bishop of Detroit, who was a Hanoverian by birth, published stirring letters in the Detroit Journal and Advertiser, in favor of free schools, with a statement of his own aspirations toward contribution to their foundation. Conrad Krapf, a Hessian, who joined the Ann Arbor colony, in 1836, knew both French and Latin, and taught both to some of his neighbors' children. A little later Andreas Stulle was principal, and John Finke and Alois Wirth, the teachers of the higher classes in a private school conducted by the German Catholics in Detroit, they being lay teachers.

196   THE GERMANIC INFLUENCE

CHAPTER XXII

THE CONTRIBUTIONS TO SCIENCE

Indian Etymology and Grammar—The Compiler of the Geological Survey—The Work of Raphael Pumpelly—The Developer of the Copper Mines—The Work of General Weitzel—A Coterie of Geniuses—The Father of Reforestration—The Founder of Detroit Observatory—A Great Naval Astronomer—Colonel Shoemaker's Collection of Maps—A German Map-Maker of 1720—Charles Frederick Robert Wappenhans.

The contributions to culture and to practically applied science that have been made in Michigan by persons of all breeds and races have been both extensive and remarkable, and their results constitute the common heritage of all the people. It is quite impossible to overlook the field of contributors without acknowledgement of the number of them who were of German birth or extraction, or who brought to their work direct German training and culture. Their various fields of activity cover a great area of effort. The results of their activities have added much to the culture, wealth, prosperity and comfort of the citizens.

One of the earliest of these was the Roman Catholic Bishop, Frederick Baraga, who is elsewhere referred to in these pages, a devoted missionary to the Indians and a director of missionary and ecclesiastical activities in the Northern Peninsula of the state. Frederick Baraga was a native of Dobernick, Unterkrain, Austria, born in 1797, and on his father's side was probably of Slavic ancestry. He studied law in Vienna. He had a right to the paternal domain of

IN THE MAKING OF MICHIGAN 197

Treffen in Unterkrain, but renounced it to study theology, that he might go to the Indian missions in America. His character was marked mostly by the influence of his mother, who was of German blood, and who was a deeply religious and cultured woman. She was a relative of the German*poet, Auersperg, whose pseudonym was "Anastasius Grau."

His education in Vienna completed, he was ordained to the priesthood, and early formed the idea of carrying Christianity and civilization to the Indians. He came to America in 1830, and put himself under the authority of the Roman Catholic Bishop of Cincinnati. In that city he met a young Ottawa Indian student, learned his tongue, and plunged into the practically unknown territory of the northwestern part of the Lower Peninsula of Michigan, and later into that of the south shore of Lake Superior. Here he came into contact with Indians of the Ottawa, Potowattamie and Ojibway, or Chippewa tribes. The French had already reduced the language of the Algonquins to written words and had made text-books and catechisms in their language, but these were unavailable for Bishop Baraga among his Indians, who did not know the Algonquin tongue, and who, moreover, despised it as the speech of a foreign clan and of their periodical enemies.

Indian Etymology and Grammar

Bishop Baraga found it necessary to collate and classify their words; to reduce them to writing, using the Roman characters in their fixation into print; to analyze the etymology which governed their use and to determine their conjugations and declensions, and eventually to put them into scientific form in lexicons and treatises on their grammar. He taught the Indians to read and write their own tongues; to record numbers, under the Arabic system, and to count, both in the decimal and duodecimal methods, so that they became cognizant of the relative values both of American and British monies. He wrote a grammar of the Chippewa tongue and a reader in Ottawa; compiled a dictionary of the Chippewa language, and wrote his own text-books and catechisms in Chippewa.

He wrote a treatise on "The History of the Characteristics and Manners of the North American Indians," in the German language. When, in 1836, he went back to Europe to solicit help for his missions, he preached, while in Paris, to the Germans residing in the French capital.

Among those skilled in its difficulties very much credit has been given Bishop Baraga for this monumental work, by such ethnologists as Schoolcraft, Mooney and Hemans, and the man who performed it and his work thereupon have been compared to Sequoiah and his fixation of the language of the Cherokees. Without detracting from the glory of the learned Cherokee, it is worthy of noting, by way of comparison, that the work of Sequoiah was done with his own ancestral language, while that of Bishop Baraga had to do with strange tongues for which he had none of the roots or bases; and that Sequoiah did his work in comparative comfort, while the research and analysis of Father Baraga had to be carried on in the forest, the tepee or the rudest of log cabins. Bishop Baraga's contribution to the science of etymology alone entitles him to a place among scholars.

The Compiler of the Geological Survey

Carl Ludwig Rominger was another man of German blood to whom Michigan owes much in another field of human effort. He came into the state in 1860, when he was forty years of age. He was a Wurtemburger, born on Brenz River, in 1820, a Doctor of Medicine of Tubingen in 1842. Before his graduation he was a prize winner for an essay on the circulation of sap in plants and for a map of his neighborhood of Tubingen. From 1845-48 he had an annual grant of 400 gulden for geological study in Germany, the Tyrol, Switzerland, North France and Belgium. When the '48 movement was agitating the students and the people, Dr. Rominger was mildly sympathetic, and, honest fellow that he was, he told on himself to the Minister of the Interior, his patron. The latter bade him continue his stipend for a year, and then go to America and stay there. He got to America in 1849, had little money and less English, geologized the valley of the Hudson and Genesee, was attracted to the neighborhood of Cincinnati by his love of paleontology, settled for a while in Chillicothe, Ohio, and in 1860 landed in Ann Arbor. There he developed a modest medical practice among the German families. Some of his fellow patriots who had settled around Saginaw helped him eke out a living from his profession by periodical visits to their locality. Meantime, he was a geological expert.

Prof. Alexander Winchell employed him in the Geological Survey of Michigan in 1869. He was associated with Raphael Pumpelly and Thomas W. Brooks, the former in charge of the Lake Superior iron country survey, the latter on the survey of the copper deposits. Winchell resigned in 1871 and the German doctor-geologist was given full charge of the Survey. Brooks and Pumpelly continued to work under Dr. Rominger, and when they had finished their task, he kept on with his, completing the Geological Survey of Michigan. Under his direction the iron and copper ranges of Northern Michigan were completely explored and mapped, so far as they were known in that early day, which was pretty far. In 1884 he retired to Ann Arbor, where he kept up his scientific work until his death, in 1907, his later years being devoted to private explorations in the lead and zinc regions of the southwest until his eyesight gave out.

Dr. Alfred C. Lane, who was later his successor as State Geologist, summed up the character of the man when he said: "All those who worked over his reports can testify to the conscientious character of his descriptions. Go where he went and you will see what he described."

Of the practical results of Dr. Rominger's work it may be said that no careful investments in Northern Peninsula lands of potential iron-carrying values are made even today, without reference, on the part of the investigating engineers, to the monumental work which he carried out for Michigan. And this is true, despite the fact that Dr. Rominger, a most exact geologist, really had little love for this branch of science, but was rather a devotee of paleontology and its revelations of early forms of life on the globe.

The Work of Raphael Pumpelly

Associated with Dr. Rominger in the work of the Geological Survey of Michigan was another who helped carry the Germanic influence into the making of Michigan. Raphael Pumpelly was born at Oswego, New York, in 1837, a descendant of one of those earlier German settlers of the Mohawk Valley who have been referred to herein. His father was a soldier in the French and Indian wars, from the Siege of Lewisburg to the Heights of Abraham, and thence through the American Revolution. He was educated at the Royal Mining Academy of Freiburg, Baden, studying under Professors Cotta, Fritsche, Goetschmann, Scherer and Winkler, in that day the recognized authorities on geology and the recovery of mineralized ores. He came to Michigan in the late '60's of the nineteenth century as the representative of the Portage Canal Company, which had been granted 400,000 acres to construct a canal across the Keweenaw peninsula. That he had good standing in his profession is evidenced by the fact that at that early date he got a salary of $12,000 a year. He studied the iron ranges with Major T. B. Brooks, whose name is linked with that of Pumpelly in the work of the Geological Survey, and in 1870-71 he made an exploration of the Gogebic iron range, the results of which appear in the reports of the Survey. Mr. Pumpelly's later career as a mining engineer brought him into practically every part of the world, his experiences and adventures in these travels forming the subject matter of two volumes of reminiscences which he published in his old age.

Louis John Rudolph Agassiz, the eminent naturalist, was of German blood, born at Neufchatel, in Switzerland, and educated as a naturalist and geologist at Zurich, in his native land, and at Heidelberg and Munich. In 1847 he came to America, becoming a Professor of Zoology at Harvard. With him came his son Alexander, to whom he himself taught geology. The son became a graduate of Harvard, and devoted himself to a variety of scientific pursuits until 1866, when he began to confine his activities to geological observation and study. In that year he began his researches of the Calumet and Hecla mining operations, eventually being made president of the company which combined the properties under a single control. To Alexander Agassiz' scientific attainments are to be credited the development of the copper mining industry in Michigan, and, in particular, the turning of the Calumet and Hecla properties from an unpromising prospect into one of the greatest copper mining operations of history.

The Developer of the Copper Mines

His work was not solely commercial. He humanized the lives of the miners in what was for long a rather desolate region, providing them creature comforts for themselves and educational advantages for their families, that would have been quite without their reach under other conditions. He was wonderfully daring as a mining operator. His son, bearing part of the name of his distinguished grandfather, Rudolph Agassiz, succeeded Alexander Agassiz as the executive head of the Calumet & Hecla Company upon the death of the latter.

These were the greatest of the developers of the mineralized country in Northern Michigan. Many others were contemporaneous with them and succeeded them, both of their own racial strain and of other breeds, but to Rominger, Pumpelly and Agassiz belongs the greatest share of the credit for the earlier and later determinations made upon this prolific source of the wealth of the state.

The opening up of the iron and copper ranges of Northern Michigan began the development of the extensive inland marine commerce of the Great Lakes. That commerce had a barrier presented to its economical and convenient conduct by the Falls in St. Mary's River, connecting Lake Superior with Lake Huron. The American Fur Company at an early date made an essay at a canal and lock to replace the dangers, labors and expense of portages around the Falls, providing sufficient capacity for the passages of batteaux and small vessels. This was later replaced by a lock built by a private company to which a land grant was given for its enterprise in undertaking the work, the company, in due season, turning the canal over to the state for control and upkeep, minus the land grant, which later on formed the basis for some very profitable iron and copper operations.

The demands of commerce, incident to the necessity of cheapening the transport of down-bound iron and copper ores and the silver ores, which were later discovered in the general mineralized district, led to the undertaking of control and development by the general government. Forthwith plans were made for a comprehensive scheme of betterment of the water-ways between Lakes Michigan and Huron.

The Work of General Weitzel

The basis of that work was already in progress in the way of a general survey of the Great Lakes and their connecting waters, inaugurated as a large project shortly before the beginning of the American civil war, suspended during its progress and resumed after its close.

Godfrey Weitzel was the son of an early Ohio family of German origin which had settled in Cincinnati. His father had come out from Prussia. The younger Weitzel was born in 1835, and brought to America in his babyhood. He graduated from West Point in 1855, with high honors, which determined, in the policy of the army, his assignment to the Engineer Corps, in which he became a First Lieutenant in 1860. He was on the staffs of Generals Butler and Banks, in the civil war. In 1865 he was in charge of all the troops north of the Potomac in the final operations against General Lee at Richmond. At the end of the civil war he was brevetted a Major General. In 1866 he was returned to the regular service in the peace-time army as a Major of Engineers. He was assigned to the charge of the improvement of rivers and harbors in the Great Lakes district and the completion of the Great Lakes survey.

This survey had been going on since 1847. It was initiated by Col. Albert, Chief of the Engineers, himself of German extraction; and it earliest work was done under the direction of Lieut. S. P. Heintzleman, a West Pointer, afterwards a famous civil war general. Prior to its initiation and during much of its early progress, the data concerning depths of water, obstructions to navigation and similiar matters essential to safe sailing was very largely in the heads of the pilots and shipmasters, who conducted their craft through the lakes and their connecting waters.

A Coterie of Geniuses

Gathering around him some brilliant young men, Weitzel organized the completion of the survey of the Great Lakes. Among these youngsters was Alfred Noble, a Plymouth lad who had just completed his engineering course at the University of Michigan after an interruption occasioned by his running away from school to participate in the civil war, and who later in life was one of the designers of the hydraulic operating machinery of the canal at Sault Ste. Marie, as well as a determining factor in the selection of the Panama route for the Panama Canal. Still later in life he was the engineer who designed the East River under-water entrance of the Pennsylvania Railroad into New York City.

Another of Gen. Weitzel's youngsters of this period was

a young civilian in whom Gen. Weitzel saw merit, named Robert Simpson Woodward, who came from a farm near Oxford, in Oakland county. He was later Dean of the School of Pure Science at Columbia University, and died after a long service as the head of the Carnegie Institute of Original Research.

With such help and his own ability as a directing engineer, Gen. Weitzel practically completed the Survey of the Great Lakes, the charts of which remain, with few amendments, the guides of the mariners who traverse these inland waterways. Later on, as the engineer in charge of River and Harbor Improvements, it fell to Gen. Weitzel to construct the first modern lock at the St. Mary's Falls, in St. Mary's River, connecting Lake Superior with Lake Huron, and to plan and partially carry out the comprehensive channel improvements in Lake George and the Neebish Rapids which were later completed under General Poe.

It is noteworthy that in this and subsequent work of the Lake Survey a most valuable contribution in the way of making and amending the maps of the Survey was rendered by Edward Molitor, a Wurtemburger by birth, as a cartographer, and by Clemens Schauroth, a civilian, who managed the expenditure of funds and kept the progress of work within the appropriations

The Father of Reforestation

Filibert Roth, the leading proponent of reforestration in the United States, was a Wurtemburger, born in 1858, who came to Ann Arbor, in 1871. He graduated from Michigan in 1890, had experiences as a timber expert for the United States government from 1893 to 1898, was Assistant Professor of Forestry at Cornell, and in 1903 became the first Professor of Forestry of his Alma Mater. He held his position for twenty years when he was made Professor Emeritus He organized the first forestry association in Michigan and started the work on the first state forest. He died in 1925.

He was described by his contemporaries as being the foremost man in his field, especially in silviculture and forest management.

Writing of Prof. Roth after his death, Albert Stoll, a Michigan journalist, himself of Germanic ancestry, said:

> The name 'Roth' has always been synonymous with forestry in Michigan. No one who ever had personal contact with him can forget his enthusiasm and intenseness on this subject. His great desire to bring back to the state the forest growth it once possessed was a dominating motive in his life. What progress has been recorded in tree restoration in Michigan will have been found to have had its incentive in the teachings, the sacrifices and hard work of Professor Roth. It was he who started us on our way toward the forest utilization of our waste lands. No man will do in the future what Professor Roth did in the past in forest pioneering.

At this writing it is proposed that the Higgins Lake Forest Reserve, on which Professor Roth did his first planting of pine seedlings, be named the "Roth State Forest."

The Founder of Detroit Observatory

In the chapter of this work dealing with the presence and usefulness of Germanic professors on the faculty of the University of Michigan, the details of the life of Professor Carl Brunnow and of his selection as the founder of the Astronomical Observatory of the University of Michigan, are given. The influence which he exerted on the progress of astronomical science in the United States remained to be measured by President Robert Simpson Woodward, the same herein referred to as having served on the Lake Survey under General Weitzel, and himself a graduate of the University of Michigan in the class of 1872. Speaking at the seventy-fifth anniversary of the founding of the University in 1912, Prof. Woodward said, in connection with a discussion of the merits of Prof. James C. Watson, the disciple and student of Brunnow:

Though Watson has descended in America from the greater Brunnow the present generation of men who represent one of the two distinctively American schools of astronomers. Perhaps most of you are aware that in the science of astronomy, including all its branches, Americans have been the leaders for more than fifty years. Two classes have been founded in America, the first, by Professor Benjamin Pierce of Harvard University, and the second by Professor Brunnow, who introduced in America, before 1860, the methods of the illustrious Gauss and the incomparable Bessel, the German astronomers who laid the foundations of modern spherical and observational astronomy. From Brunnow were descended directly some of the most distinguished American astronomers. Among his first students were Asaph Hall, the discoverer of the moons of Mars; C. A. Young, a Professor of Astronomy at Dartmouth and Princeton; the veteran meteorologist, Cleveland Abbe, and DeVolson Wood.

John Martin Schaeberle divides with Professor James Watson and Admiral Albert Gustavus Winterhalter, the honors won by Michigan men in the field of astronomical science. Professor Schaeberle was born in Germany in 1853, the son of Anton Schaeberle and Catherine Voegele. They came to Michigan when their son was a year old, settling at Ann Arbor. From his fifteenth to his eighteenth year he was an apprentice at a machine shop in Chicago, out of which city he was driven homeward by the great fire of 1871. He studied at Ann Arbor high school and the University of Michigan, graduating as a civil engineer in 1876. Meantime he was interested in astronomy, became a private assistant to Prof. Watson, and later an instructor and Acting Professor of Astronomy at the University. From 1888 to 1897 he was Astronomer of Lick Observatory in California, and had charge of its expeditions to observe the eclipses of 1889, 1893 and 1896, these pursuits taking him to Cayenne, Chile and Japan. Prof. Schaeberle, who retired to live at Ann Arbor, was himself the discoverer of three comets.

Albert Gustavus Winterhalter was born just outside Detroit in 1856. His father, Michael Winterhalter, was a Mexican war veteran and a modest inn-keeper. His son won in a competition for a Naval Academy Cadetship in 1873 and made a brilliant career in the navy. His scientific attainments were most prominent in the fields of astronomy and hydrography. In 1887, when he was a junior grade Lieutenant and only ten years out of the academy, he was made observer for the United States Navy at the International Astrophotographic Congress of Paris, at which the work of photographing the heavens and building a catalogue of the stars from the results, a work which has been going on ever since, was first practically planned. Following this conference, Lieut. Winterhalter made an inspection of European scientific institutions for his branch of the service, making a report on this whole tour which was published in 1889.

A Great Naval Astronomer

He was in charge of the Naval Observatory at Washington in 1907-1908, and was the Navy Department's Hydrographer in 1908-1909.

Apart from this scientific work, which is his chief glory, Winterhalter, who came to be a Rear Admiral in 1915, had a splendid naval history. He was on the Philadelphia in the Spanish-American War in 1898. Later in the same year he helped arrange the transfer of the Hawaiian sovereignty to the United States. He commnaded a division of gun boats from Cavite to China in 1903, was a member of the Navy's General Board in 1911, commanded the Asiatic Fleet and station in 1915-1917, and in this capacity, represented the United States on the accession of the Emperor of Japan in 1915, being the only foreign naval representative present with a fleet. Admiral Winterhalter died at Washington in 1924.

Col. Shoemaker's Collection of Maps

The best collection of the early maps of Michigan extant is that made by Col. Michael Shoemaker, of Jackson, the same who distinguished himself in the civil war, and who was a descendant of the early German settlement in the Mohawk Valley, including in his ancestry General Herkimer. Col. Shoemaker was a student of Michigan's early history, and, in addition to a long time membership therein, served the Michigan Historical Society as its President. His genius and taste ran in the direction of collecting early maps upon which the present area of Michigan was more or less correctly delineated. The complete collection which he presented to the Michigan Historical Society is priceless, and has formed the subject matter of an interesting study by Mr. William L. Jenks, of Port Huron, himself an eminent devotee of Michigan history. In describing the Shoemaker collection, Mr. Jenks recalls that the earliest map is one issued in 1648 by Jean Blaeu, a German cartographer of Amsterdam, one of the most famous of map-making families, whose business, begun in 1612, was carried on by his sons and grandsons. This map is entitled "Americae Nova Tabula." It is on a small scale, but is clear and distinct. It shows the state of knowledge in Europe concerning America when it was published. None of the Great Lakes is shown, but the St. Lawrence River starts far in the interior of the continent. The plate from which this map was printed was used in issuing a map at about the same time by Jan Jansson, under the title "America Noviter Delineata."

Next in point of age of the Shoemaker collection is a rare French map made by Pierre Duval and issued in Paris about 1670. The first edition of the map was made in 1653 and differs very little from this. The configurations of the Great Lakes are very curious, Lake Ontario measuring about one-and-a-half inches in length while Lake Erie extends only about half an inch. Lake Huron seems to be part of a series of lakes and bears the name in French, "Fresh Water Sea, or Great Lake of the Horons and Atigoatan, which has flow and ebb."

Next oldest is an English map of 1680 by William Berry, probably the largest and most authentic English map up to that date. It was based upon Sanson's map of 1650, but has a few alterations in the shapes and names of the lakes. A rare map is the English map of Daniel, covering the English empire in the continent of America and issued in 1685. The map shows three of the Great Lakes. "Huron" lies between 44 degrees and 45 degrees north latitude, and just west of 77 longitude, which would locate its easterly shore in the neighborhood of Rochester, N. Y. About one degree due south is "Lake Ontarius" and south of that and connected with it by a river is "Lake Erius or Felis." The two upper lakes are connected by streams to the St. Lawrence River.

A French map of 1649, Jaillot's "North America," is a reproduction of the first map ever published which showed all the Great Lakes. On the map of Sanson of 1650, the lakes are not completely shown. Of Superior and Michigan only the lower parts appear. All are distorted and not correctly placed with relation to each other, yet they indicate a knowledge of the interior of the continent far in advance of the English geographers of 1650.

An English map of 1695, by Morden, shows the lakes in relatively proper positions This same map, with a slight change in the text, was issued again in 1719 under the authorship of Senex, a well known geographer of that date. Another English map, made in 1710 by John Senex, covers territory beyond the Mississippi and shows the new discoveries in that region beyond the Great Lakes. A French map, undated and bearing no name, was issued probably in 1718 by N. deFer, "Geographer to His Catholic Majesty." This map is entitled "Map of New France," and gives the Great Lakes in more detail than any other up to this date. DeFer is also responsible for a beautiful map issued in 1719 and bearing the name in French, "A Very Curious Map of the South Sea." It covers all of North and South America and therefore shows the Great Lakes on a small scale.

Two of the maps bear date of 1720. One is by Herman Moll, the English geographer, who was of German birth, and shows the lakes on a large scale. It contains as an insert, an elegant engraving of "Sasquesahanok Indian Fort." The other, which is undated, seems to belong to this same period. It is by J. B. Homann, of Nuremburg, and based upon the travels and book of Father Hennepin.

A German Map-Maker of 1720

The collection includes two maps by d'Anville, a famous French geographer. One is of North America and is dated 1746. This is usually considered the best French map of the whole of North America up to this date. The one dated 1755 includes Canada, Louisiana and the English territories. Its scale is larger than that of the preceding, and it is a fine record of this region. A well detailed and larger map covering this same territory is that of Robert de Vaugondy, fils, issued in 1750, with the title in French, "Map of the Country known by the name of Canada." An important map was that of Jeffry's issued in 1775, based upon d'Anville's Map of the North America with corrections. It contains several columns of descriptive text engraved in the part depicting the ocean.

Four English maps complete the collection. These are: Kitchin's map of 1763, made after the close of the French and Indian war; Pownell's map of 1783, made after the treaty of peace between Great Britain and the United States; which shows the boundary line between the two countries; a map by Blair made in 1790, and one by Laurie and Whittle in 1794.

Charles Frederick Robert Wappenhans

An important contributor to the science of meteorology, some time a citizen of Michigan, was Charles Friedrich Robert Wappenhans. He was a native of Berlin, born in 1834, and immediately on coming to America he entered the navy, as a master's mate in 1862, rising to be a master in 1865. During the civil war he was on the Frigate Savannah, of the

North Atlantic squadron; on the Flagship Ticonderoga, of the
West India squadron; on the Matabasset, Eolus and Tacoma
of the North Atlantic squadron; on the Osceola, of the West
India squadron and on the Idaho, Kansas and Huron, of the
India squadron, and on the Idaho, Kansas and Huron, of the
his retirement from the navy he joined the Signal Service of
the army, to which the duties now performed by the Weather
Bureau were originally assigned, and in that capacity he was
Inspector of the Detroit office from 1879 to 1883, when he
was assigned to duty at Indianapolis. There he served for
30 years, returning to Germany after his retirement, where
he died. Mr. Wappenhans was one of the most learned men
in the service and his contributions to the science of meteorology through years of careful observation and deduction were
very substantial. He trained many younger men in the service, was highly esteemed for his social qualifications both
in Detroit and Indianapolis, and in the latter city was the
intimate friend of President Benjamin Harrison and his
family.

David Friday

One of the most distinguished native-born economists of
Michigan is David Friday, born at Coloma in 1876, the son
of Jacob Friday and Elizabeth Butzbach. He graduated
from Michigan in 1908, immediately became an instructor of
economics and was steadily advanced until he became full
Professor of Economics in 1919, succeeding Prof. Adams.
He was a very popular teacher with his students. He was
later made President of the Michigan Agricultural College,
but failing to adapt his teaching to the predilections of the
politicians, he resigned, to engage in economic consultancy.
He was a statistician of the Michigan Tax Inquiry Commission
of 1911; appraiser of franchises for the Michigan Tax Commission in 1914 and 1915; and statistical adviser to the United
States Telephone and Telegraph Administration in 1919. In
later years he has been a general economic consultant for

street railway, steam railroad and other public service corporations.

These constitute some of the great contributors to human knowledge who have been German-American citizens of the state. The variety of the fields in which they worked furnishes a good measure of the value of their service. They have had good company in many other equally earnest but less distinguished contemporaries of their race and blood.

CHAPTER XXIII

THE CONTRIBUTIONS TO ART

The Religious Paintings—The Public Collections—The German-American Painters—German-American Sculpture—Julius Theodore Melchers—Famous Artist Sons of Michigan.

America's classical art is not old. Benjamin West, Rembrant Peale, Gilbert Stuart and some of their contemporaries are the earliest of the nation's great in this field. Their immediate successors studied abroad. In time examples of early classical art served as the models for American students who sought to achieve excellence at home. These were practically all brought from abroad.

American galleries have many fine collections of representations of the various national schools and their respective periods. These were the models of the American school. France, Italy, England, Spain and Germany have been generous contributors to these collections, not the least of their precious items being those of German origin, which have served their purposes in the development of culture among the general public and as models for study by the ambitious disciples of art. The artistic sense of the general public has gotten its greatest stimulus from these examples which were most familiar to the larger number.

In Michigan these earliest models were most generously offered in the form of altar-pieces and religious pictures, most of them by artists who did not scale the heights of fame, but who were good men at their work, nevertheless. In the earlier history of Michigan these works found their way into the Lutheran and Roman Catholic churches. Most of them were produced by students at Munich and Dresden, and in the forms of Lutheran altar pieces and Roman Catholic "Stations of the Cross" they were about the best art that the common people had for study for a long time. In addition, the procurement of such paintings furnished an opportunity for patronage of young art students by their American friends. A striking example of this kind is a copy of Murillo's Immaculate Conception, which was the gift of Mr. Edward W. Voigt to St. Mary's Hospital in Detroit, and was the work of the student period of Joseph W. Gies, who attained repution.

The Public Collections

Later on the public and private collections began to be available for observation and study. Among these the collections of the Detroit Institute of Arts are particularly rich in examples of the work of German artists. The most ancient painting of the German school in its possession is the "Virgin and Child," of Lucas Cranach, painted in 1536. Of this period of art the Hackley Gallery at Muskegon, contains another example by George Pencz (1500-1550), "The Portrait of a Lady," of whose engravings the Detroit Institute has some fine examples. Christian William Ernest Dietrich (1712-1774) is represented in Detroit, by "The Expulsion of Hager," painted on copper and dated 1767. This was presented by the late Mr. James E. Scripps. Among the moderns perhaps the most noted piece is "The Last Hours of Mozart," painted by Michael Lieb, more familiarly known as Munkaczy. It is a gift of the heirs of Gen. Russell A. Alger. Adolph Schreyer's "Old Hungarian Mail" is the single example of this famous painter, the gift of Mr. Dexter M. Ferry, Jr. Mr. W. W. Murphy, of Jonesville, who was long Consul at Frankfort-on-Main, presented a landscape by C. Morgenstein, of Frankfort.

IN THE MAKING OF MICHIGAN

Among the other works of German artists which have been deemed worthy of purchase or acceptance by this institution are "Side-Wheeler," 1913, by Lionel Feininger; "The Crucifixion," by Ruland Frueauf; "Frau," 1920, by Ernest Heckel; "Dunes near Fehmarn," 1912, by E. I. Kirchner; "Landscape near Dresden," by Otto Kokescha; "Bathing," 1921, by Otto Mueller; "Blessing of the Earth," 1921, by Alfred Partikel; "Under the Tree," 1911, by Max Peckstein; "Hochsommer," 1906, by Leo Putz, which was from the collection of Hugo Reisinger; "Cactus Still Life," 1919, by Karl Schmitt-Rotluff; "Two Girls," by Carl Schwalbach; and "Konigsee," by Wilhelm Wex, this the gift of Mr. Emil S. Heineman. The profits of the first exhibition in the Museum were invested in F. K. M. Rehn's picture, "The Missing Vessel," as the best example exhibited at that time.

In the same Institute's collections of engraving and etchings are characteristic works of Schonhauer, Israel von Mechenem, Albrecht Durer, Altdorfer, Lucas Cranach, Barthel and Hans Sebold, Behams, George Pencz, H. Aldegrever, Lucan Von Leyden and A. Hirschvogel, who flourished during the fifteenth and sixteenth centuries. In its collections of ancient sculpture is a wood carving of the sixteenth century Suabian school, "The Saint with Sword and Book," attributed to Jorg Syrlin, the younger. Gregor Erhart, who plied his art about 1500, is represented by a group in wood, "The Virgin and Child." Examples of ninth century artistry are present in plaster reproductions of the carved panel of a reliquary and a diptych leaf, showing Christ in a seated posture, both from German sources. A fifteenth century wood carving, unnamed, is of the Madonna and the Infant Jesus. A sixteenth century piece, in wood, painted and gilded, shows a female saint, holding a floral bouquet. The Middle Rhenish period, of about 1620, is shown by a "Saint Bartholemew" carved in wood. George Kolbe's bronze, "Aspiration," is a worthy example of Greman sculpture in this material.

Of the modern and American-born painters of German birth or descent the most distinguished producers represented were two Michigan artist who achieved international recognition, Gari Melchers and Jules Rolshoven. Mr. Melchers is represented by six examples, these being "Vespers," presented by the Witenagemote Club; "The Wedding," a "Portrait of Mrs. Melchers," "The Marvel" and "The Fencing Master," all four being the gifts of the late Mr. Edward Chandler Walker; and "A Child with an Orange," presented by the Founders' Society of the Institute. Mr. Rolshoven's representation is "The Refectory of San Damiano, Assisi," which was purchased by popular subscription.

Charles Waltensperger, another Detroit artist, is represented by three of his works, "The Man with the Staff," being a copy on canvas of Rembrandt's original in the Louvre; "Fete Day in Paris," a water color, and "A Humble Meal," in oil on a panel of wood.

The German-American Painters

In addition, as productions of German born and German-American artists, the Institute possesses a portrait of himself, by Frederick E. Cohen, who was an odd sort of fellow who lived in Detroit at the time of the Patriot War, was ready for any adventure and dressed like a fop. There is one of Leon Dabo's pictures, "The Seashore," and one by his brother, Theodore Scott Dabo, "The River Seine," each of the latter being the gift of the artists. Both the Dabos are Michigan men, their mother having been an Oberly, a German Swiss. There is an example, "The Blue Gown," of Frederick Carl Frieseke, N. A., who was born at Owosso, in 1874, whose father was a pioneer German resident of Shiawassee County, and who studied in Paris under Whistler. His work won the 1904 medal at Munich. Of the work of Joseph W. Gies, there are "Lady in Pink," a pastel, and the "Portrait of Robert Hopkin," a canvas. There are also, "A Dutch Canal," by Carl Paul Gruppe; "In the Country," by Leon Kroll; "An October

Morning in New Hampshire," by William Louis Sonntag, N.
A., and "The Pool," by John Twachtman. E. Anger Irving
Couse, a Saginaw man who studied and exhibited successfully
in Germany, is also represented.

Dr. W. R. Valentiner, Curator of the Detroit Institute of
Arts, is the authority for the statement that there are few
examples of the Germanic school of painting in the private
art collections of citizens of Michigan. Mr. Julius H. Haass,
of Detroit, is the owner of some fine examples. Mr. Ralph H.
Booth, of Grosse Pointe, who is President of the Detroit Art
Commission, has specialized, to a considerable extent, in the
acquisition of examples of the German school, both in painting and in sculpture in wood. In his private collection are
two pictures by Lucas Cranach (1530-40), the subjects being
a boy and a girl, the children of the King of Saxony. These,
with Cranach's "Virgin and Child," some of his engravings
in the Detroit Institute, and an example in the ownership
of Mr. Haass, make a very creditable presentation of the genius
of this mediaeval colorist. The Haass example is a painting,
the subject being St. Paul, writing at a table, a fine bit of landscape showing through the window. It was painted in the
first part of the Sixteenth Century. The Booth collection also
contains Ambrosius Holbein's "Portrait of a Young Man";
and two portraits of a man and his wife by Ambrosius Benson. In the sculpture collection of the same owner are a
life-sized Madonna, in oak, by Hans Lienberger, and a corresponding figure in the same material representing St. John.
Two portraits, of a man and his wife, are by Bernard Scrigel.
The Booth collection also includes a carving, in ancient wood,
of the Madonna and Child, by Pilman Remenschneider, and
some examples of German sculpture and stained glass.

Mr. Haass, already mentioned, has in his private collection another example of the early Germanic school of statuary.
The subject is St. Florain extinguishing a conflagration in a
Castle. It is a polychromed wooden statuette, is a well known
subject and was done sometime in the fifteenth century. In

the most recent accessions of the Detroit Institute are some altarpieces of German origin and considerable antiquity.

German-American Sculpture

Isadore Konti, who studied under Karl Kundman, in Vienna and who is noted for his sculptural work at the Chicago and St. Louis International Expositions and in St. John's Cathedral and Trinity Church, New York, is represented by his "Genius of Immortality." In bronze, Alvin Polasek, who was born in Moravia, and who modeled the Theodore Thomas memorial at Chicago, has two examples, "Aspiration" and "Maternal Love." Frederick George Richard Roth, Brooklyn man who studied in Bremen, is represented by three of his famous bronze conceptions of polar bears.

Adolph Alexander Weinman, native of Karlsruhe, in Baden, is the sculptor of a bronze bas-relief portrait, mounted on marble, of Julius Theodore Melchers, the early sculptor-teacher of Detroit. Charles Grafley, Philadelphian of German descent, is represented in the sculpture collections of the Detroit Institute.

Randolph Rogers, famous American sculptor, was a druggist's clerk in Ann Arbor in his youth. His intimates were the older and younger Germans of the vicinity, and as young Rogers disclosed some ability at drawing, these urged him to go abroad and study art. They had intentions of making a painter out of him. Instead he developed into a master of plastic art. His famous work is the bronze doors of the Capitol at Washington. The figures on the Soldier's Monument in Detroit are of his design, as is also a monumental piece in Elmwood Cemetery, Detroit.

Of the public art of the state several leading examples are the work of Germans. When Michigan entered the Union in 1837, one of the earliest acts of the Legislature was to provide for the purchase of a portrait, now in the State Library, of Gen. Lafayette. It was delivered in 1840, and was the work of an artist named Ary (Arius) Scheffer, a personal

friend of the Marquis, who copied the portrait presented to
Congress by Lafayette himself. The bronze equestrian groups
and figures which are placed on the Wayne County Court
House are the work of Edward Wagner. Adolph Alexander
Weinman, born at Karlsruhe in 1870, modeled the memorial
of Gen. Alexander Macomb, which was set up in Detroit in
1906, and that of Mayor William Cotter Maybury, which was
placed in the same city in 1912. The statue of Governor Stevens Thomas Mason, which stands on the site of the original
State Capitol, in Detroit, was the work of Albert Weinert,
born in Leipsig in 1863 and educated there. Johannes Sophus
Gellert, a native of Schleswig, born 1852, was the sculptor
of the portrait statue of C. W. Post, eminent Michigan industrialist, which is his memorial at Battle Creek. The statue of Governor Hazen S. Pingree, in a Detroit park, was
modeled by Rudolph Schwartz, of Indianapolis.

In another field of art, that of painted and stained glass,
Ignatius Schol, a Detroiter, was one of the earliest practitioners. His ideal grouping of the Holy Trinity with "The
Last Supper" has been the altar piece of Holy Trinity Catholic
Church, in Detroit, for more than fifty years. The Munich-made stained-glass windows of the Polish Church of St. Mary,
Detroit, took the prizes for such art work at the Chicago
World's Fair of 1893. For years the leading producers stained and painted glass in the west were two German artist producers, Friedrichs and Staffin, of Detroit.

Julius Theodore Melchers

Few men have had so considerable an influence on the art
education of their communities as Julius Theodore Melchers,
who lived in Detroit from 1855 to 1903. He was born at
Soest, Prussia, in 1830, was an apprentice wood carver and
modeler when the revolution of 1848 broke out and he was in
the midst of it as an enthusiastic youngster. The movement
failing, he fled to America, remained about New York for five
years and came to Detroit. There he eked out a living by

carving wooden figures of Indians for signs for tobacco merchants. The "cigar store Indian," then and later a rather popular creation, has gone out of vogue, but there was many an artistic job of wood-carving done in its production. Melchers had higher ideals than such work involved. He was, above all, a fine master of drawing, and very early in his career he organized and taught Sunday morning classes in drawing in a German society hall in Detroit. He is remembered as an exacting but encouraging master. Among his pupils was his own son, Julius Garibaldi Melchers, named jointly after his father and his father's idol, the Italian revolutionary leader. "Gari" Melchers, as he became generally known, has for long been an artist of international fame. Other pupils of Mr.. Melchers were Myron Barlow, Michigan born artist of fame, who had a Germanic origin; Joseph W. Gies, widely known painter, and a group of men who carried their artistic training into the fields of design and illustration. Joseph L. Kraemer, famous cartoonist and newspaper illustrator, was one of his pupils. John M. Donaldson, famous architect, learned modeling in his atelier. Albert B. Wenzel, nationally known illustrator, was another of the products of his teaching, as was Harry V. Goodman, Detroit born artist, who has spent much of his life in Paris.

It was as a sculptor that Mr. Melchers really wished to be eminent, and to a considerable extent he was. He not only modeled but cut from sandstone the figures of Justice, Industry, Art and Commerce, which ornament the clock-tower of the City Hall in Detroit. Later on when Mr. Bela Hubbard provided for the placing of statues of the historic pioneers of Michigan on the facade of the same building, these being figures of Cadillac, La Salle and Fathers Marquette and Richard, the modeling of Marquette was entrusted to John M. Donaldson and of the rest to Melchers, who executed all four of the figures in marble.

A bas-relief of Mr. Melchers executed by Adolph Alexander Weinman and the memorial of his pupils and friends, is appropriately placed in the Detroit Institute of Arts.

Herman Wehner, a German born sculptor, worked in Detroit for many years and produced many pieces of merit, largely in the class of bas-relief portraits. He was for many years a pupil and collaborator with J. Q. A. Ward, a famous American sculptor whose genius ran mostly to the production of equestrian statues, and many examples of whose work are to be found in the eastern cities. Mr. Wehner's only public work in Michigan is the portrait bust of Gen. John J. Bagley, which was placed on the Campus Martius in Detroit. He also modeled and cut in marble a portrait bust of Solomon Davis, Detroit's earliest foundryman, for his son George S. Davis, one of the founders of the pharmaceutical manufacturing trade in his native city.

Famous Artist Sons of Michigan

Two American artists who enjoy international reputations were sons of Michigan German-Americans. Jules Rolshoven was born in Detroit in 1858, the son of Frederick Rolshoven and Maria Theresa Hubertina Hellings. He studied at Copenhagen, Dusseldorf, Munich, Florence and Paris, and received honors at the expositions of Munich, Berlin and other art centers. He gave life classes in Paris from 1890 to 1895 and in London from 1896 to 1902. His works are scattered world-wide in the greater collections.

Gari Melchers was also born in Detroit in 1860. His father, Julius Melchers, a sculptor and instructor in drawing, brought up a score of artists and modelers in his time, some of them of the first class. Gari Melchers was a student in Duesseldorf before he was eighteen. He received the gold medal of the Paris Salon in 1886, the Grand Medal of Honor of Berlin in 1891, and later the Grand Gold Medals of Munich, Vienna and Dresden. His scope has been very wide. He has painted many portraits, among the most notable one of President Roosevelt. A number of others, of less notable people, are placed in Detroit. The great mural paintings of "The Conspiracy of Pontiac" and of "The Arrival of Mmes. Cadillac and Tonty," which are placed in the main hall of the Detroit Public Library, are from his hand. No great collection either in America or Europe is lacking in at least one example of his work.

Frederick Carl Frieseke was born in Owosso in 1874. His parents were German people. He studied art in the Luxembourg and Paris, and in the Modern Gallery at Vienna. He has spent most of his life abroad. He is represented in the Detroit Institute collections, and recently he presented a painting to his native city.

A Germanic influence in this cultural field was exerted through Harry Muir Kurtzworth, Detroiter born in 1877, who studied art at Munich, was director of art work in Muskegon from 1911 to 1916, and founder and director of the Art Institute at Grand Rapids from 1916 to 1920. His best work was done in the development of industrial art. Mr. Kurtzworth later became Director of the Art Institute of Kansas City. John Antrobus, a portrait painter who was quite the vogue in the '70's and '80's in Detroit, was an Englishman, of supposed German antecedents.

Francis Petrus Paulus, a fine teacher and a painter of merit, was Detroit born, got his art education at Munich, studied in the Royal Academy of Fine Arts for two periods, from 1886 to 1888 and again from 1890 to 1893. He was for several years instructor of drawing in the school of the Detroit Museum of Art and was director of the Detroit Art Academy from 1895 to 1903.

CHAPTER XXIV

THE CONTRIBUTIONS TO MUSIC

The First Formal Concert—The Advent of Wilhelm Yunck—The Little German Bands—The German-Trained Music-Masters.

> Home of my heart, I sing of Thee
> Michigan, My Michigan,
> Thy lake-bound shores I long to see,
> Michigan, My Michigan.
> —Mrs. Lyster.

The Germanic influence in the development of music in Michigan reached into high places. The state song, "Michigan, My Michigan," is sung to a German air. The words were written by Miss Winnifred Lee Brant, afterwards the wife of Dr. Henry Lyster, and the poetical composition was written to fit the metre of "Tannenbaum." This was a popular German song, which was translated into English by the poet Longfellow, in his "Translations of German Songs." The original words and music were by Carl Anschutz, Royal Director at Coblenz, and they first appeared in that city about 1840. This is their history as given in August Hartell's Cyclopedia of German Song, Hartell being himself of Leipsig. Another state hymn, "Maryland, My Maryland," was also given the same musical setting.

In the Michigan hymn the lines in the fifth stanza

> "Their strong arms crumble in the dust"
> "Their bright swords gather rust"
> "Their memory is our sacred trust"

are a quotation from Theodore Koerner, the famous poet, who was a German.

The beginnings of music in Detroit were simple. Dr. Harpfy was a German doctor at the military post when the British went out in 1796. He moved across the boundary and settled at Amherstburg. About all that is recorded of him is that he was the possessor of a harpsichord sadly out of tune, which was finally transported to Detroit to furnish music for assemblages. It was ill-received and was finally sold for junk. This was the first pretentious musical instrument in Michigan, Mrs. Soloman Sibley's piano having not arrived from the East until 1803, while Father Richard imported an organ a few years later. There was little of formal music in the community life of Michigan so early. A fife and drum band gave step to the military and there were some violinists.

The First Formal Concert

It was not until 1833 that a formal concert was given in Detroit. On June 21, of that year, the Tyrolese singer, Blisse, who is said to have had a phenomenal voice, was in Detroit en tour, and he appeared, supported by a number of local Germans in chorus, in the main hall of the State's Capitol, which was then located in Detroit. Out of this effort grew a primitive brass band, which in 1834, played every summer evening in the Michigan Garden, which was around Col. Brush's home and was a place of popular amusement. In 1847 a quartet of German singers gave concerts in the Old National Hotel, in Detroit, on the present site of the First National Bank building. These were so much appreciated that they were repeated in the following year. This laid the foundation for the earliest German singing society in Michigan, in 1849, the Harmonie Society of Detroit, all the founders of which were German. These were John Fritz, Stephen Marx, Gottlieb Frey, Carl Welde, A. Stutte, C. Hensler and J. Bremer. By 1856 this society had one hundred and twenty-five members, including many persons prominent then and later in business and professional life. For the first twelve years of the Society's history, John Marx was its musical director. He was followed by Carl Stein for three years; Herman Bischof for five years, and Carl Hurz for two years, passing into 1873 when Fritz Abel became director.

Prof. Abel was born at Landau, in the Rhine Palatinate, in 1824, and studied music and voice in his native land, coming to America in 1849. He had spent eleven years in Cleveland, ten in Milwaukee and one in Chicago, when he was invited to Detroit, to become Director of the Detroit Musical Society, a general organization of devotees of music. He served the Harmonie Society as its Director until 1886, when Wilhelm Yunck succeeded him.

Wilhelm Yunck

Wilhelm Yunck was a Cassel man, born in 1853, the son of a German army colonel. He was first in his class at the Vienna Conservatory for five years. Then he studied under Joachim at Prague, was for four years in the Court Orchestra of Berlin, and frequently played and sang for the first Kaiser Wilhelm, who was a great admirer of his art. He made two tours of the United States with the American Opera Company, and then became head of the violin department of the New York Conservatory.

The Harmonie Society brought this great artist to Michigan where he was for thirty years easily the most distinguished musical leader of his period. He organized the Philharmonic quartet, which included, besides himself, Louis F. Schultz, Herman Bruckner and Walter Voigtlander, a grouping which was later changed by the admission of Herman Heberlein as the 'cellist in place of Bruckner. In addition he played the organ in a Catholic Church in Detroit. where he frequently added to the musical quality of his services by playing violin obligatos. A deeply religious man, he invariably made these performances acts of devotion, always kneeling a moment in prayer before he proceeded with his renditions. Herman Bruckner took over the direction of the Harmonie Society in Yunck's place in 1889, continuing therein for many years.

To go back a bit, again, while this organization was living its life as a center for musical development, and even before, there were contributions by the German Americans to musical culture. In 1869 the foundation was laid for the first large orchestra in Detroit by Max Bendix. He gave subscription concerts which barely paid the orchestra's way. Meantime, Bendix was training his young son, a younger Max, who was born in Detroit in 1886. When this youngster was twenty years old he became a concert master for the famous Theodore Thomas' orchestra, a position which he held from 1886 to 1896. When Theodore Thomas laid down the baton, Max Bendix, Jr., became assistant conductor of the Orchestra, being specially engaged as concert master for the Wagnerian operas as presented in the Metropolitan Opera House, at New York. He also had some merit as a composer.

The first German ball was given in Detroit in 1837. The Brothers Orth, who were from Bavaria, furnished the music. These same Orths were musicians for the Scott Guard, which was organized in 1841, by John V. Ruehle, Nicholas Greusel, John Greusel, Michael Martz, Conrad Ling, Michael Winterhalter and some others for frontier defense.

In 1845 the Detroit City Directory showed John Schick as the only music teacher in the city.

The Brady Guard, of Detroit, which went into the Mexican war, had Peter Hess for bandmaster, and the Light Guard, of the same city, had Karl Stein in the same capacity in the middle '50's.

Pastor Hattstadt, who was a pioneer at Monroe, had a son, John James Hattstadt, whom he sent over to Germany to "get" his music, in 1870. When John James was nineteen, he was teaching piano in Detroit, as he continued to do for several years. In 1886 he founded the American Conservatory of Music in Chicago.

During this time a good many orchestral directors of merit came on the scene, most of them into Detroit. Their list included such men as Heinrich Kern, Herman Bischoff, Henry Lucker, Emil Singer, Emil Schremser, who directed the Fort Wayne Military Band; Charles Graul, Rudolph Speil, Fritz Kalzow, Fritz Abel and Franz A. Apel. Among the more famous of the organists of Detroit have been Christian Heinrich, who composed as well, John N. Arens and Engelbert Andries.

The German Bands

No humble efforts in the field of art exercised a greater popular influence upon musical taste in Michigan than an institution now pretty well passed out of the life of the state. This was the "little German band," as it was described, composed of four or five strolling instrumentalists, usually performing on the brass or wood-wind, and playing for the gratuities of street crowds or neighborhoods. The group was usually composed of a seasoned immigrant of a year or two of familiarity with the country and a remnant of "greenhorns" to fill out the quartet, quintet or sextet which rendered music for the edification of the householders and the street urchins. Amusing as these quaint performers were, they knew only the classical music of Europe, and their renditions were the first of the kind ever heard by many a Yankee or Irish-American urchin of their period. They came to be as well known harbingers of the springtime as the returning song birds, and while many a joke was made about their unfamiliarity with the country, the quaintness of their dress, and the occasional "blue notes" which were blown to the distress of their conductors, they were received good-naturedly, and made a decided impress upon musical education.

Many Michigan practitioners of the musical art have studied in Germany, some of them with very famous masters. Of the conductors Johan Heinrich Beck, born in Cleveland, who was director of the Detroit Symphony Orchestra, in 1889-90, was a student of the Leipsig Conservatory. Max Bendix, who was born in Detroit, and who attained the distinction of being concert master for Theodore Thomas, studied in Berlin. George Parker Buckley, Battle Creek concert violinist, was taught in Berlin, and played with the Philharmonic and Opera Orchestra of Prague. John Baptiste Martin, Battle Creek conductor, was born in Baden, and was the pupil of Prof. Ebann and Bernard Listerman.

German-Trained Music Masters

Among the piano teachers, John Blackmore, of Vassar, studied and made his debut in Berlin. Katherine Burrows and Hattie Colburn of Detroit, were pupils of Karl Klindworth, of Berlin. Mary Wood Chase, of Ludington, was a student of Oscar Raif, in Berlin. Emma Clarkmottl, Armada solo pianist, studied under Heinrich Barth. Rossiter Bleason Cole, of Clyde, won a scholarship under Max Bruch, of Berlin. John Grinnell Cummings, Centerville man, studied piano and organ at Scharwenka's conservatory in Berlin. Louise Freyhofer was trained in the Stern Conservatory, in the same city. Bendetson Netsorg, the pianist and composer, who was born in Mecosta, was the pupil of Hugo Kaun in Berlin, and taught there for two years. Faith Helen Rogers, from Grand Junction, studied under Adele aus Der Ohe.

Many other music teachers of Michigan received German musical educations. Among them, James Francis Cooke, of Bay City, studied in Wurzburg Conservatory under Herman Ritter and Max Meyer-Olbersleben. Clara Bradley Dawson, of Detroit, was a pupil of Grazziani in Berlin. Peter William Dykema, of Grand Rapids, was trained by Cooper, in the same place. Lillian Ruth Shimberg, of Detroit, studied under Godowsky and Burmeister. Harrison Albert Stevens, who came from Whitmore Lake, was also one of Godowsky's pupils. These typical names can be added to until they run into hundreds.

One of the most distinguished musical critics of the United States during the past forty-six years is Henry Edward Krehbiel, of the New York Tribune. He has been its critic since 1880 and has made and unmade reputations. He was born of German parents at Ann Arbor, educated there, studied law, and became the musical critic of the New York Tribune over fifty years ago. He is the author of more than a score of books on music, ranging from "Reviews of the New York Musical Seasons," through "Afro-American Folk Songs" to a translation of Carl Courvorsiers "Technics of Violin Playing." His studies of Wagner and three volumes on operas are classics of the American literature of music.

CHAPTER XXV

FAECKEL - TRAEGER

The Bearers of the Lights—Distribution of Michigan German Scholars—Two Famous Engineers.

The sons and daughters of Michigan, natural or by educational adoption, of German blood or training, have brought her much honor in the field of education outside her borders. Many of them are leaders in their respective fields. John Jacob Meyer was a Frankenmuth man, born in the first missionary colony of Saginaw county. He went through Concordia College, of the Lutheran church, at Fort Wayne, and spent two years later at the University of Chicago, which gave him his Ph. D. in 1900. He is perhaps the leading American authority on the Finnish and Sanscrit languages and is Professor of German and the Structure of Sanscrit at Chicago. Much of his writing on these subjects is in the German language. His translations of the Finnish tales of Koskenniemi and the Hindoo tales of Maharashtri are classics.

Louis Ernest Fuerbringer was also a Frankenmuth product. After serving as a professor at various Lutheran seminaries, he finally became Professor of Bible Introductions and Literature at Concordia College, St. Louis.

Christian Gauss, born at Ann Arbor in 1878, and the son of Christian Gauss and Catherine Bischoff, graduated from Michigan in 1898 and was an instructor of the Romance Languages there from 1899 to 1901. He has been chairman of the Department of Modern Languages at Princeton since 1913.

Max Killner, born in Detroit in 1861 and the son of Prof. Charles Frederick Killner, went to Hobart College and thence to Harvard, where, in the Cambridge Theological School, he is Professor of Old Testament Languages.

Armin William Leuschner, born in Detroit in 1868, graduated from the Royal Wilhelm Gymnasium at Cassel, Germany, in 1886 and took his A. B. at Michigan two years later. His Alma Mater gave him her honorary Doctorate of Science in 1913. He has been Professor of Mathematics, Director of the Student Observatory, Professor of Astronomy and Dean of the Graduate School of the University of California. He has written several publications on mathematical science in German and has made a table of the minor planets discovered by Prof. James C. Watson, who was Professor of Astronomy at Michigan, and a pupil of Brunnow.

Bernard Conrad Hesse, a Saginaw man who graduated as a Pharmaceutical Chemist at Michigan in 1889, spent the years 1896-1906 as research chemist at Ludwigshaven-on-Rhine, and has later been consulting chemist of the General Chemical Company in New York. Charles Francis Haanel, Ann Arbor born, has been a developer of sugar-growing in Mexico and of grape-growing in California, and now writes philosophy at his home in St. Louis. Otto Charles Glazier, who was born in Wiesbaden, and who was instructor in Biology at Michigan (1905-1918) has been Stone Professor of Biology at Amherst College since 1918. Ernest Carl Johannes Heinrich Voss, born in Mecklenburg in 1860, and educated at Rostock, Marburg and Leipsig, was professor of German Philology at Michigan (1891-1896) and has held a similar professorship at the University of Wisconsin since that time. Otto Edward Lessing, born in Wurtemburg, A. B., of Michigan in 1896, was instructor of German there in 1896-1898, and is professor of German at Williams College. Ernest Heinrich Mensel, born in London, England, instructor in Michigan (1892-1900) has been Professor of Germanic Languages at Smith College since 1901, and in 1904-1905 was lecturer on Germanic Philology at Harvard. Florence Buck, Ypsilanti woman, whose mother was a Reznor, taught science at Kalamazoo College and is Director of the Tuckerman School, at Boston. George David Birkhoff, who was born at Overisel, is an Assistant Professor of Mathematics at Harvard.

Charles August Behrans, whose mother was a Borneman, received three degrees from Michigan and has been an engineering professor at Purdue University since 1914. Louis Bergemen, who graduated from Michigan in 1889, is head of the Department of Physics and Chemistry at Iowa State College. Bertha Baur, of Ann Arbor, is principal of the Cincinnati Conservatory of Music. Charles Russell Bardeen, born at Kalamazoo, though not of German ancestry, but who studied anatomy and medicine at the Teichman School, in Leipsig, is Dean of the Medical School of the University of Wisconsin. John Auer, Rochester man, who got his B. Sc., from Michigan in 1898, has been Professor of Pharmacology at the St. Louis University School of Medicine since 1912.

Distribution of Michigan German Scholars

James Edward Church, whose mother was an Eisenbrey, out of a Pennsylvania family, was a Holly man. He graduated at Michigan in 1892, did post graduate work at Munich later and is Professor of Latin at the University of Nevada. Besides his classical work he is an authority on the meteorology of the west and has made many contributions to the literature of snow conservation and stream flow in his adopted state. Catherine Elizabeth Dopp, who got her Ph. D., from Michigan in 1993, is Lecturer on Education Extension at the University of Chicago. Richard Fischer, whose mother was Anna Holstein, graduated as a Pharmaceutical Chemist from Michigan in 1892, has been Professor of Chemistry since 1909 at the University of Wisconsin, and is State Chemist in addition.

Melville Best Anderson, a Kalamazoo man of American ancestry, graduated from Gottingen in 1876, and is Professor of English Literature at Leland Stanford University in California. Mellen Woodman Haskell, Massachusetts man, was a Gottingen Ph. D., of 1889, and Professor of Mathematics at Michigan for a time. Since 1901 he has been Dean of the College of Letters at the University of California. Edward L. Hardy, an Owosso man, whose mother was Cordelia Cromer, made his secondary education in Germany and is President of the California State Teacher's College at San Diego. Kate Brousseau, who was born at Ypsilanti and whose mother was a Yakely, studied in Germany and is Professor of Psychology in Mills College, at Oakland, California, Frank Bohr, Kansas man, took his A. B., at Michigan in 1907, and has been in the American Consular Service at Cienfuegos, Cuba, since 1919. Royal Samuel Copland, Dexter man who got his M. D. at Michigan in 1889, took his post graduate work in German schools. He is now United States Senator from New York. Frederick H. Abbott, Niles man whose mother was a Steinbeck, has been for long Secretary of the United States Board of Indian Commissioners. Frank Bulkley, a Monroe man, whose mother was Fidelia Groendycke, has been a famous mining engineer in Colorado gold, silver and lead developments for forty years. John Jacob Abel, son of George M. Abel and Mary Becker, was a Cleveland man, who took his Ph. B. at Michigan in 1883, his A. M. degree in 1903, and was honored with the Doctorate of Science in 1912. He studied very extensively abroad for seven years, spending his time at Leipsig, Strassburg, Heidelburg, Vienna, Berne, Wurzburg and Berlin, returning to Michigan to become lecturer on Materia Medica and Therapeutics for the years 1891-1893. Since that time he has been Professor of Pharmacology at John Hopkins University in Baltimore and has become one of the most famous men in his special field.

Homer Leroy Schontz, a Kent county man, born 1876, became Botanist for the Bureau of Plant Industry at Washington. John Zedler, born in the Rhineland in 1864, an A. M., of Michigan in 1908, became Professor of History and Political Science at Albion and then Dean of the Morristown,

Tenn., Normal and Industrial College. William Frederick
Wunsch, Detroit born, and an A. B., of Michigan in 1908, became
principal of the New Church Theological School at
Waltham, Mass.
 Samuel Ottmar Mast, a Washtenaw county man whose
mother was a Staebler, took his B. Sc., from Michigan in
1889, and is Professor of Biology at Johns Hopkins University.
William E. Lingelback, who studied at Toronto, Leipsig and
Chicago, was Professor of History at the Michigan Military
Academy in 1908-09, and became Professor of Modern European
History at the University of Pensylvania. Ezra Jacob
Kraus, an Ingham county man whose mother was Catherine
Baumgras, took his B. Sc., in Michigan Agricultural College
and has been successively Professor in Oregon Agricultural
College, Syracuse University, and Wisconsin State University.
He did some earlier work in Mineralogy and Pharmacy
at Michigan. George Wells Knight is a Michigan A.
B., of 1878, who studied at Freiburg, Halle and Berlin, and became
Dean of the College of Education of Ohio State University.
Gustav Adolph Kleine, who left the U. of M. after
graduation in 1891, to study at Berlin and Tubingen, is Professor
of Economics in Trinity College at Hartford. Lyme
Frederick Kobeler, a Washtenaw county man whose mother's
name was Gomper, and who took his pharmacy degree in
Michigan in 1890, is Professor of Pharmacology and Materia
Medicine in Georgetown University at Washington.
 Frederick Eugene Wright, a Marquette man, studied in
the Real Gymnasium of Weimar and took his Ph. D. from
Heidelberg in 1900. He was instructor of Petrology at the
Michigan College of Mines (1901-1904), became Assistant
Geologist, and is associated with the United States Geological
Survey.
 Paul Frederick Voelker, Evart man by birth, became
President of Olivet College in 1920. Louis Ernest Schmidt,
who got his B. Sc., at Michigan in 1892, is a leading American
urologist. John Henry Schaffner, who was a Professor of

Botany at Michigan, is the head of the department of the same science at Ohio State University. Frederick Blackmar Mumford, a Moscow, Michigan, man who finished at Michigan Agricultural College in 1893, studied at Leipsig in 1900, and Zurich in 1901, and qualified for Director of Agricultural Experiment Station of Missouri, a place which he has held since 1909. Arthur B. Moehlman, a Wisconsin man who was made a Ph. D., of Michigan in 1923, is the statistical director of the Detroit school system.

Two Famous Engineers

George Henry Benzenberg, who graduated from Michigan in 1867 as a civil engineer, and who was made a Doctor of Engineering in 1912, was a national authority on water supply and sewerage disposal. He practically built the Milwaukee water and sewer systems. A similiar service was rendered the city of Detroit by Theodore A. Leisen, a German-American engineer of national standing, who designed and installed the filtration and water purification system which serves the city.

J. Harlan Bretz, an Ionia county man who graduated from Albion, is Professor of Geology at the University of Chicago. Bernard Hildebrandt, of Davison, in Genesee county, is astronomer of the observatory of the National University of Argentina. William Louis Eichenberg, who took his B. Sc. from Michigan in 1894, is Professor of Botany at the University of Kansas. Frank A. Ahrenveld, a Ph. D., of Michigan, is a consulting metallurgical engineer in Cleveland. Dr. Isadore Greenwald, Michigan B. Sc. of 1898, is biological chemist of the Harriman Research Laboratory of New York. Eugene Emil Felix Richard Haanel, born in Breslau in 1841, Professor of Science at Adrian College in 1866 and at Albion from 1868 to 1872, became Director of the Department of Mines of Canada, and the authority on electrothermic smelting of iron ore.

Thus there have gone out to the world from Michigan,

as contributors to the treasury of human knowledge in other parts of the world, a large number of German-Americans, some born within the boundaries of the state, some others educated in its schools, still others men of foreign birth who left part of their store of wisdom, or added to it, in Michigan. The names cited are far from all that are capable of inclusion in the list. They are recalled largely for the purpose of exemplifying the variety of contributions and the sources thereof.

CHAPTER XXVI

THE RELIGIOUS LEADERS

The Catholic Dioceses—Pioneer Catholic Missionaries.

The religious development of Michigan began with the first foreign arrivals. The earliest explorers were the French missionaries. They were in the territory of the Great Lakes in little more than a century after Columbus discovered America. They had the mission field all to themselves for a long period.

It is doubtful whether any of the pioneer missionaries were of German origin. Most of these were members of the Society of Jesus, and the Jesuits, at least those who came out to New France, were very largely men of French birth and training. When Michigan's part of the world was in the way of being colonized the French were the governing race, and the French Jesuits came across seas on missionary duty. The German Fathers of the Society were doing their work in other parts of the world. Work in America was also done by French Sulpician and Recollet priests, whose life work is written into the earliest history of the regions adjacent to the Great Lakes.

Historically the Catholic Church was the first organized system of religion whose influence was felt in the Northwest, to which the territory, which has come to be known as Michigan, belonged. That church has divided the state, for its ecclesiastical administration, into three dioceses. Of the Bishops who have ruled these, four personally represented the fruition of the efforts of an Austro-German missionary society, the Leopoldine Association, organized through the piety and assistance of an Austrian Archduchess, to send missionaries to the new lands, principally for the conversion of the Indians.

The Catholic Diocese of Detroit

The Protestant denominations were not regularly represented in Michigan until the early part of the nineteenth century. The Roman Catholic church was the first to attain its full ecclesiastical organization in the state, by the erection of the See of Detroit in 1832, the first incumbent of which, the Right Reverend Frederick Rese, was a Hanoverian by birth, who had achieved eminence in the work of his Church in Cincinnati. He resigned, went back to Europe, died in 1871, and is buried in Hildesheim. His immediate successor was Belgian-born, while his, in turn, the Right Reverend Caspar Henry Borgess, was a native of Addrup, in Oldenburg, born in 1824, who was brought to America by his parents in 1834. He was ordained and saw his earliest ecclesiastical service in Cincinnati. He was made Administrator of the Diocese of Detroit in 1870 and its Bishop in 1871, on Bishop Rese's death. Dr. Borgess' service to his church, apart from his spiritual activities, was most distinct in his putting the fiscal affairs of his diocese on an orderly basis and his development of higher education among his people. He was responsible for the founding of Detroit College by the Jesuit Fathers in 1877, an institution which has since grown into the University of Detroit. Bishop Borgess resigned his office in 1889. The ruling Bishop of the Diocese at the time of this writing, the Right Reverend Michael James Gallagher, was educated by German-speaking professors at Innspruck, in the Austrian Tyrol.

The Catholic Diocese of Grand Rapids

When the western part of the state was separated for ecclesiastical organization from the Diocese of Detroit, the

first Bishop chosen was the Right Reverend Henry Joseph
Richter, who was also an Oldenburger, born at Neuenkirchen,
in 1838. He was educated in Cincinnati and at the American
College in Rome, and after having been ordained a priest, was
long a university professor at Cincinnati. He became Bishop
of Grand Rapids in 1883. When Dr. Richter's age called for
assistance, he was given an Auxiliary Bishop in 1911, in the
person of the Right Reverend Joseph Schrembs, born in
Regensburg, Bavaria, in 1866, brought to America in 1877,
and educated at Laval University in Quebec. After a few
months service at Grand Rapids, Bishop Schrembs was appointed Bishop of Toledo, and in 1921 was made Bishop of
Cleveland. The present Bishop of Grand Rapids, the Right
Reverend Joseph Gabriel Pinten, was Michigan born, of German parents, Joseph Pinten and Anna Kloeckner, was educated in Rome, and was Bishop of Superior, Wisconsin, before his assignment to duty in his native state.

The Catholic Diocese of Marquette

As early as 1852 the Catholic authorities had provided
for an initial territorial ecclesiastical government for the
church in the Upper Peninsula, then the scene of much missionary activity. The authority over this territory was given
to the Right Reverend Frederick Baraga, a native of Austria, of German ancestry on the maternal side, who was appointed Bishop of an extinct see, and given the authority of
a Vicar-Apostolic in Upper Michigan. Later on he was appointed Bishop of the Diocese of Sault Ste. Marie, now
known as the Diocese of Marquette and Sault Ste. Marie,
an office which he held until his death in 1868. He was succeeded by his fellow-countryman, the Right Reverend Ignatius Mrak. Dr. Mrak was born in Laibach, Austria, educated
in the local gymnasium, ordained in 1837 by the Prince Bishop
Anton Aloys Wolf, and had been in Michigan since 1845, devoting his energies to the civilization of the Indians. He
accepted the episcopal office reluctantly, held it ten years, and

laid it down in 1879 to resume the work among his beloved Indians, whom he served in the neighborhood of Cross Village, in Leelenau County, until his eighty-first year. He survived his missionary activities two years.

His successor, in turn, the Right Reverend John Vertin, was a native of the same diocese of Laibach, Austria, in which his predecessor was born, and like Bishop Mrak, was of Teutonic ancestry. Dr. Vertin received his classical education at Dobelswert, in his native land. After his arrival in America, Bishop Baraga sent him in 1863 as a young student to St. Francis Seminary, Milwaukee, for training under the Rev. Dr. Joseph Salzman, the great Catholic ecclesiastical teacher of his time and of the west. Dr. Vertin was Bishop of Marquette for twenty years, when he died and was succeeded by the Right Reverend Frederick Eis. This ecclesiastic was a native of Arbach, near Coblenz, in the Diocese of Trier, Germany. When twelve years of age he was brought out to America with his family, who settled successively in Wisconsin, Minnesota and Upper Michigan. He was also a pupil of Dr. Salzman at Milwaukee until the civil war broke up the college course and he received the remainder of his education in the seminary of Joliet, Quebec. He spent twenty-nine years in missionary and pastoral work before he succeeded Bishop Vertin. In his episcopal career Bishop Eis, who was a man of wonderful physical vigor, travelled more than 200,000 miles in the Upper Peninsula on foot, on horseback and by rail in the course of his work, which he laid down by resignation in 1921, to be succeeded by the Right Reverend Paul J. Nussbaum, a native of Philadelphia, and the son of German parents. Bishop Nussbaum had been Bishop of Corpus Christi, in Texas, before he was transferred, to the Michigan scene of his duties.

Thus it is recorded that in the development of the Roman Catholic organization in Michigan two of the four Bishops of the Diocese of Detroit, three of the four Bishops of Grand Rapids and the five Bishops of Marquette and

IN THE MAKING OF MICHIGAN 241

Sault Ste. Marie were of German blood, birth or extraction. In addition, the area of Michigan produced a native-born Bishop for the Catholic Diocese of Nashville, Tenn., in the person of the Right Reverend Henry Joseph Rademacher, who was born at Westphalia, in Clinton county, in 1840, and who became Bishop of Nashville in 1883, succeeding later, by transfer, to the Diocese of Fort Wayne.

Pioneer Catholic Missionaries

The same proportion held good among the Roman Catholic clergy who served in Michigan in the days which followed the distinctively exploratory period. For instance, in the list of pioneer priests of the Northern Peninsula, the fondest memories cluster around the names of Francis Xavier Pierz, Francis Haetscher, August Kohler, George B. Weikamp, Martin Fox, Edward Jacker and Gerhardt Terhorst. Among the pioneers of the Grand Rapids diocese were Father, afterwards Bishop Baraga; Father Viscoczki, a Hungarian, who preached in German and English; the Reverend Matthias M. Mario, who came from Schellstadt, and who went back there to die; Ferdinand Allgeyer and Henry Beerhorst. John George Ehrenstrasser was an Innspruck man, who attended thirty-five missions in Western Michigan, and Joseph Schaeffer, a Redemptorist father, served in many places in 1860. Father Simon Sanderl was in the West Michigan as a missionary as far back as 1831, when he assisted Father Samuel Mazzuchelli, an Italian missionary to the Indians. He was with the Indians at Arbre Croche in 1833 to 1838.

Otto Skolla and Blasius Krake, who were priests of the Franciscan order, worked among the Menominee Indians out of Grand Rapids, in 1852, and later in 1881-1884, another Franciscan, Zephyrin Engelhardt, made a dictionary of the Menominee tongue and wrote linguistic treatises upon it.

Father Pierz was from Laibach, Austria, fruitful birthplace of so many Michigan religious pioneers. He was in

Cross Village in 1836 and at Arbre Croche in 1838, remaining there until 1852. He labored for thirty-eight years among the Michigan Indians, retiring in his eighty-eighth year and going back to Austria, where he lived to be ninety-three. The eminent Jesuit, Francis Xavier Weninger, made two missionary tours of Western Michigan, one in 1862 and the other in 1866.

Among the pioneer families whom these men served in Grand Rapids were some named Nachtegall, Schenkelburg, Hake, Klauber, Hause, Schickel, Hammerschmidt, Schiedel, Cordes and Wuerzburg.

Father Schilling was at Mendon in 1850.

In the Detroit diocese the earliest German priest was Martin Kundig, the hero of the cholera epidemic of 1834, who was the founder of the Wayne county poor-house organization, and the builder of the first German Catholic Church in 1833. His most eminent successors were Anthony Kopp, who came from Ruethen, in Westphalia; and Clemens Hammer, Peter Godez, Otto Skolla, Martin Hasslinger, Eugene Butterman, August Theodore Benedict Durst, who studied in Duesseldorf and Louvain; and John F. Friedland and Bernard J. Wermers.

The two last mentioned were outstanding men. John Ferdinand Friedland was a Saxon, born in Erfelt in 1833, who studied at Paderborn, Westphalia, and Louvain, and who began his work in Detroit in 1862. Bernard Joseph Wermers was a Westphalian, who also studied in Louvain and who came to Michigan in 1865, going first to Grand Rapids. His later activity was in Detroit. In the current clergy list of the diocese 32 per cent of the priests are of German birth or lineage.

IN THE MAKING OF MICHIGAN 243

CHAPTER XXVII

PASTOR LOEHE, OF NEUEDETTELSAU

The Foresight of Pastor Schmid—Antedated the '48 Movement—Other German Protestant Pastors—The Early Jewish Rabbinate.

The sources of the springs of influence, like those of their physical counterparts, are often hidden in faraway hills. A man who never saw America and an organization in Europe to whose management the state was only a patch on a map, had more to do with the settlement of people of German blood than either they or their progeny appreciate. The organization was the Basle Mission Society of Switzerland, an activity of the Lutheran church which was quite active in the very beginning of the nineteenth century. The man was a modest pastor at Neuedettelsau, Bavaria, by the name of John Konrad Wilhelm Loehe. He was a pastor as early as 1825. He lived in a period when the religious tenets of his own and the other divisions of the Christian church were being attacked by the materialists. He was a man of good learning from the schools. There is a tradition that he was a University man. Today he would be designated a fundamentalist in his theology.

The attacks upon the church aroused in him a determination to make its activity more vigorous and more effective. He preached against the assaults upon the foundations of belief and determined to do his share toward the cultivation of new fields in which the church might gain other spiritual dominion to offset that which might be lost in the older provinces of its kingdom. America, with its thousands of heathen Indians, offered to his mind the field for religious cultivation.

This program of mission work was not solely inaugurated by Pastor Loehe. The Basle Mission Society was working along the same lines, with this difference, that it had attempted its work by sending its men for work directly with the savages, much after the manner of the earlier Roman Catholic priests. The pioneers of this movement found that the Indians were too nomadic for this style of contact and advised the Basle Mission House that a better method was to organize small colonies of religious peasants, willing to take up life anew in a strange part of the world, with the double motive of doing better for themselves and of forwarding the mission enterprises.

It was at this stage that word was received in Basle from Heinrich Mann, who was already settled at what is now Ann Arbor, asking that a missionary be sent out to a small community of Germans which had settled there in 1829. So Pastor Frederick Schmid was sent out in 1833. He was 27 years of age, a native of Waldorf, in Wurtemburg, a student of the Mission House, and a man of great energy and youthful religious enthusiasm. He got into Ann Arbor in 1833, where he married Heinrich Mann's daughter, and began a missionary career that lasted for a little more than fifty years, during which time he founded two churches in Ann Arbor, fifteen in Washtenaw county, and many upstate. Incidentally, his son, Emanuel Schmid, graduated from the University of Michigan in 1854 and in 1856 became Professor of History at Ohio State University.

Pastor Schmid was a contemporary of Pastor Frederick Wyneken, of Fort Wayne, Indiana. Both appreciated the need of more missionaries and kept appealing for them. Pastor Schmid kept in communication with the Basle Mission House and with Pastor Loehe, of Nuedettelsau. He was an early advocate of colonization for church extension purposes, and he was ever writing for missionaries and colonists, particularly to Pastor Loehe, who was very devoted to the work. The latter gathered into his Bavarian home a few young men of religious aspirations and proceeded to fit them for the foreign ministry with as much fervor as any Jesuit master of novices ever exhibited to his potential Marquettes or Dablons. For William Loehe was, after his measure, a sort of Lutheran Ignatius.

The Foresight of Pastor Schmid

Pastor Schmid travelled far, for then, in his missionary tours. He had a good eye for land and he spied out many a fertile valley. In due course of time Pastor Loehe had another missionary's training finished, and this man, Friedrich August Craemer, who had learned English in England, was ordained and selected for the American mission. Lorenz Losel, a servant of Loehe, volunteered as a colonist. On April 20th, 1845, these men with thirteen other emigrants set out from Bremerhaven in a sailing vessel, the Caroline, arriving in New York June 8, and without delay they started to the Saginaw Valley of Michigan. Here Pastor Schmid had discovered the location on the Cass River which they named Frankenmuth.

Lorenz Hubinger, the elder, was the man of business of the group, a distinction in the community which later passed to his son, Lorenz Hubinger, the younger. The first winter was a hard one. The colonists cut the hardwoods and burned them in windrows to clear the lands. Next spring one hundred new settlers came. Within six years there were eighty families.

Thus began the virtual theocracy of Frankenmuth, of which more is written on other pages. Pastor Craemer, mindful of his mission, established a school for Indian children in 1846. He himself learned the Chippewa language. In 1847 a new Loehe-trained missionary, Emil Baierlein,

joined him in his work, and getting over to the Pine River, in
Gratiot County, in 1849, established Bethany Indian mission
there. In 1850 Pastor Craemer went to the theological seminary of his church at Fort Wayne as a professor. By 1852
Pastor Karl Augustus Wilhelm Roebbelen had three hundred
and forty-five communicants at Frankenmuth. There were
eight hundred and sixty in 1857 when Pastor Huegli took
charge. Pastor Roebbelen lost his health and went back to
Germany, dying in Baden.

In 1846 Pastor Loehe conceived the idea of a new colonizing group. He chose as its religious leader a candidate
in theology, Johann Heinrich Phillip Graebner. The group
had $4,000 in American money with which to buy land. They
arrived in New York June 1, 1847, came west to Buffalo by
rail and by water to Detroit. They consumed four days in
travelling from Detroit to the Saginaw country. There they
took up government land, founding Frankentrost.

A Hanoverian, Ferdinand Sievers, next offered himself
to Pastor Loehe for the American missions. A group of
sixteen families came out with him in 1848. They founded
Frankenlust, twelve miles north of Saginaw. In 1850 still
another Loehe-directed group of colonists, led by Pastor Herman Kuehn, was started out to found a new colony, Frankenhilf. All but one family passed no farther than Detroit, and in
the following year Pastor Deindorfer was sent out with reinforcements. In all, Pastor Loehe sent out a dozen missionaries, if Schmidt be counted as one of his. In addition to those named were Pastor John Heinrich Schwab, who
was sent out to help Pastor Schmid in 1836, and who went to
Monroe later; Pastors George William Haettstadt and Albert
Saupert, who took the neighborhood of Monroe as their field,
Haettstadt going to Adrian in 1847; Pastor Wilhelm Kremke,
who helped found Riga, and Pastor Heinrich Shaler, who was
established at Trinity Church, Detroit. Pastor Ottmar Cloester took on the Lutheran work in the Saginaw country in

1849, going from there in 1857 as a missionary to the Indians in Minnesota.

Antedated the '48 Movement

Most of these men and their colonists, it will be noticed by the dates, came to Michigan before the revolutionary movement had begun in the Fatherland, and its participants were scattered to the ends of the earth; so that they must be given due credit as pioneers of a German settlement in Michigan which was not a sequel of the '48 movement. When the revolution did occur, these out-posts of German settlement in America came into their own as pointers for the direction in which the newer exiles might journey.

Taken all in all, much of the Michigan settlement of the last mid-century traces itself back to the earnest clergyman 'of Neuedettelsau to whom it was never given to look upon America.

Pastor Schmid, from Ann Arbor, served a German Lutheran group in Detroit as early as 1833. He founded the St. John's Church of his denomination. Out of his activities and those of the Loehe-trained pastors of this communion in the middle '40's grew very much of the Lutheran foundation in Michigan. When to the names already are added those of Pastor Winkler, the first locally established Lutheran pastor in Detroit, and of Pastor John A. Huegli, the list of pioneer missionary pastors is pretty well completed.

Other German Protestant Pastors

Outside the Lutheran religious section of the early Germanic settlement of the State, there were a few adherents of the other Protestant organizations. There were also some German Jews. The German names that creep into the history of these denominations, while few, were of earnest men who did their share for the foundations of their respective churches. The Germanism of some of them was derived from the eighteenth century settlements on the Atlantic seaboard.

For instance, in 1825, the Rev. John A. Baughman, who was out of a German colony in Hereford County, Maryland, was a Methodist pastor in Nankin, and was transferred to stations all over Southern Michigan during many succeeding years. Bela Hubbard, of Detroit, an early explorer, was his son-in-law. In 1830, the Rev. Henry Colclazer appeared as a Methodist missionary in the Ann Arbor district. He was also out of the Maryland settlement. In 1837 the Rev. John Irkenbach was presiding elder of the same church in the district in which the southern tier of the state's counties were placed for the government of the church. Later on, the two famous Methodist preachers John Hood Jacokes, and Daniel C. Jacokes, were of German origin. Daniel Jacokes was admitted to Michigan conference in 1840 and John, who was sometimes called Thomas, in 1845. Both men became famous in the work of their church in Michigan. They were from Geneva N. Y., and their parentage was German.

In 1844 a mission Sunday School of this church was organized in Detroit, a layman named Charles Helwig, being in charge. He developed into an ordained pastor in 1846.

John Harris Foster tells of a German Methodist minister, the Rev. John H. Pitizel, who was in the Upper Penninsula in the '40's as a contemporary and friend of Bishop Baraga. Mr. Pitizel was a pastor in Tecumseh in 1836.

The first Free Will Baptist church in the state was organized near Ypsilanti in 1831. Its first elder and pastor was Henry S. Limbocher, from Monroe county N. Y., whose forbears spelled the family name "Limbacher." He planted churches in Calhoun, Jackson and adjacent counties. He is described as a man of limited education, of good presence, but with a poor preaching voice, and a most enthusiastic singer. Withal he was logical and argumentative in his speeches. He was a farmer and supported himself. As early as 1835 he, with two other associates, took a pronounced stand for an educated ministry and for denominational schools. Out of this beginning grew Michigan Central College at Spring

Arbor, the forerunner of Hillsdale College. Elder Limbocher raised a large share of the money for the foundation of this pioneer school. He was a trustee of Hillsdale until 1861. He removed to Kansas later on.

David Wirt, a German-ancestored clergyman from Canton, O., began preaching in Michigan in 1858. He was educated at Oberlin, but was put out of the Miami classis of his church, because he would not promise to preach and defend the Heidelberg Catechism as the word of God. He was a pastor at various times at Allegan, Lamont, Portland and South Haven, and then became a general missionary along the new line of the Northern Pacific Railroad in Dakota, Oregon and Washington. His sons and daughters went as missionaries to Siam.

Of the clergy of the Episcopal church, the Rev. James Selkrig, of German antecedents from Columbia county, N. Y., was pastor of the church at Niles in 1834. He also founded churches at St. Joseph and Michigan City. He finally gave up parochial work to become an Indian missionary in Allegan county. Rev. George Schetky, D. D., was rector of Trinity Church in Saginaw from 1874 to 1877. The Rev. Paul Zeigler, of a Detroit German family, was from 1885, and for nearly forty years onward a leading pastor, missionary and educator of the same church in the Diocese of Michigan. In 1871 the Episcopalian Church at Ontonagon was in charge of Rev. Dr. De Low, German born, and with a tradition of having been cut off by his Jewish parents when he joined with the Gentiles. Rev. William Frederick Faber, who was pastor of St. John's Episcopal Church in Detroit, 1905-1914, became Bishop of Montana in the last mentioned year. He was a Buffalo man of German ancestry, his mother having been Carolin Schoenthall.

Rev. William Hogarth was pastor of Jefferson Avenue Presbyterian Church in Detroit from 1858 to 1873.

The Jewish rabbinate in Michigan began its history in Michigan in 1854 when Rabbi Adler, Bavarian born, took up the work in Detroit which he carried on until 1861. Among his successors from then to now were several men of prominence in the councils of their own religious organization and in general scholarship. The early outstanding one of these was Kaufman Kohler, who was Rabbi of the Temple Beth El in Detroit 1869-1871. Rabbi Kohler was born at Furth, in Bavaria, in 1843, and was educated at Munich, Berlin and Leipsig, taking his doctor's degree from the University of Erlangen in 1869. He was called to Detroit that year, passing on to Chicago in the third year thereafter. He called the Rabbinical Conference of 1885 at Pittsburgh, at which the platform of the Reformed Judaism of America was adopted.

The Early Jewish Rabbinate

His writings on doctrinal and ethical topics were voluminous, ranging from his contributions as editor of the Jewish Encyclopaedia's department of Theology and Philosophy, through the field of scriptural criticism, Semitic studies, lectures and periodical publications, to "Jewish Theology Systematically and Historically Considered" (1917), which was an English version of his "Systematische Theologie des Judenthums Auf Geschichtlicher Grundlage." This he wrote some years before for the Berlin Society for the Promotion of Jewish Literature. Dr. Kohler was one of the first modernists among the Jews and the first American Rabbi to declare his belief in the historic existence of Christ, which he did in the early '70's. This caused quite as much controversy at the time as was the more recent one on the same subject by Rabbi Wise, of New York.

Dr. Kohler, in addition to his special fitness in the field of Jewish theology, was a devotee of Dante, and wrote at some length in exposition of the meanings of the Divine Poet. His son, Max James Kohler, born in Detroit, became a New York lawyer of prominence, a writer on the criminal law, and an interesting exponent of Jewish racial characteristics.

The Author of "Kassandra"

Rabbi Heinrich Zirndorff was Dr. Kohler's successor in Detroit. Dr. Zirndorf was a German poet and rabbinical scholar, born at Fuerth, Bavaria, in 1829. He died in Cincinnati in 1893. He was educated privately for trade, but his studies of German and English classics inspired him to continue studying them. At the age of nineteen, he went to Munich, where he attended gymnasium until 1855, and then to Vienna, where he devoted two years chiefly to poetry. Some of his best verse was written during that time, "Kassandra," a tragedy in five acts, being published at Vienna in 1856. In 1857 he obtained the position of Rabbi of Lipso-Szent-Miklos, Hungary, but soon resigned and moved to Frankfort-on-the-Main. In 1860 he published a selection of his poems at Leipsic, and in the same year he went to London as a private tutor. There he lived for thirteen years, writing and teaching, and mingling with the best society of the English capital. In 1873 he returned to Germany as rector of the Hebrew Teachers' Institute at Munster, and in 1876 accepted the rabbinate of Congregation Beth-El, Detroit. In 1884 he became Professor of History in the Hebrew Union College at Cincinnati. Dr. Zirndorf contributed to "Deborah," of which he subsequently became associate editor. In 1889 he was chosen Rabbi and preacher of the Ahabath Achim Congregation in Cincinnati, and held this position until his death.

Dr. Zirndorff was succeeded by Rabbi Louis Grossman, a native of Vienna, educated in the University of Cincinnati and the Hebrew Union College of Cincinnati, who served for several years, until he became professor of Theology, Ethics and Pedagogy at Hebrew Union College, where he taught until his death. He was a most voluminous writer on theological, anthropological and ethnological subjects, was the biographer and editor of the works of Rabbi Isaac Wise, and a devotee of the study of folk-lore. He exerted a very great influence in Michigan in the direction of creating tolerant opinion among religionists, a work which was continued by his successor, Rabbi Leo M. Franklin, himself the son of a German father, and for more than a quarter of a century the Rabbi of his congregation.

CHAPTER XXVIII

THE FIELD OF BENEVOLENCE

Irish Famine—The Deaf-Mute Institute—Borgess Hospital—Varied Public Benefactions of German-American Citizens.

In the field of philanthropic effort in Michigan German-Americans have not held aloof from their fellow-citizens but have been, generally, participants in such movements as have been going on. Distinctive contributions there have been, however. One of the earliest was the giving, in 1848, by what was at the time a small community of German-Americans in Detroit, of a substantial sum, for the relief of the Irish famine sufferers. The donation of the fund by which the German-American Seminary in Detroit was established was an attempt at racial rather than general benevolence.

In many places in Michigan the general public enjoys values derived from the largest philanthropies. At Menominee the public library was the gift of August Spies, a lumberman of much wealth. At Monroe the public library is housed in the older home of Dr. Edward Dorsch, a modest and learned physician whose outstanding quality was not wealth. At Ypsilanti the public hospital is a memorial to William Beyer, of German ancestry, and in his active career an Ohio steelmaker, who retired to the city which he made the beneficiary of this generosity. At Kalamazoo a hospital perpetuates the memory of Bishop Casper Henry Borgess, of the Catholic diocese of Detroit, who left the savings of his lifetime to continue the association of his name with good works. In Detroit the nurses' home of Providence Hospital is the donation of Frederick J. Fisher, a prosperous manufacturer of German antecedents.

In Menominee the public park of the city was the provision of John Henes, German born, who did well in the city which he benefitted. In Detroit Perrien Park, a square in the heart of a congested area of homes, testifies to the thoughful beneficence of Dominick Perrien, German miller of three decades ago; while a quarter of a million dollars was left by William C. Stoepel, of Detroit, in 1924, to provide additional play-ground area for the nerthwestern part of his home city. In the purely cultural field the family of John P. Fleitz, of Detroit, provided the marble high altar of the Catholic Church of Ss. Peter and Paul, and George Osius was responsible for the Schiller memorial. Maurice Black's monument is a library of commercial economics in the University of Detroit, and William C. Weber's contribution of valuable land was the deciding factor in the location of the Detroit Institute of Arts on the site which, in 1927, will be occupied by its newly completed structure.

In the field of charity Altenheim, an old peoples' home at Monroe; the German Protestant Orphans and Old Peoples' Home at Detroit; the Lutheran Children's home, at Bay City, and the Lutheran Deaf Mute Institute at Detroit are the benefactions of a group of German-Americans of a distinctive belief.

The Deaf Mute Institute

The last named institution has had an interesting history. It was not the pioneer institute in the state for the teaching of the deaf. That work had been inaugurated by the state, in its institution at Flint, as early as 1854. In 1874 Pastor Gottlieb Speckhardt was charged with the duty of establishing an orphan asylum for church dependents at Royal Oak. He was a mature young man, who was born in Friedberg, in the Grand Duchy of Hesse-Darmstadt, where he was well educated and where, before entering the ministry, he was a teacher of the deaf along the lines of early German systems organized for this work. His earlier American experiences were at Sebewaing, in Michigan, before his assignment to the foundation at Royal Oak, and at Sebewaing he undertook the education of two mute children of his parish. These he brought with him to Royal Oak and continued to instruct them there.

A change in the church policy of benevolence centralized the care of the orphans, leaving Speckhardt foot free to carry out a project of his own for the more extensive education of the deaf. One thing led to another, until finally he acquired means enough to start his institute at Norris, then a small place outside of Detroit, now within the city's boundaries. His means were limited, but by 1875 he was able to establish his school in adequate structures and began his work. Originally his educational subjects were taught by the oral or lip reading method, of which Pastor Speckhardt was himself a master, but with the development of the sign language, which was taken up by the National Deaf Mute College at Washington, the Institute began to use it as well, employing a special teacher from Washington, Miss Thompson, to develop instruction by this method. The Institute continues to the present day, having during the intervening years done a valuable and humane work for the silent by qualifying them for communication with each other and with those who were not afflicted like themselves.

The social side of the German group developed a good many benevolences through organizations of fraternal, co-operative and religious characters, the primary motives of which usually had engrafted upon them systems of sick and funeral benefits, which were of much service before the demands for them came to be the purposes of the commercial insurance organizations by which these earlier co-operative societies have been very largely replaced. Some survivals of these still remain, particularly in the cases of mutual fire insurance societies organized by the earliest agricultural groups. Examples of this class of survivals may be cited from the cases of the German Farmers Mutual Fire Insurance Company, of Washtenaw county, which has been doing business since 1859 and carries $15,000,000 of risks; the German Farmers Mutual Fire Insurance Company of Macomb; and that of Wayne County, organized in 1874, which has an equal volume of risks. The earlier fraternal societies have become largely merged with purely commercial insurance organizations or have gone out of business.

CHAPTER XXIX

THE PROFESSION OF MEDICINE

Dr. Anthon's Service at Detroit—Dr. Herman Melchior Eberts — Other Pioneer Physicians—The First Operator for Strabismus—Dr. Peter Klein—Dr. Herman Kiefer—Dr. Brumme and Dr. Carstens—Dr. Edward Dorsch—Dr. Michael Carl Theodore Plessner—Dr. John Flinterman and Dr. Spranger — The Discoverer of Podophyllin—The Early Work Horse Doctors—Pioneer Work.

All races and kinds of people have entered the learned professions in the modern period of the history of Michigan, among them, naturally, many German-Americans. The exiles from their fatherland at the close of the '48 rebellion were, in considerable number, of the student class, many of them graduates, the remainder well on the way to their degrees. These, generally, applied their trainings to their prospective life work in the new country to which they had come. The medical men and the engineers found a demand for their services in the fast-growing commonwealth of which they had become a part. The lawyers' lives were not cast in such pleasant places. Michigan was a common law state and the law men educated in German universities had been trained in the civil law and made more familiar with the Codex Justiniana than with the institutes of Sir William Blackstone or the theories of Chancellor Kent. The journalists, too, found a different institution in America from that with which they had been familiar in Germany. Theirs was an institution devoted to discussions of philosophy, of statecraft and of the more elevated topics of human discussion. The American institution, by the time they came on the scene, was becoming more and more devoted to narration than comment, to the news rather than to the editorial field. Therefore those Germans who came into the state with a journalistic training had to find expression for themselves in the first instance, at least, in German language newspapers and periodicals.

Of the four estates the medical men and engineers came into the country equipped to talk the universal language of their professions. The lawyers and the journalists were restricted to their own. This explains a good many of the results.

The Profession of Medicine

The medical profession began to be represented in Michigan almost at the beginnings of its provincial history. The original dispensers of physic and the practitioners of what used to be described as "chirurgerie" were brought in as attaches of the military establishment. So Dr. Eustace Chapoton, ancestor of a line that has produced other eminent disciples of Esculapius, came a little later than Cadillac; and, after him, some others to serve the fort and the troops when they were served at all.

When the British wrested control from the French, Gen. Henri Bouquet, was in command at Montreal. He, being a Franco-German Swiss, leaned to the German side of his ancestry, rather than to the French, with whom he had been in conflict. He selected Dr. Anthon to be the surgeon of the post at Detroit. For that matter, the selection may not have been entirely that of Bouquet, but of English officers at New York, who having Anthon on their hands as the results of an English privateering adventure on the high seas, were desirous of putting the evidence as far out of sight as possible.

George Christian Anthon was born at Salzungen, in Saxe-

Meiningen, August 25, 1734. His grandfather, John Caspar Anthon, was Rathsmeister of the town council. His father, George Michael Anthon, was a clergyman and a teacher in the town school for boys. His mother was Elizabeth Kramer. George Michael Anthon died soon after George Christian's birth, and his widow remarried, becoming the wife of John Gottlieb Baumhardt, a surgeon of Salzungen. Under Dr. Baumhardt as his first teacher, later under Dr. Kackel, at Gerstingen, and then at Eisenach, the young student qualified in medicine and surgery, and was examined and passed at Surgeon's Hall in 1750. Sixteen-year old surgeons were probably more usual then than they are now. At 20 he engaged as surgeon on a Dutch ship in the West Indies trade. This ship was captured by a British privateer, which brought its crew as prisoners and its cargo as booty into the port of New York in 1757.

Dr. Anthon's Service in Detroit

Anthon was rather too conspicuously important a young person to be just the kind of witness the English cared to have around at a time that the colonies were beginning to question the virtue and saving grace of British rule, so he was found a job in the colonial military service. He was made an assistant surgeon of the British in 1758 and sent to Detroit in 1760. He made a prompt complaint to Gen. Bouquet that the post was short of medical supplies. He got along famously with everybody, was a good liver and entertainer and bought a cask of sherry every year. Chief Pontiac made him a grant of land adjoining his village near Detroit. He returned to New York in 1764, was sent out west with Col. Croghan's expedition in 1765, and was promptly captured by the Kickapoo Indians at the Wabash. By 1767 he got back to Detroit, where he was made surgeon of the fort in Gen. Haldiman's time.

In Detroit he married Mary Navarre, who died childless and was replaced by a new wife, her niece Genevieve

Jadot, the widow of a young Lieutenant. Three of his children, two of them sons, were born in Detroit. George became a Lieutenant in the Navy and commanded a gun-boat in the war of 1812. John Anthon, born in 1784, became President of the New York Law Institute. In 1786 Dr. Anthon moved back to New York, where his sons Henry and Charles were born. Henry became rector of St. Marks-in-the-Bowery and held his place for 50 years. Charles Anthon became a most eminent Greek and Latin lexicographer and translator of texts, and was known to every youthful classical scholar of the last century.

Despite his brief training and early graduation Dr. Anthon seems to have been a man of much ability. He spoke English fluently and without accent, but had his troubles when he began to wrestle with the language in writing. He was one of the first to maintain that yellow fever was not contagious. He went to New York in 1786, bringing with him a comfortable fortune. He was there one of the Governors of the Lying-in-Hospital in 1802, and a leading member of the Episcopalian Church. He left an estate of $15,000 after having lost a considerable sum in an adventure in the China trade, and having lived up to his station as a gentleman so lavishly that it was noticed in his day.

It will interest his present-day brethren to know that on Sept. 10, 1772, General Gage sent a complaint from New York to Lieut. Col. Smith at Detroit that Dr. Anthon was charging too much for taking care of the Tenth Regiment.

Dr. Herman Melchior Eberts

The next doctor of German lineage to impress himself on the growing community of Michigan was Herman Melchior Eberts. There is no doubt of his Germanic ancestry, because it is traceable back to 1592, when his forbear, the Count Caspar Eberts, of Augsburg, was rewarded by Charles V., of Austria, for meritorious service rendered two years before against the Turks who had invaded Austria. The Count of the sixteenth century is described as having been skilled in medicine. His great-grand-son, Henry Joseph Melchers, was a doctor in Augsburg, a good deal of a social lion and a military man.

Of this Dr. Eberts, Herman Melchior Eberts was the son, born in 1753, achieving his license to practice in 1776, and almost immediately receiving an appointment as surgeon to the Hanau regiment of Hessians, which was sent out to America in the employ of the British. He arrived in America in 1777. Disliking the nature of the conflict into which he was introduced, he resigned at Quebec. He lived a while at Sorel and Boucherville, at which latter place he married Francois Huc, daughter of a French army officer. He got into trouble at Montreal, over an unauthorized autopsy on a young woman who died of a mysterious disease, which he and two of his fellow practitioners wanted to investigate, and had to run off to Detroit in 1791. Prior to that time he used the family name of "von Ebertz." This he changed to "Eberts."

For the standards of his day Dr. Eberts was a man of good professional education. He was a learned botanist and applied his knowledge to searching out the medicinal virtues of native herbs and roots, of which many appeared in his materia medica. In 1796 he became Sheriff at Detroit, by appointment of Gov. Winthrop Sargeant, holding for two years. In his official position he was accustomed to stage himself quite picturesquely, wearing a "billy-cock" hat, breeches and hose, a brocade vest and a velvet coat, the whole outfit backed up by a highly decorated sword.

He got along badly with his wife, who left him and went to a nunnery in Montreal. He had a home in Windsor later on, and when the war of 1812 came about he accepted a surgeon-majorship on the British side under Gen. Brock, his sons, John and Richard, being also commissioned officers who participated in the capture of Detroit. Another son, Henry, was an American soldier under Gen. Scott, and was killed at Lundy's Lane. He died March 14, 1819, at Windsor.

During his life-time he was a Lutheran. On his death-bed he became a Roman Catholic. He had been a member of Zion Lodge of the Masons, but the members thereof gave him the cold shoulder for his British sympathies during the occupation by Brock.

Other Pioneer Physicians

Dr. William Harpfy was surgeon of the British forces at Detroit when they evacuated in 1796. He retired across the river to Malden, or Amherstburg, as it is now called. Little is told of him except that he was German-born and German educated and was the owner of a harpsichord. With Harpfy passed out the last of the medical representatives of the old regime. Doctors who for the next thirty years kept Michigan people in good health or cured them when they were ailing were largely men of American birth and training from the east, earnest and well educated disciples of Esculapius who found a wide and promising field in the new West then opening up. Among these, naturally, were some scions of the German families which had early settled in New York, Pennsylvania and other of the original states. Some of them had a good deal of history and learning behind them. They were all of the "work-horse" doctor type, who rode their horses and carried their saddlebag supplies of physic over a vast territory.

In 1841, one of these, Dr. Philip Kephart, came to Berrien Springs, with his wife, Susanna Krimmel, whom he married in Somerset county, Penn., the year before. She had been sent back to Pennsylvania from her birthplace in Berrien county for a better education than was then available in Michigan. By way of showing the extent of operations in land in those days, Susanna Krimmel's father, who had come into Berrien in 1829 with his wife, Mary Lobengeyer, pre-empted 10,000 acres of land in Oronoko township. His son-in-law, Dr. Kephart, was of a family that had come to Pennsylvania in 1754. He was born in Tarrytown, Maryland, in 1807, and graduated from Baltimore, Memphis and Somerset County, Penn., whence he removed to Berrien Springs in 1840. In addition to his professional work he was the first village president of Berrien Springs and was associated with all the enterprises of the growing community. His practice was through the entire area of Berrien County. The form of his name indicated the variations of German names, "Kephart" being an ancient dialectical variant of "Gebhardt," which itself was a derivation of the Old High-German "Gebahard," contracted into a bi-syllabic form as the New High-German developed.

A queer contribution to the medical professional history of Michigan was Dr. Isaac Lamborn, a Quaker from Louden Co., Virginia, whose ancestors were German. He graduated from the University of Pennsylvania, taking medicine under Prof. Gibson, and later studied at William and Mary College. He preached for a while, was a stenographer in Washington during John Quincy Adams' administration and came to Michigan in 1830, undertaking a roving practice of medicine, which extended through thirty active years. He travelled the entire southwesterly area of Michigan, with Battle Creek as a center. He was active in the politics of his time, saw the hard side of life in his old age, and died in Cass County infirmary in 1873.

The First Operation for Strakismus

Dr. Joseph Tunnecliffe, Jr., of Jackson, born in Monroe in 1818, was the son of a German-American farmer, who came to Michigan earlier than that and then went back to Herkimer county, N. Y. His son graduated from Castleton Medical College, in Vermont, and came west again to Jackson in 1841, practicing there for some years, until he went to California. In 1852 he returned to Jackson, became surgeon of the Fourth Michigan Infantry at the outbreak of the civil war, and in 1863 became Military Agent of the state at Washington. In 1841 he performed the first recorded operation in Michigan for strabismus. He was so successful that it brought him prestige. He operated on 50 other cases in the following year.

There was an addition to the medical faculty of the state in the mid-century of a group of outstanding German physicians and surgeons who made a great impress, not only on their fellow-citizens, but upon medical education as well. In those early days access to the practice of medicine was gained through either of two avenues, formal instruction and graduation in the schools or tutorship under a preceptor actively engaged in the practice of the medical art. There were no examining boards or registration officers in those days, and it rested with the qualified practitioners themselves to keep the profession clean. To that end they organized in Detroit first, the Sydenham Society, and later the first Wayne County Medical Society. This group granted certificates of proficiency in medicine and surgery. The first modern German doctor whose name appeared on these documents was Dr. Klein.

Dr. Peter Klein

Peter Klein was a very early physician in the modern period of German-American settlement in Michigan. He settled in Detroit as a practitioner in 1846, fresh from the medical courses of King's College, Toronto, and Geneva, N. Y. College of Medicine. He came from Dormagen, on the Lower Rhine, where he was born in 1813. His mother and stepfather brought him across the ocean when he was 15, the trip taking 88 days. The family took up a farm near Buffalo. When he was 21 he studied medicine four years under a physician, practiced in Western New York, following this experience with two years of study in the institutions named. He was splendidly ethical, and was one of the earliest members of the Sydenham Association, predecessor of the Wayne County Medical Society, both organized by the regular practitioners of his period to maintain the integrity of medical ethics. Dr. Klein was an ardent Democrat, and his fervor brought him into the foundation of the Michigan Volksblatt newspaper in 1854, of which he was the editor. During the civil war, when past his fiftieth year, he was surgeon in charge of the Exchange Barracks of the federal army, which preceded Harper Hospital, Detroit, and left behind him a record of hard work among the wounded and disabled soldiers of the war who were returned to Michigan for treatment. Dr. Klein was a city physician of Detroit when that was a "thank you" job.

The Career of Dr. Kiefer

Herman Kiefer's professional training has been related in earlier pages in connection with his regency of the University of Michigan. He got into practice in Detroit in 1851, and was a founder of the German-American Seminary, of which he was president from 1861 to 1872. Later he was a member of the Detroit Board of Education. He was the distinctly representative German of his community, having been president of the Saengerfest of 1857, the Centennial of Schiller, in 1859; the Festival of Humboldt, 1869, and the Peace Celebration at the close of the Franco-German War in 1871. He was as ardent a Republican as Peter Klein was a Democrat. In 1854 he was President of the German-American Republicans of Michigan. In 1872 he was one of the Presidential Electors of the state, and in 1876 he was a delegate to the Republican National Convention which nominated Gov. Hayes, of Ohio, for the presidency. Taken all in all, Dr. Kiefer was one of the most distinguished citizens of Michigan of his period, regardless of race. He was an active practitioner until his old age.

Carl Conrad George Brumme began the practice of Medicine in Michigan immediately upon his arrival in Detroit in 1852. He was a Hanoverian, born at Gottingen, in 1817, and was the product of the schools of his native city. His grandfather had been a senator, a silversmith and church organist, and on the death of Dr. Brumme's father, became his guid-

ing spirit, determining for him a career in medicine. His
mother remarried, to a dentist, and young Brumme was apprenticed to his step-father for dentistry and surgery for
six years. He matriculated as a student of surgery in 1840,
and of medicine in 1842. In 1843 Prof. Edward Von Seibold
made him assistant physician, during his medical course, of
the Royal Lying-in-Hospital of his home city, a place which
he held until his coming to America. Dr. Brumme was a
particularly hard-working physician, especially among his
fellow-countrymen, during the early years of the German settlement in Detroit.

Dr. John Henry Carstens

John Henry Carsten's father was in prison when John
Henry was born in June, 1848, at Kiel, in Schleswig-Holstein;
for the father had been a revolutionist, which was a really
dangerous profession in Germany in those days, and especially so where those who professed were mature men. Somehow
or other the powers that were looked upon revolutionary
sentiments as being much more dangerous when entertained
by grown-up men than when they found lodgement in the
brains and enthusiasms of youngsters of the student age. So
it was for America for the senior Carstens and his brood, and
1849 found him in the Springwells part of Wayne County,
in Michigan, just opposite the military post of Fort Wayne,
which was then being constructed.

The elder Carstens was a pharmacist by profession, but
became a gardener on his arrival. One of the fruits of his
disturbance of the new soil to which he attached his fortunes
was the discovery of a quantity of Indian remains. He had
planted himself right on one of the Indian burial-grounds
which Prof. Henry Gilman later made famous by his reports
on the Springwells mounds to the Smithsonian Institute.

John Henry Carstens became a doctor at the Detroit College of Medicine, being one of its first products in this line,
and he plunged at once into all the phases of his profession,

including the teaching of his art. He was a fine surgeon, became a specialist on gynecology, and above all a splendid instructor. He lectured on almost every branch of his profession. The most constant reaction on the minds of his students, as they told of it in their years mature, was that he was a very honest teacher. He was not satisfied with the sum of medical knowledge at any period of his professional career, but was constantly advising the search after more of it. He was a continuous translator of medical literature from the German and the French, and his original writings were copied abroad in much volume. Dr. Carstens was a hearty and genial man, took an active interest in politics and earned the respect and affection of his community. He ran for Mayor of Detroit once, but, having none of the practical arts of the office-seeker, was defeated.

Dr. Edward Dorsch

A German-American doctor who was very useful to his adopted state, largely as an influence for culture, was Dr. Dorsch, of Monroe. Edward Dorsch was born in Bavaria in 1822, his father having been an attache of the court. In 1830 he was sent to a celebrated Catholic institute, where for many years he was the only Protestant pupil. He left in 1840, at the age of eighteen, to attend Munich University, graduating therefrom in his twenty-third year. By order of the Bavarian government he was sent to Vienna, to perfect his theoretical knowledge by actual practice in the hospitals. In addition he took up the study of philosophy, botany, natural history and kindred sciences. Being an active thinker and ready writer the government in power took offense at the tone of his articles, and in the spring of 1849, with a large number of others he was driven out, coming to America in the capacity of surgeon to the other emigrants.

He came to America, intending to settle in Detroit, but was diverted to Monroe by a friend. He arrived there in the fall of 1849, and practiced until his death in 1887. From his earliest citizenship he was a staunch Republican. In 1860 he was Presidential Elector from the Second District, on the ticket headed by Mr. Lincoln. He refused all local offices, accepting for one term an appointment on the state board of education. In 1868 he was appointed examining physician for the pension board, which position he held up to the time of his death. While pension examiner he prepared a draft showing the course and effects of a rifle ball on the human body, which was afterwards adopted and is still in use by the pension department.

Outside of contributions to magazines he published a book of poems in German, never translated, entitled "Hirten Briefe an Mein Volk". Critics speak in terms of the highest praise of his masterly handling of words, although they claimed that the thinker over-ruled the poet. His translations of the English poets into the German have called forth only the highest words of praise from the critics.

Personally Dr. Dorsch was of a retiring disposition. A careful student, generous to a fault, beloved by those who knew him, he had few intimates. His warmest and truest friends were his books. A connoisseur in art, he gathered a fine collection of artistic works, many of which were given by his wife to the library of the University. The family residence was also left to the city of Monroe for a library, called the Dorsch Memorial Library.

Dr. Michael Carl Theodore Plessner

Michael Carl Theodore Plessner was one of the pioneer physicians of the Saginaw Valley. He was a Prussian, born in 1813. His father, Henry Plessner, was a professor in the University of Breslau. He studied medicine from 1833 to 1837 at the University of Berlin, graduated as a Doctor of Medicine, and was immediately appointed surgeon of the Cholera Hospital, serving in and about Berlin for four years. He was next a Royal Officer of Health at Friedland and Stettin, successively. He was a revolutionist, with the usual sequel, and August 10, 1849, found him in Saginaw. He immediately entered into the affairs of his new home. In 1852 he was a Free-Soil advocate of Hale, but thereafter he was a Republican. He was a Justice of the Peace for eight years, Superintendent of the Poor for the same period, President of the City Board of Education for 10 years and a Presidential Elector in 1868, in the Electoral College which elected General Grant to his first term in the presidential office.

He was one of the early proponents of German immigration into Michigan and is credited with the composition, in German, of the "Emigrants' Guide to the State of Michigan" published by Commissioner Thompson in 1849. The occasion of his death, after 45 years active practice in Saginaw, was made the occasion of many public appreciations of his qualities as a medical man and a citizen.

Silas Farmer, the historian of Detroit, is the authority for the statement that Johnson and Priscilla Book, of Palermo, Ontario, the parents of Dr. James Burgess Book, of Detroit, were "both of German descent." Dr. Book was born in 1844, took his medical courses at Jefferson Medical College in Philadelphia, the Medical School of Toronto University and Guy's Medical School in London. He came into Detroit about 1855, built up a large practice and associated himself with both the Michigan and Detroit Colleges of Medicine, successively, as Professor of Surgery. In this capacity he made some delicate experiments on nerve stretching, then a new departure in medical practice. In 1882, at the Michigan College of Medicine and Surgery, he performed an operation involving the removal of Mechel's ganglion. It was the first successful operation of the kind in the west. He quit medical practice upon his marriage to the daughter of Francis Palms, a wealthy citizen, and devoted the latter years of his life to the care of the family fortune. His sons are leading capitalists of Detroit, engaged in carrying out a most remarkable improvement in the construction of edifices facing

Washington Boulevard, with the conception of which Dr. Book is credited.

Dr. Flinterman and Dr. Spranger

Johann Flinterman, who started a practice at Detroit in which he continued for 45 years following 1867, was born in Amsterdam in 1840, but was the son of German parents, Rudolph Flinterman and Margaretha Regenbogen. He got his primary education at Schuettdorf and Lingen, and studied medicine at Gottingen, where he was licensed and married, coming immediately to America and Michigan. He built up an enormous practice in all classes of professional work, and was a devoted and hard-working member of the professional societies. He was one of the originators of the Detroit Board of Health, a member thereof for several years and its president in 1881. He was the first apprentice of Schiller lodge of Masons.

Francis Xavier Spranger, who came to Detroit in 1862, was the pioneer disciple of Hahneman in the profession in Michigan, having been a graduate of the Homeopathic Medical College of Cleveland. He was born in Bavaria, given a classical education in Pennsylvania, and later studied medicine under practitioners, one of them being the noted Dr. J. M. Parks, of Cincinnati. His degree obtained, he established himself in practice in Detroit, where he was long the sole representative of his school of medicine. He had an immense practice and was constantly on the go. He once related that for a period of fifteen years his office prescriptions averaged seven thousand annually and his daily professional visits varied from thirty to forty per day. He was a devotee of music and excelled in performance on the zither.

The Discoverer of Podophyllin

Dr. John Kost got into Adrian in 1867 by his selection as Professor of Chemistry and Geology in Adrian college. He was an Ohio man, born in 1819, his great-grandfather having

IN THE MAKING OF MICHIGAN 271

been an emigrant from the Palatinate, and his grand-father, Michael Koss, a forage-master in the army of the Revolution. He began studying medicine when he was sixteen, under Drs. McGowan and Tuttle, of Coshocton, O., was licensed to practice, leaned toward the eclectic school, started a program of reform in medicine, became Professor of Materia Medica and Therapeutics in the University of Cincinnati, and published books on these subjects and upon the theory and practice of medicine. The latter were translated into German and circulated abroad. During this period he was also a professor for some months of each year, in the Medical College of Worcester, Mass. He left Adrian in 1867 to become President of Marshall College, in Illinois, but returned to Adrian, where he retired. He was a minister of the Methodist Church for 35 years, serving irregularly in this capacity.

He was the discoverer of several alkaloids and resinoids which have found their places in Materia Medica. Among these there is claimed for him the extraction of podophyllin from the mandrake root, which he exhibited to classes at Worcester in 1848, and in Cincinnati in 1849, before any other claimant to the discovery had asserted himself.

The Early "Work-Horse" Doctors

Dr. Charles C. Dillenbaugh, whose father was a doctor also and a native of Switzerland, made an early occupation of Clinton county in a professional way, settling there in 1863, after a year's study at Michigan, another at Buffalo, and six years experience in the Erie County Hospital. He was 13 years at Westphalia and then went to Portland, in Ionia county. He was one of the old-fashioned general practitioners, whose work carried him over the territory of several counties. Although not of their faith and a Mason, he got along famously with the Bavarian Catholics of Westphalia, whose professional stand-by he was for a generation.

Among the early practitioners of Ionia county was Frederick Gundrum, born in Pirmasens, in the Bavarian Palatinate, in 1843. After an experience in Indiana, where he learned English and read medicine for three years privately, he attended Michigan University for one year and Miami Medical College for another, and graduated in 1868. He immediately went into practice at Ionia. He made a good reputation as a surgeon, and, like Dr. Dillenbaugh, was called upon to traverse a wide area in his practice. His brothers, Godfrey and George, of the same birth, were pharmacists during the same period in Ionia, George Gundrum later being president of the State Board of Pharmacy.

C. N. Ege was the county physician of Wayne in 1844 and Henry Lemcke in 1845 and 1846. Peter Klein held the position in 1848, 1851, 1854 and 1855. One of their contemporaries in practice was Dr. Brockhauser.

By the early '60's there was a good sprinkling of German medical men in Michigan. Besides those already named in Detroit there were Charles A. Hanmer, George Huenert, M. J. Klein, S. Joseph Merendorff, Carl Otto, Edward Schroeder, Casper Schulte, Edward Steeger, Heinrich Thuener and Benjamin Rudolph. In Grand Rapids Eugene Mainhan was in practice; in Saginaw Theodore Crouse, J. J. Lutze and Franz Massbacher; in Bay City, F. W. Walthausen and Charles Kindemann; in Jackson Drs. Schott and Selphe; in Ann Arbor Carl Rominger, Conrad George, J. Krapp, and Bernhardt Hesse. Henry Geissmar practiced at Belle River; Dr. Rinehardt, at Pontiac; Edgar Hamm at Danville; M. D. Senter at Eagle River; Wilhelm Godeke at Leland; Dr. Lewis Kleine at Midland; Dr. Felke at Cedar Rapids, Franz Schott at Marshall; Dr. Laukenstein, at Grand Rapids; and Edward Dorsch at Monroe. Dr. Dorsch was a man of great brilliancy, and his library is part of the collection of the University of Michigan.

Among the later additions to the medical faculty of the state from German scources was Dr. Karl A. Kanzler, who came to the state in 1884, settling first in Saginaw and later in Detroit. Dr. Kanzler was a Bavarian, a native of Munich, who took his first training in medicine at the University of his native city, where he received his degree and where he was for a time a demonstrator of anatomy. He supplemented his studies at Munich by further work at the Universities of Berlin and Strassburg. Dr. Kanzler died in Detroit in 1920. His son became vice-president of the Ford Motor Company.

Pioneer Work of the German Physicians

These were the pioneers who made the way a little easier for those who followed, and who in addition to individual service, assisted in the attack on the conditions which threatened to delay settlement. They were all in the early battle against malaria, the bane of an undrained state. Some of them were in the battle against cholera. They had their full share in the recurrent campaigns against small-pox. Later some of them were pioneers in the early contests against tuberculosis and cancer.

They had worthy successors. In the current lists of the medical profession hundreds of names are borne by practitioners of German birth and ancestry. Besides these a considerable number of the earlier and later members of the profession have derived some of their knowledge from courses of instruction or post-graduate attendances at the German and Austrian universities. One of the earliest and best beloved of these was David Osborne Farrand, of Detroit, of pious memory among the remnant of the older generation of his city. After graduating in literature in Michigan, Dr. Farrand took his medical training in Munich. One of his associates, who was studying pharmacy at the time and who finished his medicine at home, was Dr. Samuel P. Duffield, who was the founder of the pharmaceutical industry in Detroit. In the practice of his profession in his home city during his short life—he died at forty-nine—Dr. Farrand was literally the slave of the poor. His devotion was compensated by their trust and affection, frequently by little else.

To enumerate the medical men of Michigan who have received the whole or a part of their training in German and Austrian schools would be to leave the field of narration for an excursion into that of professional biography; and at the same time, it might, by inclusion or exclusion, furnish a sufficient basis for complaint of improper valuations of the work of the professional men who now serve the afflicted.

IN THE MAKING OF MICHIGAN 275

CHAPTER XXX

THE PROFESSION OF LAW

George Morell—The Abels—John Van Armin—Otto Kirchner—Franz Christian Kuhn—Edwin F. Uhl—Early German-American Advocates.

During the history of the state many citizens of German birth or extraction have attained judicial office. In 1887 Emil Glaser was Probate Judge of Delta county. In 1889 the first German-American Judge of the Wayne Circuit Court was George Gartner. The following year Morse Rohnert and William Look were on the same bench. In 1912 George E. Weimer became Judge of the Kalamazoo Circuit. In 1922 Adolph F. Marschner and Theodore J. Richter were added to the Wayne bench.

There were not many German lawyers in the early history of the settlement of their race in Michigan. A good many men came from abroad with a legal training in the German universities, but they were trained in the civil law rather than the common law, and few of them pursued their profession under the new conditions. Otto Roeser, for instance, who came to Saginaw in 1849, with as full an equipment in the law as a young man of his age might get, turned to farming, and accomodated his neighbors by being a justice of the peace. He was typical of a considerable group. Some of them advanced to the stage of being legal "handy men," who gave counsel and drew papers, but no great number took the bar.

The first lawyer of German extraction, and that rather remote, who made his impress upon the law of the state was George Morell. He was one of the Judges of the United States Court for the Territory of Michigan from his appointment in 1832 until Michigan became a state in 1836. In that year he became Associate Justice of the Supreme Court, and in 1842 its Chief Justice. He was a Massachusetts man, his ancestry derived from a family that left France at the time of the Edict of Nantes, living in Germany for some generations, and finally getting into New England. He was a Williams College man, a lawyer of some importance and a common pleas judge in the east before he was appointed a judge in the west. He died in Detroit in 1845.

Arnold Kaichen came to Detroit in the '50's after having taken a law course in Germany in the University of Giessen. He achieved prominence at the Detroit bar and in politics. Prior to his death in 1873, he had been for four years United States Land Agent for Michigan and for eight years United States Pension Agent.

There were some early German-American lawyers upstate. Among the first members of the bar of Washtenaw county was Sylvester Abel, a descendant of the early settlement of Ann Arbor. Julius Caesar Abel, believed to have been Sylvester's brother, was the first practicing lawyer in Kent county, settling in 1834. In 1843 he was attorney for the defense in Kent county's first recorded murder trial. He was a self-made lawyer, and did some land surveying. He died in 1871. In 1851 John Van Armin, of mixed Dutch and German ancestry, was a lawyer in Kalamazoo. He was then considered the ablest Democratic campaigner in the state. Later on, as a practitioner at Chicago, he achieved great prominence as a criminal lawyer. John Van Armin was a Michigan soldier in the Black Hawk War, and was Captain of a company recruited for the Mexican War which never got into action. In the middle '60's John H. Kimboldt was in practice at Eaton Rapids, Peter Koch at Grand Rapids, James B. Gott at Ann Arbor, Emil Anneke at Lansing, J. F. Stuch at Allegan, and G. M. Bachman at Adrian.

Otto Kirchner

The two most prominent lawyers of the race in Michigan's earlier legal history were Otto Kirchner and Franz Christian Kuhn. Mr. Kirchner's legal training is set forth in these pages in connection with his teaching of law at the University of Michigan. He was a young Prussian whose first opportunities were gained at Lansing, while a clerk in the office of his uncle, Emil Anneke, who was Auditor-General from 1863 to 1866. Mr. Anneke was also from Prussia, and had received a training in the law, was rather active in politics and practiced some in Grand Rapids and later in the Saginaw Valley. Later Mr. Kirchner studied law in Detroit, and made his first adventure as a practitioner as the associate of Walter Elliott, another youngster who deserted the law for the priesthood and became prominent in his church work.

Mr. Kirchner was active in politics and became Attorney-General, serving from 1877 to 1880, inclusive, during the administration of Gov. Croswell. Later he practiced alone. He was exceedingly well grounded in the law and was very thorough. As counsel for the state he initiated the proceeding for Gov. Pingree which led to the surrender of nearly all the special charters of the railroads granted in the early days of the state's history, bringing them under the general law, and eventually under the ad valorem system of taxation. An example of his thoroughness is found in his preparation for a mining case involving a large interest in a Michigan copper property. Prior to the trial of the case he spent nearly a year at the Massachusetts Institute of Technology in preparation on the technique of the industry. With this equipment he won his case, and with it the largest law fee paid up to that time to a Michigan practitioner.

Franz Christian Kuhn, Detroit born and Mt. Clemens raised, studied law at Michigan, graduating in 1894. He was appointed Attorney-General in 1910, was subsequently elected to the same office, and in 1912 was appointed to the Supreme Court of the state to succeed Mr. Justice Blair. He was elected in the same year, and resigned in 1919.

Edwin F. Uhl

Edwin F. Uhl, a great lawyer whose career was largely in Grand Rapids, was of mixed Dutch and German ancestry, from Avon Springs, N. Y., where he was born in 1841. His father was of German descent, his mother a De Graff, of an ancestry reaching back to the Dutch settlers. Both were born in Duchess Co., N. Y. The family moved to a farm near Ypsilanti in 1844, and in 1862 Mr. Uhl took his A. B. from Michigan. He was Prosecuting Attorney of Washtenaw county in 1871 and 1872, and in 1876 he moved to Grand Rapids, where he achieved great professional success. He was one of the leading Democrats of the state, was Mayor of Grand Rapids in 1890, and during the administration of President Cleveland became Assistant Secretary of State. He was later made Ambassador to Germany by Mr. Cleveland. Mr. Uhl's daughter married Earl D. Babst, Ohio born man whose maternal ancestry was German, who graduated in law from Michigan in 1894, practiced in Detroit with Otto Kirchner until 1904, later became President of the National Biscuit Company, and later still, President of the American Sugar Refining Company, being at present Chairman of the Board of the latter company, with his residence in New York.

Contributions to Other States

Quite a few Michigan born and Michigan trained men of Germanic extraction achieved excellence in the law in other parts of the country. Among them were Franz Chadbourne Eschweiler, an upper peninsula man who graduated from Michigan in law 1886, and became a Justice of the Supreme

Court of Wisconsin. William Andrew Holzheimer, Saginaw man out of Michigan in 1898, became a District Judge in Alaska. Theodore Brentano, Kalamazoo born in 1854, was sent to Germany to be educated and became a Judge of the Superior Court of Chicago and Minister to Hungary in 1922. John Jacob Lentz, famous Ohio Congressman and Democratic leader, was a Michigan law student of 1882. Obadiah Gardner, born in Port Huron in 1852, and whose mother was Maria Strebils, of a German family in St. Clair county, went east, practiced law and became, as a freak of politics, a Democratic Senator from Maine. After his retirement he was made a member of the International Joint Commission, and in that capacity laid the foundation of facts for the Great Lakes-St. Lawrence Waterway proposition.

Henry Herman Rolapp, born in Flensburg, educated in a German realschule, came to Michigan, studied law and went to Utah, where he is a Justice of the Supreme Court.

William Kettner, John Kettner's and Fredericka Lang's son, from Ann Arbor, became a lawyer and a congressman from the San Diego, Cal., district, from the Sixty-third to the Sixty-Sixth Congresses.

Frederick W. Kerner, a Karlsruhe man born in 1829, came into the state with an old country legal education, but the lure of military life attracted him and he joined up with Gen. Scott's forces in the Mexican War, followed up by enlistment in the regular army, and was a soldier of the Civil War. After its close, he practiced for 21 years at Jackson.

Daniel P. Sagendorph, of Charlotte, a noted up-state lawyer, was the son of Jacob Sagendorph, who was himself of German parentage and who lived in Columbia county, N. Y., in 1840, where his son was born. He was a prohibitionist candidate for office in 1870. Daniel Striker, of Hastings, another well-known Michigan lawyer, was out of a Wayne County, N. Y., German descended family.

William Purdy Yerkes, who was admitted to the bar in

Pontiac in 1843, and began practice in Detroit two years later, was twice elected Probate Judge of Wayne County. He was descended from a Hanoverian family of German extraction.

In the current generation of lawyers in Michigan so many German-Americans are at the bar that it would be obviously impossible to enumerate them or attempt to compare their excellences in their profession.

CHAPTER XXXI

THE PROFESSION OF ENGINEERING

The Early Surveyors—A Descendant of Muhlenburg—A Developer of Hydro-Electric Power.

There were many Germans who came into Michigan with a knowledge of engineering, some of its confined to land surveying. Joseph Wampler, Deputy Surveyor-General of Michigan in 1816, was an itinerant Methodist minister of German extraction from Tuscarawas county, Ohio. He is known to have subdivided towns on Ranges 10 and 11 in Oakland County. There is a Wampler Lake in Jackson County named after him. In 1831, Utter Brink surveyed that part of Wayne County which is now Wisconsin. He was a brigade officer in the Michigan contribution to the Black Hawk war. In 1821 a young Ohio German surveyor named Hester was assigned to the survey of ten townships between Flint and the Cass River. The surveyor who first reached the Tobacco River in the Saginaw country in 1829 for the purpose of subdividing the townships found some town corners that had been marked by an earlier surveyor, Samuel Steinbrook, who had surveyed the meridian and the correction lines. Steinbrook later was a surveyor in Oakland county, as one of a group including William Broockfeld, who surveyed 5,400 miles of town and section lines in Michigan territory, including areas in Livingstone, Lenawee, Jackson, Calhoun, Midland, Bay and Genesee counties. Philip Bigler surveyed the road from Saginaw to Kawkawlin in 1829. Later on Ferdinand Diechman, a Westphalian, who settled in Saginaw in 1849, laid out a good deal of the land in Saginaw and Tuscola counties. Lewis Leffler, born at Frankfort-on-Rhine in 1811, settled in Kochville and did land surveying in Saginaw county in 1849 and 1850. In 1860 one of the party that laid out the plank road from Bay City to Saginaw was Christopher Heinzman.

In the survey of the lakes several German-American names appear. To begin with, the first suggestions for a comprehensive survey were made in 1838 by Col. John Abert, chief of engineers, who was of German ancestry, and was a West Pointer of 1811. His son, James William Abert, was actually engaged on the survey in 1843-1844. A preliminary survey of the coast of Lake Huron was made in 1833 under the direction of a Lieutenant and two cadets from West Point. The Lieutenant was Samuel P. Heintzleman, afterward a distinguished General in the civil war. The largest amount of the lake survey work was done under the direction of Gen. C. B. Comstock, but it was completed under the direction of Col. Godfrey Weitzel in the late '60's and the '70's.

A Descendant of Muhlenberg

Among the men who made part of their careers on the survey of the Great Lakes was Lieut. Lewis Muhlenburg Haupt, a descendant of the original Muhlenburg family, who having graduated in 1867, was an engineer officer in the survey until 1869, with his headquarters at Detroit. He was then just out of West Point, and later made a great name for himself as a teacher and consultant. He devised a plan for saving eroded beaches from the action of the sea, thereby preserving several ocean pleasure resorts, and saving Barnegat light, off the coast of New Jersey, from destruction by the elements.

The great cartographer of the service at Detroit during fifty years was Edward Molitor, a Wurtemburger. As the work progressed and its various charts were reduced to form they were send to Baltimore for reproduction by Julius Bien, a German lithographer who had set up his establishment at that city, largely for the production of government work of this character. For years Mr. Bien was alone in the country in his ability to produce lithographic and copper engraved maps of the quality required by the government standards. Mr. Molitor's son, David Albert Molitor, born in Detroit in 1866, achieved distinction in his profession by service with the United States army engineers, under General Orlando M. Poe, on canal and channel work at Sault Ste. Marie, as designing engineer on the Panama Canal project and as a Professor of Civil Engineering at Cornell University from 1908 until 1911. Edward Molitor's nephew, Frederick Albert Molitor, also Detroit born in 1868, became a civil engineer, specializing in railroad work, and was the railway expert for the United States Government in the Philippine Islands during 1906, 1907 and 1908. Clemens Schauroth, a civilian engineer employe of the service during many years, was partly responsible for the drainage of the marshes on the Detroit river south of Detroit and their reduction to the purposes of industry.

Lieut. Lugenbeel, who was stationed at Fort Gratiot, and who later became a major-general in the army, also did some engineering work for the government in the Michigan field.

Montgomery Meigs was a Michigan man who owed his eminence in engineering to German teachers. His father, General Meigs, of the army, was building Fort Wayne, at Detroit, when his son was born in Detroit in 1847. At the age of 20 he was sent to the Royal Polytechnic School of Stuttgardt. As a youngster in the profession he helped survey the Northern Pacific Railroad and later became the engineer on the power and navigation development of the Mississippi river in the neighborhood of Keokuk.

Hermann Kahlman, German born, an engineer on railway construction in the old country, gained a Missouri record in the civil war which mortises in with those of Stifel, Siegel, Osterhaus and Hassendeubel, came to Michigan as one of the government river improvement engineers, and had to do, during his active career, with the development of the Lime Kilns Channel at the westerly entrance of Lake Erie and the ship canal across Lake St. Clair. He was also the inspector of materials entering into the Weitzel Lock of St. Mary's Falls Ship Canal. In his later years he designed and built the first bridge between the city of Detroit and the Belle Isle Park in Detroit river. In the Light House Service Commander Samuel P. Heyerman, Prussian born, and with a fine civil war naval record, was for long Superintendent of the district which had the Great Lakes in its care.

A Developer of Hydro-Electric Power

Among the engineers to whom Michigan owes a considerable of her growth, traced through the results of the construction of the canal at the Falls of St. Mary's River and the foundation of the water-power industry at Sault Ste. Marie, was Hans August Evald Conrad Von Schon, a native of Prussia, a graduate of the Royal Prussian Academy of Berlin, a Sub-Lieutenant in the Third Rhenish Infantry, 29th Regiment, in the Franco-Prussian war, and almost immediately thereafter a practitioner of engineering in the United States. He is accountable, as engineer adviser to the state of Alabama, for the earliest accurate estimates of the water power values of Muscle Shoals and the Warrior river. Mr. Van Schon was in general civil engineering until 1891, when he became connected with the United States Engineering Corps, having to do with construction of the locks at St. Mary's Falls. From 1897 to 1902 he was chief engineer of the Lake Superior Power Company, which constructed a hydro-electric power at the Soo, the effective work of which created the carbide industry at that place. He had considerable to do with the development of the ambitious iron and steel industrial projects of Francis H. Clergue on both the American and Canadian sides of St. Mary's River, and later devoted himself to general consultancy in hydro-electric engineering. Among his creations is the water supply system of Highland Park, Michigan.

CHAPTER XXXII

THE PROFESSION OF ARCHITECTURE

William Himpel—Frederick Spier and William C. Rohns—Albert Kahn —Louis Kamper—Emil Lorch.

In the contributions to architecture in Michigan some of the German-American practitioners of the profession were prominent. As a matter of fact there was little early architecture in the state. Such important building as was done was planned by the builders themselves, except in rare cases. Father Gabriel Richard is credited with designing old St. Anne's church in Detroit, and Robert T. Elliott and Alphaeus White, two Irishmen trained in engineering, are given credit for some early Catholic churches. It was not until the generation of Gordon W. Lloyd, James Anderson, Mortimer L. Smith and their contemporaries in formal architecture that the profession came into its own in the state.

The first costly public building in the state was the present State Capitol at Lansing. It was designed by Elijah W. Myers, a Springfield, Illinois, man with a remote German ancestry, who finally settled in Detroit. Myers had a genius for designing acceptable public buildings, coupled with a good bit of political ability in getting the commissions in charge of their construction to accept his plans. He designed, in addition to the Michigan State Capitol, similar buildings for Texas and Colorado and a rather costly courthouse for Stockton, California.

In the '70's William Himpel, a New York architect who

was an accomplished renderer of modern construction in the Gothic forms, designed St. Joseph's Catholic church, in Detroit, said to be one of the best Michigan examples of pure Gothic wholly wrought in stone, and St. Andrews Cathedral in Grand Rapids. Later, when the spire was added to St. Joseph's church, the design was carried out by John M. Donaldson and Henry Meier, the latter a German-American architect of much distinction. Peter Dederichs, German born and German trained, practiced architecture in Detroit for many years, designing St. Albertus church for the pioneer Polish Roman Catholic congregation.

As a matter of fact there was not enough money spent on construction in the earlier days in Detroit to warrant good architectural talent being employed, and, in addition, a good deal of the designing of public work was left to the engineers. In the '80's there was a change in conditions. Fortunes had been accumulated and monumental building, such as it was, came into favor as a form of investment. Cyrus W. Eidlitz, a New Yorker whose name indicates his ancestry, designed the Michigan Central Station in Detroit which preceded the one built in 1910.

Later on Frederick Spier and William C. Rohns, German-born and German-trained, made it known that railroad stations could be structures of beauty as well as utility, and designed the Michigan Central Railroad's Stations at Ann Arbor and Niles, working them out in the favorite building material of the period, Lake Superior red sandstone; and for the Grand Trunk Railway they designed the stations at Battle Creek, Durand and Lansing. All of these buildings retain their style and adaptability to the present time Later on, in 1891, the same architects designed the first important steel frame building for Detroit, for the Chamber of Commerce of the city. They had many original problems to work out in the matters of foundations, wind-bracing, distribution of light, adequate mechanical equipment for heating, artificial lighting and elevation, which they did very well. Meantime other architects of German birth or extraction did much private work of lesser pretense and cost, among them Julius Hess, Richard Raseman, and Gustav Mueller. The latter, prior to the legal banning of the brewing industry, was a specialist in the construction of buildings for its purposes, but he designed many other structures as well. His excellence lay in the field of ornament, of which he is a master. Among his more pretentious pieces of design is that, yet to be carried out, for a civic center for the city of Fordson, one of the seats of the Ford motor car industry. Mr. Mueller's most distinguished creation in public architecture is the Hurlbut memorial gateway at Detroit Waterworks Park.

A great deal of the work, of these German-American architects, as well as that of their American contemporaries, was wrought into actuality by German-American builders of prominence, of whom Albert A. Albrecht and Henry Spitzley were types.

Albert Kahn and Louis Kamper

In the most recent constructional period in Michigan German-born architects practicing their profession in the state have stood up well with their brethren in the profession. Of this modern group easily the most prominent have been Albert Kahn and Louis Kamper. Kahn was born at Rhaunen, in Westphalia, in 1869, received a public and partial high school training in his native land, was brought to America in 1881, and was educated in Michigan schools. In 1890 and 1891 he held a traveling scholarship for study abroad and in 1904 engaged in the practice of his profession at Detroit. The list of his creations of the modern type is very lengthy. The buildings of the Detroit News and Detroit Free Press, the Detroit Athletic Club, the Temple Beth El, in Detroit and the Michigan University Hospital are among his most striking works in the field of public buildings, while in the commercial and industrial field the Burroughs Adding Machine, Packard Motor Car, Hudson Motor Car, Ford Motor Car and Lozier

Motor Car factories in Detroit were revelations of style introduced into the housing of manufacturing organizations. With his brother, Julius Kahn, born at Munstereiffel, Germany, in 1874, and who has been Albert Kahn's associate, he developed the use of reinforced concrete in building and the design of steel reinforcing material to a high degree, most of their work incorporating the newer structural resources into its construction. Julius Kahn has had, in addition to his architectural engineering experiences, a brilliant career in general engineering, serving in the United States Navy as a civil engineer, later on the United States Engineering Corps and from 1900 to 1903 as chief engineer of the sulphur and iron mines of the Futuyami Shokai, of Tokio, in Japan.

Louis Kamper, who was born in Rheinphaltz, Bavaria, in 1861, was educated in the German technical schools before he came to America at the age of 21, and began his architectural career with McKim, Mead & White, of New York. He came to Detroit as the associate of John Scott, in 1888, and began to practice alone in 1890. His first piece of notable work was the residence of Col. Frank J. Hecker, in Detroit, then a most striking example of ornate domestic work. He planned the Michigan building for the Buffalo exposition, designed Providence Hospital and the rebuilding of St. Mary's Hospital in Detroit, and the Roseland mausoleum, the largest in the country and the subject of much favorable comment. His recent work has been almost wholly in connection with the building projects of the Book interests of Detroit for whom he has created the Cadillac Square Building, the Book-Cadillac Hotel, the Book Building, the Industrial Bank Building, the 1200 Washington Boulevard building, and the Book Tower, the last mentioned of thirty-five stories; and he is engaged, at the time of this writing, on a second Book Tower, which will be more than eighty stories in height, and which is to be the tallest structure ever erected in the world. Besides these. Mr. Kamper, whose son, Paul Kamper, is his present associate, has designed important buildings erected in other parts of the United States.

Emil Lorch, Detroiter born of German parents and Michigan educated, has made a most important contribution to the advance of the profession as the head of the School of Architecture of the University of Michigan.

Louis Mendelsohn, later in life famous as a manufacturer of motor car bodies in association with the Fisher interests, began his career as an architect, in association with Albert Kahn.

Most of the German-American architects who have attained prominence in Michigan have practiced their profession at Detroit. The reason for this localization was that Detroit has always been the center of Michigan capital and the opportunities were greatest there.

CHAPTER XXXIII

THE PROFESSION OF JOURNALISM

Carl Schurz—Robert Reitzel—The German Language Press—August Marxhausen—Engelbert Andries.

Men of German birth and extraction have had more or less to do with the press of Michigan for nearly a hundred years. At least three names among these are outstanding, those of Carl Schurz, August Marxhausen and Ferdinand Weller. The first daily issued in Detroit, the Advertiser and Tribune, appeared June 11, 1836. It was the outgrowth of a Whig Weekly called the Northwestern Journal, which was edited by various people, among them George Corselius, who was put in charge of the paper in 1838 by Col. Samuel Dexter, an eastern man with a land promotion activity, who wanted his particular brand of politics discussed in its columns. Corselius appears to have come from Buffalo, is said to have had German ancestry, and lived for some time in Ann Arbor.

In 1861 Benjamin F. Geiger, a New Yorker of German descent, joined James E. Scripps, in the purchase of the Detroit Advertiser and consolidated it with the Detroit Tribune.

In 1866 prominent Michigan Republicans, aiming to find a mouthpiece for the radical and aggressive element of the party, financed the Detroit Daily Post, and brought Carl Schurz to Detroit as its editor. Mr. Schurz was a German soldier, statesman and editor, and a champion of freedom in two countries. In the words of former President Eliot,

of Harvard, he was "the greatest American citizen of German
birth." He was born at Liblar, Prussia, and educated at
Bonn, where he aided in the publication of a newspaper of
liberal tendencies. He escaped arrest during 1848 by hurry-
ing to Switzerland, and there worked his way to Paris, where
he served as correspondent to German papers. He next went
to London and then emigrated to America in 1852. He became a citizen of Wisconsin, found support as a journalist
and lawyer, and became celebrated as an eloquent orator,
for he had acquired a remarkable command of English. He
was a delegate to the Republican National Convention which
nominated Lincoln, and was rewarded for his campaign services by appointment as Minister to Spain. This position he
resigned on the outbreak of the civil war. He was commissioned Brigadier-General in 1862 and Major-General in
1863, and took part in the battles of Bull Run, Chancellors-
ville, Gettysburg and Chattanooga.

Carl Schurz' Career in Michigan

In 1866, finding the Detroit Advertiser and Tribune too
conservative a Republican paper to suit them, Senator
Zachariah Chandler, James F. Joy and other leading Michigan Republicans founded a new paper, the Detroit Post,
and brought Mr. Schurz into Michigan to be its editor. He
surrounded himself with a brilliant staff, but did not make
a success of the paper, for one of the reasons already cited,
that the newspaper institution of America was not the kind
of one that existed in his native land, which was still his ideal.
His first year of management dissipated the capital and the
proceeds of a $40,000 mortgage, and he had yet to find his
place in the German language newspaper field. He did find
it a little later when St. Louis capitalists assisted him in
establishing a German paper in St. Louis, the Westliche Post,
which became a power in the west. In 1869 he took his
seat as United States Senator from Missouri, being the first
American citizen of German birth to enter the Senate. He

was one of the first to oppose Gen. Grant's re-election and presided over the convention which nominated Greeley for the presidency. When Mr. Hayes became President, Schurz was appointed Secretary of the Interior, serving from 1877 to 1881. In the latter year he became editor-in-chief of the New York Evening Post, formerly edited by William Cullen Bryant. He died in New York City, May 14, 1906.

Among the working newspaper men of Detroit have been numbered many men of German birth or blood. Joseph Greusel, son of the John Greusel who came out from Bavaria and helped found the Scott Guard in Detroit back in the '40's, was for many years a writer on the Detroit Free Press and its legislative correspondent at Lansing. His son, in turn, John Hubert Greusel, followed in his father's footsteps, and eventually deserted journalism for general literary pursuits. George Frank Helwig was for many years a writer on the Detroit Free Press, as was August F. Kersten on the Detroit News, becoming finally the managing editor of the Grand Rapids Democrat. Edward F. Kranich long did editorial work and reporting on the Detroit News. Jan Schmedding, a Hollander who wrote fluently in German, vibrated between the Abend Post in Detroit and the English language newspapers. One of his works of a permanent character was his translation of the papers of Cadillac in 1905, for the Michigan Pioneer and Historical Society. A similar contribution to permanent history was made by Rudolph Worth and Dr. Frederick Krustz, editor of the Volksfreund, of Jackson, who made a number of translations from original French sources for the same society. Alphonse Balcke, who was a Detroit Abend Post man, and who went to the Spanish-American war, was a particularly graceful writer of prose and verse.

Robert Reitzel

An odd genius, and one of the most brilliant writers of the Detroit group of German-Americans, was Robert Reitzel, a Baden man, born in 1849; named after Robert Blum, who was

executed because he had been a revolutionist; the son of a poor
teacher; a student of philosophy and theology at Heidelberg;
a devotee and panegyrist of love, wine and freedom; an emigrant to America at 21, and in the succeeding year the youthful
pastor of the German Reformed Church in Washington, where
he dreamt vague imaginings of uniting religion and science,
and becoming a new Luther to reform a church already reformed. He did not last long as a pastor. Being an ardent
thinker along lines of social reform, as well as a remarkably
well trained man on literary subjects, he spent several years
as a public lecturer on these topics, being finally set up in Detroit, in 1884, as the editor and publisher of a weekly newspaper, Der Arme Teufel,—the Poor Devil. This adventure
gave Reitzel a poor living, but was his medium for the publication of his literary work. In this field he was a man of varied
talent. He could and did discuss German literature with the
highest information and ability. He wrote poetry, in a diction
and meter and with a loftiness of thought which caused even
his conservative admirers to liken him to Heine. He was
extremely radical on the subjects of government and theology,
and attacked their various phases with biting sarcasm. He
was the friend of all the oppressed, whether they were or not
making little difference if he believed they were. He was by
turns a Christian, a Socialist and an Anarchist, but never con-
sistently one or the other for long. He himself said that as
the Christians had driven him to forsake Christianity, so the
Socialists spoiled socialism for him, and the Anarchists, anar-
chism. However, he continued to publish his Poor Devil with
pretty much regularity, to the delight of his various classes of
admirers, from those who enjoyed his poetry and literary
criticisms to those for whom his political, economic and religious radicalisms were a comfort. He led the life of an ardent
Bohemian, divided what he had in excess, from time to time,
with whoever needed it worse, and passed away in middle age
in 1898, at 49, after a year of incapacity caused by illness. His

fugitive works have been compiled and printed in three volumes by his admirers and his life formed the theme of a thesis by Adolph Edward Zucker, of the Graduate School of the University of Pennsylvania, in 1917.

George E. Miller, for many years connected with the Detroit News, had a Pennsylvania German ancestry.

In the journalistic institution of the state German-American editors have done much pioneer and later work. Frederick Weller was one of the strong men of his profession. He came to Howell in the '50's and had before him the double duty of perfecting himself in England and learning to be a printer. He mastered both and in 1865 became the editor of the Muskegon News, a place which he held until his death many years later. Mr. Weller was one of the great journalistic supporters of the Democratic party and was high in its councils during his editorial career.

Henry B. Miller, a "Pennsylvania Dutchman," from Lebanon county, established the Kalamazoo Telegraph in 1844 as a Whig paper. He staid with it a year, going to Buffalo where he started the Buffalo Telegraph as a German language paper. Later he became superintendent of lighthouses on the lakes.

In 1873 Edward Kroenche was one of the group who founded the Bay City Tribune, which was published for over 40 years. Kroenche was a publisher rather than a writer. The paper was started in the interest of the Republican party, but the Democrats got hold of it within a year and held it until 1876, when it once more became the exponent of Republican doctrine.

Charles H. Richman, a Saginaw newspaper man long connected with the Courier, of that city, was the son of Charles L. Richman, who was of the Canadaigua, N. Y., German settlement, and who arrived in Saginaw in 1836. The younger Richman gained the reputation of being a thorough going reporter.

J. R. Roth edited the Benzie County Journal in 1883.

In 1886 the Adrian Expositor was owned by Dr. Koss, of that city. Lee & Kurz acquired the Monroe Monitor in 1875. In 1844 the Paw Paw Free Press was established by Geiger & Gantt.

The German Language Press

The German language press of the state had some very good journalists in its service. These men were of a type different from the English newspaper men. The latter were affected in favor of the news features of their publications. Even from the start of modern journalism in the state, the English language papers leaned toward news. The German language press was more distinctively literary and didactic. A German newspaper could live a month without a murder, a robbery or a great fire; contenting itself with its political news and editorials, a good essay or two and a continued story. The two schools of journalism produced two kinds of journalists in the earlier years. In modern days they show a closer identity in editorial styles.

The first German language paper of the state was the Allgemeine Zeitung, published at Detroit in 1844. It was a Democratic paper in politics. When it was 10 years old it was merged with another paper, the Michigan Demokrat, to which Dr. Peter Klein was giving his energies and his intellect. Four years later the Demokrat was combined with the Michigan Volksblatt, established in 1855 by August Marxhausen and his brother. Emil Anneke, who had been on the New York Staats-Zeitung, and who was later Auditor-General of the state and who was Otto Kirchner's uncle, was one of the writers on this publication. The following year Mr. Marxhausen founded a weekly newspaper, the Familien-Blaetter. This was particularly the period in which the weekly newspaper was the vogue among the new citizens of all extractions. The Germans had their New York Staats-Zeitung, the Irish their Boston Pilot, and the newly arriving French their Courier des Etats Unis, and so the newly settling groups of

Germans in the west found their mental pabulum and their news from the old country in the Familien-Blaetter. It circulated extensively, not only in Michigan but in Indiana and Wisconsin as well. In 1868 Mr. Marxhausen began a daily edition of the Abend Post. At this period there were three German daily newspapers in Detroit, the Michigan Journal and the Volksblatt as well as the Abend Post. In 1878 the last mentioned absorbed the Journal, and in 1910 the Volksblatt.

August Marxhausen

August Marxhausen was a native of Kassel, in Hesse. He was born in 1833. He was too young to be in the revolution of 1848, but as it passed away, and he became mature, he accepted the convictions of those who participated in it. He was only nineteen when he came to America, and twenty when he came to Detroit. With his brother he got a place on the Michigan Democrat, whose policy did not suit the mature judgment of this youth of ?2. Like many another young newspaper man before and after his time, he conceived that the elders were running their paper wrongly, and, this being a free country, proceeded to start one of his own, as the exponent of his own convictions. This was the Michigan Journal, a daily started in 1855, by a partnership composed of Mr. Marxhausen and his brother, and continued for 13 years, when they sold the paper and dissolved the partnership. In 1865, August Marxhausen alone started the Familien Blaetter, out of which grew in 1868, the daily German newspaper, the Detroit Abend Post, which continues until the present time. Mr. Marxhausen died in 1910, after 64 years of activity in Michigan newspaper work.

Mr. Marxhausen was a man of high intelligence, good economic information, and very simple political convictions. He was essentially democratic, in the sense that he believed in the expression of the popular will, and in the largest personal liberty consistent with the necessary surrenders to government. This was emphasized by his separation in

1872, from the regular Republicans. He was the friend and political follower of Schurz, and with him he joined the liberal wing of the party in the nomination of Greeley for President. In spite of that he was twice, later on, selected by his party, the Republicans, to their national convention. He was a very brave journalist in his expressions, and a wonderful writer of strong German prose. A man of great simplicity, he was exceedingly genial, and possessed all the social characteristics, an exemplification of which was that, for twenty-seven successive years, he was president of the Harmonie Society of Detroit.

Wilhelm Wiethoff was for more than 20 years prior to 1912 a voluminous writer on both the German and English newspapers of Detroit.

William Eichelsdoerfer started the Staats-Zeitung in Grand Rapids in 1874. It lasted but three years.

Edna Ferber, Kalamazoo born, and the daughter of Jacob Charles Ferber and Julia Neumann, has achieved eminence as a newspaper writer in Milwaukee and Chicago, and has written a considerable number of short stories of merit.

Mary Louise Obenauer, Saginaw woman who took her A. B., at Michigan in 1893, became an editorial writer on newspapers and Director of Industrial Survey and Research Service for the National War Board at Washington.

A distinguished figure in a special field of Michigan journalism was Engelbert Andries, born in the Rhineland in 1842, and who settled in Detroit in 1875, immediately establishing himself as the publisher of the Stimme der Wahrheit, a German Catholic weekly newspaper of high literary and philosophical merit. Associated with John B. Mueller as editor for most of the time, he continued in the direction of this publication for 43 years, the paper closing its career July 4, 1918. In the years following 1894 they were assisted by Mr. Andries' son, Henry A. I. Andries, American-born and German university educated, as editor, whose work in the field of religious journalism was recognized by honors from Pope Benedict. In addition to his journalistic eminence the elder Andries was one of the leading American promoters of the Cecilian school of church music, and he was the first to introduce it in Michigan. He was an accomplished student of music and an organist of much artistic excellence.

CHAPTER XXXIV

THE CONTRIBUTIONS TO COMMERCE AND INDUSTRY

John Jacob Astor—Importance of His Business—A Group of Mid-Century Business Men—Colonel Frank J. Hecker—German Adaptability to Industry—Many Industrial Pioneers—Up-State Industrial Founders—The Development of New Industries—Adventures in Scientific Industry—Western Michigan Industrial Pioneers— Beginners of Motor Industry.

The first great business man of German birth or blood to operate in Michigan was John Jacob Astor, of New York. He actually ran his business in the state and frequently visited his various headquarters within its borders, although he had a multitude of local managers and subalterns.

Astor was German born, a native of Waldorf, near Heidelberg, in 1763, and by the time he was 20 was a skillful handler of animal hides. He came to America at that age and at once went into the business of handling furs, which he prepared for their market condition with his own hands. By 1789 he was worth $200,000, and well set in the fur trade, growing more important therein and wealthier every year. By 1810 he was one of the wealthiest men in America. The following year he founded Astoria, in Oregon, this foundation being one of the muniments of the sovereignty of the United States over that portion of its present dominion. While he made money there, Oregon was pretty far away from New York; the Hudson Bay Company, a powerful competitor, was not a nice neighbor, and the British captured Astoria in 1813 and let in their own fur trader, the Northwest Company. So Astor withdrew from that quarter and began to transfer his activities to Michigan, where he had been doing some business already.

His American Fur Company had been chartered in 1808. A very powerful English corporation, the Mackinaw Company, operating in the region of the Great Lakes with Mackinaw as its headquarters, was his competitor in the London market. Astor had a good opinion of the Great Lakes fur-gathering territory, so he purchased a two-thirds interest in the Mackinaw Company, and took an option on the remaining third for five years. He purchased it under his contract. His first entry into the business in Michigan had been in 1810. When the war of 1812 came the British captured Mackinac and interrupted his traffic, by diverting the trade to themselves, and threatened him with grave loss. In 1813 he was unable to purchase any fur worth speaking about. The Northwest Company was here his competitor again.

The fortunes of war turned his way, the American Fur Company got the upper hand when the English merchants were ousted, and Astor's company operations were extended from the Great Lakes to the Pacific Ocean. He was a bit of a politician and had influence enough with Congress to have a law passed, in 1816, restricting the fur trade to American citizens. He absorbed the Northwest and Southwest Fur Companies in that year, made the region about the Great Lakes a department of his greater organization, reformed the whole fur-gathering and trading industry, covered the producing areas with local agents in a way that would do credit to modern systems, crushed out the independent traders by underselling them or hiring their men away, and had at Mackinac the center of his business organization.

It was no small one at that. It covered the Lake Michigan and Lake Superior country, the upper reaches of the Mississippi, the valleys of the Chippewa and Flambeau Rivers of Wisconsin and the St. Croix River territory in what is now Minnesota.

Importance of the Astor Business

By 1822 he had seven traders working with him on joint account out of Mackinaw, thirty-two more who were independent but who bought their supplies and naturally turned over their pelts to his company, three direct buyers on company account, and 22 others with various kinds of contracts, making 64 in all. Besides these, he had a constant force of nearly 300 men, factors, clerks, boatmen, carpenters, tailors, graders, packers and what not in his employ, to whom he paid wages varying from $140 to $2,400 a year, in addition to their supplies. The magnitude of his business was enormous for his day, or for that matter, for a much later one. He made two profits, one on the furs which he purchased, the other on the goods which he paid for them. Money rarely entered into the transactions. His currency was calico, blankets, brandy, ammunition, food stuffs, and trinkets. The double turn-over is said to have averaged $3,000,000 a year. Every July and August from 3,000 to 4,000 Indian traders, trappers and bush-rangers generally came in to Mackinaw with their peltries and went out of it with their year's supplies.

He had strong men for agents. Ramsay Crooks and Robert Stuart were his main men. At the Grand Rapids location he had Rix Robinson; at Grand Haven, Madame La Framboise, who was a wonderful business woman; at Muskegon, Martin Ryerson, who became a lumber king and whose posterity are Chicago millionaires; at Saginaw, Patrice Reaume and Ephraim and Gordon Williams, and James Abbott at Detroit. A trader named Austin served him at Kalamazoo, John Parish in Mecosta, and one Chappee was his agent with the Menominee Indians.

Competition came and he began to retire in 1827. He was followed by the Buhls and other German-Americans from Detroit, and various others who got into the business. Astor sold out his Michigan interests in 1864.

During Astor's time another Mackinaw merchant of importance was Michael Dousman, of Mackinaw, who was of German descent from Quebec. Dousman was a British subject who continued to reside at Mackinaw after the surrender of the Northwest posts in 1796, and by the Treaty of 1794 he became an American citizen. In 1812 he was forced to aid the British against his will and was taken to Montreal, where he was finally released under bond of $4,000. He became a member of the firm of David Stone & Co., after the war. He was with the American Fur Company but was debarred as a foreigner from fur trading under the Act of 1816. He was permitted to resume in 1819. He was President of Mackinac Village, 1824-25, and Probate Judge of Mackinaw County, 1833-40.

Enter Kanter, the Buhls and Others

The American Fur Company's assets were sold to a trader named Hubbell, who lived at St. Paul, and who carried on the business under the same name, finally failing to meet his obligations and getting into financial trouble. The company's creditors made an arrangement with Edward Kanter, a young German-American, then in business at Mackinaw, to work out the debts and carry on. This Mr. Kanter did, made some money, left Mackinaw and reappeared in Michigan business life later on among the bankers at Detroit.

The Buhls appeared as successors of Astor in the fur trade because they were hat-makers in Detroit and hats were made of beaver-skins. They got into Detroit in the '30's from Pennsylvania, whither their parents had immigrated from Saxony. They were two brothers, Christian

Henry and Frederick. Later on they parted company, Frederick to continue his hat-making and fur-dealing and pass it on to his son Walter; Christian to go into the hardware trade and found a fortune that is not yet through growing. Christian Buhl, in addition to running a great hardware business, was interested in banks, started the Detroit Locomotive Works and actually built railroad engines in Detroit; started the Detroit Copper & Brass Company; and was a promoter and builder of the Hillsdale & Indiana Railroad, the Detroit & Eel River Railroad, and the Detroit & Butler Railroad, which connected the Wabash lines with Detroit, Frederick Buhl initiated the first hat-making industry in the state.

The next great business men of the race to appear in Michigan and do well were three who were contemporaries, Traugott Schmidt, Peter Henkel and Henry Weber. Schmidt was a man from Reuss, born in 1830, whose ancestors had been leather finishers for twelve generations, and whose sole wealth when he arrived in America in his nineteenth year was his familiarity with tanning. He worked in a small tannery at Flint in 1850, joined Gottlieb Beck in Detroit as an employe in the succeeding year, and in 1853 started a leather producing business for himself, which still continues. To the ordinary leather trade he added a traffic in deer skins, fur and wool, and his business became so important that he became Michigan's first modern exporter, shipping his productions to Germany, where he eventually established a branch house. The volume of his exports is credibly reported to have run as high as half a million dollars a year in early days and to a point very much above that figure later on. He travelled the northwest, traded with the Indians, bought valuable Detroit real estate and became one of the earliest of the savings bankers in his home ctiy.

His contemporary, Peter Henkel, was the son of a wooldyer from Beilstein, in Westphalia, who, with his parents and his brother Frederick came to Michigan in 1842. He started as a retail grocer, graduated into milling and was in pork-packing in the middle '50's. He was the first Detroiter to engage in this trade on a large scale, developing both his milling trade and provision trade into large exportations. By 1860 he was doing a million dollars a year of business.

Henry Weber, the contemporary of both, was a cabinet maker who, assembling some other Germans of his trade about him, essayed the making of furniture on a large scale. At first he employed hand labor, but later installed machinery so that, in 1872, when his establishment was wiped out by fire, he had the largest furniture factory in Michigan and was doing an annual business of three quarters of a million dollars.

In the development of transportation in the state several German-Americans were prominent. Andrew J. Earling, who as President of the Chicago, Milwaukee & St. Paull Railroad, had much to do with the development of the mineralized sections of the Upper Peninsula, was the son of a German immigrant. Mr. Earling never lived in Michigan. Eugene Zimmerman of Cincinnati, son of an immigrant, brought about the consolidation of the Pere Marquette Railroad with the Cincinnati, Hamilton & Dayton Railroad a union which did not prove permanent. Zimmerman was about the last of the race of American railroad exploiters, who preceded the stable and conservative operators.

Frank J. Hecker

The railroad industry developed a great manufacturer in the person of Frank J. Hecker, son of a Freedom township, Washtenaw county, German family. He got into the civil war in its last year as a youngster and immediately thereafter went west to engage in the work of the building of the Union Pacific Railroad under General Dodge. That experience led to his engagement by some Detroit capitalists who had built the Eel River Railroad in Indiana, to become their superintendent. Later he engaged in car-building at Adrian in a modest way and his earlier railroad employers joined their capital with his in the formation of the Peninsular Car Company at Detroit. He got into the business at a time that American railroad expansion was being rapidly carried on, made and sold hundreds of thousands of freight cars, and finally consolidated his works with those of his principal competitors, Messrs. Newberry and McMillan. Consolidation being greatly in vogue at the time this union of interests was taken into a greater corporation, of which it was the major part at the beginning, and which became the American Car and Foundry Company. Col. Hecker, by this time a great capitalist of Detroit, invested his fortune in various manufacturing enterprises, in banking interests and in real estate developments, which he continues to manage at an advanced age.

Col. Hecker's public services were very conspicuous. At the beginning of the Spanish-American War he was charged with the duty of providing a transport service for the United States for the movement of its troops into Cuba, a task which he performed with promptness and success. Later he served on the Panama Canal Commission, while that great national work was in the making.

In later years the commercial career of Sebastian S. Kresge, of Detroit, became spectacular. He was of a German-Swiss family which settled in Monroe county, Pennsylvania, in 1745. His first American ancestor was Konrad Kresge. His own mother was Catherine Kurkle. From the ownership of a single store, selling a variety of merchandise at cheap prices, he developed a national chain-store organization, headed by himself, which does a hundred million dollars worth of business a year. Mr. Kresge developed national notice, apart from his mercantile career, by being one of the foremost American proponents of the doctrine of prohibition, as applied to spirituous liquors.

The Germans who came into Michigan from 1830 onward

brought with them some peculiar adaptabilities to industry. The peasantry among them, as is recited herein, took to the land in great numbers and became a part of the agricultural population of the state, usually grouping themselves into colonies where they found expression for their social, religious and nationalistic characteristics. There were, however, many others besides peasants in the immigration. Among these were artisans skilled in distinctive trades. Many Germans were woodworkers. The old country industrial segregation of such artisans into Zimmermann, or house builders, and Tischler, or carvers and finishers, was continued in America. Hence early German cabinet-makers became the founders of the furniture industry, the wood finish trade and the business of pattern-making for metal castings.

German Adaptability of Industry

There was practically no baking industry when the Germans came. Many of them were skilled in the trade and practiced it. They went further in food production. They were the earliest confectioners. They introduced preserved, spiced and smoked cooked meats to the American menu. They taught conservation of food supplies which had therefore been wasted, or at least not been prepared for consumption in savory and attractive forms. They were wagon makers and blacksmiths, and if they came from North Germany, they were skilled ironworkers. It goes without saying that many of them were adept in the brewing of malt beverages. They were millers of wheat, oats and rye. Indian corn or American maize was at first a good deal of a mystery to them as an article of human consumption. Many of them were leather dressers. There were some who were wool workers and weavers. They had an old country experience in leaching the alkaline constituents of wood ashes and they knew how to combine the products of their leachings with non-edible fats; so they were early in the business of making soap and other detergents.

They were in Michigan before the days of camphene and kerosene lamps. Therefore, candle-making for domestic illumination was added to soap-making. The raw materials of both were derived from identical sources. Stearin had not yet been cheaply separated from tallow and the separation of paraffine was still in the womb of science. They were the first musical instrument makers.

So the German artisans brought a good deal to productive industry in Michigan in the way of knowledge. They added to this knowledge, discipline, industry and a determination, on the part of most of them, to get ahead. There were a good many of them who were pioneers of Michigan industry.

Marcus Stevens, Steuben county, New York, "Dutchman", began to manufacture furniture in Detroit in 1842. His partner was Samuel Zug, three generations away from Palatinate ancestors who had settled in Pennsylvania. Henry Bremer, who left Germany in 1839, had a soap and candle factory in Detroit in 1841, which he maintained until he moved to Grand Rapids in 1855. Archibald Soloman, German descended, came from Erwin, New York, to Detroit in 1833, where he had a furniture shop. He went to Grand Rapids four years later and made the first wooden-seated chairs seen in Kent county. William Haldane, son of a Delaware county, New York, German family, first settled in Grand Rapids in 1836, and he brought to that city in 1840, the first machinery for chair making that was brought into the state. It was run by horse-power.

Many Industrial Pioneers

John C. Zeigler, who came to Michigan in 1852, was the first jeweler of Saginaw. He was also a private in Company "H" of the Second Michigan Volunteers in the civil war. Henry Brestefeld, born in Hanover in 1815, spent some years in the employ of the Knabes, piano manufacturers in Baltimore, and started furniture making in Saginaw in 1855. Carl

Miller, a Saginaw pioneer of 1854, was one of the earliest wood finish makers. Rudolph Schnacker, in Saginaw in 1847, was the first cabinet maker in the place. Frederick Koehler, Mecklenburger, was Saginaw's leading blacksmith in 1852. Henry Failing, Herkimer county, New York, man, was a brickmaker in Marshall in 1832. Heinrich Mann, one of the founders of the Ann Arbor colony of 1830, was a tanner and made leather. The very first German in Ann Arbor, Conrad Bessenger, was a baker from Mannheim, in Baden. Adam Leitelt, who was of German ancestry, and from Bohemia, founded an iron works in Grand Rapids in 1854, that is still in existence. August Posner made both potash and brick in Mt. Clemens in 1854. John Dittmar, a Prussian, began making farm wagons in the same place the year before.

German artisans brought book-binding as an industry into Michigan in the '50's of the nineteenth century. Arouet Richmond and Frederick Backus began a business in 1850 in Detroit that has survived through three quarters of a century.

Giving these industrialists a few years to get started it is found that by 1863, the Germans practically monopolized the tannery business in Michigan. Christian Goetz had a tannery at Hillsdale, Ludwig Struber one at Owosso, Henry Krause was in the business at Ann Arbor, Christ Ziegle at Lansing, Andrew Kerschner at Monroe, Gottlieb Josenhans at Owosso, George Unterkercher at Manchester, and the establishments at Detroit were owned and operated by Traugott Schmidt, John Karrer & Brother, Henry Koester, J. & A. Schehr and Andreas Badenbach.

In cabinet making, Henry Weber, who had already begun to assume prominence as a furniture manufacturer, became eventually the first of the quantity producers of household furniture in the state. He advertised that he made his product of rosewood, mahogany, walnut and oak, and offered library, office and dining room furniture, showing great variety for his period. When his works were destroyed by fire in 1872 the loss was over a quarter of a million dollars, making it the largest fire loss in the city since the great fire of 1805. His contemporaries in this line were then Wilhelm Kalkbronner, Martin Federlein and Stevens & Zug, already mentioned.

In the same year the cooperage trade in the metropolitan city of the state was monopolized by Philip Kling, Nicholas Senninger, John Reutschler and August Dorman. J. P. Weiss, Adam Couse and Peter Grimm were building pianos in Detroit and Charles Schulenburg was constructing billiard tables. Schulenburg's creation was not the club table of the later period, but the big English model, twelve feet by six in dimensions. John Bornman and F. A. Schober were in the printing business. Jacob and William Darmstaetter and Bernhardt Stroh had established lager beer breweries, destined to supplant the ale and porter brewing establishments theretofore operated by Irishmen and Scotchmen.

Dr. Samuel P. Duffeld, with his recently finished German education in pharmaceutical chemistry, was applying it in the modest establishment that in sixty years has grown into the plant of Parke, Davis & Co.

By 1880 German-American bakers had grown into a majority of the purveyors of breadstuffs in the state. In the milling trade, by the same time, the establishments of Henkel, Lauhoff and Perrien, in Detroit; Allmendinger, in Ann Arbor; Stock in Hillsdale and Voight in Grand Rapids were the leaders in the industry in the state, not counting a large group of lesser operators of the breed in the same trade.

Up-State Industrial Founders

Upstate German tradesmen were getting into business for themselves. At the beginning of the '60's among the machinists of the state were Frank Huetteman at Detroit, who later developed glass-lined steel tankage; Jacob P. Gwinner, at Ann Arbor; John Kanause, at Saline; Joseph Wuertzner, who was settled at Three Oaks; A. H. Schaeffer, at

Plymouth; Robert Grahn, at Sand Beach; Adolph Leitelt, at Grand Rapids; Conrad Rade, at Trenton, and Melchior Bettinger, at Woodland. George Helliker had a foundry at Farmington; a Hildebrand one at Hartland; a Whitmer one at Goodrich; a Willings one at Niles; Michael Pheff one at St. Joseph and Rossman & Feak one at Allegan. These were the early plow-makers.

Thus, there were at this period, many industrial foundations by German-Americans in Michigan which illustrated in their beginnings the truth of the adage that great oaks from tiny acorns grow. These were of the usual types of western American industry of the period. In addition there were new and unusual industries founded by German-Americans. In Detroit the Laitner brothers had introduced the new industry of brush-making, Philip Welz was fabricating saw-making machinery and C. D. Widman was producing picture mouldings. Theodore Becker had founded a flower pot industry, and Peterman & Sharpstein had a fairly important laboratory for patent medicine making at Marshall.

The lumber industry was opening up big. There were many large operators, but there were none of more consequence than Charles L. Ortman, of Saginaw, whose son-in law, Wilhelm Boeing, followed in his steps; or than Weideman & Wright of Saginaw; or Engelman & Salling, of Muskegon. John Lents was running early upper peninsula camps at Eagle River; J. L. Bearinger at Lapeer; Charles Reitz and his brothers at Manistee; H. Reidler at Muskegon; Armin, Bruster and Kindinger at Sebewaing; the Laderach brothers at Salzburg; Solomon Suppen at Manistee; Zink & Stover at Exeter; Philip Mauer at Norwalk, and there was a host of smaller operators, capitalist working shoulder to shoulder with woodsman, or taking his place with the teams or on the drives. The lumber operations were carried on with mining camp speed and exertion. The harvest of money could not come too quickly. In the later days the master timberman, Frederick Weyerhauser, had his camps in Michigan as well as in Wisconsin and Minnesota.

The Development of New Industries

While these business transactions called for daring, there were enterprises which were of greater risk in which German-Americans were conspicuous as pioneer investors. When electric lighting was beginning to promise to be commercial, Edward W. Voigt, of Detroit, found great difficulty in getting the more conservative investors to join him in making Mr. Edison's invention useful to his fellow citizens. Mr. Voigt was a brewer who had acquired a competency. Most people who knew him in this capacity were not aware that he had taken almost a full course at the University of Wisconsin and followed it up by a sailing voyage to the countries of the Pacific. He had a natural bent for giving a promising new process or invention a fair try-out. Hence his pioneer interest in electric lighting. When Hugo Matullath brought his process for making veneer barrels into Michigan, which promised great economy of the timber raw material, Mr. Voigt was one of his backers. He was also among the earliest Americans to appreciate the values of the Mitscherlich process for making paper pulp and invested largely in the establishment of mills for using it. Later when electric traction was demanded he became a very heavy investor in that form of transportation.

Improved processes for tanning leather have been devised and applied by Carl Ernest Schmidt, and the greatest tanneries in the state have borne the names of German owners and operators. In beet sugar refining one company was called, distinctively, the "German-American," and the first seeds for the Michigan plantings came from Germany. The development of the chicory trade and the fabrication of the root in Michigan is wholly in control of a German company.

Fred Hubel devised gelatine capsules for medical doses and was for years their sole producer in the United States.

The brothers, Robert and Frank Kuhn, sensing the coming importance of electrical heating devices, were the pioneers in the design and production of this class of merchandise, in the fields of domestic appliances and mechanical tools.

Apart from the early adventures of Edward Voigt in the development of the Mitscherlich process of producing sulphite pulp for paper-making, many other German-American names appear in the development of this industry in Michigan. Herbert Everard, whose progenitors were Eberhardts, had a great deal to do with this line of manufacturing, both at Munising and Detroit; and E. W. Kiefer at Port Huron; Dr. H. A. Frambach at Cheboygan; and Jacob Kindelberger, Felix Pagenstecher, Hale P. Kauffer and A. E. Curtenius in the Kalamazoo Valley were prominent in the trade.

In the field of industrial chemistry, Walter K. Schmidt, of Grand Rapids, with a Spanish War experience behind him, and C. K. Schmidt, of the same city, are the outstanding modern developers of furniture wood finishes, the latter having produced, in addition to the formulas for the earlier stains, the lacquer and nitro-cellulose finishes applied in more modern times. The names of members of the Stroh family appear in the development of the Portland cement and heavy chemical industries. Those of Osius and Stroh are connected with the growth of ammonia distillation.

The history of the motor car industry fairly bristles with the names of German-American pioneers, occupying position as producers, engineers and designers.

Adventures in Scientific Industry

The daguerrotype had hardly been supplanted by the process of photography through the use of the negatives rather than positives before Gottlieb Grelling was practicing the art in Detroit. Gmeiner, Van Leyen and Hochgraef were the early engravers on wood, Van Leyen devising a process of photographing the matter to be engraved on box-wood before the days of the half-tone engraving. In this same line of illustrative art Max Levy, born in Detroit in 1857, took to photography in 1890, and introduced the screen halftone process. In 1917 he invented a counting chamber for the Haemocythometer, an instrument for the counting of blood corpuscles, which was adopted by the army surgeons. He was also the government's expert during the World War on its optical instruction program.

When electric refrigeration was first attempted in Detroit, Herbert Horace Bunzel, born in Prague and a professor of bio-chemistry, was the chief chemist of the Isko Corporation, which essayed it.

Fred Sanders was a Baden man who learned his trade as a confectioner in Karlsruhe, where he remained until he was 27 years of age He came to America in 1875, settled in Detroit, and established himself in his business, in which he became very successful, and which now engages the second and third generations of his family. Sanders is credited with the introduction of the "ice cream soda" beverage to the American public.

In varied industry, William Philip Beyer, son of John Bartholomae Beyer, was one of the earliest steel-plate engravers in Detroit, retiring in 1887, while Frederick Huetwold was one of the first of the modern school of lithographers in Detroit.

Samuel Zug, who went into the furniture manufacturing business in Detroit in 1843, was a Cumberland county, Pennsylvania man. He was one of the earliest abolitionists in Michigan. His ancestors came from the Palatinate in 1727. His business associate was Marcus Stevens, from Steuben county, New York, whose original family name was Steuben.

Thomas McGraw, long known as Michigan's leading dealer in wool, was an Irishman from Limerick. His mother, Elizabeth Faught, was born in Germany and married Redmond McGraw in Ireland. She brought her family to Michigan in 1835 ard died in Oakland county.

IN THE MAKING OF MICHIGAN 315

Jacob Beller was well settled in Detroit in the '60's, when he pulled up stakes and went to Chicago. He lost nearly a million dollars by the Chicago fire in 1871, and returned to Detroit to become a brewer and boniface. He came from Moosackn, Hamburg, and his original family name was Bachler.

The Lesher family, old-time tailors of Detroit, were Pennsylvania German from Pennsylvania. Their great-uncle was a captain in the Revolution.

Fred Carlisle, old-time Detroit capitalist and historian, tells of his mother Polly Carlisle, who was a daughter of John Croul, of Montgomery county, New York. He was the son of Frederick Croal, or Krull, who came from Prussia in 1718, and being a cripple was bound out as a redemptioner for six years for his passage money. John Croul was in the War of 1812. Jerome Croul, who was one of the original owners of the gas works in Detroit, was out of this ancestral strain.

Western Michigan Industrial Pioneers

In the metropolis of western Michigan, Grand Rapids, Elias Matter, a German-American cabinet-maker from Uniontown, Pennsylvania, began making furniture in 1855, his modest beginning growing into important production. Adolph Leitelt, a Bohemian of German blood, started an iron works that has been controlled by three generations of his family. Frederick Hartman engaged in the same trade in 1872, with the same continuity of management. Carl G. A. Voight and William G. Herpolsheimer founded their retail dry goods business in 1870. Herpolsheimer was born in Carlsruhe in 1842. Henry Froelich started the Grand Rapids Chair Company in 1872. Julius Berkey, one of the founders, in 1872, of a great furniture producing establishment of the present day, was of German descent. The Voights were early millers as well as merchants. Christopher Kusterer was a leading brewer. The Wursburg family, descended from the pioneers of the '30's, continued to be represented in commercial business through the third generation. Willard Barnhart, a Grand Rapids business pioneer of 1870, was a great-grandson of Peter Barnhart, who came from the Palatinate in 1771 and settled in Philadelphia. William Hake, arriving in Grand Rapids in 1853, and becoming an important manufacturer, was born in Westphalia in 1828. Godfrey von Platen, who achieved success in the timber and lumber business, both in the upper and lower peninsulas of the state, making his home at Grand Rapids, was German born in 1857. Conrad G. Swensberg, better known as an educator, was one of the earliest founders of the furniture industry in Grand Rapids after the close of the civil war, in which Prof. Swensberg served with distinction.

In the Upper Peninsula the sugar industry was practically established in the neighborhood of Menominee by John Henes and Gustavus A. Blesch, while an important stained glass industry at the same place owes its origin to Jacob Leisen and his son, Lewis Leisen.

The innkeepers of the early period was largely eastern men, of English lineage, but they had no monopoly. William Bohling kept hotel at Adrian, Joseph Schneckenburger at Chelsea, Charles Kunz at Eagle Harbor in the copper country, Jacob Stauber at East Saginaw, Martin Heibisch at Frankenmuth, C. Schulte at Houghton, Nicholas Kemp at Muskegon, Peter Scharz at New Baltimore, Jacob Eberly at Owosso, and Peter Hiller at Ypsilanti. Andrew Nagel was a brewer at Coldwater.

Albert Strelow was one of the original incorporators of the first Ford Motor Company, in company with the Dodges, John S. Gray and the other founders. He sold out too early to realize a fortune. Raphael Herman, a Konigsburger, born in 1865, developed gas and steam specialties and laid the foundation for a prosperous industry in Detroit. H. Mueller, who built the German Benz car in 1895, founded a great alloy metals institution in Port Huron. August F. Blesch, born in

Baden in the year of the revolution, came to Detroit at his maturity, became head of a brass manufacturing establishment, and was president of the Detroit Employers' Association in 1906.

Pioneers in the Motor Car Industry

Albert Strelow has been mentioned as one of the original incorporators of the Ford Motor Company. He was far from being the only German-American who participated in the foundation of Michigan's leading industry. J. C. Danziger, of Detroit, was one of the earliest mechanical engineers who applied himself to the solving of the problems presented by the new method of mechanical transportation. The earlier and later history of the industry, which has been most largely centered in Detroit and Michigan, carried in its pages scores of German names, most of them persons of American birth and Germanic descent. Among these may be cited Frank L. Klingensmith, long associated with Ford industry; William E. Metzger, one of the pioneer manufacturers; J. G. Utz, an early designer; J. G. Bayerline; Martin L. Pulcher, a pioneer in motor truck building; Edward V. Rickenbacker, famous as well in aviation; Henry Timken, designer of axles; J. H. Newmark, who was associated with the Durant interest; Christian Girl and V. R. Heftler, who devoted their talent to accessory development; William F. V. Neumann, an early manufacturer; Arthur von Schlegel, whose application was to the commercial side of the business; S. I. Fekete, an Austrian, who has done a great deal of refinement in motor engineering, and Rudolph Friedrich Flinterman.

To these must be added the Fishers, six brothers in all, who became the outstanding manufacturers of motor car bodies in the country.

CHAPTER XXXV

PARTICIPATIONS IN BANKING

The Savings Bank Founders—The Career of Edward Kanter—Other German-American Bankers.

German-American names appeared in Michigan banking at a very early date. Michael Dousman, the fur trader of Mackinac, and Christian Clemens, the founder of Mt. Clemens, are named in the original charter of 1834 as organizers of the Michigan Insurance Company, which was incorporated to operate a bank at Detroit. The Michigan State Bank was a successor to this institution and both Christian H. Buhl and Frederick Buhl were stockholders in it.

An early director of the First National Bank of Detroit was a millionaire merchant from Boston, William F. Weld, said to have been of German antecedents, although this is disputed. When the Second National Bank was organized in Detroit both the Buhls were among its founders. When the American Exchange National Bank was organized in 1865, Edward Kanter was one of the directors.

The era of saving banks began in Michigan when the Savings Bank Act was passed in 1871. The Wayne County Savings Bank was one of the first organized, its first Vice-President being Herman Kiefer, and, among its Trustees, Paul Gies, Jerome Croul and Traugott Schmidt, all of immediate or remote German ancestry. The People's Saving Bank's foundation was almost contemporaneous, with Anton Pulte,

Wilhelm Boeing, Sigmund Rothschild, and John Mark as directors. Frank A. Schulte, who joined its forces in the earliest years, spent over 50 years in its service. The Michigan Savings Bank, an almost equally early foundation, had Julius Stroh, Joseph Kuhn and John H. Kaple among its organizers. The Home Savings Bank, a creation of the early '80's, had John S. Schmittdiel, Augustus Ruoff, Frederick Guenther and George Clippert as its founders. Julius H. Haass, a young clerk in its service at its beginning, eventually became the President of its successor, when it united with the Wayne County Savings Bank.

Edward Kanter's Career

Edward Kanter, Breslau born in 1824, son of a linen merchant, stowaway on a sailing ship from Havre to New Orleans, apprentice there in a drug store where one of his experiments blew up the shop, waiter on a Mississippi river steamboat, victim of yellow fever and a boiler explosion and survivor of both, added to the sum of his youthful experiences by getting into Detroit in 1844 and being refused a job in the Detroit Savings Fund Institute. He passed on to Mackinaw to become a clerk for the American Fur Company. In two years it withdrew, leaving him to face the creditors and contractors. He arranged with the creditors and started business on a capital of $200, staying five years and building up the beginnings of a fortune. He tried ship-chandlery in Detroit next, and being located at the main wharf, added banking for the sailors. He went into banking exclusively in 1868, first privately, then, in 1871, as the German-American Bank, with his two sons as his staff and directors. In course of time he retired and other German-American names were added to his bank's directory, including Louis Blitz and Philip Breitmeyer. George H. Kirchner, who began as a clerk with the bank, finally became its President. During the World War the directors changed the name of this bank from the German-American to the First State Bank. Mr. Kanter's sons and a grandson followed their ancestor in the banking business. He himself died in 1896.

When the State Savings Bank was first reorganized Frank J. Hecker became a director. The Peninsular Savings Bank of Detroit was organized in the late '80's. Paul Weidner, Simon C. Karrer, Caspar Schulte, Sigmund Simon and Joseph Perrien were on its first board of directors. The Union National Bank, later consolidated with another, had Valentine Hilsendegen, Carl Schmeman, Adam Ochsenhirt, August Goetel, Theodore Gorenflo, Henry Wunsch and Albert A. Albrecht on its board, and John B. Padberg was its cashier.

Other German-American Bankers

In Grand Rapids William G. Herpolsheimer was a founder of the Grand Rapid's National Bank and David M. Amberg of the National City Bank. The Fourth National Bank, of that city, had Christian Bertsch among its organizers. In Saginaw William Seyffardt and August Melze helped build up the Commercial National Bank, and August Schuppe was the first treasurer of the Savings Bank of East Saginaw. Mr. Schuppe was a Baden man, college bred at Carlsruhe, who came to America in 1849 and to Saginaw in 1859. William Peter was an original stockholder of the Bay City Bank in 1871. In Adrian, the name of R. A. Kaiser; in Albion those of W. S. Kessler, W. H. Rodenbeck, and G. W. Snyder; in Calumet those of August Mette, Joseph Herman and Peter Ruppe; in Hudson that of Edward Frensdorff; in Grand Haven that of John A. Pfaff; in Hastings that of Daniel Striker; in Lansing those of Jacob Stahl and Fred Stable; in Marine City, those of John F. Zimmerman and W. F. Sauber; and in Mt. Clemens those of the Ulrichs and Lungerhausens, appear among the early bankers and bank capitalists

In Ann Arbor, Christian Mack, Wurtemburger born in 1834, and into Michigan in 1851, founded the Ann Arbor State Bank, of which he was for 26 years president. He was succeeded by Michael J. Fritz, son of one of the pioneer families, and himself a student of Tubingen. Edwin F. Mack, Christian's son, became a banker in Detroit and later in Chicago. Louis G. Kaufman, president of the Chatham-Phenix National Bank of New York, was the son of Samuel Kaufman, who came into Marquette in 1852, ran a general store and iron mines, and directed his son into a Marquette savings bank to learn the the business. George L. Maltz, who founded a private bank at Alpena, later converted into a state bank, was one of the banking commissioners of the state.

The savings bank idea appealed to thrifty German-Americans in Michigan from the beginning. For that reason, in the earlier days and in the larger cities, where there were considerable Germanic populations, many operating officers of the banks were selected from available Germans, for the convenience of carrying on business in the tongue of these customers. As a consequence a considerable percentage of the employes of the banks of Michigan are of German birth or extraction. From these were drawn, as a general rule, the men who were trained in the handling of foreign exchange, transactions of this class becoming frequent at an early date for transmission of funds to intending emigrants to America and for assistance to needy relatives at home. Before the advent of the international money order system these exchanges were very numerous.

CHAPTER XXXVI

THE DEVELOPMENT OF NATURAL RESOURCES

Germans Who Prospered in Mining—The First Copper Mill.

Among the recoverers of commercial values from the natural resources of Michigan there were many German-American citizens. These resources included the surface earths and clays, the timber supplies and the products of the mines. In another place in this writing is shown the formal and orderly work done upon the iron and copper resources of the state in a scientific way by Dr. Carl Rominger and Raphael Pumpelly. But in the pioneering that was done before their time, there were many hardy men, of every race, who participated.

John H. Forster, whom Peter White used to classify as a descendant of the early German immigration into New York, was one of the early explorers and mining captains, and has written interestingly of the beginnings of the upper peninsula iron and copper industry. He was in the north as early as 1846 prospecting for copper at Eagle River. He says that "a few rough German miners and a Frenchman" constituted his force in 1846 and 1847. His comment on the German workers was that they were very capable miners, but that they lacked interest in the industry, preferring to go into trade. By 1860 Mr. Forster said the entire population of Hancock was composed of Cornishmen, Irish and Germans.

IN THE MAKING OF MICHIGAN 323

German-Americans had a pioneer connection with the modern mining of copper in Michigan. The first of those to locate the mineral in Keweenaw County were Dr. A. A. Rudolph, who was born in Germany and came into the copper country in 1843; Adam Haas, also German born, a Pittsburgh associate of Rudolph; Philip Schenerman, who later became superintendent of the Quincy Mine mills; and Joseph Sahl, a graduate of Freiburg, who later gave up mining engineering to study for the Roman Catholic priesthood, and still later became an agnostic.

These men were sent out by Pittsburgh and Boston mining company interests to search for copper, which they first found in an occurence of the black oxide near Fort Wilkins. This discovery became the Pittsburg & Boston mine. It was not especially rich. Pursuing their explorations further they located another deposit at Keweenaw, finding a large fissure of native copper in the face of the bluff. This became the Cliff mine.

Germans Who Prospered in Mining

Eventually they went back east, but other Germans who were in the copper country got into mining, both with their labor and their funds. Peter Sauer was a drayman at Calumet who put his spare money into Calumet & Hecla mining stock when it sold for a few shillings a share. When he died — and he kept on draying to the last — there was a million dollars worth, at the market price, of this kind of assets in his estate. Peter Ruppe, whose father started a general store at Hancock in 1863 and later went to Red Jacket, put his spare money into the copper stocks. When he died there was $4,500,000 of this mining property in his holdings. Edward Bollman, of Laurium, worked at the Cliff mine in the '60's. He became a wood contractor for the mines, furnishing mining timber for the stopes. When he died in 1915 he left an estate of $3,000,000, largely composed of mining stocks. Edward M. Leiblein, of Hancock, born at Rockland in Ontonagon

County, started with nothing and became a great wholesaler and bank stock investor of the copper country. The Mass family, of Negaunee, acquired its wealth by persistent explorations of the Negaunee iron range. The Lauerman family of Marinette got its wealth from similar foundations.

In September, 1846, Philo M. Everett, one of the pioneer iron ore men took some ore from near Teal Lake and had it smelted in an old foundry cupola at a place called Hodunk, near Coldwater. William Lemm, a German iron-worker, was the furnace man.

As early as 1846, John B. Maas, born in Germany 20 years before, was prospecting for iron in Marquette county. Capt. J. B. Schwartz, who was born in Lorraine in 1844, got into the Lake Superior iron region in 1856. He operated the Tilden mine for Gov. Tilden, of New York, who ran for the presidency in 1876 and he discovered the Barnum mine, which was owned and named after William H. Barnum, of Connecticut, who was the Tilden's campaign manager in the famous presidential contest. George Runkel operated Crystal Falls mine in 1880. He was born in Germany in 1838, and had come into Michigan from Iowa. Anthony Monnig brought a group of German miners to the copper country in the '50's, from Detroit.

Edward Breitung, from Saxe-Meiningen, where he was educated, got into Kalamazoo in 1849, was in business in Detroit in 1851, and went to Marquette in 1855. He opened up the Washington mine, explored the Menominee range in 1863, and the Negaunee range in 1870, developing the Republic mine. In 1882 he helped develop the Vermillion range in Minnesota.

First Copper Mill of German Type

The first mill for the reduction of ore in the copper country was erected in 1843, at Eagle Harbor. It was built by Charles T. Jackson, who afterwards became a United States Geological Survey man. It was called a "German pulverizer," being of the standard type used in Germany for reducing soft ores. Joseph Stahl, who settled in Copper Harbor in 1845, is said to have operated this machine. C. F. Eschweiler was superintendent of the Isle Royale copper mine in 1862. About this time, George Messersmith was writing letters from Copper Harbor to the Detroit Free Press describing the occurances on Keweenaw Point.

Many other Upper Peninsula Germans achieved wealth and importance by doing useful things in the early days. Iron Mountain was platted in 1879 by Joseph Flesheim, who was associated with Isaac and Samuel Stephenson. The beginnings of Norway came from the discoveries in a test pit made by Anton Odell, a Luxembourger, who was a shoemaker nearby. Jerome B. Schwartz, originally a Detroiter, was a mining captain in 1881 at Crystal Falls mine, the land of which had been purchased from the government a few years earlier by Guido Pfister. In 1875, Augustus Spies, who was the local grocer and butcher at Menominee, and had been investing his spare money in pine lands, built a mill at Menominee out of which he gained an immense fortune. Skanee was founded in 1871 by a colony of Wisconsin Germans. Hermansville was founded in 1878 by C. J. L. Meyer, who had come up from Fond du Lac, in Wisconsin. Emil Glaser, a Saxon, after his service in the Civil War, went to Escanaba, where he built the first lumber dressing mill.

One of the greatest fortunes accumulated in the Upper Peninsula in mining and timber lands was that of an original Lower Peninsula man, who was an early investor in and controller of such properties. This was John Munroe Longyear, who as a young Lansing man, developed a genius for acquiring cheap lands containing natural resources. The Upper Penninsula had in it a great deal of government land, some of which was granted for railroad aid, some for state roads, and all the rest of which was available for "filing," as the process was called, with scrip originally issued by the government to soldiers in the Indian and other minor wars.

This scrip was sold for a song by its recipients and was kicked around Chicago, which was its principal market, at prices as low as twenty-five cents per acre of its representative value, when it became apparent that it could be used to acquire title to land in Northern Michigan and other timbered countries. Mr. Longyear was an expert at forming syndicates and pools to acquire these lands with scrip and at small cash prices, and between personal ownership, partnerships, pools and agencies he probably controlled more mineralized acreage in the Upper Peninsula than any other one man. His operations made him immensely wealthy, his estate being among the very largest of his time in Michigan. He was very daring, so much so in fact, that he capitalized and operated coal mines at Spitzbergen, off Norway and under the Arctic Circle. Mr. Longyear was of remote German ancestry, his forefathers being from an Alsatian family which settled in Ulster County, New York, in 1730, when the name was Langjahr.

Among later day men in the copper country, Frank Klepetko, Austrian engineer, born in 1856, was engineer of the Delaware, Conglomerate, Tamarack and Osceola mines from 1880 to 1890. During 1903, Ulysses Samuel Shaw Arentz did a tour of surveying in the copper country. He moved to the Nevada mining country and his neighbors in that state sent him to the Sixty-Seventh Congress.

As early as 1843, John Cordes, a Westphalian who had settled in Clinton county in 1836, was engaged in the opening up of the plaster quarries in Kent county which have since become the basis of a great industry. Conrad Kuhl, who was born in Wurtemburg in 1819, who settled in Monroe in 1849, and later moved to Sebewaing, was one of the earliest to produce salt from Saginaw county brines.

Frank Geisen was the surface captain and Conrad Kalb the supply clerk when Capt. William B. Frue opened up Silver Islet mine in Lake Superior in 1870.

Mining and lumbering were anybody's game in Michigan

IN THE MAKING OF MICHIGAN

in the middle and latter parts of the last century, and that of German-American residents of the state no less than of others who were early adventurers in these industries. Land and labor were as cheap for them as for anybody else. There were outstanding operators like Mack, Schmitt, Ortman, Boeing, Engleman, Mark and Fleitz, who accumulated great fortunes in the timber trade, as did operators like Breitung, Maas, Kaufman and Schlesinger in the iron ore trade.

CHAPTER XXXVII

THE GERMAN-JEWISH BUSINESS MEN

The Brothers Rothschild—The Brothers Butzel—Emil Solomon Heineman—Simon Heavenrich—Julius Houseman—Louis Blitz — Jacob Seligman—The Brothers Schloss—The Jewish Pack-Peddlers.

The revolution in Germany affected a considerable number of Jews, well educated and rather financially competent people, who, having sympathized with the democratic movement, felt called upon to evade the penalties of such sympathy by voluntary exile from their native land. They scattered throughout the world, some going to South America, and some to the North American continent. Of the latter, a considerable number settled in the middle west of the United States. They were attracted to the cities as centers of trade, and very early established themselves firmly in several lines of business.

Many of these came into Michigan early, settling principally in Detroit, where they founded commercial enterprises which grew into business organizations of much importance. Among the earliest of these to arrive, and certainly the first to achieve great commercial success, were the Rothschilds. They were three brothers, Sigmund, Feist and Kauffman. They were the first merchants to develop a great business in leaf tobacco in the west. They all came from Frankfort-on-Main in 1854, and recognizing the potential growth of the tobacco trade in Detroit, both from the

IN THE MAKING OF MICHIGAN

standpoint of demand from local manufacturing and of distribution to other centers, proceeded to build up Detroit as a jobbing market, particularly for foreign tobacco from Sumatra and Cuba. They had branch houses both in Amsterdam and Havana and for years their importations of tobacco furnished a very high percentage of the revenues of the Detroit customs district. The Sutter brothers later divided the trade with them but eventually moved to Chicago, as that city began to assume importance as a distributing center. The Rothschilds went out of the business in time, leaving it to a group of Jewish and Gentile German-American tradesmen, who have dominated it until the present day.

A precursor of the Rothschilds was Magnus Israel, a native of Waldeck, who was born in 1819, and who came to Kalamazoo in 1845, starting a general store. He had the reputation of being a very learned man, especially in the physical sciences. He remained in business until his death in 1868. In 1855, Simon Rosenbaum, also a native of Waldeck, became his business partner and continued the business after Mr. Israel's death.

Magnus and Martin Butzel

The Butzels, Magnus and Martin, were Bavarians from Schesslitz. When Magnus was fourteen years old he was apprenticed to the business of making interior wood finish for buildings and doing artistic glass work. He became a journeymen in 1847 and worked at his trade for five years, when he came to America, joining his brother Martin, who was his senior by two years, had about the same old country experiences, had come six years earlier, and was already in business in a modest way at Saugerties, near Kingston, New York. The two brothers formed a partnership in the dry goods trade and went into business in Peekskill, New York, whence they came to Detroit in 1862 and became associated with their brother-in-law, Emil Solomon Heineman, who was already in business, and began the manufacture of ready-made clothing and men's furnishings. Mr. Heineman retired in 1890 and Magnus Butzel in 1893 because of failing sight. Magnus Butzel took a very active part in the community life of his city. He was a member of the Board of Education in 1882 and 1883, and in the latter year he was elected a Commissioner of the Public Library, being reelected for two successive terms in 1889 and 1895. One of the branch libraries of the city is named in his honor. He was one of the first directors of the Detroit Chamber of Commerce and a liberal giver to all public causes. Martin Butzel, his brother, was a man of the same character, though less given to participation in public affairs.

Their brother-in-law and business associate, Emil Solomon Heinemann, was a Bavarian from Schesslitz, whose grandfather had been located at Neuhaus, near Hamburg, in the eighteenth century. Heineman was one of the earliest Jewish merchants to locate in Detroit, coming in 1851 and establishing the business in which his brother-in-law Butzel joined him. In his early commercial life he was employed by a merchant named Amberg, having as a fellow clerk a young Saxon, Edward Breitung, the son of a Lutheran minister from Schalkau, in Saxe-Meinigen, who was a victim of the revolution and who later cut an important figure in the early commercial and mining history of the Upper Peninsula. Mr. Heineman's son later on became Controller of the City of Detroit.

One of Mr. Heineman's contemporaries was Samuel Heavenrich, also a Bavarian from Frensdorf, who had been trained in a commercial school at Regensburg. He, too, had to leave Germany on account of his participation in the revolution. He came to America and to Detroit in the middle '50's and after learning the ways of his new homeland he established himself in business with his brother, Simon Heavenrich, engaging in clothing manufacturing. He was the first operator in this trade in the country to introduce power machinery for the cutting of many thicknesses of cloth to a pattern.

Julius Houseman

Another of this group was Julius Houseman, whose father was a cotton and linen manufacturer in Seckendorf, in Bavaria, and who was training his son to succeed him. The revolution had its influence on the young man's life and he came to America in 1850. The beginning of 1852 found him in the clothing business in Battle Creek and Grand Rapids, where he built up an extensive business, with branches in New York, Baltimore and Savannah. Mr. Houseman's business, which was a partnership under the style of Houseman & May, survived so long that it is at this time the second oldest mercantile establishment in Grand Rapids. Mr. Houseman admitted Moses May and his cousin, Joseph Houseman, to partnership. Moses May died and Joseph Houseman acquired the May interest. The establishment is now owned by Henry, a son of Joseph Houseman, and E. W. Jones.

The original Houseman's commercial success is attributed to the generous but discriminating credit which he gave to western Michigan merchants. He once said, "I had to carry a very heavy book in the pioneer days." He was a Democrat, and was successively a State Representative from his city, its Mayor, the candidate of his party for Lieutenant Governor of the state, and a Member of Congress. He was a man of fine intellectual attainments, being especially well trained in economics and politics.

Louis Blitz, who was also a Frankforter, and whose family came to the United States in 1852, took his law at the University of Michigan, and then turned to industry. He was responsible for the foundation of the first glass factory in Michigan, established at Delray, in the late '70's, and covering the making of window glass, commercial ware, and some artistic products. After 20 years of existence, it was bought up by a larger organization. He was a leader among the

Jewish people of Michigan, and a tablet to his memory was erected in the earlier Temple Beth El in Detroit, which was built during the time of his presidency of the congregation.

Jacob Seligman

Jacob Seligman was one of the most picturesque merchants of Michigan in his time. He is said to have been born at Frankfort-on-Main. He got into Oakland county in the middle '60's, engaging in the retail clothing trade at Pontiac, where he married the daughter of Don Carlos Buckland, a pioneer of the county. Seligman was a pigmy of a man, being but five feet tall, a circumstance which he capitalized into a self-advertisement of himself as "Little Jake," by which sobriquet he was always known. He had a competitor in Pontiac in the person of an Englishman named Christopher R. Mabley, in the days before extensive newspaper advertising of commodities and when, in the absence of professional advertising writers, the ingenuity of merchants was taxed to attract customers. Seligman and Mabley were well matched in this respect, and conducted a most intense rivalry, which resulted in Mabley buying Seligman out of Pontiac, the latter going to Saginaw in 1869. Mabley later became the leading merchant of his day in Detroit, while Seligman became a leader in the clothing trade and later a banker in his new home city. He accumulated a considerable fortune and was the moving spirit in the Majestic Building enterprise in Detroit, then the greatest construction project of the state, which was later on occupied by the business successors of his early rival in Pontiac.

The panic of 1893 hit him hard and he was stripped of his fortune and his health. Later he recovered both in Colorado. He was a man of much commercial ability, a good friend and a good enemy, and had a biting wit. Once, on his return to Saginaw for a visit, all his old friends joined in a complimentary dinner, at which the good-will of his former associates was voiced by the eloquent Benton Hanchett. Seligman had developed an enmity against an old business associate and the chance to get even was too good to be lost. Mounting a chair so that he could be seen, he essayed his response with tears streaming down his cheeks. "I have a friend in Detroit," he began, "half of whose life, yes, all of it, I would gladly give to be able to speak as finely as Mr. Hanchett." The rest of his address, after this sally at getting even, was lost in laughter at his mot. Everyone knew he meant what he said. He was very vain. He built the Tower Building in Saginaw, and on the top of the tower placed a life-sized cast-iron statue of himself. It is there yet.

Mark Sloman, who was from Kevolova, in the neighborhood of Berlin, came into Detroit in 1850, and was for many year engaged with local merchants in the leather and wool trades. In 1878 he founded a business of his own largely concerned with the handling of furs, in which he was succeeded by his sons and his sons' sons. One of his sons, Adolph Sloman, born in Detroit, has been for more than forty years a leader of the Detroit bar.

The brothers Seligman Schloss and Emmanuel Schloss were Bavarians who came to Detroit in 1851, engaging immediately in the retail trade, and in 1853 in the wholesale dry goods trade, in which they continued until their retirement in 1914. Their jobbing trade was extended into clothing manufacturing, for which, for these merchants as well as many others similarly engaged, the Lake Superior mining country offered a commanding outlet in the early days.

Others of this group who engaged in similar commercial and industrial enterprises were Sigmund Simon, who served as one of Detroit's Commissioners of the Poor from 1887 until his death; the Freunds, who started the earliest department store in Detroit; Emil Heyn, who initiated a similar business in the '70's, which is still continued by his successors; the Freuds, who, having accumulated a great fortune in Lake Superior mining and mercantile enterprises, invested it in business property of Detroit, which has become very valuable; the Sellings, Schlesingers and Wursburgers, of the clothing trade, and the Kuttnauers, Rosenfelds and Teichners, of the leaf tobacco trade. These were in almost all cases, pioneer merchants of the modern period of Detroit and Michigan which began with the close of the Civil War.

The Humble Pack-Peddlers

A great many German-Jewish merchants of consequence began their mercantile careers in the state as pack-peddlers.

While an occasional sneer is made at these humble merchants, there was a good deal of economic importance to the state in their traffic. They were by no means the pioneers of this order of business. The Irish preceded them all over southern Michigan and northern Ohio, Indiana and Illinois. The particular training of the Irish pack-peddlers came from the North-of-Ireland origin of most of them, where their boyhood occupations had been in linen production and cloth-weaving mills. An apprenticeship to the linen trade, in factories and on bleach-greens, or to the broadcloth trade in weaving, tucking and finishing mills, made them rather more expert than others with these classes of merchandise, which they carried to the farmhouses of Michigan before the days of the railroad, first in packs and later with horse-drawn vehicles. They were in their time the only traders who brought the high-class materials required for table and bed linen, woman's cloaks and the farmers "Sunday-go-to-meetin" attire to the consumers who could afford to buy them. They were great "rogues" as traders, and had a fine inventiveness of hints about smuggling and other out-of-the-way performances calculated to inspire the cupidity of bargain-seekers, maintaining a fine line in their romancing between their suggestions of law evasion and actual confession thereof.

These men made the way for the Jewish pack-peddlers, whose stocks were largely of ribbons, laces, cheap personal ornaments and the general class of dry goods now known in the trade as "novelties"—such as needles, threads, tapes, insertions, buttons, buckles, beads and the like—which were not so profusely stocked at the crossroads stores, nor in such variety as those which those hard-working venders brought to the consumers' doors. The German-Jewish pack-peddler was, moreover, a real trader, where his Irish prototype was a salesman. The latter always sold for money. His Jewish follower was not averse to swapping kind for kind, providing for the making of two profits, one on his merchandise, the other on the raw furs, or the pelts, or the fleeces of wool which he exchanged for the fabricated goods which constituted his outgoing stock.

These itinerant merchants, being foreign in speech and manner, were handicapped by both, as compared to their Irish brothers of the road, except in the German settlements; but despite these handicaps they were welcomed, kindly received, and their visits became the foundations of many enduring friendships and confidences between traders and settlers. Jacob Brown, afterwards a jobber of importance in Detroit, began his business career as one of these pack-peddlers in Clinton county, where he knew practically every farmer and almost always traded his wares for furs, pelts and wool. Joseph Josephs, later a successful merchant of Grayling, "packed" over the entire northern Michigan timber area as a young man. In a manner these and their kind were worthy successors of the early French traders in the same territory.

These, again, are the high lights of the German-Jewish occupancy of industrial opportunities in Michigan. The lists of names given are only suggestive of the numbers engaged. They are far from being complete. For that matter, some of the families and the places in which they labored have passed away and the record of these pioneers is carried only in tradition.

CHAPTER XXXVIII

EXPERIMENTS IN COMMUNITY LIFE

The Frankenmuth Colony—Community Virtues—Some Other Communities—Dr. Schetterly's Experiment—"King" James J. Strang.

Germans have had a good deal to do with colonizations in Michigan. Each of these enterprises sought to realize the ideal of a homogeneous community, having mutual helpfulness as its basis, some running their courses under individual freedom of action, others organized more pretentiously and intended to be the concrete expression of some economic or religious theory. Of the first class the German settlements of the Lutherans of Frankenmuth, Frankentrost, Frankenlust and Frankenhilf, and that of the Bavarian Catholics in and around Westphalia, in Clinton county, were the most strikingly successful. They were composed of colonies of German farmers, content to carve their homes in community out of the wilderness and to preserve their habits and customs so far as was consistent with their new environments and the genius of the new form of government to which they had given allegiance. The bond of unity between the constituents of these particular colonies was uniformly religious. Indeed in some of the Lutheran colonies the religious phase was so dominant that they were essentially theocratic in their community governments up to twenty years ago.

The most extensive and successful of these colonies was that at Frankenmuth, in Saginaw county, and the characteristics ascribable to it were to be found in all the other colonies, though in less marked degrees. Up to 1905 everybody living in Frankenmuth was of German birth or descent save one Welshman named Eugene Williams and an Indian, who spoke German. Every family owned its own farm or village homestead. From 1853 onward for 40 years there had never been a dollar of tax on property in the township returned to the county as unpaid. There had never been a pauper supported by the county. The poor and infirm were provided for by private or church charity. There were no lawsuits before the local justices. The differences between the townspeople were composed by the pastor of the church, and, once the differences were decided, the parties to the controversy went away from their ecclesiastical tribunal in good-natured rivalry in their competitive compliments to their peace-making pastor. Mortgages were taboo. Titles to property passed rarely by deed, generally through probate from parents to sons and daughters in common tenancy. When the daughters of such families prepared to become wives their brothers bought out their shares, and, if they hadn't money enough loans were secured from better-off neighbors, at a savings bank rate of interest, with notes as the evidences of debt, mortgage security being never required.

Community Virtues

When the hand of death left children parentless, the pastor wrestled with the Spirit to guide him in his decision as to what childless family these orphans should be given for their up-bringing. Usually there were several candidates. Orphaned families were never separated. The theory was that what the Lord meant for a family should remain one. Their maintenance was provided for, in their new homes, by modest but sufficient payments from the income of farms bequeathed the church organization by people of good intent for just such purposes.

There was not a perch of bad road in the township, nor a rod of unstable fence. Three horses were a plow-team rather than a pair, an early manifestation of consideration of brute creatures. The education of exceptionally bright young men and women was made a matter of common concern and expense. A striking product of this condition was Prof. Meyer, the great Orientalist of the University of Chicago. Another was Bishop Rademacher, of Fort Wayne, a product of Westphalia, in Clinton.

Betterment of stock breeding was accomplished by communal purchases of pure-bred sires. A bank couldn't live in the community. There was no money to be made from borrowers of money. Those who had "spar-kasse" laid it away in their respective wallets in the iron safe of the trusted storekeeper, to which access might be had when it was wanted. Lorenz Hubinger, the younger, said in 1900, that if any great emergency, national or otherwise, arose upon which he and Pastor Meyer could agree upon the question of necessity, Frankenmuth could produce half a million dollars of gold from its hoards in twenty-four hours. As a matter of fact it contributed $250,000 to the World War Liberty Loan. Naturally conditions have modernized since then.

There were two breweries in the town and several taverns. The brewer concocted his product out of two bushels of malt to the barrel where the metropolitan producers used but one and a half, and it was a mortal sin to offer beer for sale before it had been aged for eight months.

The blind shoemaker was passed around between the tavern-keepers for his keep as a sort of good luck piece, and the little children led him from his cobbler shop to his abode for every meal. Strangers in the village were picked up and entertained without formality, and the little ones made pretty curtseys to them and said "Guten Tag" as they passed and repassed. The wool of the native flocks was spun into yarn and knitted at the local mill.

When the harvest was made, "Kirchwei" was celebrated on a special Sunday. The celebration consisted of open house by everybody and for everybody, at which tables were bounti-

IN THE MAKING OF MICHIGAN 339

fully laden with all manner of refections, of meats and pastry, the creations of which were household problems for weeks in advance. Nor were the offerings wholly confined to solid foods. Frankenmuth made its wines, not only from grapes, but from the dandelions, the elderberries and rhubarb, and the degrees of their fermentation were not laid down by law.

Nor was there excess. When some one developed that human weakness, some father of Israel, with official authority, put what was jocosely described as the "Indian sign" upon him. This ceremonial consisted in notifying every public entertainer that the offender might not be served, under penalty of the law. When works meet for repentance were accomplished by the culprit, the fateful sign was lifted and his personal liberty in sumptuary matters was restored.

Thus Frankenmuth continued for long to be a story out of a picture book, guided and ruled by its spiritual leaders and the elders of the laity as one succeeded another, with all the evidences of industry and thrift and none of discord or lack of kindliness. In some degree or other these characteristics marked all the other homogeneous communities cited.

Some Other Communities

There were some other attempts at community foundations that were not so successful or enduring. When Pastor Sievers brought his group of peasants from Bavaria and founded Frankenlust in 1846, he was followed for a visit by his father-in-law, Herr Koch, who was by the way of being an extensive industrialist in the home-land. Herr Koch was even then an incipient revolutionist and he foresaw the impending protest against undemocratic rule. With that foresight came the determination to move his saw mills and his woolen mills out of Germany before the hand of authority took them from him, as he feared would happen. So he provided Pastor Sievers with funds to buy some hundreds of acres for his new industrial refuge, which he decided to call Amelith, after his wife.

But man proposes. The revolution did come at home and Herr Koch was in it, body, soul and breeches, but his industrial works were not confiscated. So he never came out to create his mid-nineteenth century Pullman or Ivorydale. Sixty acres were deeded for church and school purposes and the present settlement of agricultural Amelith is where industrial Amelith was to have been.

Another of these early idealistic settlements has quite passed away. It was on the shores of Wild Fowl Bay, in Huron county, and was made in 1857, under the leadership of the Rev. Emil Baur, who purchased several thousand acres of government land for his group of pioneers, each family taking up from 80 to 160 acres. The colony was called "Ora Labora," meaning "Pray and Work." The settlement was modeled after that made earlier at New Harmony, Pennsylvania, and was a co-operative community under religious direction, though real property was not held in common. A sawmill, a tannery and workshops were erected, some of the finest cork pine in Michigan being manufactured in the saw mill. A stone-run flouring mill was operated. Hops and barley were grown for the making of domestic supplies of beer. When the civil war broke out so many of the men of the community went into the service that the community began to break up. Only a few cabins remain to mark its site.

Nearby at Port Crescent, in Huron county, a similar but smaller settlement of Germans was made in the early '60's. Christian Schlegelmilch built a flouring mill there which became quite famous for its product.

Dr. Schetterly's Experiment

Dr. George Schetterly, of Ann Arbor, might have gotten along better with his co-operative community had his material been Germanic. Schetterly was a queer kind of idealist who was established in Ann Arbor in 1842. He was Ger-

man born and German educated, and was a disciple of Fourier.
He had an idea that the world should be composed of small
colonies of people whose existence was based on kindness,
mutual forbearance and helpfulness. By the end of 1843
he had expounded his doctrine with such success that on
Dec. 14 of that year fifty-six people from Wayne, Oakland,
Washtenaw and other counties met at Clark's Lake, in Jackson county, for a three day's session for the purpose of organizing an Alphadelphia Association. They adjourned to
Jan. 3, 1843, to meet at Bellevue, and chose the southwest
quarter of Comstock, Kalamazoo county, to be their permanent home.

Those who went into the enterprise were mostly Yankee
farmers. They settled at Comstock in March, 1844. They
built a tabernacle 20x200 feet, agreed not to molest anybody's religion or political opinion, or to compel anyone to
support a church, and were to help each other in sickness.
Anybody over twenty-one who was approved by the leaders
and who had six months provisions was to be let in. The
organization was a sort of a communistic corporation, and
the plan was to reward the workers in proportion to the skill
shown. Each person's property contribution was appraised
and the amounts entered on the books as a credit to each
member as so much stock at $50 a share. There grew to
be 188 in the colony. A number of men put their farms
into the association. The scheme finally "blew up." Schetterly went to Indiana to organize a similar institution called
La Grange Phalanx, and he drifted into Wisconsin to form
another. Both had an equally unlucky history. Dr. Schetterly finally wound up as keeper of the government lighthouse on Grand Traverse Bay.

"King" James J. Strang

Another more practical idealist of the colonizing type
who is well known in Michigan history had Germanic origin
and type claimed for him, but in the later idiom of the turf

he is classifiable as a "ringer." This was James J. Strang, the Mormon King of the Beaver Islands, and the "King" of the historic "Strang" Rebellion." He came from Voree, near La Crosse, Winconsin, where he was raised in a community of Swiss and German farmers, whose descendants occupy the locality to the present time. He went to Nauvoo, Illinois, in 1844 to hear Joseph Smith preach Mormonism, became a Mormon himself, and gathered an expedition of men and women to settle on St. James Island, of the Beaver group, in upper Lake Michigan. There he set up a fantastic church organization, is said to have practiced polygamy and was finally suppressed by the law and force of arms. He combined a great deal of religious activity with successful acquisitiveness of the property of his associates. He was an intellectual man, a fascinating orator and a great religious controversialist. In his autobiography he says that "my father, Clement Strang, is the fifth son of Gabriel Strang; coming originally from a Norman stock, which having continually intermarried with the Dutch and German families of the Hudson, he partakes more of the German type than any other."

CHAPTER XXXIX

PERSISTENCE IN INDUSTRIES AND PROFESSIONS

It was a classical philosopher who wrote the parable, Ne Sutor ultra Crepidam, meaning that sensible folk should not wander beyond the limits of their capacities. But it remained for a German phrase-maker to give the same sentiment and added meaning when he wrote, Schuster, Bleib bei Deinem Leisten.

That the value of the advice has not been lost on many a family of German origin in Michigan is evident from their persistence through successive generations in the lines of business which their fathers founded. This is particularly remarked of families connected with the milling industry. The third generation of Henkels is in the trade in Detroit. The same is true of the Allmendinger family in Ann Arbor in the same industry; of the Stocks of Hillsdale; of the Voight family of Grand Rapids; of the Amendt family at Monroe, and of the Breisch's at Lansing, where the succession has been through the ancestor, Andrew Langerbacher, and his son-in-law and grandson. Frederick Thoman, in the same city and trade, was succeeded by his brother and his brother's son.

The Lauhoff family once had four flouring mills in Detroit. At the beginning of the nineteenth century Alexander Lauhoff was a water power miller at Warburg, in Saxony. He came to Detroit so early that he was disappointed with the place and went on with the Koenig family to the "copper regions", as they were called. That country didn't promise well to him, though it did to Wilhelm Koenig, who remained on Lake Superior and became rich. Alexander Lauhoff, his son, was born in Detroit in 1820, and married in 1838 to Christina Kruse Dueweke, daughter of John Joseph Dueweke, a Hanoverian then established in the grocery trade. There were two other Lauhoff boys, Edmund and Henry. Three generations of the family have been in the milling trade. They also invented and manufactured milling machinery, including a smutting machine. They invented the machinery which is used to flake grains into the forms now used for breakfast food, to toast the food, and to granulate smoking tobacco. Benjamin H. Krause, of Grand Rapids, is selling shoes to the descendants of the same merchants to whom his father and grandfather sold similar goods. Three generations of Kanters have engaged in banking in Detroit and two generations of Schupps in Saginaw. The family names of Schulte and Borgman are identified with the same business in Detroit. Three generations of Clipperts have manufactured and sold bricks in Detroit, with a collateral line at Lansing. Adam Leitelt founded an iron works at Grand Rapids in which he was followed by sons and grandsons.

Max Bendix was director of a German musical society in Detroit in 1869, and his son, Max Bendix, also, followed up his father's art, becoming concert-master in Theodore Thomas' orchestra.

Two generations of Schultes made soap in Detroit. Three generations of Marxhausens were connected with the Detroit Abend Post. John Christopher Wilhelm Greening started a horticultural nursery at Monroe, which is being managed by his grandsons, with a fourth generation growing up to continue it. His neighbor, Isaac E. Ilgenfritz, Pennsylvanian of German ancestry, made a similar foundation in the same

city in 1847, and his business succession is in the hands of
the third generation of his family.

Examples of Family Persistence

This family persistence in the industry or profession of
the founders was particularly noteworthy in the days of the
brewing industry. Three generations of Voigts in Detroit
were brewers, as were three generations of Strohs, three of
Klings, three of Martz's and three of Darmstatters, while
three generations of Schemms have done the same in Saginaw,
and three of Kusterers in Grand Rapids. Three generations
of Buhls have conducted the wholesale hardware business
in Detroit. Three generations of Hubingers have been
connected with the cheese-making industry at Frankenmuth.
There have been two generations of Pastors Haas in the
Lutheran ministry at Detroit and three of Pastors Graebner
in Michigan. Three generations of Behrs and two of
Schmidts have been engaged in tanning leather in the metropolis
of the state. The third generations of the Bornman and
Schober families conduct the printing establishments of the
founders, and three generations of Backuses have had to
do with book-binding and the making of the record books
of Michigan bankers, manufacturers and public officials.

In the baking business there have been three generations
of Wagners in Detroit and in public construction a
similar line of Poraths.

In the medical profession there has been a succession
of Doctors Carstens, Spranger and Schulte. Fred Sanders,
the Baden confectioner who invented the ice-cream soda
beverage, was succeeded by son and grandson. In floriculture,
three generations of the Breitmeyers, Pochelons, and
Gladewitz families in Detroit and three of Fruehs in Saginaw
have conducted the same business. John Henry Haberkorn,
of Allenburg, came to Detroit in 1851 and started furniture
making. His son and grandson followed him in direction
and ownership. Two generations of Molitors followed the

profession of engineering. Three generations of Widmans were represented in the various divisions of the wood-working trade in Detroit.

In the interior of the state the same persistence in identical industry or profession is familiar to smaller circles of people. The characteristic followed the participants from their homeland, where family names, once attached to an industry, were connected with it for generations.

IN THE MAKING OF MICHIGAN 347

CHAPTER XL

GERMANIC NAMES IN OFFICIAL LIFE

State Officials of German Lineage—Regents of University—German-American Senators—German-American Representatives—Representation in the Electoral College—Representation in Congress.

Germanic names begin to appear at an early date in the official history of Michigan. The first steps toward constituting a state government were taken in the Convention of 1835, which met in Detroit on May 11 and adjourned June 24th, 1835. John Biddle was the President of the Convention, whose membership was composed in the largest part, of citizens of Anglo-Saxon lineage, with an odd suggestion of Irish or French birth or descent in a few names. John Biddle himself was of German origin, not so long removed in time, at that, from the German Bittles who had come over in the first decades of the eighteenth century and settled in New Jersey, later going to Pennsylvania. Michael Dousman, of Mackinaw, who represented the fifteenth district, was of German extraction. The first Convention of Assent, held in the following year at Ann Arbor, had as one of its members Michael Stubbs, of Washtenaw, a scion of the early German settlement of that county. The second Convention of Assent, which met three months later in the same city, included in its membership George W. Hoffman, of Berrien; Jacob and Abiel Silver, of Cass; and John E. Schwartz, of Wayne. The proceedings of these Conventions put the first State Constitution into effect after the admission of Michigan as a state of the national union. It continued in effect until the Constitution was revised in 1850. The Convention which did this work met in Lansing on June 3, 1850, and adjourned August 15 of the year named. John Swegels, Jr., of German ancestry from the east, was one of its secretaries, but outside this officer it had no German-American official or member. The convention's revision was adopted by the people.

The Convention of 1867, which was held in Lansing from May 15 to August 22, did not produce a revision which met with the favor of the people. It had representatives from forty-four counties, among them Robert F. Gulick, of Keweenaw, and Peter Henkel, of Wayne. The former was a pioneer in the mining supply trade of the northern peninsula, while the latter was, by the time of the Convention, a well settled and wealthy wholesale merchant and provisioner of Detroit.

The Convention of 1873, which sat at Lansing from August 27 to October 16, was an appointive body, composed of two commissioners from each of the then existing congressional districts. Its membership included no German-American delegate.

The Convention of 1907-8, which met at Lansing from October 22, 1907 to March 3, 1908, was composed of three delegates from each senatorial district of the state. Its membership included many of the ablest and most representative men of the state. Among these Benjamin F. Heckert, of Paw Paw, and Andrew L. Deuel, of Harbor Springs, are said to have been of remote German descent, while Alfred M. Fleishauer, of Reed City, and William J. Oberdorffer, of Stevenson, are of obviously proximate ancestry of Germanic character.

State Officials of German Lineage

None of the Governors of Michigan, either in the colonial period or under the state government, derived their ancestry from the race under discussion, except the one preceding the incumbent at the time of this writing. Governor

Alexander J. Groesbeck's ancestry was Alsatian, which puts him on the border-line.

Nor were any of the Lieutenant-Governors derived from this ancestry. There is no question of the lineage of George L. Maltz, who was State Treasurer from 1887 to 1890, inclusive; nor of that of Joseph F. Hambitzer, who served in 1893-1894; nor that of John W. Haarer, who served from 1913 to 1916.

John Swegles, Jr., he who was Secretary of the Constitutional Convention of 1850, was the first Auditor-General who was selected by the people, serving from 1851 to 1854. Emile Anneke, of Saginaw, held this same office from 1863 to 1866.

The first German-American to appear in the list of Attorneys-General was one of the greatest lawyers in the history of the state bar, Otto Kirchner. He served from 1877 to 1880. Mr. Kirchner was born in Prussia, and was distinctively connected with most German-American movements in the state. His successor, Jacob H. Van Riper, has been claimed by German-Americans as one of their own, but this was not true. Mr. Van Riper was of old Dutch and Yankee ancestry. The next incumbent of the office of German extraction was Franz Christian Kuhn, of Macomb, who held office from 1910 to 1912, when he was advanced to the bench of the Supreme Court of the state. Mr. Kuhn's immediate ancestors were from Germany, coming from Hesse. The later Gov. Groesbeck held the Attorney-Generalship in 1917 and 1918.

No citizen whose name indicates German ancestry has held a commission on the State Board of Education, either during the appointive or elective period of such membership.

The records of the State Board of Agriculture show Abraham C. Prutzman as an appointive member from 1867 to 1873. William J. Oberdorffer, of Stevenson, was a member both by appointment under the Constitution of 1850, and

by election under that of 1908, having been a member of the
board from 1905 to 1911.

The Regents of the University

Membership in the Board of Regents of the University
of Michigan has always been justly considered honorable.
Until the Constitution of 1850 was adopted these places were
filled by appointment of the governor. Under this system
Michael Hoffman, of Washtenaw, was appointed in 1837, and
resigned in 1838. The Reverend Martin Kundig, of Detroit,
about whom more is written herein, was appointed in 1841
and served his full term until 1845.

The constitution of 1850 made the regencies elective.
This method in time brought George L. Maltz, of Alpena,
into office in 1879, he resigning in 1880. Dr. Herman Kiefer,
of Detroit, one of the greatest of the Regents, obtained his
place on the board first by appointment, in the place of Moses
W. Field, of Detroit, who died in 1889. Filling Mr. Field's
term, Dr. Kiefer was re-elected for and served a further
full term of six years, retiring at the end of 1901.

John E. Schwarz, who came into the state as a soldier
under General Anthony Wayne, and whose name appears
rather continuously in that part of the history of the state
recording events occurring during his lifetime, was the first
Adjutant-General of the state, serving from 1836 to 1839.
One of his successors, Frederick William Curtenius, served
from 1855 to 1861.

The Banking Department has two typical names in the
roster of its Commissioners, those of George L. Maltz, who
was appointed to fill a vacancy in 1898 and who served until
1903, and of Henry M. Zimmerman, who served from 1907
until 1911.

In the territorial legislative days there were not many
persons of German birth or ancestry in Michigan. Yet William H. Puthuff, of Michilimackinac, appears as a member
of the First Legislative Council, which held its sessions in

IN THE MAKING OF MICHIGAN 351

Detroit in 1824 and 1825. There was no similar suggestion of ancestry in any of the five succeeding legislative councils. The State Legislature succeeded the Territorial Councils even before the admission of Michigan to the Union. There has always been a consistent representation of German-American membership in both houses since the beginning of a sufficient German-American population to warrant it and to furnish citizens competent to carry on in legislative office. The history of the Senate shows the presence in its various sessions of the following persons of either suspectible or actual German blood:

German-American Representatives

The House of Representatives, being the much larger body of the State Legislature, and the one whose membership is chosen from districts of smaller areas than those of which senatorial districts are composed, has naturally included more German-American citizens of Michigan in its membership than the Senate, because it has had more members of every class and extraction. The German-American memberships of the House of Representatives since the entrance of Michigan into the Union have included, among others, the following, reported by reference to districts and legislative sessions:

Henry Acker, Jackson, 1839-1849; M. Livy Agens, Mason, 1905, 1907, 1909; Charles Angerer, Monroe 2, 1889; Moses Bartow, Clinton, 1863, Clinton 2, 1875; William B. Baum, Saginaw, 1, 1893; Jacob Bauman, Detroit, Wayne 2, 1901; Leonard Baumgaertner, Saginaw 2, 1899, 1900, 1901; Saginaw 1, 1903; William G. Baumgaertner, Manistee, 1887; John Beck, St. Clair 3, 1875; Conrad Bettinger, Wayne 1, 1883, 1887; Samuel J. Bidelman, Barry 1, 1881, 1882; Adam F. Bloom, Wayne 1, 1881, 1882; Albert H. Bosch, Ottawa 2, 1915, 1917; John E. Bonser, Bay 3, 1901; Martin V. Borgman, Wayne 1, 1881, 1882; Gus A. Braun, Huron, 1925; Edward Breitung, Marquette, 1873; John Brisks, Bay 1, 1889; Alexander Cohen Ingham 1, 1907; Barney Diehl, Macomb, 1917;

Louis Dillman, Wayne 1, 1877; Philip Eichorn, St. Clair 1,
1, 1903, 1905; Henry J. Eickoff, Wayne 1, 1897, 1898, 1899,
1900; George J. Eisenmann, Monroe, 1913; John C. Eisenmann, Monroe 1, 1885, 1887; Charles Engel, Sanilac, 1909;
Hieronymus Engleman, Macomb, 1885; Alfred M.
Fleischauer, Osceola, 1897, 1898, 1899, 1900; John W. Frey,
St. Joseph 2, 1853; Augustus H. Gansser, Bay 1, 1911; Ludger A. Gelinas, Saginaw 1, 1909; Gottfried Gettel, Huron,
1915, 1917; Paul Gies, Wayne 1, 1859, 1865, 1877; A. S.
Glesner, Branch 1, 1859; Anthony Gluechlich, Wayne 1, 1893;
August Goebel, Wayne 1, 1879; Michael Greiner, Wayne 2,
1875; John Greusel, Wayne 1, 1871, 1872, 1873; Joseph Greusel,
Wayne 1, 1903, 1905, 1907, 1913; Charles C. Groesbeck, Macomb 2, 1863, 1864; Nicholas Gulick, Shiawassee, 1853; Bernaard Haack, Saginaw 2, 1871, 1872; Gus.Theodore Hartmann;
Houghton 3, 1925; Otto Hatzenbuhler, Wayne 1, 1899, 1900;
David E. Heineman, Wayne 1, 1899, 1900; August Heinemann,
Huron, 1889; William E. Henze, Wayne 1, 1891, 1892; Peter
Herrig, Saginaw 1, 1895, 1897, 1898, 1899, 1900; Christian
Hertzler, Monroe 1, 1873, 1874, 1875; John M. Herz, Wayne
1, 1891, 1892; Emanuel Himsbaugh, Branch 2, 1883; John
Hoeft, Presque Isle, 1909; Herbert H. Hoffman, Sandusky,
1915; Charles A. Hoffmeister, Tuscola 1, 1897, 1898, 1899,
1900; Julius Houseman, Kent 1, 1871, 1872; George C. Huebner, Wayne 1, 1889; Martin Kellander, Ontonagon, 1887;
John Kalmbach, Washtenaw 1, 1911; Jacob Kanouse, Livingstone 1, 1861, 1862; Luther C. Kanouse, Livingstone, 1901;
Edward Kanter, Wayne 1, 1857; Frederick Kappler, Jr.,
Houghton 2, 1909, 1911, 1913; Charles W. Kemmerling,
Monroe, 1909, 1911, 1915; Reuben Kempf, Washtenaw, 1840;
Henry Klei, Wayne 1, 1881, 1882; Peter Kiein, Wayne 1,
1869, 1870, 1875; Herman L. Koehler, Wayne 1, 1913, 1915;
Joseph Kuhn, Wayne 1, 1879; Frederick W. A. Kurth, Wayne
2, 1879; Benjamin Laubach, Ottawa 2, 1877, 1879; Albert
T. Linderman, Muskegon 2, 1893, 1895; Peter Linderman,
Ingham 1, 1857, 1858; Frederick Lindow, St. Clair 1, 1899;

IN THE MAKING OF MICHIGAN 353

Joseph P. Maas, Wayne 1, 1913; John Makelin, Sanilac 1, 1885, 1887; Charles Manzelman, Wayne 1, 1885; William H. Martz, Wayne 1, 1911, 1913, 1915, 1917; Henry Mayer, St. Clair 1, 1883; Louis Meyer, Livingstone 1. 1875; Joseph P. Munne, St. Clair, 1851; Joseph T. S. Munne, St. Clair 1, 1871, 1872; Christopher Mohr, Bay 2, 1893; Walter E. Molster, Wayne 1, 1897, 1898; Julius Movius, Washtenaw, 1850; William F. Nank, Macomb, 1905, 1907, 1913, 1915; Louis Neller, Ingham 1, 1913; August Neidermeier, Monroe 2, 1897, 1898, 1899, 1900; Frank Noeker, Clinton 2, 1879, 1883; Conrad John Netting, Wayne 1, 1925; William J. Oberdorffer, Menominee, 1897, 1898, 1899, 1900, 1925; Christian A. Opperborn, Alpena, 1911; Placidus Ord, Chippewa, 1846; George Orth, Arenac, 1891, 1892; Olin Pengra, Huron, 1883; Albert E. Peterman, Houghton 1, 1913, 1915, 1917; George Peters, Monroe, 1861, 1862; Anthony Paucher, Washtenaw, 1838; August Quintel, Bay 2, 1915, 1917; Richard Radebaugh, Ingham 1, 1911; Lawrence T. Remer, St. Clair 1, 1881, 1882; Theodore Rentz, Wayne 1, 1887; John Michael Riegel, Bay 2, 1901; Cel Rix, St. Clair, 1843, 1844; Albert H. Rutter Wayne 1, 1919, 1921; John G. Rummel, Saginaw 3, 1883; John C. Rauchholz, Saginaw 2, 1925; John J. Rogner, Tuscola 1, 1893, 1895; John V. Ruehle, Sr., Wayne 1844; Theodore C. Ruff, St. Clair 2, 1913; George W. Schaeffer, St. Joseph, 1913; William H. Schantz, Barry 1905, 1907, 1909; Peter Schars, Macomb 1, 1865, 1867; Casper F. Scholtler, Macomb 1, 1875; B. F Schellberg, Wayne 1, 1893; Henry L. Schmidt, Kent 1, 1917; Henry Schmidt, Saginaw 1, 1899, 1900; John Schmidt, Osceola, 1913, 1915, 1917; John E. Schwartz, Wayne, 1845; Charles Schier, Washtenaw 1, 1855, 1869, 1870; Washtenaw 2, 1865; John W. Shisler, Kent 2, 1897, 1898, 1899, 1900; Frederick Shurtz, St. Joseph, 1839, 1844; Charles A. Sink, Washtenaw 1, 1919; Henry L. Stoflet, Wayne 5, 1889; Otto Stoll, Wayne 1, 1895; William P. Strauch, Shiwassee, 1925; John Struble, Cass 1, 1875; Henry Stumpenhausen, Washtenaw 2, 1899, 1900, 1901; Jacob Summers, Macomb, 1835, 1836;

Leo Taube, Wayne 1, 1917; Isaac J. Ullman, St. Joseph, 1835, 1836; Madison J. Ulrich, Kent 1, 1885; G. Joseph Unsoeld, Wayne 1, 1909, 1911, 1913; Philip B. Wachtel, Emmet, 1889, 1891, 1892, 1893; Leo P. Wagner, Saginaw 1, 1917; Joseph Waltz, Wayne 4, 1879, 1885; Charles A. Weidenfeller, Van Buren, 1913; August J. Weier, Monroe 1, 1897, 1898, 1899, 1900; Joseph Weier, Monroe 1, 1869, 1870; Henry A. Weiss, Gratiot, 1885; Joseph M. Weiss, Wayne 1, 1907; Charles A. Weisser, Barry, 1915, 1917; Charles Wellman, St. Clair 2, 1885, 1887; Peter Wenting, Muskegon, 1913; August F. Wettlaufer, Wayne 1, 1889; Frederick Wieland, Oakland 2, 1913, 1915; Jacob M. Wiltse, Saginaw 4, 1883; John K. Yocum, Washtenaw, 1851; Henry J. Zacharias, Saginaw 1, 1907; Elisha Zimmerman, Oakland 3, 1873, 1874; Henry M. Zimmerman, St. Clair 2, 1897, 1898; John Zimmerman, Wayne 1, 1893.

German-American Senators

Sylvester Abel, Washtenaw, 1857; John E. Barringer, Macomb, 1887, 1889; Frank P. Bohn, Luce, 1925; Edward Breitung, Marquette, 1877; William M. Cline, St. Clair, 1885; Frederick W. Curtenius, Kalamazoo, 1853, 1867; Joseph Fleishheim, Menominee, 1891, 1893; Charles A. Friedlender, Iosco, 1891; August H. Gansser, Bay, 1915, 1917; Gottfried Gettell, Huron, 1925; Paul Gies, Wayne, 1867; Michael Greiner, Wayne, 1885; John Greusel, Wayne, 1875, 1881, 1883; Frank A. Groger, Lenawee, 1915; Albert O. Heine, Bay, 1905; Carl Heisterman, Huron, 1885; Christian Hetzler, Monroe, 1885; Louis N. Hilsendegen, Wayne, 1915; Reuben Kempf, Washtenaw, 1885; Herman L. Koehler, Wayne, 1917, John Leidlein, Saginaw, 1899, 1900, 1911; Hugo Charles Loeser, Jackson, 1901; Joseph Nagel, Wayne, 1889; Abraham C. Prutzman, St. Joseph, 1869, 1871, 1873; William A. Rosenkrans, Shiawassee, 1911, 1913; Anthony B. Schumacher, Eaton, 1900; John E. Schwarz, Wayne, 1847; Michael Shoemaker, Jackson, 1851, 1877, 1883, 1885; Frederick Schurtz, St. Joseph, 1857; Charles

A. Sink, Washtenaw, 1921; Albert Stoll, Wayne, 1899; Walter F. Treuttner, Gogebic, 1925; Mathew D. Wagner, Huron, 1897, 1898, 1899, 1900; Joseph M. Weiss, Wayne, 1891, 1892, 1893. Charles T. Winegar, Dickinson, 1913.

Representation in the Electoral College

In the representation that Michigan has had in the electoral college since her admission as a state of the Union, the first apparently German-American name to appear was in 1860, when Dr. Edward Dorsch, of Monroe, was in the list of the first Lincoln electors. Dr. Dorsch was a Monroe physician of much prominence who was born abroad, practiced for 34 years, and made valuable contributions to the University of Michigan.

In 1864 when Lincoln was a candidate for re-election the Michigan list of electors included Frederick Waldorf and Christian Eberbach. Mr. Waldorf, who was a native-born German, came from Welstein, Hesse Darmstadt, and had settled in Michigan early enough to have married the daughter of John Jacques Godfrey, of Monroe, an Indian and fur trader in 1844. He was Mayor in 1857, 1858, 1860, and 1866. Mr. Eberbach was one of the original German settlers of Washtenaw county, who came over in 1838. He was educated as an apothecary in Stuttgart, and was long a leading citizen of Ann Arbor. In 1868 there were among the six district electors William Doeltz, a merchant of Detroit, and Michael C. T. Plessner, who was a Saginaw physician, pharmacist and chemist. In 1872, Mr. Waldorf again appeared as an elector, and Dr. Herman Kiefer, of Detroit, who later became a Regent of the University, and Charles L. Ortman, a leading Saginaw lumberman, were in the list of those who made General Grant president. In 1876 Mr. Doeltz reappeared as a presidential elector, Charles H. Kempf being another, both of German-American extraction. It was not until 1888 that another German-American citizen of Michigan was chosen a presidential elector, this one being Edward

Burk, a manufacturer who took an active interest in furthering the fortunes of the Republican party. In 1892, Otto Ihling, of Kalamazoo, and Conrad G. Swenberg, of Grand Rapids were among the electors. In 1908 Solomon Stern was in the Michigan list of members of the Electoral College.

Representation in Congress

No citizen of Michigan of German-American extraction has achieved Senatorial honors so far in the history of the State. As the early population was rather distinctively of Eastern origin it was natural that a considerable period should elapse before one of the newer peoples could find a place in the House of Representatives from a Michigan district. Until the Forty-Eighth Congress of 1883, all the representatives from Michigan were of what might be called distinctive Yankee origins. In the Forty-Eighth Congress the outlanders broke into the representative delegation with marked emphasis. William C. Maybury, who was of Irish extraction, and Julius Houseman and Edward Breitung, both of German birth, were elected to represent the First, Fifth and Eleventh districts respectively. Mr. Maybury held out for two terms. The other two citizens named were single-termers. The next German-American to achieve such honors was Ferdinand Brucker, of Saginaw, elected to the Fifty-Fifth Congress in 1896, and serving during 1897 and 1898, a single term. In the Sixty-Seventh Congress, William H. Frankhauser represented the Third District, but he died early in his term.

In Michigan the honor of being the standard bearer for congressional honors on the part of the minority party has not been without distinction. Many an apparent forlorn hope has come pretty close to being a victory. Among the contestants for the current minority party for Congress in the state's history have been John H. Fedewa, in the Sixth District for the Fiftieth Congress in 1886; John Semec, in the Eleventh District for the Fifty-First Congress in 1890; Ferdinand Brucker, in the Eighth District, for the Fifty-Sixth Congress in 1898; Martin G. Loennecker, in the Second District for the Fifty-Seventh Congress, in 1900; William A. Bahlke, in the Eleventh District, for the Sixtieth Congress, in 1906; William W. Wedemeyer, in the Third District, for the Sixty-Third Congress, in 1913; William A. Seegmiller, in the Eighth District for the Sixty-Fifth Congress, in 1916, and the Sixty-Ninth in 1924; Henry C. Haller, in the Tenth District, for the Sixty-Fifth and Sixty-Sixth Congress in 1916 and 1918; and Frederick Kappler in the Twelfth District, for the Sixty-Eighth Congress 1922.

Perhaps the most distinguished career in the House of Representatives of any congressman from Michigan was that of Joseph W. Fordney, Representative from the Eighth Michigan district from the Fifty-Sixth to the Sixty-Seventh Congress, inclusive, Chairman of the Ways and Means Committee of the House and author of the Fordney-McCumber Tariff Law. Mr. Fordney's ancestry was remotely German, his great-grandfather, who was a resident of Alsace, having come to America with General Lafayette. The family name at that time was Fortner.

CHAPTER XLI

THE GEOGRAPHICAL IMPRESS OF THE RACES

Beginnings of Modern Place Names—The Impress of German Settlement—Townships, Cities and Villages with Germanic Names.

Where the footsteps of men fall on the paths and roadways of new country they leave their impress, but not more surely than do the races of men which contribute to the making of the populations of the same new countries. The Romans left their "chesters" all over England, the "chesters" being the "castra" or camps which the legions formed and in which they rested. In a later day the English, the French and the Spaniards left their marks on the names of the locations in the various territories of the United States of whose dominion they were the pioneer contestants with the native savages.

New England's Bostons, Newports, Cambridges, Surreys, Norfolks, Hartfords, Plymouths, Northamptons, Middlesexes, Bristols and similarly named cities and towns are the monuments of the race of the first English arrivals in that territory, as are Bangor, Belfast, Limerick, Derry, Londonderry, Antrim, Sullivan and others of equally traceable extraction the marks of the first abiding places of transported Irish settlers in Maine, New Hampshire and Vermont; and, as, again, the early French marked New England with new editions of Calais, Lubec, Barre and St. Croix, when they first traversed the wilds of its most northerly states.

In much the same manner have the various races that have successively or concurrently inhabited Michigan left their unmistakable impresses upon the geographical nomenclature of the state. The Indians today survive largely in the names of places to which they gave, in the words of their various tongues, descriptive names and titles of poetic suggestion.

The French, first foreign comers, queer compounds of piety and amiable deviltry, made the next markings of this character. Their missionaries, imbued with the spirit of their faith, fairly exhausted the litany of their saints in their appellations of geographic places, bestowing them with wonderful propriety. The placid lake was put under the protection of the gentle St. Claire. The Indian mission site was given to the care of the more martial St. Ignatius. The falls between Superior and Huron were named after the Blessed Lady, while the more dangerous islands and rocks were given to the sturdier spiritual attention of St. Michael, St. Martin and St. Vital. Meantime to the Coureur du Bois the rivers were all red, or black, or white, and so we have them as the Rouge, or the Sable or the Blanc. The points were either Aux Chenes, or Au Sable or Au Pins, depending upon their physical characteristics and resemblances.

Beginnings of Modern Place Names

The advent of the English, in their turn, produced no marked impress upon the geographical nomenclature of the territory of Michigan. They held not long at a time, and none too securely ever.

Still other marked influences were the wars of the Revolution and of 1812—1813, producing as they did scores of national heroes who found their Valhallas in the names given cities, towns and villages, such as those named after Washington, Madison, Monroe, Adams, Jefferson, Lafayette, Livingstone and other great figures of the earlier days of the Republic, the names in most cases having been transported into Michigan from the earlier places, similarly called, out of which proceeded the New York and New England immigrants who helped settle the state in its early days. Later on a returned veteran of the Mexican war gave his home locality the name of Delrey, its identity now lost by consolidation with Detroit. Thus the state was marked with names indicating the locality origins of the early divisions of the settlers. There are traces of New York origins in **Albion, Fenton, Troy, Holly, Lansing, Monroe, Rochester and Hudson,** as there are of New England in **Chelsea, Lowell, Plymouth, Howell, Ovid, Quincy, Manchester, Hartford, Bangor** and scores of other similarly named places.

Then came the Irish with the days of the makings of canals and railroads. There weren't so many places left for them to name as the earlier pioneers had to christen, but they recalled their ancestral land in the county names of **Antrim, Clare, Emmet, Wexford and Roscommon** while **Boyne, Blaney, Carrollton, Curran, Emmet, Fergus, Lennon, McBrides, McGinn, McIvor, Markey, Mt. Morris, Riley Center, Roscommon, Sheridan, Sullivan, Nestoria and Waterford,** among the postoffices and towns, and **Kearney, Baltimore,** three or four **Sheridans, Breen, Brady, Grattan,** two **Tyrones, Powell, Larkin, Sullivan, Waterford, Nester, Flynn, Moore, Doyle and Emmet,** among the townships, have unmistakably Celtic flavors and origins.

The Impress of German Settlement

The Germans constituted the next large mass immigration to Michigan after that of the Irish. To a great extent the larger accessions to the population of the state from the two races were contemporaneous.

Of the counties Baraga bears the name of a great German-American missionary.

Of the townships the names of Germanic origin include **Mathias** in Alger; **Overisal** in Allegan; **Custer** in Antrim; **Baraga** in Baraga; **Frankenlust** in Bay; **Newburg** in Cass; **Koehler** in Cheboygan; **Westphalia** in Clinton; **Frederic** in Crawford; **Breitung** in Dickinson; **Vienna** in Genesee; **Sigel**

IN THE MAKING OF MICHIGAN 361

in Huron; Berlin and Sebewa in Ionia; Stambaugh in Iron; Hanover in Jackson; Weber in Lake; Hamburg in Livingstone; Stronach in Manistee; Custer in Mason; Meyer in Menominee; Hillman and Vienna in Montmorency; Otto in Oceana; Klacking in Ogemaw; Bearinger, Bismarck, Krakow, Metz, Moltke and Posen in Presque Isle; Blumfield, Brandt, Frankenmuth and Kochville in Saginaw; Custer and Minden in Sanilac; Germfask and Mueller in Schoolcraft; Berlin and Cottrell in St. Clair; Mendon in St. Joseph; Hamtramck in Wayne and Hanover in Wexford.

Of the post offices the German-named ones in the state include Bonifas in Gogebic; Brant in Saginaw; Brohman in Newaygo; Brunswick in Muskegon; Carlshend in Marquette; Custer in Mason; Dolph in Missaukee; Doster in Barry; Engadine in Mackinac; Eckermann in Chippewa; Frankenmuth in Saginaw; Frankfort in Benzie; Freda in Houghton; Frederic in Crawford; Gera in Saginaw; Goetzville in Chippewa; Hamburg in Livingstone; Hamtramck in Wayne; Hanover in Jackson; Herman in Baraga; Hermansville in Menominee; Hessel in Mackinac; Humboldt in Marquette; Interlocken in Grand Traverse; Jacobsville in Houghton; Johannesburg in Chippewa; Kinde in Huron; Klingers in St. Joseph; Luther in Lake; Levering in Emmett; Luzerne in Oscoda; Mendon in St. Joseph; Minden in Sanilac; Nessen in Benzie; Oberlin in Gladwin; Oden in Emmett; Posen in Presque Isle; Raber in Chippewa; Ruth in Huron; Rumely in Alger; Schaffer in Delta; Schomberg in Leelanau; Schultz in Barry; Steiner in Monroe; Steuben in Schoolcraft; Strasburg in Monroe; Walhalla in Mason; Waltz in Wayne; Weidman in Isabella; Winde in Delta, and Winegars in Gladwin.

Of the incorporated villages bearing German names the examples are Custer in Mason; Frankenmuth in Saginaw; Hanover in Jackson; Luther in Lake; Mesick in Wexford; Posen in Presque Isle; Stambaugh in Iron; Webberville in Ingham and Westphalia in Clinton.

CHAPTER XLII

SOME "FIRST" PEOPLE AND THINGS

There have been some more or less intimate contacts of Germans with the early public life of Michigan, which was then, for the most part, Detroit.

Dr. Eberts, elsewhere referred to, was the first Sheriff of Wayne County in 1796.

The first seal of the city of Detroit was made by a German engraver, William Wagener, of York, Pennsylvania.

The first movement for a public school system, made in 1841, was promoted by Father Martin Kundig, of Detroit. There was then one French and one German school in the city.

The first train on the Erie & Kalamazoo Railroad, which was the precursor of the Lake Shore system, was brought into Monroe in 1836, drawn by horses, with John Barrager as their driver.

The first modern saw-mill at Mackinac, driven by steam, was Michael Dousman's, built in 1830. The first mill at Muskegon was Joseph Stronach's waterdriven mill, built in 1842.

The first iron foundry in Grand Rapids was constructed and operated in 1838 by W. S. Levake, an eastern German-American.

There were two women fur traders of fame in the history of that traffic in the west. One was Madame Laframboise, at Grand Rapids. The other, not so famous, was Teresa Schindler, at Mackinaw, a woman of German-Canadian extraction whose ancestors lived at Montreal.

In 1827 Gen. John E. Schwartz owned and operated the largest schooner on the Detroit River and the connecting lakes. It was the Emily, of only 34 tons burthen.

The earliest organization of city mail distribution in Michigan in Detroit was in 1864. In the first squad of letter-carriers appointed was Henry Tenwinkle, born in Prussia in 1818.

The first distinctive German cornet band organized in Michigan was that of Battle Creek. Gustave Brucker was its director.

The first Philharmonic Quartet for the presentation of chamber music was that which Wilhelm Yunck directed in Detroit in the '80's.

The earliest extraction of commercial ammonia from gas-house liquors was made in Detroit by George Stroh and George Osius in Detroit.

The first brewer in Western Michigan was Peter Weirich, from Coblenz, who started production at Grand Rapids in 1852.

Titus Hutzel, son of August Hutzel, who married the pioneer Heinrich Mann's daughter at Ann Arbor, built at Ann Arbor the waterworks for his home city and operated it for years, one of the few examples of such privately owned utilities in the state.

Among the founders of the Republican party at the meeting held "under the Oaks" at Jackson, July 6, 1854, was Valentine Hilsendegen, who represented Wayne county at the session.

Among the curiosities of political life in Michigan have been the election of three clergymen in active service to the executive direction of their cities. These three happened to be Roman Catholic priests, one being Reverend Patrick R. Dunigan, of Lapeer, the other two of German extraction. Rev. Charles J. Koenig was Mayor of New Baltimore in the 1900's and Rev. Frank A. Seifert is the current (1926) President of the Village of Daggert, in the Northern Peninsula.

ERRATA

¶ The home of Pastor Loehe, spoken of on page 243 and elsewhere, and given as Neuedettelsau, should appear as Neuendettelsau.

¶ The doubt about Pastor Loehe having been university-trained is resolved by later information that he was so educated.

¶ The selection of Frankenmuth as a German mission settlement, credited to Pastor Schmid, of Ann Arbor, was not wholly due to Pastor Schmid. His helper, Pastor Auch, of Sebewaing, is entitled to part of the credit, at least.

¶ The reference to the pioneer Hubinger, of Frankenmuth, as the elder Lorenz Hubinger, is incorrect. His name was John Matthias Hubinger.

¶ The name of Carl Ernest Schmidt, is incorrectly given in one place as Carl Eugene Schmidt. The former is the correct version.

EPILOGUE

The story of the migrations to and settlement in Michigan of a single race contained in the foregoing pages has no claim of completeness made for it. It is a running commentary rather than a perfect Index Hominum et Rerum. From its pages are lost the names of German settlers whose neighbors and fellow-citizens have corrupted them beyond identification by phonetic spellings; and those other family names which have been abbreviated or which have lost the original forms by being translated into English equivalents.

Much more might be written in the same strain, bringing out the contributions to the making of Michigan, by men of German birth, blood and ancestry, many of which have been forgotten, or have been rendered in modesty, or have been so wrought in humility and sacrifice, albeit always with industry and good humor, that their actual and relative values have not been fully appreciated; and, maybe, some day, more will be written.

These things have not been set down to furnish the basis for any claim that this group has exceeded its neighbors and contemporaries in patriotic, civic, cultural or commercial effort; but, rather, to show that in the honorable competition of contribution toward the building of the state and the nation it has given its full share to the sum of the common efforts of life; been generous in particular lines where its peculiar psychology and training made that possible; and has done many useful and profitable things for itself and the common citizenship, all of them important, some of them rising to the standards of glory.

From the nature of the subject, and the self-imposed limitations of the writer, much of what has been written has been local and personal; and the treatment thereof has been cursory and racy, rather than profound or elaborate. Perhaps there have been inaccuracies of inclusion or exclusion, but none of them have been wilful; and, as to them who may have been mistakenly included, let it be said that they are in good company, while those who have been forgotten or omitted may be remembered at another time.

At any rate, the pages now ending are not the results of any attempt to scale the heights of racial enthusiasm, for the writer is not of the blood of those whom he has sought to discuss, is not a Teuton but a Celt, the son of an Irish merchant sailor, for whom the lakes that surround Michigan were the scenes of the activities of a life-time. His strain and its experiences have taught his breed that no harm can come from occasional reversions to the facts of history.

IN THE MAKING OF MICHIGAN

BIBLIOGRAPHY

Much of the matter contained in this volume has been derived from local sources, such as the home history publications of newspapers, and more from the incomparable Michigan Pioneer Collections, with some other matter from the resources of the Burton Historical Collection of the Detroit Public Library. Beyond these sources the published works consulted constitute the following bibliography:

Adams, Mrs. F. L.	Pioneer History of Ingham County. Lansing, 1923.
Andreas, A. T.	History of St. Clair County, Michigan. Chicago, 1883.
Bailey, J. R.	Mackinac, formerly Michilimackinac. Third edition, Lansing, 1897.
Beakes S. W.	Past and Present of Washtenaw County, Michigan. Ann Arbor, 1906.
Beers, F. W.	History of Washtenaw County, Michigan. 1881.
Bek, William G.	The German Settlement Society of Philadelphia, 1916.
Benjamin, Gilbert Giddings	The Germans in Texas. Philadelphia, 1916.
Biographical Publishing Company	Portrait and biographical album of Washtenaw County, Michigan. Chicago, 1891.
Biographical Publishing Company	Portrait and biographical record of Muskegon and Ottawa Counties, Michigan. Chicago, 1893.
Biographical Publishing Company	Portrait and biographical record of Saginaw and Bay Counties, Michigan. Chicago, 1892.

Bosse, George Von	Das Deutsche Element in Dem Vereinigten Staaten unter Besonderer Berucksicktigung seines Politischen, Ethischen, Sozialen und Erzieherischen Einflusses. 1908.
Brook, Andrew Ten	"Our German Immigrations." Michigan Pioneer and Historical Collection. 1894.
Bulkley, J. McC.	History of Monroe County, Michigan. Chicago, 1913.
Burton, Clarence M.	City of Detroit.
Burton, Clarence M.	Scrapbook. (Burton Historical Library, Detroit.)
Butterfield, G. E.	Bay County Past and Present. Bay City, 1918.
Carlisle, Fred	Wayne County Historical and Pioneer Society. Chronograph of Notable Events in History of the North-West Territory and Wayne County, 1531-1890. Detroit, 1890.
Catlin, G. B. and Ross, Robert B.	Landmarks of Wayne County and Detroit. Detroit, 1898.
Chapman, C. C.	Portrait and biographical album of Ingham and Livingstone Counties, Michigan. Chicago, 1891.
Chapman, C. C.	Portrait and biographical album of Isabella County, Michigan. A complete history of the county, from its earliest settlement. Chicago, 1884.
Chapman, C. C.	Portrait and biographical album of Jackson County. Michigan. Chicago, 1890.
Chapman, C. C.	Portrait and biographical record of Kalamazoo, Allegan and Van Buren Counties, Michigan. Chicago, 1892.
Chapman, C. C.	History of Kent County. Chicago, 1881.
Chapman, C. C.	Portrait and biographical album of Midland County, Michigan. Chicago, 1884.
Chapman, C. C.	Portrait and biographical album of Oakland County, Michigan. Chicago, 1891.
Chapman, C. C.	History of Washtenaw County, Michigan, and biographies of representative citizens. Chicago, 1881.
Chapman, C. C.	Portrait and biographical album of Barry and Eaton Counties, Michigan. Chicago, 1891.
Chapman, C. C.	Portrait and biographical album of Clinton and Shiawassee Counties, Michigan. Chicago, 1891.

Chapman, C. C.	Portrait and biographical record of Genesee, Lapeer and Tuscola Counties, Michigan. Chicago, 1892.
Chapman, C. C.	Portrait and biographical album of Gratiot County, Michigan. Chicago, 1884.
Chapman, C. C.	History of Kent County. 1881.
Collin, H. P.	A Twentieth Century History and biographical record of Branch County, Michigan. New York, 1906.
Cook, S. F.	Drummond Island. The story of the British Occupation, 1815 - 1828. Lansing, 1896.
Cook, S. F.	Mackinaw in History. Lansing, 1895.
Coolidge, O. W.	Twentieth Century History of Berrien County, Michigan. 1906.
Courier, Ann Arbor	Branch County Directory and Historical Record. 1871.
Crampton, E. J.	History of the Saint Clair River. St. Clair, 1921.
Dewey, F. S.	Alpena County, its shore-lines and terraces, its rocks and hills, its giant wells and subterranean river, its resources and curiosities. (n. d.)
Dillenback, J. D.	History and Directory of Ionia County, Michigan. Grand Rapids, 1872.
Dillenback, J. D.	History and Directory of Kent County, Michigan. Grand Rapids, 1870.
Disturnell, John	Island of Mackinac, giving a description of all the objects of interest, also an account of the early settlement of the country. Philadelphia, 1875.
Durant, S. W.	History of Ingham and Eaton Counties, Michigan. Philadelphia, 1880.
Durant, S. W.	History of Kalamazoo County, Michigan. 1877.
Ensign, D. W.	History of Allegan and Barry Counties, Michigan. Philadelphia, 1880.
Ensign, D. W.	History of Berrien and Van Buren Counties, Michigan. Philadelphia, 1880.
Erickson, Robert E.	Histories of the Evangelical Lutheran Church in Various Michigan Counties. Detroit, 1920-21-22.
Everett, Franklin	Memorials of the Grand River Valley. Chicago, 1878.

Everts, L. H.	History of Calhoun County, Michigan. Philadelphia, 1877.
Everts, L. H.	History of Oakland County, Michigan. Philadelphia, 1877.
Everts, L. H.	History of St. Joseph County, Michigan. Philadelphia, 1877.
Everts and Abbott	History of Genesee County, Michigan. Philadelphia, 1879.
Everts and Abbott	History of Livingstone County, Michigan. Philadelphia, 1880.
Everts and Abbott	History of Hillsdale County, Michigan. Philadelphia, 1879.
Farmer, Silas	History of Detroit and Wayne County and Early Michigan. Detroit, 1890.
Farmer, Silas	History of Detroit and Michigan; or, The Metropolis Illustrated, including a full record of territorial days in Michigan, and the annals of Wayne County. Detroit, 1884.
Farmer, Silas	History of Detroit and Michigan, including a full record of territorial days in Michigan and the annals of Wayne County. Detroit 1889.
Faust, A. B.	The German Element in the United States. 1909.
Flohrer, William W.	Liberty Writings of Dr. Herman Kiefer. New York, 1917.
Fogel, Edwin M.	Beliefs and Superstitions of the Pennsylvania Germans. Philadelphia, 1915.
Forster, John H.	Life in the Copper Mines of Lake Superior. Michigan Pioneer and Historical Collection, 1887.
Fox, T. B.	History of Saginaw County, from the year 1819 down to the present time. East Saginaw, 1858.
Fox, T. B.	History of the Saginaws and the settlement of Saginaw County from 1819 to the present. East Saginaw, 1879.
Fulda, Ludwig	Amerikanische Eindrucke. 1914.
Fuller, G. N.	Economic and Social Beginnings of Michigan. 1916.
Glover, L. H.	A Twentieth Century History of Cass County, Michigan. Chicago, 1906.

IN THE MAKING OF MICHIGAN 371

Graebner, Th. — The Bavarian Settlements of the Saginaw Valley. St. Louis, 1919.

Grover, F. R. — A brief history of Les Cheneaux Islands; some new chapters of Mackinac history. Evanston, Ill., 1911.

Gulley, O. S., Bornman & Co. — Wayne County, Michigan, Historical and Pioneer Society. Chronography of notable events in the history of the North-West Territory and Wayne County, 1531-1890, with biographical sketches of the early explorers and pioneers.

Gansser, A. H. — History of Bay County, Michigan, and representative citizens. Chicago, 1905.

Henry, Alexander — Alexander Henry's Travels and Adventures in the years 1760-1776; edited with historical introduction by M. M. Quaife. Chicago, 1921.

Hogaboam, J. J. — The Bean Creek Valley, Hudson, Mich., 1876.

Howland, C. P. — An Historical Sketch of Sand Lake.

Herald Printing Co. — St. Clair County Centennial Celebration, 1821-1921. Pt. Huron, 1921.

Hartwick, L. M. — Oceana County Pioneers and Business Men of Today. Pentwater, Mich., 1890.

Interstate Publishing Company. — History of Jackson County, Michigan.

Jenks, W. L. — St. Clair County, Michigan. Its History and Its People. Chicago, 1912.

John, S. A. — Jubilaeumsschrift zum Fuenfundsiebzigsten Jahrestag der Gruendung der Deutschen Evang. 1908.

Kalamazoo Publishing Company — The Centennial Celebration at Kalamazoo, Mich., July 4, 1876. Kalamazoo, 1876.

Kellog, L. P. — The Capture of Mackinac in 1812. Madison, Wis., 1913.

Kelton, D. H. — Annals of Fort Mackinac. Revised edition. Detroit, 1883.

Knapp, J. I. and Bonner, R. I. — Illustrated History and Biographical Record. Lenawee County, Mich. Adrian, 1903.

Kohl, John George — Travels in America, New York, 1855.

Leach, M. L. — A History of the Grand Traverse Region. Traverse City. 1884.

THE GERMANIC INFLUENCE

Learned, Marion Dexter Americana Germanica. Philadelphia, 1917.
Leeson, M. A. History of Saginaw County, Michigan. Saginaw, 1918.
Leeson, M. A. History of Macomb County, Michigan. Chicago, 1882.
Michigan Immigration, Commissioner of; "Des Auswanderer Wegweiser."
Michigan Immigration, Commissioner of; "Michigan, Seine Vorzuege." Lansing, 1875.
Michigan Immigration, Commissioner of; "Michigan und Seine Hilfsquellen." Lansing, 1882.
Michigan Volksblatt Semi-Centennial Issue, Detroit, 1902.
Millard, A. L. Early History of Lenawee County and of the City of Adrian. Adrian, 1876.
Mills, J. C. History of Saginaw County, Michigan. Saginaw, 1918.
Newton, Stanley The Story of Sault Ste. Marie and Chippewa County. Sault Ste. Marie, Mich., 1923.
Oliver, D. D. Centennial History of Alpena County, Michigan, 1837-1876. Alpena, 1903.
Page, — History of Manistee County, Michigan. Chicago, 1882.
Page, — History of Muskegon County, Michigan, with illustrations and biographical sketches of its prominent men and pioneers. Chicago, 1882.
Page, — History of Bay County, Michigan. Chicago, 1883.
Page, — History of Lapeer County, Michigan. Chicago, 1884.
Palmer, Frend "Germans in Michigan." (Palmer Scrapbook) Burton Historical Library, Detroit.
Parkin, A. E. Historical geography of Detroit; Michigan and its resources, 1881; Michigan and its resources, 1883.
Potter, W. W. History of Barry County. Grand Rapids, 1912.
Reitzel, Robert Des Armen Teufel. (Reprint) Detroit, 1913.
Robinson, George History of Cheboygan and Mackinac Counties, Detroit, 1873.
Rogers, H. S. History of Cass County from 1825 to 1875. Cassopolis, Mich., 1875.

Rosengarten, J. G.	The German Soldier in the Wars of the United States. 1886.
Ross, R. B., and Catlin, G. B.	Landmarks of Wayne County and Detroit. Detroit, 1898.
Rowland, O. W.	A History of Van Buren County, Michigan. Chicago, 1912.
Ruff, Joseph	Michigan History Magazine. Joys and sorrows of an emigrant family. (n. d.)
Rust, E. G.	Calhoun County Business Directory for 1869-70. Battle Creek, 1869.
Schneck, J. S.	History of Ionia and Montcalm Counties, Michigan. Philadelphia, 1881.
Sprague, E. L. and G. N. Smith	Sprague's History of Grand Traverse and Leelanaw Counties, Michigan. 1903.
Strang, J. J.	Ancient and Modern Mackinac. St. Ignace, 1885.
Strickland, W. P.	Old Mackinaw; or, the Fortress of the Lakes and its surroundings. Philadelphia, 1860.
Taylor, H.	Compendium of History and Biography of the City of Detroit and Wayne County, Michigan. Chicago, 1909.
Tappan, Harvey	Pioneer History of St. Clair County. Algonac, Mich., 1910.
Tucker, W. D.	Gratiot County, Michigan; Historical, Biographical, Statistical. Saginaw, 1913.
Utley, H. M.	Michigan as a Province, Territory and State. 1906
Van Fleet, J. A.	Old and New Mackinac. Second Edition. Cincinnati, 1874.
Wait, S. E.	Old Settlers: An Historical and Chronological Record of the Grand Traverse Region. Traverse City, 1918.
Williams, M. C.	Early Mackinac: "The Fairy Island." St. Louis, Mo., 1897.
Wing, T. E.	History of Monroe County, Michigan. New York, 1890.
Whitney, W. A.	History and Biographical Record of Lenawee County, Michigan. Adrian, Mich., 1879-80.
Wood, E. O.	Historic Mackinac. New York, 1918.
Zucker, Adolph Edward	Robert Reitzel. Philadelphia, 1917.

Varia

Michigan Pioneer and Historical Collections. Lansing, 1877 et seq.
Catholic Encyclopedia, New York, 1909.
Michigan Manual, Lansing, 1876-1925.
Michigan State Gazeteer, Detroit, 1863-1926.

APPENDIX A

THE GERMAN-AMERICAN OFFICERS OF THE CIVIL WAR

These are the names and records of German American officers of Michigan Regiments and from Michigan in other branches of the service, who were engaged in the Civil War, 1861—1865.

Alberti, Alexander, East Saginaw, 1st Lieut. 5th Inf. June 19, 1861. Captain, July 7, 1862. Discharged July 9, 1864

Arndt, Albert F. R., Detroit, 2nd Lieut., Battery "B" 1st Light Artillery, Sept. 10, 1861. Taken prisoner in action at Shiloh, Apr. 6, 1862 Exchanged Nov. 19, 1862. 1st Lieut. May 1, 1862. Capt. Sept. 3, 1863. Wounded in action at Griswold, Ga., Nov. 22, 1864. Major, March 14, 1865. Mustered out, July 29, 1865.

Bachman, Augustus, Detroit. Entered Service May 28, 1861. Sergeant Battery "A" 1st Light Artillery. 2nd Lieut. November 24, 1862. 1st Lieut. Sept. 21, 1863. Discharged for disability, March 30, 1864.

Baer, Henry C., Castleton. Entered service Aug. 21, 1861. Sergeant Company "H" Sixth Inf., 2nd Lieut. June 4, 1864; 1st Lieut. Mar. 7, 1865. Mustered out Aug. 29, 1865.

Barse, George R., Detroit. Entered service May 1, 1861, as Private Company "A" first three months, Infantry. Mustered out August 7, 1861. Supernumery Lieut. Fifth Cavalry Aug. 14, 1862. 2nd Lieut. Jan. 1, 1863. 1st Lieut. Aug. 18, 1863. Taken prisoner in action at Ruckland's Mills, Va., October 19, 1863. Escaped May 7, 1864. Retaken July 3, 1864. Escaped Nov. 23, 1864, and finally reached the picket line of the Michigan Engineers and Mechanics on the Sherman march to the sea. Discharged for disability March 22, 1865.

Baroth, Herman, Ionia. Captain Twenty-First Infantry, July 30, 1862. Resigned January 13, 1863.
Beilman, Frederick, Port Huron. Entered service August 9, 1861, as Sergeant Company "H" First Cavalry. 2nd Lieut. September 12, 1862. Taken prisoner at Bull Run, Va:, August 30, 1862. Exchanged. Resigned April 15, 1863.
Beisel, William H., Exeter. Entered service August 14, 1862. Sergeant Company "K" Eighteenth Infantry. 2nd Lieut. January 24, 1865. Mustered out June 26, 1865.
Berger, John A., Frankenmuth. 1st Leiut. Twenty-Ninth Infantry, July 29, 1864. Mustered out Sept. 16, 1865.
Burger, Joseph, Detroit. Entered service May 25, 1861, as Sergeant Company "A" Second Infantry. 2nd Lieut. 1st Lieut. September 1, 1862. Resigned May 15, 1863.
Berger, Otto A., Franklin. Entered service August 28, 1861. Sergeant "D" Company Fifth Infantry. 2nd Lieut. August 18, 1864. 1st Lieut. May 8, 1865. Mustered out July 5, 1865.
Berringer, Christopher, Charlotte. Entered service June 10, 1861. Sergeant Company "D" Third Infantry. 2nd Lieut. Fifth Infantry September 16, 1864. 1st Lieut. October 25, 1864. Mustered out July 5, 1865.
Birkenstock, A. E., Grand Rapids. Captain Third Infantry May 13, 1861. Resigned on account of disability, August 7, 1861.
Bogardus, Peter A., Grand Rapids. 2nd Lieut. Thiid Infantry, May 13, 1861. 1st Lieut. August 11, 1861. Resigned Jan. 1, 1862.
Boffinger, Peter, Bay City. Entered service August 28, 1861. Sergeant Company "K" Fifth Infantry. 2nd Lieut. June 19, 1864. 1st Lieut. October 8, 1864. Discharged for disability as 2nd Lieut. Nov. 29, 1864.
Bolza, Charles E., Grand Rapids. 2nd Lieut. Sixth Cavalry, October 13, 1862. Killed in action at Falling Water, Md., July 14, 1863.
Borgman, Martin V., Detroit. 2nd Lieut. Sixteenth Infantry, July 16, 1862. 1st Lieut. November 8, 1862. Wounded in action at Gettsburg, July 2, 1863. Resigned June 2, 1864.
Bosembark, John Hillsdale, Captain Eleventh Infantry, March 1, 1865. Resigned May 31, 1865.
Brand, Charles R., Detroit. Entered service August 15, 1861, as Sergeant Company "G" Ninth Infantry. 2nd Lieut. August 7, 1863. 1st Lieut. October 15, 1864. Mustered out Sept 15, 1865.
Braidenback, Henry, Lexington. First Lieut., Twenty-Second Infantry. July 31, 1862. Captain June 7, 1864. Mustered out June 26, 1864.
Breitschneider, Robert, Niles. Captain Second Infantry, Apr. 25, 1861

IN THE MAKING OF MICHIGAN

Resigned Dec. 14, 1861. Captain Twelfth Infantry, to rank from Oct. 1, 1861. Resigned Sept. 3, 1862.

Brickner, Charles, Detroit. Entered service Sept. 1, 1861. Sergeant Company 'K" Fifth Infantry. 2nd Lieut. Oct. 9. 1864. Mustered out July 5, 1865.

Brink, George, Nankin. Entered service June 17, 1862. Sergeant Company "K" Seventeenth Infantry. 2nd Lieut. May 26, 1865. Not mustered as an officer. Discharged June 3, 1865.

Brogle, Frantz, Detroit. Second Lieut. Second Infantry, Sept. 22, 1861. Resigned May 4, 1862.

Bross, Herman, Canandigua. 2nd Lieut. Eighteenth Infantry, July 27, 1862. Resigned March 5, 1863.

Burger, Mathew B., Odessa. 2nd Lieut. Eleventh Cavalry, August 1, 1863. Wounded in action at Saltville, Va., Oct. 2, 1864. 1st Lieut. Jan. 30th, 1865. Mustered Aug. 19, 1865.

Busch, John G., Saginaw. Entered service May 25, 1861. Commissary Sergeant Second Infantry. 2nd Lieut. Feb. 24, 1863. 1st Lieut. May 25, 1864. Killed in action near Petersburg, Va., July 30, 1864.

Clutz, Charles, Grand Rapids. Chaplain Eleventh Cavalry, August 31, 1863. Mustered out Aug. 10, 1865.

Colblenz, John J., Sturgis. Entered service Aug. 8, 1862, as Sergeant Company "E" Nineteenth Infantry. 2nd Lieut. Jan 12, 1864, Resigned Aug. 8, 1864.

Conn., Charles G., Elkhart, Ind. 2nd Lieut. Sharp-Shooters, Aug. 8, 1863. Taken prisoner near Petersburg, Va., July 30, 1864. Captain April 11, 1865. Mustered out July 28, 1865.

Coshun, Joseph, Kalamazoo. Entered service July 29, 1862. Sergeant Company "F" Nineteenth Infantry. 2nd Lieut. June 15, 1865. Not mustered as an officer. Discharged June 10, 1865.

Cramer, Peter, Woodland. 1st Lieut. Sixth Cavalry, Oct. 13, 1862. Resigned Feb. 18, 1863.

Curtenius, Frederick W., Kalamazoo. Colonel Sixth Infantry, June 10, 1861. Resigned June 20, 1862.

Custer, Thos W., Monroe. Corporal Twenty-First Ohio Infantry. 2nd Lieut. Sixth Cavalry, July 11, 1864. Brevet 1st Lieut. Captain and Major U. S. Volunteers, March 13, 1865, for "distinguished and gallant conduct." Mustered out April 24, 1866.

Despeldan, Peter, Grand Haven. Entered service Oct. 3, 1861. Sergeant Company "I" Sixteenth Infantry. 2nd Lieut. May 8, 1865. 1st Lieut. July 7, 1865. Mustered out as 2nd Lieut. July 8, 1865.

Dillman, Lewis, Detroit. Captain Second Infantry, April 25, 1865. Major March 6, 1862. Lieutenant Colonel July 26, 1862. Resigned July 30, 1863.

Ditman, Augustus, Romeo. Entered service August 13, 1861. Sergeant Company "A" Ninth Infantry. 2nd Lieut. Nov. 23, 1864. 1st Lieut. April 20, 1865. Mustered out Sept. 15, 1865.

Duesler, Benjamin, Quincy, Captain Company "C". First U. S. Sharp-Shooters, Aug. 21, 1861. Resigned Oct. 18, 1861.

Duesler, Daniel, Quincy. 1st Lieut. Fourth Cavalry, Aug. 13, 1862. Captain Feb. 1, 1863. Discharged for disability, June 27, 1863.

Duesler, Jeremiah, Coldwater. Entered service Aug 1, 1862, as Sergeant Company "G" Fourth Cavalry. 2nd Lieut February 18, 1863. Resigned 21, 1864.

Dubendorf, Edward, Coldwater. 2nd Lieut. First Michigan, (One Hundred and Second U. S.) Colored Infantry, Nov. 14, 1863. 1st Lieut. May 5, 1865. Quartermaster Aug. 18, 1865. Mustered out Sept. 30, 1865.

Dyckman, Barney, Paw Paw. 2nd Lieut. Third Cavalry, Sept. 7, 1861. 1st Lieut. Jan. 13, 1862. Resigned Oct. 26, 1864.

Efner, Joseph H., West Springfield, Mass. 2nd Lieut. First Michigan (One Hundred and Second United States) Colored Infantry, Jan. 20, 1865. Mustered out Sept. 30, 1865.

Eidelbuss, George, Washtenaw. Entered service Aug. 5, 1861. Sergeant Company "B", Sixteenth Infantry. 1st Lieut. May 8, 1865. Mustered out July 8, 1865.

Ernst, Casper, Nunica. 1st Lieut. Fourteenth Infantry. Nov. 18, 1861. Captain July 27, 1863. Major Feb. 13, 1865. Mustered out July 18, 1865.

Ewalt, Jacob, Berrien Springs, 1st Lieut. Twenty-Fifth Infantry, Aug. 10, 1862. Captain, March 13, 1863. Discharged for disability, Oct. 28, 1864.

Faner, Julius D., Grand Rapids. Entered service June 10, 1861, as Sergeant Company "C" Third Infantry. 2nd Lieut. Sept. 26, 1862. Wounded in action at Mine Runs, Va., Nov. 30, 1863. Discharged for disability, May 28, 1864.

Frey, William H., Burr Oak. Entered service Sept. 9, 1861. Sergeant-Major, First Infantry. 1st Lieut. May 8, 1854. Brevet Captain U. S. Volunteers, Aug. 6, 1864, "for gallant and distinguished services during the operations on the Weldon Railroad." Mustered out July 9, 1865.

Eberhard, John P., Burr Oak, Entered service Aug. 22, 1861, as Sergeant Company "K" Seventh Infantry. 1st Lieut. April 15, 1862. Killed in action at Antietam, Md., Sept. 17, 1862.

Friedlander, Charles, Detroit. Entered service March 11, 1862. Sergeant Battery "H" First Light Artillery. 2nd Lieut. May 29, 1865. Not mustered as an officer. Discharged July 22, 1865.

Funke, Moses A. Jonesville. Captain Fourth Infantry, May 26, 1861 Resigned Sept. 7, 1861.
Gager, Frank, Detroit. Entered service Aug. 13, 1861. Sergeant-Major Sixteenth Infantry. 2nd Lieut. June 28, 1864. Brevet Captain U. S. Volunteers, Sept. 30, 1864, "for gallant services at the battle of Peeble's Farm, Va.," Captain, May 8, 1865. Mustered out July 8, 1865.
Geismer, Henry, Newport. Assistant Surgeon Twenty-Second Infantry, Oct. 7, 1862. Resigned July 12, 1863. Assistant Surgeon Twenty-Ninth Infantry March 19, 1863. Mustered out Sept. 6, 1865.
Gies, Paul, Detroit. 1st Lieut. Twenty-Seventh Infantry, Oct. 10, 1862. Resigned May 25, 1863.
Goebel, Augustus, Detroit. 1st Lieutenant, Second Infantry, Sept. 22, 1861. Captain Aug. 25, 1862. Resigned Feb. 14, 1863.
Goetz, Joseph, Mt. Clemens. Captain Twenty-Second Infantry, July 31, 1862. Discharged for disability, May 17, 1865.
Gogan, Julius, Houghton. Entered service July 21, 1862. Sergeant Company "I" Twenty-Third Infantry. 2nd Lieut. July 11, 1865. Not mustered as an officer. Discharged June 28, 1865.
Graverat, Garrett A., Little Traverse. 2nd Lieut. First Sharp-Shooters July 22, 1863. Died July 10, 1864, of wounds received in action near Petersburg, Va., June 17, 1864.
Greble, Charles E., Almont. 1st Lieut. Eight Cavalry, Nov. 1, 1862. Captain August 31, 1863. Mustered out July 20, 1865.
Gruner, Charles F., Sturgis. Entered service June 20, 1861, as Sergeant Company "C" Fourth Infantry. 2nd Lieut. Sept. 1, 1861. 1st Lieut. September 1862. Mustered out Aug. 18, 1864.
Guest, Adolphus A., New York City. 2nd Lieut., Company "B", Second U. S. Sharp-Shooters, April 2, 1862. 1st Lieut., April 2, 1862. Captain Oct. 14, 1862. Mustered out Oct. 10, 1864.
Gundlach, William, Detroit. Entered service May 25, 1861. Sergeant Company "A" Second Infantry. 1st Lieut. April 25, 1865. Mustered out July 28, 1865.
Gunderman, John, Essex. Supernumery Second Lieutenant, Fifth Cavalry Aug. 14, 1862 2nd Lieut. Nov. 25, 1862. Chaplain Oct. 9, 1863. Mustered out June 22, 1865.
Haling, Eugene, Detroit. Entered service May 25 1861. Sergeant Company "D", Second Infantry. 2nd Lieut. July 22, 1865. Not mustered out as an officer. Discharged July 28, 1865.
Hartmeyer, Louis, Detroit. Entered service May 1, 1861, as Sergeant Company "A" First (Three Months) Infantry. Taken Prisoner at Bull Run, Va., July 21, 1861. Mustered out Sept. 25, 1862.
Haas, Christian, Hudson. Entered service Aug. 18, 1862. Sergeant

380 THE GERMANIC INFLUENCE

Battery "B" First Light Artillery. 2nd Lieut. Feb. 3, 1864. 1st Lieut. Sept. 20, 1864. Mustered out July 14, 1865.
Hautsch, Frederick, New York City. 2nd Lieut. First Michigan (One Hundred and Second U. S.) Colored Infantry Jan. 18, 1865. Mustered out Sept. 15, 1865.
Heidt, Lewis, Detroit. Entered service Oct. 21, 1862, as Sergeant Battery "K", First Light Artillery. 2nd Lieut. Sept. 21, 1863. 1st Lieut. March 8, 1864. Died of disease at St. Mary's Hospital, Detroit, Michigan, Aug. 9, 1864.
Heine, Charles, Marshall. 2nd Lieut. Sixth Infantry, August 19, 1861. 1st Lieut. Oct. 9, 1861. Resigned Sept. 25, 1862. Captain Fourteenth Battery Light Artillery Sept. 19, 1863. Mustered out July 1, 1865.
Herkner, Joseph C., Grand Rapids. 1st Lieut. First Engineers and Mechanics, Sept. 12, 1861. Captain Jan. 1, 1864. Mustered out Sept. 22, 1865.
Hetz, Theodore, Grand Rapids. Entered service June 10, 1861, as Corporal Company "C" Third Infantry. 2nd Lieut Jan. 2, 1862. 1st Lieut. Jan. 1863. Mustered out June 20, 1864.
Heylauf, Andrew, Ionia. Entered service August 7, 1862. Sergeant-Major First Infantry. 2nd Lieut. Oct. 29, 1864. Not mustered as an officer. Discharged June 17, 1865.
Hoag, Edward H., Tecumseh. 2nd Lieut. Eighteenth Infantry, July 27, 1862. 1st Lieut. Dec. 27, 1862. Resigned Dec. 31, 1863.
Holshaeur, Frederick, Detroit. Entered service Nov. 12, 1862. Sergeant Battery "K" First Light Infantry. 2nd Lieut. Feb. 24, 1863. Mustered out July 22, 1865.
Hubert, Walter, Sr., Grand Rapids. Entered service Sept. 19, 1861. Sergeant Company "B" First Engineers and Mechanics 2nd Lieut. Nov. 3, 1864. Mustered out Sept. 22, 1865.
Hupert, Christopher, Detroit. 2nd Lieut. Battery "K" First Light Artillery, Feb. 20, 1863. Resigned Sept. 21, 1863.
Hyser, Willis, Plainfield. Captain Sixth Cavalry, Oct. 13, 1862. Discharged for disability Oct. 22, 1863. Recommissioned Captain Sixth Cavalry 16, 1864. Discharged March 21, 1865.
Hyzer, William W., Ypsilanti. Entered service Oct. 14, 1861. Corporal Battery "C" First Light Artillery. 2nd Lieut. June 30, 1863. 1st Lieut. Feb. 20, 1864. Captain Dec. 18, 1864. Mustered out June 21, 1865.
Jacks, John, Edwardsburg, 2nd Lieut. Sixth Infantry, Aug. 19, 1861. 1st Lieut. September 1, 1862. Discharged Oct. 27, 1863.
Jasnowski, Saturnin, Detroit. Entered service Nov. 4, 1862, as Sergeant Company "E" Twenty-Seventh Infantry. 2nd Lieut. Nov. 17, 1864. Wounded in action near Petersburg, Va., June 18, 1864. 1st Lieut. May 15, 1865. Mustered out July 26, 1865.

IN THE MAKING OF MICHIGAN 381

Jott, Joseph H. Jackson. Entered service May 1, 1861, as Private Company "B" First (three months) Infantry. Mustered out Aug. 7, 1861. 1st Lieut. Ninth Infantry Oct. 12, 1861. Died at Elizabethtown, Ky., Feb. 15. 1862.

Kanouse, Luther C., Cohoctah. Entered service Sept. 4, 1862, as Sergeant Company "D" Sixth Cavalry. 1st Lieut. July 1, 1864. Mustered out Nov. 24, 1865.

Karp, Peter, Entered service Aug. 13, 1861. Sergeant Major First Cavalry. 2nd Lieut. Nov. 1, 1862. Discharged April 25, 1864.

Karrer, Benjamin, Detroit. Entered service Aug. 24, 1861, as Private Company "K." First Cavalry. 1st Lieut. Ninth Cavalry, Nov. 3, 1862. Resigned Jan. 17, 1864 for disability.

Kast, Gustav, Detroit. 2nd Lieut. Second Infantry, April 25, 1861. Resigned Sept. 22, 1861. Captain Sixteenth Infantry Feb. 1, 1862. Resigned July 29, 1862.

Kath, Theodore, Ray. Entered service Aug. 9, 1862. Sergeant Company "G" Second Infantry. 2nd Lieut. Sept. 25, 1863. Mustered out June 26, 1865.

Kauffman, Peter, Charlotte, 2nd Lieut. Twentieth Infantry, July 29, 1862. Resigned March 5, 1863.

Keller, Frank, East Saginaw. Entered service Aug. 1, 1861. Sergeant Company "D" Sixteenth Infantry. 2nd Lieut., April 26, 1863. Mustered out Sept. 10, 1865.

Keltner, Dion B., Sault Ste. Marie. Entered service Aug. 28, 1861. Sergeant "F" Company, Fifth Infantry. 1st Lieut. June 10, 1864. Captain May 8, 1865. Brevet Captain United States Volunteers, April 9, 1865, "for gallant and meritorious service during the recent campaign terminating with the surrender of the insurgent army under General R. E. Lee." Mustered out July 5, 1865.

Kealer, Theodore P., Bronson. 2nd Lieut. Eleventh Infantry, Aug. 24, 1861. Resigned Feb. 12, 1862.

Keyser, Sylvester, Niles. Entered service May 25, 1861. Sergeant Company "E" Second Infantry. 1st Lieut. July 7, 1864. Captain, Sept. 30, 1864. Brevet Major U. S. Volunteers, April 2, 1865, "for gallant and meritorious services before Petersburg, Va." Discharged July 29, 1865.

Kilmer, Peter B. Napoleon. 1st Lieut. Twenty-Eighth Infantry, Aug. 15, 1864. Mustered out June 5, 1866.

Kiletz, George F. Lexington. Entered service Nov. 15, 1862, as Private Company "E" Sixteenth Infantry. 1st Lieut. Jan. 20, 1864. Brevet Captain U. S. Volunteers, July 6, 1864, "for gallant and distinguished service at the battle of the Wilderness, Va., and during the present

THE GERMANIC INFLUENCE

campaign against Richmond, Va.," Captain July 16, 1864. Discharged for disability March 14, 1865.

Kimmel, Edward F. Berrien Springs. 2nd Lieut. Twenty-Fifth Infantry, Aug. 10, 1862. 1st Lieut. March 13, 1862. Resigned Sept. 23, 1864.

Kimmel, Henry T., Niles. Entered service Aug. 14, 1862, as Private Company "F" Twenty-Fifth Infantry, 2nd Lieut. Twelfth Infantry, Feb. 18, 1863. First Lieut. March 15, 1864. Resigned July 3, 1864. Captain Thirtieth Infantry, Nov. 22, 1864. Mustered out June 23, 1865.

Kimmle, Edgar A., Niles, 1st Lieut. Twenty-Fourth Infantry, Sept. 27, 1864. Mustered out June 30, 1865.

Kimberk, Fred W. Brighton. 2nd Lieut. Fifth Infantry June 19, 1861. Resigned May 27, 1862. Captain Twenty-Second Infantry July 31, 1862. Resigned Dec. 8, 1863.

Kingscott, Wm. G., Warren. Entered service September 7, 1861. Sergeant Company "H" Second Cavalry, 1st Lieut. Sept. 20, 1864. Transferred to One Hundred and Thirty-Sixth U. S. Colored Troops, June 22, 1865.

Knoblock, John, Detroit. Entered service Feb. 17, 1864, as Corporal Company "F" First Infantry. 1st Lieut. Nov. 1, 1854. Mustered out July 9, 1865.

Kramer, John Holland. Entered service Aug. 14, 1862, as Sergeant Company "I" Twenty-Fifth Infantry. 2nd Lieut. Feb. 17, 1863. 1st Lieut. June 17, 1863. Mustered out June 24, 1865.

Lainberg, Carl A., Detroit, 1st Lieut. Battery "C" Light Artillery Dec. 6, 1861. Resigned March 23, 1863.

Levy, Nathan, Rochester, N. Y. 2nd Lieut. Tenth Infantry Oct. 1, 1861. 1st Lieut. April 25, 1863. Resigned Jan. 12, 1864.

Lieber, Albrecht, Chicago, Ill. Appointed from Eighth Illinois Cavalry as 2nd Lieut. First Michigan (One Hundred and Second United States) Colored Infantry, May 15, 1865. Mustered out Sept. 30, 1865.

Limbocker, Thomas J., Trenton. 2nd Lieut. Battery "I" First Light Artillery, Aug. 14, 1862. Resigned for disability Feb. 3, 1864.

Lind, John C. East Saginaw, 2nd Lieut. Fourteenth Infantry, Nov. 18, 1861. Captain July 9, 1862. Died at East Saginaw, Mich, Aug. 9, 1863.

Ludlim, John, Saginaw. 2nd Lieut. Second Infantry, April 25, 1861. 1st Lieut. Dec. 1, 1861. Resigned Sept. 17, 1862.

Lum, Charles M., Detroit. Captain First (Three months) Infantry, May 1, 1861. Wounded in action at Bull Run, Va., July 21, 1861. Colonel Tenth Infantry Nov. 20, 1861. Mustered out April 1, 1865.

Lungerhausen, Charles, Detroit. Entered service May 25, 1861. Sergeant Company "A" Second Infantry. 1st Lieut. Nov. 5, 1864. Mustered out July 28, 1865.

IN THE MAKING OF MICHIGAN 383

Lusk, George W. 2nd Lieut. First Cavalry, Aug. 22, 1861. Captain Oct. 1, 1862. Mustered out Nov. 28, 1865.
Maetzke, William A., Manchester. Entered service Aug. 24, 1864. Quartermaster-Sergeant, Twenty-Eighth Infantry. 2nd Lieut. April 11, 1865. Mustered out June 5, 1866.
Maltz, George L., Detroit. Entered service June 20, 1861. Sergeant-Major Fourth Infantry. 2nd Lieut. Dec. 13, 1862. 1st Lieut. March 21, 1864. Wounded in action at Coal Harbor, Va., June 3, 1864. Mustered out June 28, 1864.
Maltman, John S., Ypsilanti. Entered service Aug. 4, 1862, as Sergeant Company "E" Seventeenth Infantry. 1st Lieut. June 30, 1864. Mustered out June 3, 1865.
Marks, Leopold, Detroit. Entered service Jan. 2, 1863. Sergeant Company "G" Ninth Cavalry. 2nd Lieut. Jan. 18, 1864. Discharged Aug. 27, 1864
Mayerbeck, Charles, Detroit. Entered service Sept. 26, 1861. Sergeant Company "C" Fourteenth Infantry. 2nd Lieut. March 14, 1865. Mustered out July 18, 1865.
Maus, Jacob, Hastings. 2nd Lieut. Eighth Infantry. Aug. 29, 1861. Resigned Jan. 9, 1862.
Mauch, Bernard, Detroit. 1st Lieut. Three Months Infantry, May 1, 1861. Wounded and taken prisoner at Bull Run, Va., July 21, 1861. Not mustered as an officer. Mustered out June 5, 1866.
Melchor, Thaddeus, W., Paw Paw. Captain Fourth Cavalry, Aug. 13, 1862. Resigned April 6, 1863.
Meyer, Charles G. East Saginaw. Captain Twenty-Ninth Infantry, July 29, 1864. Mustered out Sept. 6, 1865.
Mickley, Henry L., Adrian. Entered service Nov. 5, 1861. Sergeant Company "F" Fifteenth Infantry. 1st Lieut. Nov. 1, 1864. Captain, March 30th, 1865. Mustered out Aug. 13, 1865.
Miller, Jacob W., Fentonville. Entered service Sept. 19, 1861, as Sergeant Company "I" Third Cavalry. 2nd Lieut. Sept. 18, 1864. Discharged June 6, 1865.
Miller, Henry, Saginaw. Captain Fifth Infantry, June 19, 1861. Discharged Feb, 18, 1863.
Miller, Clement F., Kalamazoo. 1st Lieut. and Adjutant First Engineers and Mechanics, Sept. 12, 1861. Resigned March 21, 1864.
Millershaum, Stephen W., St. Clair. Entered service March 14, 1862. Sergeant Company "F" First Cavalry. 2nd Lieut. March 7, 1865. Not mustered as an officer. Discharged March 25 1865.
Mizner, John K. Detroit. Captain Eighteenth U. S. Infantry, May 14, 1861. Colonel Fourteenth Michigan Infantry, Nov. 11, 1862. Brevet Major U. S. Army, Dec. 31, 1862, "for gallant and meritorious

services in the battle of Murfreesboro, Tenn." Brevet Lieut. Colonel U. S. Army Sept. 1, 1864, "for gallant and meritorious services during the Atlanta campaign, and in the battle of Jonesboro, Ga.," Brevet Brigadier General U. S. Volunteers, March 13, 1865, "for gallant and meritorious services during the war." Mustered out of volunteer service July 18, 1865. Major Twentieth U. S. Infantry Feb. 22, 1869. Transferred to Twelfth United States Infantry, March 15, 1869. Transferred to Eighth U. S. Infantry, May 14, 1877.

Mizner, William, London. Entered service Aug. 6, 1861. Sergeant Company "F" Sixteenth Infantry. 2nd Lieut. May 8, 1865. 1st Lieut., July 7, 1865. Mustered out as 2nd Lieut. July 8, 1865.

Mogk, George C., Ann Arbor. 1st Lieut. Three Months Infantry, May 1, 1861. 1st Lieut. First Infantry, Aug. 17, 1861. Taken prisoner at Bull Run Va., Aug. 30, 1862. Exchanged. Captain Aug. 30, 1862. Mustered out Sept. 26, 1864.

Morseman, John J., Coldwater. Entered service July 28, 1862, as Sergeant Company "H", Nineteenth Infantry. 2nd Lieut. June 15, 1865. Not mustered as an officer. Discharged June 10, 1865.

Muhlburg, Franz. Grand Rapids. Entered service June 10, 1861, as Sergeant Company "C" Third Infantry. 1st Lieut. Fifth Infantry, Feb. 1, 1864. Wounded in action May 5, 1864. Wounded in action near Petersburg, Va., June 16, 1864. Mustered out July 5, 1865.

Muma, Charles A., Flint. Entered service Aug. 4, 1862. Sergeant-Major Twenty-third Infantry. 2nd Lieut. March 8, 1864. 1st Lieut. Nov. 12, 1864. Mustered out June 28, 1865.

Myers, Joseph W., Detroit. Entered service Nov. 10, 1861, as Sergeant Company "D" Fourteenth Infantry, 2nd Lieut. July 4, 1862. 1st Lieut. May 30, 1863. Adjutant, July 3, 1863. Captain, July 10, 1864. Mustered out July 18, 1865.

Myers, Charles, Detroit. Captain Sixteenth Infantry, Aug. 9, 1861. Wounded in action at Gaines' Mill, Va., June 27, 1862. Discharged for disability, Oct. 1, 1863.

Myers, Frederick, Houghton. Captain Twenty-Seventh Infantry, Oct. 10, 1862. Wounded in action at Wilderness, May 6, 1864. Major, July 8, 1864. Discharged for disability, May 15, 1865.

Neff, William Monguagon. 2nd Lieut. Ninth Cavalry, Nov. 3, 1862. Died at Knoxville, Tenn., Oct. 15, 1863.

Negus, Edward L., Chelsea. Entered service May, 1861, as private Company "D" First (three months) Infantry. Mustered out Aug. 7, 1861. Sergeant Company "B" First Cavalry, Aug. 30, 1861. 2nd Lieut. Sept. 7, 1862. Mustered out Nov. 7, 1865.

Neff, Cady, Trenton. 2nd Lieut. Ninth Cavalry, Nov. 3, 1862. Resigned Feb. 17, 1864.
Noteman, David, Coldwater. 1st Lieut. Eighth Cavalry, Nov. 1, 1862 Resigned for disability June 21, 1864.
Nuhfer, Andrew, Cleveland, Ohio. Entered service Aug. 15, 1861. Sergeant Company "G", Ninth Infantry. 2nd Lieut. Nov. 23, 1864. 1st Lieut. July 15, 1865. Mustered out Sept. 15, 1865.
Nunnely, George, Mt. Clemens. Entered service Nov. 4, 1862, as sergeant Company "D" Eighth Cavalry. 2nd Lieut. May 14, 1864. Mustered out Sept. 22, 1865.
Neyman, A. J., Bangor. Entered service Aug. 1, 1862, as Sergeant Company "G", Nineteenth Infantry. 2nd Lieut. June 1, 1864. Taken prisoner Oct. 27, 1864. Paroled. Resigned April 24, 1865.
Ohls, Henry J., Dowagiac. Entered service Aug. 8, 1862. Sergeant Company "A" Nineteenth Infantry. 2nd Lieut. May 8, 1865. Mustered out June 10, 1865.
Ottman, Joseph, Manchester. Entered service June 16, 1862, as Sergeant Company "A" Seventeenth Infantry. 1st Lieut. Oct. 22, 1864. Mustered out June 3, 1865.
Papst, Rudolph, Lexington. Entered service Oct. 25, 1861. Sergeant Major Tenth Infantry. 2nd Lieut. March 31, 1863. 1st Lieut. Aug. 26, 1864. Adjutant Feb 24, 1865. Captain, May 8, 1865. Mustered out July 31, 1865.
Pistorius, Fred, Detroit. 1st Lieut. and Adjutant First Cavalry, Feb. 20, 1864. Discharged Sept. 11, 1864.
Prutzman, Ed. M., Three Rivers. Entered service Sept. 11, 1862, as Sergeant Major Twenty-Fifth Infantry. 2nd Lieut. Feb. 6, 1863 1st Lieut. and Adjutant, June 17, 1863. Killed in action at Resaca, Ga., May 14, 1864.
Rauser, John G., Lodi. Entered service May 1, 1861, as private Company "E" First (Three Months) Infantry. Taken prisoner at Bull Run, Va., July 21, 1861. Exchanged. Mustered out May 20, 1862. Re-entered service Dec. 27, 1862., Sergeant Battery "K" First Light Artillery. 2nd Lieut. April 11, 1865. Not mustered as an officer. Mustered out July 22, 1865.
Rath, Christian, Jackson. 2nd Lieut. Seventeenth Infantry, June 17, 1862. Wounded in action at Antietam, Md., Sept. 17, 1862. 1st Lieut. Dec. 6, 1862. Captain, Aug. 4, 1863. Taken prisoner in action at Spottsylvania, Va., May 12, 1864. Escaped May 12, 1864. Brevet Major and Lieut. Col. U. S. Volunteers, July 8, 1865. "for special efficient services during the confinement, trial and execution of conspirators." Discharged July 19, 1865.

THE GERMANIC INFLUENCE

Reisdorf, Benjamin, Monroe. 2nd Lieut. Eleventh Infantry Aug. 24, 1861. 1st Lieut., March 12, 1862. Resigned Dec. 16, 1862.

Richter, George, Ann Arbor. Entered service Dec. 12, 1862, as Sergeant Battery "K" First Light Artillery. 2nd Lieut. March 8, 1864. 1st Lieut. Aug. 9, 1864. Mustered out July 22, 1865.

Richman, Charles, H., Saginaw City. Capt. Tenth Infantry, Oct. 1, 1861. Mustered out Feb. 6, 1865.

Risdorph, Charles H., Battle Creek. Entered service May 25, 1861. Sergeant Company "C" Second Infantry. 2nd Lieut. July 22, 1865. Not mustered as an officer. Mustered out July 28, 1865.

Ritter, Peter, Angola, Ind. Entered service Aug. 15, 1864. Sergeant Company "F". Third Infantry. 2nd Lieut. Nov. 28, 1865. 1st Lieut., June 30, 1865. Mustered out May 25, 1866, as Sergeant.

Ritter, Charles H., Detroit. Entered service, Aug. 28, 1861. Sergeant Company "D" Fifth Infantry.

Roehm, Ernest G., Detroit. Entered service July 1, 1861. Sergeant Company "A" First Infantry. Wounded in action at Bull Run, Va., Aug. 30, 1862. 2nd Lieut. May 30, 1865. 1st Lieut. July 15, 1865. Not mustered as an officer. Mustered out July 9, 1865.

Rose, Charles B., Westphalia. 1st Lieut. Fourteenth Infantry, Nov. 18, 1861. Died of disease at Farmington, Mass., June 11, 1862.

Roth, William F., Ann Arbor. Captain Three Months Infantry, May 1, 1861. Mustered out Aug. 7, 1861.

Ruddiman, George, Muskegon. Entered service June 13, 1863. Sergeant Company "F" Second Infantry. 2nd Lieut. July 22, 1865. Not mustered as an officer. Mustered out July 28, 1865.

Ruehle, John V., Detroit. Lieut. Col. Sixteenth Infantry, Aug. 21, 1861. Resigned July 6, 1862.

Ruehle, John V. Jr., Detroit. 1st Lieut. Second Infantry, April 25, 1861. Captain, September 22, 1861. Resigned April 19, 1864.

Ruehle, Martin, East Saginaw. Entered service May 25, 1861. Sergeant Company "H" Second Infantry. 2nd Lieut. July 22, 1865. Not mustered as an officer. Absent wounded on muster out of regiment.

Ruff, Joseph, Jackson. Entered service Dec. 17, 1861. Sergeant Company "D" Twelfth Infantry. 2nd Lieut. June 14, 1865. 1st Lieut. Nov. 18, 1865. Mustered out as 2nd Lieut. February 15, 1866.

Salter, Charles H., Detroit. Entered service May 1, 1861, as private Company "A" First (Three months) Infantry. Mustered out Aug. 7, 1861. 2nd Lieut. Sixteenth Infantry Aug. 9, 1861. 1st. Lieut. Aug. 30, 1862. Captain Dec. 16, 1863. Brevet Major U. S. Volunteers, Sept. 30, 1864, "for gallant and distinguished services at the battle of Peebles' Farm, Va., Mustered out Jan. 13, 1865.

IN THE MAKING OF MICHIGAN 387

Sanger, Joseph P., Detroit. 2nd Lieut. First (three months) Infantry, May 1, 1861. 2nd Lieut. First U. S. Artillery, Aug. 5, 1861. 1st Lieut. Oct. 26, 1861. Brevet Captain May 28, 1864, for gallant and meritorious service in action at Bermuda Hundred, Va., Brevet Major, March 13, 1865, "for gallant and meritorious service in the battle of Russell's Mills, Va., Aug. 16, 1864." Regimental Adjutant, Jan. 31, 1866. Captian Feb. 7, 1875.

Schram, LaRue, Burton. Captain Twenty-Ninth Infantry, July 29, 1864. Discharged for disability, March 22, 1865.

Schill, Adolph, Detroit. 1st Lieut. Battery "K" First Light Artillery, Feb. 21, 1863. Captain April 11, 1865. Mustered out July 22, 1865.

Scheick, Carl, Marengo. Entered service Oct. 21, 1863. Sergeant Fourteenth Battery Light Artillery. 2nd Lieut. March 17, 1865. Mustered out July 1, 1865.

Scheutz John C., Saginaw. Entered service May 25, 1861, as Sergeant Company "H" Second Infantry. 2nd Lieut. Dec. 4, 1861. 1st Lieut. Feb. 7, 1862. 1st Lieut. Battery "K" First Light Artillery, Nov. 21, 1862. Captain Feb. 21, 1863. Major First Regiment Light Artillery, April 11, 1865. Mustered out July 29, 1865.

Schefnicker, Joseph, Saginaw. 1st Lieut. Fourteenth Infantry Nov. 18, 1861. Resigned Nov. 16, 1862.

Schimpf, Charles, Rockland. Entered service Aug. 13, 1862. Sergeant Company "A" Twenty-Seventh Infantry. 2nd Lieut. May 15, 1865. Mustered out July 26, 1865.

Scheffler, Carl B., Jackson. 2nd Lieut. Third Cavalry, Sept. 7, 1861. 1st Lieut. June 10, 1862. Captain, Oct. 17, 1864. Mustered out Feb. 12, 1861.

Schneider, Frederick, Detroit. Entered service May 25, 1861, as Sergeant Company "A" Second Infantry. Sergeant Major May 14, 1864. 1st Lieut. June 6, 1864. Wounded in action in front of Petersburg, Va., June 18, 1864. Captain July 30, 1864. Taken prisoner July 30, 1864. Escaped July 30, 1864. Wounded and taken prisoner in front of Petersburg, Va., Oct. 27, 1864. Exchanged Feb. 22, 1865. Lieut. Col. Dec. 18, 1864. Colonel April 18, 1865. Mustered out as Lieut. Colonel July 28, 1865.

Seibert, Jacob, E., Lansing. Entered service Aug. 9, 1862. Sergeant Major Twentieth Infantry. 1st Lieut. and Adjutant, June 18, 1864. Killed in action at Weldon Railroad, Va., Sept. 30, 1864.

Seigfried, Franklin B., Mason. Entered service Aug. 22, 1861, as Sergeant Company "B" Seventh Infantry. 2nd Lieut. Dec. 30, 1862. 1st Lieut. May 1, 1863. Wounded in action at Gettysburg, Pa., July 2, 1863. Discharged for disability April 20, 1864.

Shafer, Sylvester, Lapeer. 2nd Lieut. First Cavalry, Aug. 22, 1861. Resigned Feb. 16, 1862.
Shaffer, George T. Calvin. 1st Lieut. Nineteenth Infantry, July 28, 1862. Captain, May 15, 1864. Wounded in action June 22, 1864. Major Twenty-Eighth Infantry, Aug. 15, 1864. Lieut. Colonel Dec. 10, 1864. Brevet Colonel and Brig. Gen. U. S. Volunteers, March 13, 1865. "for gallant and meritorious services at the battle before Atlanta, Ga., and at Wise Fork, N. C." Mustered out June 5, 1866.
Sheffert, Robert, Burr Oak. Entered service Feb. 8, 1862. Sergeant Company "A" Fifteenth Infantry. 1st Lieut. June 6, 1865. Mustered out Aug. 13, 1865.
Shelt, John, Rome. 1st Lieut. Eighteenth Infantry. July 27, 1862. Resigned Dec. 13, 1862.
Shiffer, William H., St. Johns. Entered service Dec. 14, 1861. Sergeant Company "K" Fourteenth Infantry. 2nd Lieut. July 7, 1865. Mustered out July 18, 1865.
Shontz, John, Byron. Entered service Aug. 28, 1861. Sergeant Company "H" Fifth Infantry. 2nd Lieut. Oct. 1, 1864. 1st Lieut. Nov. 7, 1864. Mustered out July 6, 1865.
Shoemaker, Michael, Jackson. Colonel Thirteenth Infantry, Jan. 28, 1862. Taken prisoner Sept. 7, 1862, near Tyre Springs, Tenn., and confined in Libby Prison. Exchanged Sept. 27, 1862. Resigned May 26, 1863.
Shriver, Frederick Grand Rapids, 1st Lieut. Third Infantry, May 13, 1861. Captain Aug. 1, 1861. Wounded in action at Groveton, Va., Aug. 29, 1862. Resigned Oct. 25, 1862.
Siegel, Bartholomew, Shiawassee. Entered service Sept. 13, 1861, as Sergeant Company "I" Eighth Infantry. 1st Lieut. April 25, 1865. Mustered out July 30, 1865.
Singler, Isaac, Berlin. Entered service Aug. 30, 1862. Sergeant Company "D" First Engineers and Mechanics. 2nd Lieut. Nov. 3, 1864. Mustered out Sept. 22, 1865.
Sillick, Henry L., Quincy. 2nd Lieut. Eighth Cavalry, Nov. 1, 1862. Captain Aug. 21, 1863. Resigned on account of disability Oct. 27, 1864.
Slack, Joseph B., East Saginaw. Entered service Aug. 1, 1861. Sergeant Company "D" Sixteenth Infantry, 2nd Lieut. April 22, 1863. Mustered out Sept. 9 1864.
Slafter, Albert, Tuscola. Entered service Aug. 22, 1861. Quartermaster sergeant Seventh Infantry. 2nd Lieut. Feb. 10, 1863. Killed in action at Gettsburg, Pa., July 3, 1863.
Slight, Jacob P., Bath. Entered service Sept. 4, 1861. Corporal Com-

pany "B" Third Cavalry. 2nd Lieut. First Michigan (One Hundred and Second United States) Colored Infantry, Dec. 23, 1864. Mustered out Sept. 30, 1865.

SlEght, William E., Bath. Entered service as Private Company "C" Sixty-Fifth New York Infantry. Wounded in action May 3, 1863. 2nd Lieut. First Michigan (One Hundred and Second United States) Colored Infantry, Jan. 20, 1864. 1st Lieut. May 6, 1864. Mustered out Sept. 30, 1865.

Smith, Theodore F., East Saginaw. Entered service Aug. 22, 1861, as Sergeant Company "A" Second Cavalry. 2nd Lieut. Jan. 1, 1863. 1st Lieut. May 27, 1863. Resigned May 4, 1864.

Smith, Julius W., Grand Rapids. Entered service Dec. 29, 1863. Sergeant Company "I" First Engineers and Mechanics, 1st Lieut. Nov 3, 1864. Mustered out Oct. 1, 1865.

Spang, Charles D., Muskegon. 1st Lieut. Third Infantry, May 13, 1861. Resigned Oct. 28, 1861.

Stauber, Silas, J., Monterey. Entered service Aug. 1, 1862, as Sergeant Company "L" Fourth Cavalry. 2nd Lieut. April 21, 1864. Brevet Captain U. S. Volunteers, May 10, 1865, "for meritorious services in the capture of Jeff. Davis." Mustered out July 1, 1865.

Steiner, William, Detroit. Entered service Oct. 16, 1861. Sergeant Company "G" Fourteenth Infantry, 2nd Lieut. Feb. 13, 1865. 1st Lieut. July 5, 1865. Mustered out as 2nd Lieut. July 18, 1865.

Swart, Menzo, Flushing. Entered service July 30, 1861, as Sergeant Company "C" Sixteenth Infantry. 2nd Lieut. April 27, 1863. Wounded in action at Tolopotomy, Va., June 1, 1864. 1st Lieut. Aug. 3, 1864. Mustered out as 2nd Lieut. Sept. 26, 1864.

Swimm, George T., St. Charles. Captain Twenty-Ninth Infantry, July 29, 1864. Resigned March 27, 1865.

Swobe, Thomas, Bertrand. Entered service Oct. 16, 1861. Sergeant Company "E" Twelfth Infantry. 2nd Lieut. April 12, 1865. **Mustered out Feb. 15, 1866.**

Symald, Ernest. Lyons. Entered service June 10, 1861, as Sergeant Company "E" Third Infantry. 2nd Lieut. Fifth Infantry Sept. 1, 1864.

Theill, James H., Hillsdale. Entered service July 27, 1864, as Sergeant Company "A" Fifth Infantry. 2nd Lieut. Oct. 24, 1865. Not mustered as an officer. Mustered out May 26, 1866.

Vosburg, Bernard, Galesburg. Captain Thirteenth Infantry, Oct. 3, 1861. Resigned July 12, 1862.

Wager, Albert, Prairie Ronde. Entered service Aug. 7, 1862. Sergeant Company "H" Twenty-Fifth Infantry, 2nd Lieut. Jan. 4,

1864. 1st Lieut. January 5, 1864. Discharged for disability, Oct. 28, 1864.

Wager, Martin, Battle Creek. 2nd Lieut. First Sharp-Shooters, June 3, 1863. Killed in action in front of Petersburg, Va., June 23, 1864.

Weber, Peter A., Grand Rapids. Battalion Adjutant Second Cavalry Sept. 2, 1861. Mustered out June 1, 1862. Captain Sixth Cavalry, Oct. 13, 1862. Killed in action at Falling Waters, Md., July 14, 1863.

Webber, Jacob, Lansing. 1st Lieut. Sixteenth Infantry, Aug. 9, 1861. Resigned Jan. 19, 1863.

Weimer, George, Saranac. Entered service Aug. 5, 1862. Sergeant Company "I" Twenty-First Infantry. 2nd Lieut. Dec. 16, 1862. 1st Lieut. Feb. 3, 1863. Captain, Aug. 24, 1863. Mustered out June 8, 1865.

Wesener, Hugo, Saginaw. 2nd Lieut. Fifth Infantry, June 19, 1861. Resigned April 16, 1862.

Wideman, Henry, Lexington. Entered service Dec. 4, 1861, as Sergeant Company "D" Tenth Infantry. 2nd Lieut. Nov. 8, 1864. 1st Lieut. Feb. 24, 1865. Captain June 7, 1865. Mustered out July 19, 1865.

Wild, John L., Caledonia. Entered service Sept. 10, 1863. as Chief Trumpeter, Tenth Cavalry. 2nd Lieut., April 1, 1864. 1st Lieut. Jan. 7, 1865. Mustered out Nov. 1, 1865.

Winegar, William, Grass Lake. 2nd Lieut. Seventeenth Infantry, June 17, 1862. 1st Lieut. Dec. 28, 1862. Captain Sept. 14, 1863, Resigned Dec. 24, 1863. on account of disability.

Winegar, Ira, Saranac. Assistant Surgeon Third Infantry July 29, 1864. Resigned March 6, 1865.

Wirts, John R., Hudson. 2nd Lieut. Company "C". First U. S. Sharpshooters, Aug. 31, 1862. Resigned Feb. 25, 1863.

Wirts, John M., Hudson. Entered service Oct. 3, 1861, as Sergeant-Major Third Cavalry. 2nd Lieut. Feb. 27, 1862. 1st Lieut. Aug. 13, 1862. Captain Sept. 22, 1864. Mustered out Feb. 12, 1866.

Wiselogal, Frederick G., Albion. Entered service Dec. 24, 1861. 1st Lieut. Dec. 20 20, 1864. Captain April 12, 1865. Mustered out Feb. 15, 1866.

Zeigler, Augustus, F., Detroit. Entered service Aug. 4, 1862. Sergeant Major Twenty-Fourth Infantry. 2nd Lieut. Oct. 14, 1864. Mustered out June 30, 1865.

Zoellner, Frank, Detroit. Entered service May 25, 1861. Sergeant-Major Second Infantry. 2nd Lieut. Feb. 24, 1863. Died Dec. 2, 1865, of wounds received Nov. 24, 1863.

Curtenius, Edward A., Kalamazoo. 1st Lieut. Fifteenth U. S. Infantry May 14, 1861. Brevet Captain, April 7, 1862, "for gallant and meritorious services at the battle of Shiloh, Tenn." Died at Buffalo, N. Y., Nov. 9, 1862. (Regular).

Custer, George A., Appointed from Military Academy, 2nd Lieut. Second U. S. Cavalry, June 24, 1861. Lieut. Fifth U. S. Cavalry, Aug. 3, 1861. 1st Lieut. June 17, 1862. Brigadier General U. S. Volunteers, June 29, 1863. Assumed command of Michigan Cavalry Brigade at Hanover, Penn., June 30, 1863. Brevet Major U. S. Army, July 3, 1863, "for gallant and meritorious service at the battle of Gettysburg, Pa.," Captain Fifth U. S. Cavalry, May 8, 1864. Brevet Lieut. Colonel U. S. Army, May 11, 1864, "for gallant and meritorious service at the battle of Yellow Tavern, Va.," Brevet Colonel U. S. Army, Sept. 19, 1864, "for gallant and meritorious service at the battle of Winchester, Va.," Major-General U. S. Volunteers, Oct. 19, 1864. Brevet Brigadier General U. S. Army March 13, 1865, "for gallant and meritorious service at the battle of Five Forks, Va." Brevet Major General United States Army, March 13, 1865, "for gallant and meritorious service during the campaign ending with the surrender of the insurgent army of Northern Virginia." Mustered out of volunteer service Feb. 1, 1866. Lieut. Colonel Seventh U. S. Cavalry July 28, 1866. Killed with his whole command June 25, 1876, in action with Sioux Indians on little Big Horn River, Montana Territory. (Regular).

Custer, Thomas W., Monroe. 2nd Lieut. First U. S. Infantry, Feb. 23, 1866. 1st Lieut. Seventh U. S. Cavalry, July 28, 1866. Brevet Captain March 2, 1867, "for gallant and distinguished conduct in the engagement with the enemy at Wayensboro, Va., March 2, 1865." Brevet Major, March 2, 1867," "for distinguished conduct in the engagement with the enemy near Namozine Church, Va., April 3, 1865." Brevet Lieut. Colonel March 2, 1867, "for distinguished courage and service at the battle of Sailor's Creek, Va." Captain Dec. 2, 1875. Killed June 25, 1876, in action with Sioux Indians on Little Big Horn River, Montana Territory. (Regular).

Deitrich, C. J. Captain and Commissary Subsistence Volunteers, Feb. 19, 1863. Resigned July 14, 1865. (Regular).

Clitz, John M. B., Born in New York, March 10, 1823. Appointed from Michigan, Aug. 12, 1837. Attached to sloop "Ontario" West India Squadron, 1837-42. Naval School Philadelphia, 1843. Passed Midshipman, June 29, 1843. Sloop "St. Mary's" Mediterranean Squadron, 1844-45. Sloop "Falmouth" Home Squadron 1845-46. Commander Brig. "Hecla" Home Squadron, 1847. Capitulation of Castle San Juan d' Uloa, and capture of Tuspan. Steamer "Perita,"

THE GERMANIC INFLUENCE

Home Squadron 1847-47. Frigate "Cumberland" Mediterranean Squadron, 1849-51. Lieut. April 6, 1851. Coast Survey, 1851-52 Steam Frigate "Mississippi" East India Squadron, 1852-56. Special duty, Washington 1856. Sloop "Decatur" Pacific Squadron 1858-59. Steam Sloop "Iroquois" 1861. Commander, July 15, 1862. Commanding "Penobscot" North Atlantic Blockading Squadron, 1853. Commanding Steamer "Osceola" North Atlantic Blockading Squadron (Brazil) 1868-69. Commanding Frigate "California" Pacific Squadron 1870-72. Commodore, Dec. 28, 1872. Commanding Naval Station, Port Royal, S. C. 1876-77. Light House Inspector, 1878-80. Rear Admiral, March 13, 1880.

Heyerman, Oscar F. Born in Prussia. Appointed from Michigan, Nov. 29, 1861. Naval Academy, 1861-64. Steam Frigate "Colorado," Flagship Mediterranean Squadron 1866-67. Master Dec. 1, 1866. Steam Sloop "Canandaigua," European Squadron, 1868-1869. Lieut. March 12, 1868. Lieut. Commander, Oct. 13, 1869. Steam Frigate "Colorado" Flag-Ship Asiatic Fleet, 1870-1873. Ordnance duty, New York, 1873-74. U. S. Ship "Alert" cruising with Naval Cadets, 1875. Steam Sloop "Marion," 1876. Steam Sloop "Swatara," North Atlantic Station, 1877-78. U. S. Store-Ship "New Hampshire" Port Royal, S. C. 1879-1880.

Ahlen, Charles T. Entered service May 1, 1861, as Corporal Company "D", First (three months) Infantry. Mustered out Aug. 7, 1861.

APPENDIX B'

THE GERMAN-AMERICAN DEAD OF THE WORLD WAR

This is the list of Michigan German-American names that appears in the Roll of Honor of the dead of the Thirty-Second Division of the American Expeditionary Force, engaged in the World War, this being the Division to which most of the soldiers from Michigan were assigned. Other divisions engaged in the conflict contained other Michigan German-Americans, some of whom paid the supreme sacrifice. The initialings represent these meanings: D. W., died of wounds; K. I. A. killed in action; D. D., died of disease.

Name.	Service.	Cause and Date of Death
Bartels, Herman J.	Pvt 1 cl Co D 126 Inf.	K. I. A. 8-30-18.
Becker, Gustave G.	Pvt 1 cl Co A 126 Inf.	K. I. A. 10-17-18.
Berg, Alex.	Pvt Co B 128 Inf.	D. D. 3-13-18.
Bergann, Frich A.	Sgt Co 128 Inf.	K. I. A. 10-9-18.
Beuthin, Clarence	Pvt Med Det 125 Inf.	K. I. A. 8-6--18.
Bierschbach, Wm. T.	Corp Co E 125 Inf.	K. I. A. 10-9-18.
Blankertz, Walter T.	Sgt Co C 120 Mg Bn	K. I. A. 8-1-18.
Bohacz, Joe. W.	Corp Co A 126 Inf.	K. I. A. 8-2-18.
Boneburg, George	Corp Co K 126 Inf.	K. I. A. 10-16-18.
Boraback, Charles H.	Pvt 1 cl Bat A 119 F A	K. I. A. 8-12-18.
Borle, Omer	Sgt Co D 126 Inf.	K. I. A. 10-5-18.
Borst, James R.	Pvt 1 cl Co I 126 Inf.	K. I. A. 10-9-18.
Brandt, Herman A.	Pvt 1 cl Co L 126 Inf.	K. I. A. 10-6-18.
Breningsthall, George	Pvt 1 cl Co M 128 Inf.	K. I. A. 11-8-18.
Bush, Maurice J.	Pvt 1 cl Co B 126 Inf.	K. I. A. 10-5-18.
Cline, David E.	Corp Co L 125 Inf.	K. I. A. 8-31-18.

THE GERMANIC INFLUENCE

Name.	Service.	Cause and Date of Death
Clinefelter, Clyde C.	Sgt Co A 126 Inf.	K. I. A. 7-31-18.
Clinefelter, Robt O.	Pvt 1 cl Co A 126 Inf.	K. I. A. 8-4-18.
Crist, Jessie	Corp Co G 126 Inf.	K. I. A. 10-5-18.
Cunningham, Charles	Sgt Co K 126 Inf.	D. D. 7-3-18.
Dausman, Leroy L.	Sgt Co D 126 Inf.	K. I. A. 10-4-18.
Demund, Jacob H.	Corp Co E 125 Inf.	K. I. A. 10-11-18.
Dorenburg, Frank A.	Pvt Co H 127 Inf.	D. W. 10-13-18.
Drabenstott, Alvia R.	Pvt Co 126 Inf.	K. I. A. 9-4-18.
Dressell, Egerett C.	Corp Mg Co 125 Inf.	
Duerwearder, Alberic J.	Corp Co H 126 Inf.	K. I. A. 10-8-18.
Engle, Charles W.	Pvt 1 cl Co C 126 Inf.	K. I. A. 10-5-18.
Euper, Charles A.	Pvt Bat C 125 F A	
Ewald, Edward A.	Pvt Co D 127 Inf.	K. I. A. 10-11-18.
Falk, Oscar	Capt. Co. F. 125 Inf.	D. W. 8-1-18.
Fett, Paul	Sgt Co L 126 Inf.	K. I. A. 8-28-18.
Fisher, Peter W.	Pvt 1 cl Co L 128 Inf.	D. W. 9-3-18.
Frede, Arthur	Pvt Co L 125 Inf.	D. W. 9-3-18.
Frank, Edward	Pvt Co A 128 Inf.	K. I. A. 8-1-18.
Gehring, Thomas	Pvt Mg Co 126 Inf.	K. I. A. 10-8-18.
Gietzen, William	Corp Co E 123 Inf.	K. I. A. 8-31-18.
Graf, Ernest	Sgt Co E 126 Int.	K. I. A. 10-4-18.
Guzal, Anthony J.	Pvt Co L 125 Inf.	K. I. A. 7-31-18.
Hansen, Ray H.	Pvt 1 cl Co C 125 Inf.	K. I. A. 8-29-18.
Harm, Ufkie	Pvt Co I 127 Inf.	K. I. A. 9-3-18.
Hartman, Leland O.	Corp Co I 126 Inf.	K. I. A. 10-2-18
Haslick, Charles	Pvt Co E 125 inf.	K. I. A. 9-4-18.
Henning, William	Pvt Co D 126 Inf.	K. I. A. 7-31-18.
Henninger, George	Pvt Co 128 Int.	D. W. 11-11-18.
Hiler, Edward	Pvt 1 cl Co L Inf.	D. W. 7-31-18.
Hilferink, Hubert	Pvt Sup Co 125 F A	D. D.
Hoffman, Edward A.	2nd Lt. 125 Inf.	D. W. 10-10-18.
Hollonsbad, Hoyt	Corp Co E 125 Inf.	K. I. A. 7-31-18.
Hosler, Clifford C.	Pvt Co H 125 Inf.	K. I. A. 10-9-18
Hottinger, Benedict J.	Mech Co G 126 Inf.	K. I. A. 8-28-18.
Hovercamp, John	Pvt Co L 125 Inf.	K. I. A. 8-2-18.
Hunsinger, William A.	Pvt Co A 127 Inf.	K. I. A. 10-7-18.
Jager, John	Corp Co L 126 Inf.	D. D. 10-29-18.
Janke, Otto W.	Pvt Co D 127 Inf.	K. I. A. 10-15-18.
Johns Lewis C.	Pvt Co F 125 Inf.	K. I. A. 8-9-18.
Kierschke, Edward G.	Pvt Co C 128 Inf.	K. I. A. 8-1-18.
Kimmel, Donald K.	Corp Co G 126 Inf.	K. I. A. 8-27-18.

IN THE MAKING OF MICHIGAN 395

Name.	Service.	Cause and Date of Death
Kingsburg, Leo F.	Sgt Co D 125 Inf.	K. I. A. 8-4-18.
Klebba, August J.	Corp Co F 125 Inf.	K. I. A. 10-9-18.
Kline, Anthony	Pvt Co E 125 Inf.	K. I. A. 10-9-18.
Klinker, Gilbert	Corp Co I 126 Inf.	D. W. 10-17-18.
Kosal, Eli	Pvt 1 cl Co H 125 Inf.	K. I. A. 10-15-18.
Koster, Thomas	Pvt 1 cl Co H 125 Inf.	K. I. A. 7-31-18.
Kremer, John F.	Sgt Co F 126 Inf.	K. I. A. 8-29-18.
Krueger, William J.	1st Sgt Co M 127 Inf.	K. I. A. 10-3-18.
Krull, Reubin	Pvt Co I 126 Inf.	K. I. A. 8-1-18.
Larges, Walter W.	Pvt Co H 126 Inf.	K. I. A. 9-1-18.
Le Buda, Emil	Pvt Co G 128 Inf.	D. W. 8-6-18.
Lehmann, Wilford	Pvt Co G 127 Inf.	K. I. A. 8-3-18.
Lemke, Gustav C.	Corp Co K 128 Inf.	K. I. A. 11-7-18.
Lemke, William C.	Corp Co D 126 Inf.	K. I. A. 7-31-18.
Linegar, William	Sgt Co I 126 Inf.	K. I. A. 10-9-18.
Linna, George H.	Pvt Co G 125 Inf.	K. I. A. 10-14-18.
Loibl, Anthony T.	Sgt Hq Co 126 Inf.	K. I. A. 8-31-18.
Lukeman, Joseph	Pvt 1 cl Bat F 119 F A	K. I. A. 10-3-18.
Lueskow, Arthur	Pvt Co L 125 Inf.	K. I. A. 7-31-18.
Lutz, Anthony E.	Sgt Co A 125 Inf.	A. C. C. 9-19-18.
Lutz, William B.	Pvt 1 cl Bat A 119 F A	K. I. A. 8-10-18.
Lymburner, Robert H.	Pvt Mg Co 125 Inf.	K. I. A. 8-4-18.
Markel, George	Pvt Co H 125 Inf.	D. W. 9-1-18.
Marks, Rex V.	Corp Co M 126 Inf.	K. I. A. 8-2-18.
Melcher, Edward	Sgt Co C 120 Mg Bn	K. I. A. 8-28-18.
Messner, Fred	Pvt Co G 125 Inf.	K. I. A. 10-8-18.
Michel, Henry A.	Mech Co A 125 Inf.	K. I. A. 8-6-18
Miller, Leo A.	Pvt 1 cl Co K 126 Inf.	K. I. A. 8-29-18.
Miller, Raymond E.	2nd Lt Co B 120 Mg Bn	K. I. A. 7-31-18.
Minus, Alex.	Pvt Mg Co 126 Inf.	K. I. A. 10-5-18.
Myers, George W.	Corp Co K 125 Inf.	K. I. A. 7-31-18.
Neverdahl, L. W.	Sgt Co L H 128 Inf.	K. I. A. 10-20-18.
Pada, Walter	Corp Co L 125 Inf.	K. I. A. 7-31-18.
Perlick, Otto	Sgt Co H 128 Inf.	K. I. A. 11-11-18.
Pietras, Walter	Pvt Co I 128 Inf.	K. I. A. 9-1-18.
Poet, John W.	Corp Co D 125 Inf.	K. I. A. 8-4-18.
Preiskorn, Erwin	Corp Co E 126 Inf.	D. W. 8-31-18.
Rasp, Charles J.	Pvt 1 cl Co C 128 Inf.	K. I. A. 7-2-18.
Rieck, Victor I.	Pvt Mg Co 125 Inf.	K. I. A. 10-9-18.
Ritz, Charles	Pvt 1 cl Mg Co 125 Inf.	K. I. A. 10-18-18.
Romes, Stephens	Pvt Co H 125 Inf.	K. I. A. 10-15-18.

THE GERMANIC INFLUENCE

Name.	Service.	Cause and Date of Death
Rorabacher, Clare	Corp Co F 126 Inf.	K. I. A. 10-9-18.
Rosenzweig, Henry F.	Pvt Co I 126 Inf.	K. I. A.
Rothfus, Adrian	Sgt Mg Co 126 Inf.	K. I. A. 7-31-18.
Ruchti, Alfred	Pvt Co G 127 Inf.	D. W. 8-2-18.
Ruedisale, William	Corp Co C 125 Inf.	D. W. 8-5-18.
Saltin, William	Pvt Co L 126 Inf.	K. I. A. 10-10-18.
Sawcheck, Gregory	Pvt Co L 126 Inf.	D. W. 8-28-18.
Schafke, Albert	Pvt Co H 125 Inf.	D. W. 10-20-18.
Schmees, Leo	Pvt 1 cl Co G 126 Inf.	K. I. A. 10-14-18.
Schmitz, Joseph	Pvt Co B 125 Inf.	D. W. 10-16-18.
Schniers, Leo	Pvt 1 cl Co G 126 Inf.	D. W. 10-14-18.
Schoof, Clark W.	Pvt Co D 126 Inf.	K. I. A. 8-1-18.
Schulz, John E.	Pvt Co K 125 Inf.	K. I. A. 7-31-18.
Schultz, Harry W.	Pvt Co F 126 Inf.	K. I. A. 10-4-18.
Seifert, Herbert J.	Pvt Co D 128 Inf.	K. I. A.
Selschotter, Julius	Pvt Co 125 Inf.	K. I. A. 8-29-18.
Sole, Arthur A.	Pvt Co F 128 Inf.	K. I. A. 9-1-18.
Solomon, Max	Pvt Co D 125 Inf.	K. I. A. 8-28-18.
Stauber, John	Pvt Co L 125 Inf.	K. I. A. 7-31-18.
Steffe, Paul E.	Corp Co F 126 Inf.	K. I. A. 8-31-18.
Struber, Herman	Pvt Co D 128 Inf.	K. I. A. 9-1-18.
Teichler, John	Sgt Co I. 125 Inf.	K. I. A. 7-31-18.
Thomas Emil	Pvt Co C 125 Inf.	K. I. A. 8-27-18.
Udych, John	Pvt Co A 128 Inf.	K. I. A. 9-1-18.
Ulrich, Dan F.	Pvt 1 cl Co C 128 Inf.	K. I. A. 8-1-18.
Weisgerber, Clifton G.	Sgt Co C 126 Inf.	K. I. A. 8-30-18.
Weiss, Adolph C.	Pvt Med Det 125 Inf.	K. I. A. 8-6-18.
Wenzel, Byron W.	Pvt Co A 126 Inf.	K. I. A. 8-27-18.
Wolfe, Lawrence	Corp Co A 125 Inf.	D. W. 10-5-18.
Wortz, Peter P.	Corp Co G 126 Inf.	K. I. A. 8-27-18.

INDEX

INDEX

Abbott, Frederick H., 233
Abel, Frank Lawrence, 171
Abel, Fritz, 225, 227
Abel, John Jacob, 233
Abel, Julius Caesar, 276
Abel, Sylvester, 276
Abert, Col. John, 282
Abert, James William, 282
Ackie, Stephen, 105
Adamy, Peter H., 105
Adelbert, Brother, 187
Adendorf, John, 172
Agassiz, Louis John, 201
Ahrenweld, Frank A., 235
Alber, Frederick, 142
Alberti, Alexander, 113
Albrecht, Albert A., 288, 320
Allbright, Egbert, 78
Allen, Eben, 45
Allgeyer, Rev. Ferdinand, 241
Allmendinger, Daniel Frederick, 89
Almerian, Brother, 188
Alton, Frederick, 96
Amberg, David M., 320
Ambruster, Jacob, 91
Ameis, Nicholas, 86
Amelung, Frederick, 25
Amian, Brother, 187, 188
Ammeling, Gilbert Pastor, 24
Ammerman, 80
Amrhein, 70
Amrhein, John, 74
Anderson, Melville Best, 232
Andries, Engelbert, 227, 298
Andries, Henry A. I., 298
Andres, Paul Gerhardt, 171
Andrew, Brother, 188
Angell, James R., 159
Angler, William R., 157
Annecke, Emil, 94, 277, 296
Anthon, George Christian, 259
Antonius, Frederick W., 350
Antrobus, John, 222
Apel, Franz A., 227
Arendt, Pastor F. W. M., 184
Arends, Robert M., 188
Arens, John N., 227
Arentz, U. S. S., 326
Arets, 19
Argus, George, 83
Arnd, Hugo E. R., 157

Arndt, Albert F. R., 116
Arndt, Christopher, 80
Arndt, Jacob, 80
Askin, John, Jr., 45
Askin, John, Sr., 45
Asman, John, 88
Astor, John Jacob, 300
Atterbury, Rev. John G., 152
Auch, Pastor John J., 184
Auer, John, 232
Azarias, Brother, 187
Babst, Earl F., 278
Bacher, 19
Backus, Frederick, 309
Bade, Henry, Sr., 97
Bader, Bernhard, 76
Baer, Christopher, 75
Bahlke, Wm. A., 367
Baierlein, Emil, 246
Balcke, Alphonse, 293
Ballen, Frederick, 142
Bandholz, Harry H., 170
Baraga, Rt. Rev. Frederick, 196, 239
Barath, Herman, 115
Barbour, Levi L., 153
Bardeen, Charles Russell, 232
Barie, Wm., 70
Barlage, Anton F., 69
Barnetz, D., 25
Barnhart, Peter, 316
Barnhart, Willard, 316
Barrager, John, 362
Barth, Heinrich, 228
Bauck, Paul, 188
Bauer, Emil, 340
Bauer, Family, 70
Bauerlein, J. G., 317
Baugham, Charles, 116
Bauman, Rev. John A., 91, 248
Baum, Jesse, 105
Baur, Bertha, 232
Baur, John C., 74
Beaman, Wooster W., 157
Benringer, J. L., 311
Bechard, David, 77
Beck, Gottlieb, 304
Beck, Johan Heinrich, 228
Becker, Francis, 50
Becker, Melchior, 43
Becker, Matthias, 187
Becker, Theodore, 311

INDEX

Beckman, 38
Beerhorst, Henry, 241
Behagel, Daniel, 19
Behaum, Martin, 17
Behr, Lorenz, 70
Behrans, Charles August, 232
Beisel, Peter Jr., 105
Beller, Jacob, 315
Bellheimer, Joseph, 83
Belser, Carl William, 166
Beltenbender, Heinrich, 78
Beltenbender, Peter, 78
Belzer, Family, 70
Bendix, Max, 226, 344
Beninghoff, Frederick, 116
Bent, Frederic, 83
Bentzen, Frederick Whelpley, 170
Benzenberg, George Henry, 235
Berberich, Prof. Francis, 178
Bergemen, Louis, 232
Berger, Jacob, 116
Berghle, Elmer, 170
Berkey, Julius, 315
Bernhardt, Martin, 105
Bers, Abraham, 108
Bertz, George B., 86
Besie, Family, 70
Bessinger, Conrad, 53, 89, 309
Bettinger, Melchior, 311
Betterle, "Deacon," 80
Betzing, Christian, 83
Beyer, William, 253
Biddle, John, 347
Bigler, Philip, 281
Bird, Capt. Henry, 47
Birkhoff, George David, 232
Birkinstock, Adolph, 113
Bischoff, Catherine, 230
Bischof, Herman, 225
Bischoff, Herman, 227
Bishop, Levi, 68
Bittenbender, 83
Bittner, Walter Simon, 170
Blackmore, John, 228
Blein, Joseph, 68
Blesch, August F., 316
Bliset, Peter, 80
Blitz, Louis, 319, 331
Bloomberg, Michael, 82
Bochman, Christian and Poly, 81
Bock, Joseph Carl, 170
Bockharst, Rev. Aloysius J., 178

Boeing, William, 311, 319, 327
Bogard, Jacob, 47
Bogling, Pastor Freidrich, 184
Bohling, William, 316
Bohr, Frank, 233
Boliman, Edward, 323
Bolza, Charles, 117
Bertsch, Christian, 320
Book, Dr. James Burgess, 269
Book, Johnson, 269
Borgess, Rt. Rev. Caspar H., 175, 238
Borgman, Sylvia Irene, 172
Borick, William C., 23
Borneman, Dedrich, 69
Bornman, John, 310
Borse, James R., 154
Bosche, Rev. Aloysius F., 176
Bosksche, Julius, 95
Bouquet, Henry, 35
Bour, John, 69
Bouquet, Henri, Gen., 258
Bourland, Benjamin Parsons, 166
Bowerfind, K. S. 181
Bradley, Clara, 228
Braidenback, Henry, 115
Brakeman, Peter F., 195
Brandt, Otto, 83
Breggy, Louis, 169
Brehm, Derich, 39
Breitschneider, Robert, 111
Breitung, Edward, 324, 327, 330, 356
Breitmeyer, Philip, 319
Bremer, Henry, 308
Bremer, J., 224
Brentano, Theodore, 279
Brestefeld, Henry, 308
Bretz, J. Harlan, 235
Brinck, Aaron, 103
Brink, Utter, 281
Brockhauser, Dr., 70
Broockfeld, William, 281
Broman, 83
Brown, Jacob, 335
Brucker, Ferdinand, 356-357
Brucker, Gustav, 363
Bruckner, Herman, 225
Bruckner, Pastor, 184
Brueggeman, Frank, 71
Brum, Christopher, 75
Brumme, Carl C. G., 265

INDEX

Bruner, Charles Theodore, 171
Bruner, Jacob, 80
Brunold, Peter (Brother Eucarius) 189
Brunnow, Franz Fredrich, 153, 205
Brunschweiler, George L. Dr., 114
Bruske, Rev. August F., 180
Bruske, Gottlieb R., 94
Buck, Daniel, 45
Buck, Florence, 232
Buckley, George Parker, 228
Buehler, 88
Buhl, Christian Henry, 304, 318
Buhl, Frederick Augustus, 115, 304, 318
Bulkeey, Frank, 233
Bunzel, Herbert Horace, 314
Burk, Edward, 356
Burkhardt, Catherine, 80
Burkholder, Abraham, 85
Burrows, Katherine, 228
Busch, John J., 112
Butterman, Eugene, 242
Butzel, Magnus, 329-30
Butzel, Martin, 329-30
Cady, Calvin B., 157
Camber, Emilian (Brother Anselm, 188
Campau, Louis, 74
Campbell, Capt., 37
Canfield, Arthur G., 160
Canfield, R. Bishop, 163
Carleton, Gen. Sir Guy, 35
Carlisle, Fred, 315
Carstens, Dr. John Henry, 194, 266
Cartagh, Brother, 188
Casper, 83
Casterlein, Jacob, 104
Cattrell, Henry, 74
Chapoton, Dr. Eustace, 258
Chase, Mary Wood, 228
Chauvin, 34
Christensen, George Luther, 173
Church, James Edward, 232
Clarkmottl, Emma, 228
Claus, 69
Clause, William, 47
Clem, John Lincoln, 112
Clemens, Christian, 68, 85, 318
Clergue, Francis H., 284
Clippert, George, 319
Cloester, Ottmar, 246
Closter, Ottmar, 183
Cohen, Frederick E., 216
Colburn, Hattie, 228
Colclazer, Rev. Henry, 248
Colclazer, Jacob, 77
Cole, Frank Nelson, 166
Cole, Rossiter, 228
Comegys, Cornelius, 25
Connor, Richard, 84
Conrad, Charles Frederick, 74
Conrad, John, 74
Cooke, James Francis, 228
Cooley, Dr. Thomas Benton, 166
Copland, Royal Samuel, 233
Corbus, Gottfried, 52, 76
Corbus, James Godfrey, 87
Corbus, Richard, 77, 108
Cord, Ferdinand, 116
Cordes, John, 326
Cornell, Jacob, 75
Corselius, George, 291
Cottrell, Henry, 87
Couse, Adam, 310
Couse, E. Anger, 217
Craemer, 58
Craemer, Pastor, 90, 183, 245
Crager, Jacob, 75
Craig, James A., 160
Cramer, Peter, 117
Crary, Isaac E., 151
Crell, Joseph, 28
Cremer, Henry, 103
Crissman, Michael, 85
Cron, Lieut. Anton Caesar, 171
Cross, Arthur Lyon, 166
Croul, Jerome, 318
Crouse, 88
Crouse, Theodore, 272
Cummings, John Grinnell, 228
Curtenius, A. E., 313
Curtenius, Frederick William, 77, 113
Custer, Abel, 105
Custer, George Alexander, 117
Custer, Thomas W., 142
Czizek, Augustus, 115
Dabo, Leon, 216
Dabo, Theodore Scott, 216
Danziger, J. C., 317
Darmstaetter, Jacob, 310
Darmstaetter, William, 310
Dederichs, Peter, 287

INDEX

Deindorfer, Pastor, 183
Dellenbaugh, Dr. Charles C., 271
De Longuiel, M., 50
De Low, Rev., Dr. 249
Dennison, Walter, 164
De Peyster, Col., 40
Dethoff, Carl C., 172
Deuel, Andrew L., 348
Dewey, Willy A., 160
Dickhaus, Prof. Joseph H., 178
Dieckhoff, Thomas Johann, 165
Diechman, Ferdinand, 282
Dieckman, Frederick, 94
Diegel, Henry, 69
Diehl, Francis, 43
Diemer, Hugo, 170
Dierstein, Samuel, 77
Dilbeck, 19
Dillenback, John, 84
Dillenback, Laura, 84
Diefenbach, John (Brother Damian), 189
Dittmar, John, 309
Dobbreton, John, 83
Dock, George, 159
Dodder, Jacob, 79
Doctitz, William, 355
Donner, William, 86
D'Ooge, Martin L., 155
Dopp, Catherine Elizabeth, 232
Dorchester, Lord, 36
Dorman, August, 310
Dorsch, Dr. Edward, 168, 253, 267, 272, 355
Dousman, Michael, 303, 318, 347
Dow, Earl W., 164
Dove, Joseph, 96
Drake, Joseph H., 163
Drexelius, Frederick, 95
Dubendorf, Edward, 116
Duengle, 88
Dueweke, Christina K., 344
Dueweke, John J., 344
Duffield, Rev. George, 152
Duffield, Dr. Samuel P., 274, 310
Dumser, Pastor Simon, 184
Durst, August Theodore Benedict, 242
Dyema, Peter William, 228
Earling, Andrew J., 305
Etherage, Anna, 113
Eberbach, Christian, 92, 355

Eberdt, Pastor Julius, 184
Eberhard, John P., 114
Eberle, Herman Roth, 173
Eberle, Jacob, 83
Eberstein, Conrad, 81
Eberstine, Henry, 80
Eberts, Dr. Herman Melchior, 49, 117, 260
Eberle, Jacob, 316
Eddy, Joseph, 82
Edelman, John D., 93
Edwards, missionary, 84
Effinger, Rev. Augustine M., 176
Effinger, John R., 165
Ege, C. N., 272
Eggert, John, 85
Egler, Philip, 116
Ege, Dr., 70
Eggeman, David Bernard, 69
Ehrenstrasser, John George, 241
Eichelsdorfer, William, 298
Eichenberg, William Louis, 235
Eicher, Rev. Michael, 177
Eidlitz, Cyrus, W., 287
Eilett, Jacob, 82
Eisenach Family, 70
Eldred, Julius, 68
Elliot, Mathew, 47
Elliott, Richard R., 59
Elias, Edward A. M. Ph. D., 181
Endlich, John, 116
Engel, Johannes, 105
Engelhardt, Rev. Zephyrin, 241
Engleman, Michael, 327
Eppling, Pastor F., 184
Erley, Rev. Hugo J., 176
Ermatinger, Lawrence, 43
Ernest, Caspar, 114
Eschweiler, Franz Chadbourne, 278
Esper, Jacob, 74
Etherington, Capt., 37
Evans, Edward P., 155
Everard, Herbert, 313
Everts, Mr., 68
Ewalt, Jacob, 115
Eyme, Ludwig, 181
Fabor, Rev. William F., 249
Failing, Henry, 309
Falckner, 19
Falkstein, John, 83
Fangboner, Daniel, 82
Farrand, David Osborne, 273

INDEX

Faser, Maria, 49
Fasquelle, Louis, 154
Faulkner, Martin, 25
Faust, Albert Bernhardt, 17
Fedewa, John H., 356
Fedewa, Morris, 76
Federlein, Martin, 310
Fekete, S. I., 317
Feldner, Edward, 194
Felker, Peter H., 169
Fenstermacher, Saul, 105
Ferber, Edna, 298
Ferguson, Wilbert, 181
Ferle, Henry, 96
Fernekes, Gustave, 173
Ferners, Joseph (Brother Amerian), 188
Feske, 88
Feuerhak, George, 170
Fick, Pastor Herman, 185
Finan, Brother, 188
Finzel, George, 185
Firehaudt, Wilhelm, 68
Firmilian, Brother, 188
Fischer, Gotthelf, 170
Fischer, Peter, 70
Fishback, Richard, 78
Fischer, Richard, 232
Fischer, William, 70
Fisher, Frederick J., 254
Fisher, John, 50
Flanders, Francis, 108
Fleischauer, Alfred L., 348
Fleitz, John P., 254
Fleitz, John P., 327
Flescheim, Joseph, 325
Flinterman, Johann, 270
Flinterman, Rudolph F., 317
Flugel, Charles, 87
Fogle, Floyd Eard, 172
Fogle, Josephine Rena, 172
Folz, Leroy Stewart, 172
Fordney, Joseph W., 357
Foster, John Harris, 248, 322
Fouts, Minerva, 171
Fox, Jacob, 74
Fox, Martin, 241
Francis, Peter, 34
Fralick, Henry, 74
Fralick, Peter, 74
Frambach, H. A., 318
Frank, John, 74

Frank, John Peter, 102
Franke, Emil Arthur, 173
Frankhauser, Wm. H., 356
Franklin, Leo M. Rabbi, 252
Frappe, Martin, 49
Fredenburg, John, 81
Fredenburg, Sylvester, 77
Freer, Paul C., 158
Freideman, Otto Herman, 172
Freidhoff, John, 86
Frelinghuysen, Frederick, Gen., 24
Frelinghuysen, Rev. Theo. J., 24
Fremont, John C., 30
Frends, 333
Frensdorf, Edward, 320
Freyhofer, Louise, 170, 228
Frey, Gottlieb, 224
Friday, David, 211
Frieden, John Peter, 176, 177
Friedland, John F., 242
Frieseke, Frederick, 83
Frieseke, Frederick Carl, N. A., 216, 222
Friess, (Rev. Mother Carolina), 12-190
Friess, Johann George, 190
Fritz, John, 224
Fritz, M. J., 320
Froebes, Prof. John B., 178, 179
Frogensus, Brother, 188
Frue, Capt. W. B., 326
Fuerbringer, Louis, Ernest, 230
Funke, Moses A., 113
Furbeck, John Phillip, 173
Fusz, Prof. Vincent A., 178
Gall, Peter, 105
Gallagher, Rt. Rev. M. J., 238
Gardner, Obadiah, 279
Gartner, George, 275
Gauss, Christian, 230
Gayley, Charles Mills, 165
Gehrine, Rev. Henry, 87
Gehring, Herbert August, 171
Geiger, Benjamin F., 291
Geik, Nicholas, 96
Geisen, Frank, 326
Geissmor, Henry, 272
Gellert, Johannes Sophus, 219
Gentner, Louis Gustav, 171
George, Family, 70
Gephart, Capt. Henry, 114

INDEX
403

Gerlach, Christian, 86
Gerst, Francis J., 178
Getman, George Arnold, 172
Gettman, Solomon, 83
Gettering, Winnifred Sarah, 172
Geyser, Prof. Anthony F., 178
Gies, Jacob, 70
Gies, Joseph, 69
Gies, John H., 70
Gies, Joseph W., 216
Gies, Lorenz, 70
Gies, Paul, 70
Gies, Paul, 116
Gies, Paul, 318
Gies, Wilhelm, 69
Girl, Christian, 317
Girty, Simon, 47
Gladwin, Capt., 39
Glaser, Emil, 275, 325
Glazier, Otto Charles, 231
Godeke, Wilhelm, 272
Godez, Peter, 83, 242
Goebel, August, 112, 320
Goetchius, Steven, 85
Goetsch, Henry Max, 173
Goetz, Christian, 309
Gohl, Family, 70
Goldsmith, John, 115
Gomberg, Moses, 162
Goos, Valentine, 188
Gortz, Joseph, 115
Gorenflo, Theodore, 320
Gosiger, Rev. Frederick A., 178
Gott, James B., 276
Graebner, John Henry Phillip, 183, 246
Graebner, —, 58
Graebner, Pastor, 184
Graeverat, Garret, 46
Graf, Family, 70
Graffenried, Baron Christ, 26
Grafley, Charles, 218
Grahn, Robert, 311
Graul, Charles, 227
Greening, John C. W., 344
Greenwald, Dr. Isadore, 235
Greiner, Michael, 74
Grelling, Gottlieb, 313
Grenshky, Peter, 96
Gres, Henry, 85
Grettenberger, Marion Louise, 172
Greusel, Family, 69

Greusel, John, 70
Greusel, Joseph, 293
Greusel, Nicholas, 70
Greusel, Nicholas Jr., 108
Grimm, Peter, 310
Grimmelsman, Rev. Joseph F. X., 176
Groesbeck, Alex J., 349
Groesbeck, Walter D., 170
Groll, John, 69, 85
Grossman, Louis, Rabbi, 251
Gruenist, Joseph, 42
Gruenthamer, Prof. M. J., 178
Gruppe, Carl Paul, 216
Guck, Homer, A., 173
Guenther, Frederick, 319
Gulch, - 21
Guldenstein, 88
Gulick, Robert F., 348
Gundrum, Frederick, 272
Guth, Frederick, 85
Guthe, Karl Eugene, 166
Gwinnder, Jacob P., 310
Haanel, Charles Francis, 231
Haanel, Eugene Emil Felix Richard, 235
Haarer, John W., 349
Haas, Adam, 323
Haas, Jacob, 92
Haass, Julius H., 217, 319
Habenbach, Aaron, 78
Haberkorn, John H., 345
Hack, Bernard, 93
Hack, John, 143
Hackenberg, - 83
Hackman, - 83
Haettstadt, George William, 246
Hage, Conrad, 95
Hager, Daniel, 76
Hagerman, Franz Heinrich, 77
Hagerman, John, 82, 168
Hahn, J. N., 184
Haigle, Charles Edmund, 173
Hake, William, 316
Haldane, William, 308
Haldimand, Sir Frederick, 34
Haller, Henry C., 357
Hambach, Henry, 37
Hambach, Jacob D., 37
Hambach, William, 37
Hambitzer, Joseph F., 349
Haminiski, Michael, 91

INDEX

Hamm, Edgar, 272
Hammer, Clemens, 242
Hamtramck, John Francis, Jr., 101
Hands, William, 42
Haney, Charles, 75
Hanmer, Charles A., 272
Hans, Jacob P., 116
Hardenburg, Jermiah, 80
Hardenburg, Louis Martin, 173
Hardy, Edwin L., 233
Harliman, Peter, 39
Harper, Robert, 26
Harpfy, Dr. William, 262
Harsens, Bernardus, 87
Harsens, Jacob, 87
Hartline, - 88
Hartman, Frederick, 315
Hartman, Sergeant, 43
Harts, Prof. Martin M., 178
Hartscher, Francis, 241
Hartsig, John, 86
Hartzell, Susanna, 152
Haskeel, Mellen Woodman, 233
Hasselman, James Blood, 171
Hasslinger, Martin, 242
Hattstadt, John James, 226
Hattstaet, Pastor, 185
Haupt, Lieut. Lewis M., 282
Haybarger, - 83
Heavenrich, Samuel, 330
Heberlein, Herman, 225
Hecker, Col. Frank J., 289, 305, 320
Hecker, Frank J., 320
Heckert, Benj. F., 348
Heftler, V. R., 317
Heirman, Prof. Francis, 178
Heibisch, Martin, 316
Heimsch Family, 70
Heineman, Emil S., 329-330
Heinrich, Christian, 227
Heintz, - 19
Heintzen, Jacob, 74
Heine, Charles, 116
Heintzleman, Samuel, 282
Heintzman, Charles, 95
Heintzman, Christ, 95, 282
Heisrodt, Thomas, 81
Heiss, John, 70
Heitkamp, Father Aloysius, 178
Heitlaud, Freda A. M., 181
Helliker, George, 311
Hellwig, Louisa, 83

Helwig, George Frank, 293
Helwig, Charles, 248
Hemmeter, John G., 93
Hempl, George, 160
Hench, George A., 160
Henes, John, 254, 316
Henk, Anthony, 86
Henkel, Joseph, 70
Henkel, Peter, 304, 348
Henn, Edward (Lieut.), 51
Hennepin, Father, 19
Hensler, C., 224
Henzel, Herman, 171
Herbst Family, 70
Herman, August, 25
Herman, John, 75
Herman, Joseph, 320
Hermeling, John (Brother Leodicius), 188
Herpolsheimer, William G., 315, 320
Herrman, Raphael, 316
Hess, Peter, 226
Hess, Julius, 288
Hesse, - 38
Hesse, Bernhardt, 272, 231
Heydenburk, Martin, 53
Heydlauff, Christian, 91
Heyn, Emil, 333
Hetz, F. John, 95
Heyerman, Samuel P., 284
Heyl, Friederika Margretha, 171
Hiesrodt, John M., 94
Hildebrand, Charlotte, 85
Hildebrandt, Bernard, 235
Hildner, Johann Augustus Charles, 166
Hildor, Walter Gotlob, 171
Hilgard, Eugene Woldemar, 156
Hiller, Peter, 316
Hillman, Frederick H., 169
Hilsendegen, Valentine, 320, 363
Hilsendegen, Valentine, 363
Himmelberger, Ransom, 170
Himmelein, Linde Louise, 171
Hirschman, Andrew, 37
Hite, Baron John, 30
Hock, - 83
Hoeffer, Rev. George A., 176, 178
Hoexter, Prof. Samuel J., 179
Hoffend, Prof. Wm. M., 178
Hoffman, George, 52

INDEX

Hoffman, George W., 105, 347
Hoffman, John D., 173
Hoffman, Michael, 151
Hoffman, Paul (Brother Conrad Ernest), 189
Hoffman, Peter, 25
Hoffman, Philip H., 78
Hoffsteller, Christ, 74
Hogarth, Rev. William, 249
Hollenberg, Henry (Brother Boniface), 189
Holmich, Amandus, 86
Holtslander, Joseph, 93
Holzheimer, William Andrew, 279
Hommel, - 69
Honeck, Anthony A., 178
Hopphan, Karl Ernest, 170
Horger, John, 74
Houk, Henry, 75
Houseman, Henry, 331
Houseman, Julius, 96, 331, 356
Huber, Andreas, 69
Huber, Gotthelf C., 161
Hubinger, Lorenz, 245, 338
Huegli, John A., 183, 247
Huenert, George, 272
Huerman, Prof. Henry G., 178
Huetteman, Frank, 310
Huetwald, Frederick, 314
Hugh, Brother, 187
Hulett, George Augustus, 167
Hulick, Dietrich or
Humbert, Jacob, 74
Humell, Margaret, 83
Hunsiker, Silvanus, 75
Hunter, Robert, 22
Huperz, Christopher, 116
Hurz, Carl, 225
Hutzel, Titus, 363
Igenfritz, Isaac E., 344
Ihling, Otto, 356
Immel Family, 70
Ingersoll, Robert, 82
Inselman, Claus, 81
Irkenbach, John, 78, 80, 248
Israel, Magnus, 329
Jacker, Edward, 241
Jacob, Homer, 75
Jacobs, Christopher, 76
Jacobs, Hiram, 105
Jacobs, Louis, 103
Jacokes, Daniel C., 248

Jacokes, John Hood, 248
Jans, Anneke, 18
Jauch, Carl J., 173
Jawert, 19
Jelsch, Joseph, 70
Jennings, Herbert Spencer, 166
Johannes, 80
Johannes, Henry, 39
Jones, Edward D., 164
Jones, Elisha, 157
Jones, Robert, 45
Josenhans, Gottlieb, 309
Josephs, Joseph, 335
Jung, Frank, 95
Jungman, 84
Kagey, Henry, 26
Kagi, John Henry, 26
Kahlman, Hermann, 283
Kahn, Albert, 288
Kahn, Julius, 289
Kaichen, Arnold, 276
Kaiser Family, 70
Kaiser, R. A., 320
Kalb, Conrad, 326
Kalkbronner, Wilhelm, 310
Kallenbach, 69
Kaius, Anthony, 70
Kalzow, Fritz, 227
Kamerer, Charles, 74
Kamp, Joseph B., 143
Kamper, Louis, 288, 289
Kanause, John, 310
Kanause, William, 91
Kanitz, Louis (Col.), 121
Kanter, Edward, 303, 309
Kanzler, Dr. Karl A., 273
Kaple, John H., 319
Kappler, Frederick C., 357
Karrer, Simon C., 320
Kast, Gustave, 111, 115
Kauffer, Hale P., 313
Kauffman, Calvin H., 163
Kauffman, Louis G., 321
Kauffman, Peter, 115
Kauffman, Samuel, 321
Kaufman, Fritz, 70
Kaufman, L. G., 327
Keeler, Henry, 70
Keider, John, 92
Keifer, E. W., 313
Keiff, Lorenz, 91
Keiser, Christian, 85

Keller, Dr. H. F., 173
Kellinger, Father Louis, 178
Kellner, Charles Frederick, 231
Kemp, Nicholas, 316
Kemper, Sebastian (Brother Felan), 188
Kempf, Charles L., 355
Kempf, Michael, 81
Kempff, Nicholas, 95
Kephart, Dr. Philip, 262
Keplius, 19
Kern, Heinrich, 227
Kerner, Frederick W., 279
Kernper, Joseph L., 178
Kerschner, Andrew, 309
Kersler, Fred, 95
Kessler, W. S., 320
Kettner, William, 279
Kiefer, Carl, 170
Kiefer, Dr. Herman, 35, 152, 265, 318
Kierstede, Dr. Hans, 18
Kies Family, 70
Killner, Max, 231
Kindelberger, Jacob, 313
Kindemann, Charles, 272
Kineske, Hannah, 77
Kinipel, Henry Joseph, 188
Kimbaldt, John H., 276
Kimmel, Edward F., 115
Kimmel, Henry, 91
Kirchner, Adolph, 93
Kirchner, George H., 319
Kirchner, Otto, 158, 194, 277, 349
Klawater, Jacob, 46
Klein, 83
Klein, Dr. Peter, 264, 272, 296
Klein, M. J., 272
Klein, Samuel, 77
Kleine, Gustav Adolph, 234
Kleine, Dr. Lewis, 272
Klem, Stephen Vincent, 170
Klepetko, Frank, 326
Klett, Sophia, 83
Klindworth, Karl, 228
Kling, Philip, 310
Klingensmith, Frank L., 317
Knaebel, Carl Henry, 173
Knapper, Louis, 169
Knight, George Wells, 234
Knipschier, Father John E., 178
Kobeler, Frederick, 234

Koch, Herr, 339-340
Koch, Peter, 276
Koch, Theodore W., 162
Koch, William, 96
Kocher, Arthur E., 170
Kocker, Peter, 81
Koehler, Frederick, 309
Koehler, Joseph, 70
Koenig, Rev. Charles J., 364
Koenig, Conrad W., 181
Koenig, George Augustus, 174
Koenig, Miss Selma S., 181
Koenig, William, 344
Koeplinger, John, 94
Koester, Michael, 117
Koester, William, 50
Kohl, John George, 72
Kohler, August, 241
Kohler, Kaufman, 250
Kohler, Max James, 250
Kohne, Prof. Christopher J. 178
Kokenge, Professor John B., 178
Konti, Isadore, 218
Kopp, Anthony, 242
Kopp, Reverend Mr., 55
Korte, Peter, 74
Kost, Dr. John, 271
Koster, 19
Krake, Blasius, Rev., 241
Kranich, Edward F., 293
Krapf, Conrad, 195
Krapp, Conrad, 92
Kratz, Leonard, 48
Kratz, Mary, 48
Kraus, Edward H., 165
Kraus, Ezra Jacob, 234
Krause, Benj. H., 344
Krause, Henry, 309
Krecke, Florenz, 193
Kregger, Michael, 105
Kreischer, Joseph Henry, 78
  Carl, 79
Krehbiel, Henry Edward, 229
Krenerich, Peter, 81
Krentel, Andrew Peter, 170
Krentkampf, Rev. Ferdinand, 179
Kremer, Conrad J., 172
Kremer, John, 68
Kremer, Professor John B., 178
Kremke, Wilhelm, 246
Kresge, Sebastian S., 306
Krezer, John M., 104

INDEX

Kroenche, Edward, 295
Kroll, Leon, 216
Kropp, Conrad George J., 272
Kuehn, Herman, 246
Kuhl, Conrad, 326
Kuhlbord, Jacob, 25
Kuhlman, Father John W., 178
Kuhlman, Professor Adolph J., 178
Kuhn, Chester Ferdinand, 172
Kuhn, Frank, 313
Kuhn, Franz C., 87, 277, 349
Kuhn, John, 86, 319
Kuhn, Robert, 313
Kuhnmuench, Professor Otto, 178
Kulp, Walter L., 171
Kunders, 19
Kundig, Rev. Martin, 152, 242, 350
Kunkle, Jane, 157
Kunz, Charles, 316
Kunze, August, 70
Kunze, Edward Joseph, 170
Kunze, Pastor, 20
Kurner, Frank W., 109
Kurtzworth, Harry Muir, 222
Kusterer, Christopher, 315
Kuttnauers, the, 334
Laible, Joseph, 69
Laitner, - 311
Lamplan, Jacob, 37
Landskroener, William, 93
Lange, Gottlieb, 94
Lange, Herman Carl, 171
Langenbacher, Andrew, 343
Lantz, 78
Lantzen, Fred, 96
Lasley, William, 95
Lauer, Nicholas, 187
Lauhoff, Alexander, 343
Laury, John, 91
Laury, Hanna, 82
Lausen, Nicholas, 78
Lautner, Robert Menzel, 171
Lederer, Henry, 96
Lederer, John, 18
Leffler, Lewis, 282
Leffler, Mabel Louise, 171
Legislators, German-American, 351
Leib, Father Charles J., 178
Leiblein, Edward M., 323
Leifert, Charles, 93
Leir, Moritz, 164
Leisen, Jacob, 316

Leisen, Lewis 316
Leisen, Theodore A., 235
Leisler, Jacob, 18
Leitelt, Adam, 309
Leitelt, Adolph, 311, 315
Lehman, Charles E., 116
Lembeck, Lucas, 188
,Lemcke, Henry, 272
Lemke, Dr., 70
Lemm, William, 324
Lendenberger, George, 25
Lents, John, 311
Lentz, John Jacob, 279
Lerich, Peter D., 86
Lernoult, Captain, 41
Lessing, Otto Edward, 231
Leuschner, Armin William, 231
Levake, W. S., 362
Levering, - 25
Levering, Joshua, 25
Levy, Max, 314
Leyenberger, John, 30
Leyenberger, Peter, 30
Liebering, Weekhart, 25
Limbocker, Elder Henry, 77, 248
Lindermans, 84
Line, John C., 114
Lineberger, David, 30
Lineberger, Walter F., 30
Ling, Conrad, 70
Lingelback, William E., 234
Linkletter, Charles S., 96
Locker, John, 76
Lodeman, Ernest G., 169
Loeffler, Egbert Theodore, 162
Loehe, John Konrad
    Wilhelm, 243
Loennecker, Martin G., 357
Lohrman, Henry, 83
Longyear, John M., 325
Look, William, 275
Lorch, Emil, 161
Lorch ,Emil, 290
Lorenz, - 21
Losel, Lorenz, 245
Louenback, Gertrude, 171
Loubacher, Michael, 71
Loveder, Clement, 91
Luchen, - 19
Lucker, Henry, 227
Lugenbeel, Lieutenant, 283
Luke, Brother, 187

Lungerhausen, Traugott, 86
Luthardt, John N., 83
Lutz, Dr. Frederick, 181
Lutze, J. J., 272
Lymburner, Adam, 43
Maas, John B., 324, 327
MacDougal, George, 40
Machris, Peter, 68
Mack, - 89
Mack, Christian, 320, 327
Mack, Edwin F., 321
Maderfield, Nicholas Hubert, 173
Maentz, Henry, 80
Maier, Martin, 76
Mainhan, Eugene, 272
Maladon, John, 69
Maltz, George L., 152, 321, 349
Mandorff, Rachel, 83
Mann, 89
Mann, Gother, 47
Mann, Henry, 89
Mann, Peter, 81
Margenau, Roy Edward, 173
Margenruth, Dora, 83
Mario, Rev. Matthias M., 241
Mark, Rt. Rev. Ignatius, 239
Mark, John, 319
Mark, John, 327
Marschner, Adolph F., 275
Martin, John Baptiste, 228
Marth, - 88
Martz, Frank, 70
Martz, Michael, 70
Marx, Stephen, 224
Marxhausen, August, 291
Massbacher, Franz, 272
Mast, Prof. S. O., 181
Mast, Samuel Ottmar, 234
Mather, Fridolin (Brother Amos), 189
Matthai, 19
Matthaus, Adam, 188
Matullath, Hugo, 312
Mauch, Bernard, 111
Mauch, Joseph William, 181
Mauer, Philip, 311
Maus, Jacob, 114
Mayer, - 25
Mayer, Augustin K., 177
Maxis, Terese, 190
McGowan, Jonas H., 152
McGraw, Thomas, 314

McKee, Alexander, Capt., 44
Mead, George Herbert, 166
Meader, Clarence Linton, 167
Medal of Honor, 142
Meier, Henry, 287
Meigs, Montgomery, 283
Meincke, Bruno, 181
Meiners, Rev. Herman, 178
Melchers, Gari, 216
Melchers, Julius Theodore, 218, 219
Meltzler, William Douglas, 171
Melze, August, 320
Menche, Alfred Herman, 173
Mendelsohn, Albert, 174
Mendelson, Louis, 290
Menninger, William, 46
Mensel, Ernest Heinrich, 231
Menter, John W., 143
Merendorff, S. Joseph, 272
Merian, Kasper, 19
Messersmith, George, 325
Metle, August, 320
Metz, Family, 70
Metzger, William E., 317
Metzler, Philip (Brother Junian), 188
Meuffels, Joseph, 176
Meyer, Prof., 338
Meyer, Augustine K., 178
Meyer, C. J. L., 325
Meyer, Lieut. Elias, 37
Meyer, John Jacob, 320
Meyers, Frederick, 116
Meyers, Henry, 103
Meyers, Jesse Jeemiah, 170
Meyers, Joseph, 105
Meyers, Michael, 119
Meyers, William J., 170
Michael, Louis, 26
Michael, William, 80
Michel, - 22
Michel, John, 170
Miege, Rt. Rev. J. B., 176
Miesel, Family
Miller, Albert, 92
Miller, Frederick, 103
Miller, George E., 295
Miller, Henry, 69
Miller, Henry, 113
Miller, Henry B., 295
Miller, John, 88

INDEX

Miller, John Peter, 86
Miller, Lewis, 96
Minnuet, Peter, 18
Miller, Peter, 70
Miller, Philip (Brother Jonas) 189
Millins, Anton, 70
Mittelberger, Gottleib, 20
Moehling, Family, 69
Moehlman, Arthur B., 235
Moeller, Father Henry, 176
Mogk, George F., 111
Mohn, Harrison B., 169
Moldenhenker, Dr. Richard Gottlieb, 173
Molitor, David Albert, 283
Molitor, Edward, 204, 282
Moll, Herman, 210
Monnig, Anthony, 324
Moore, Charles, 34
Moore, Joseph, 51
Moorman, Fr. Otto J., 178
Morell, George, 276
Moring, Frederick, 74
Morris George S., 155
Mueller, Frederich, 188
Mueller, Gustav, 288
Mueller, John B., 298
Mueller, H., 316
Muhlenberg, Heinrich, 23
Mulithner, John Balthasar, 87
Muller, Bernard (Brother Balddomer), 188
Muma, Fred, 80
Mumford, Frederick Blackmor, 235
Muntsch, Prof. Albert, 178
Murphy, William Walton, 59
Myer, Frank B., 181
Myers, Elijah W., 286
Nagel, Andrew, 316
Neberfeldt, William, 19
Neff Family, 70
Netsorg, Bendetson, 228
Netter, John, 88
Neuchterlein, H. G., 184
Neuman, Wm. F. V., 317
Neuman, Julia, 298
Newcome, Frederick C., 163
Newlander, Carl Edward, 170
Newmark, J. H., 317
Nichar, Geroge H., 108
Niswander, Frank J., 170

Noeker, John, 74
Noete, John, 49
Noll, Conrad, 143
Norris, Lyman D., 152
Novy, Frederick G., 159
Nussbaum, Rt. Rev. Paul J., 240
Nuffer, Frederick, 184
Obenauer, Mary Louise, 298
Oberdorffer, William J., 348
Obetz, Henry L., 157
Ochsenhert, Adam, 320
Odell, Anton, 325
Odren, Alexander, 81
Orth, Bros., 70
Ortman, Charles L., 311, 327, 355
Osius, George, 254
Otgen, Christian, 87
Otgen, Theobold, 87
Otten, Prof. John, 178
Otting, Rev. Prof. Bernard J., 177
Otting, Rev. Prof. Henry W., 178
Otto, Carl, 272
Ousterhaut, Cornelius, 91
Overholser, J., 181
Overmeyer, Calvin Jennings, 171
Overrocker, Adam, 103
Padberg, John B., 320
Pagenstecher, Felix, 313
Pangborn, William, 102
Parker, Walter R., 163
Parr, Philip (Brother Wilban), 189
Parsons, Philo, 168
Pastorius, Francis Daniel, 19
Pattengill, Albert H., 157
Patterson, George W., 163
Patterson, Richardson, 45
Pauli, Henry Carl, 37, 39
Pauling, William, 43
Paulus, Francis Petrus, 222
Peighthal, George, 37
Pelz, Henry, 188
Perrien, Dominick, 254
Perrien, Joseph, 320
Peter, William, 320
Peters, Charles, 94
Peterman, Albert Edward, 174
Petsch, Peter, 76
Pettee, William H., 156
Pfaff, John A., 320
Pfister, Guido, 325
Pheff, Michal, 311

INDEX

Phineas, Brother, 187
Pierz, Francis Xavier, 241
Pinten, Rt. Rev. Joseph Gabriel, 239
Pirmian, Brother, 18
Pitizel, John H., 248
Plank Family, 70
Plattenberg, Josephine Howard, 172
Plattner, Solomon, 81
Plessner, Michael C. T., 94, 268, 355
Plettel, 21
Pludderman, 88
Plumhoff, August, 95
Polasek, Alvin, 218
Porter, John Frederich, 151
Posner, August, 309
Potamian, Brother, 187
Presser, William, 70
Preuss, Prof. Francis A., 178
Printy von Buchan, John, 18
Prosser, Engins, 39
Prussia, Christian, 77
Prutzman, Abraham C., 169, 349
Publow, Henry Lantz, 171
Pulcher, Martin L., 317
Pulte, Anton, 70, 318
Pumpelly, Raphael, 200, 322
Purry, John Peter, 27
Puthoff, William H., 350
Quant, Jacob, 43, 46
Raddike, - 88
Rade, Conrad, 311
Rademacher, Rt. Rev. Henry Jos. 240, 338
Rademacher, Louise, 170
Radenhorst, Jacob Lieut., 47
Rahn, Otto, 170
Ramte, Paul, 50
Rafel, Wilhelm, 77
Randall, Robert, 45
Rangman, 43
Ransom, Epaphroditus, 56
Raseman, Richard E., 288
Rattenauer, Jacob, 103
Rauschert, Pastor, 184
Rebec, George, 164
Reichart, August, 181
Reichenbach, Henry, 69
Reid, William, 82
Reidler, H., 311

Reifschneider, 83
Reighard, Jacob E., 159
Reigle, David, 120
Reigle, Elias, 120
Reigle, John, 120
Reiker, George H., 181
Rein, Charles, 86
Rein, Wilhelmina, 86
Reinhert, Walter August, 171
Reitz, Charles, 311
Reitzel, Robert, 293
Rese, Rt. Rev. Frederick, 195, 238
Reutschler, John, 310
Rheinhard, Louis, 75
Richard, Rev., Gabriel, 286
Richman, Charles H., 114, 295
Richmond, Aroult, 309
Richter, Rt. Rev. Henry Joseph, 239
Richter, Theodore J., 275
Rickenbacker, Edward V., 317
Rieden, Frederick, 74
Rieden, Michael, 74
Riegel, Gustavus A., 93
Riesdorf, Benjamin, 114
Rigge, Rev. Joseph F., 178
Rinehart, Thos. F., 181
Roberts, Robert E., 67
Robertson, David, 45
Robertson, William, 45
Rockefeller, Johann Peter, 24
Rockefeller, John D., 24
Roden, John, 185
Rodenbeck, W. H., 320
Roebbelen, Karl Augustus,
Roemer, Prof. Charles, 178
Roeser, Otto, 94, 95, 275
Roesser, William, 93
Rogers, Faith Helen, 228
Rohnert, Morse, 275
Rohns, William C., 287
Rolapp, Henry Herman, 279
Roller, Ernest, 171
Rolshoven, Jules, 216, 221
Romeicke, Herman, 94
Rominger, Dr. Carl Ludwig, 190 272, 322
Rose, Charles B., 114
Rosing, Anton Scheel, 171
Rosenbaum, Simon, 329
Rosencrantz, Clarissa, 75

INDEX

Rosencrantz, Josiah, 105
Rosencrantz, Mortimer R., 106
Rosenfelds, the, 334
Rossman, Stephen, 82
Rosswinkel, J. Rheinhardt, 178
Rossy, Jacob, 43
Roth, Anthony, 49
Roth, Christian, 115
Roth, Filibert, 161, 204
Roth, Frederick George, 218
Roth, J. R., 295
Roth, William F., 111
Rothschild, Feist, 328
Rothschild, Kaufman, 328-9
Rothschild, Sigmund, 319, 328
Rublein, George, 97
Rudhart, George Jacob, 42
Rudolph, Dr. A. A., 323
Rudolph, Benjamin, 272
Ruehle, Fred, 70
Ruehle, Godfrey Leonard Alvin, 172
Ruehle, John V., 70, 71, 107, 114
Ruffing, Augustine J., 178
Ruland, Israel, 46
Ruland, William, 105
Rumple, Herman, 173
Runkle, George, 324
Ruoff, Augustus, 319
Rupp, Bernard H., 181
Ruppe, Peter, 320, 323
Russ, Valentine, 187
Sagendorph, Daniel P., 279
Sager, Abram, 154
Sahl, Joseph, 323
Salter, John Casper, 74
Sanderl, Father Simon, 241
Sanders, Fred, 314
Sanders, Henry Arthur, 166
Sanger, Joseph P., 111
Sateren, Martin Gerhard, 173
Sauber, W. F., 320
Sauer, Peter, 323
Saupert, Albert, 246
Schaaf, Anna Miss, 190
Schacht, William Henry, 173
Schacker, Rudolph, 93
Schade, Reverend M., 54
Schaeberle, John Martin, 206
Schaefer, Charles, 95
Schaeffer, A. H., 310
Schaeffer, Joseph, 241

Schaffner, John Henry, 234
Schafman, Rev. Henry A., 178
Schalch, F. A. (Capt.), 51
Schank, Charles, 86
Scharz, Peter, 316
Schauroth, Clemens, 204, 283
Schebosch, Missionary, 84
Scheele, Arnold, 171
Schefnicher, Joseph, 114
Schellenberger, Mary Etta, 172
Schellhaus, Lorenz, 78
Schenerman, Philip, 323
Schetky, Rev. George, D. D., 249
Schetterly, George, 340-341
Scheutz, John C., 116
Scheyrz, Henry, 75
Schick, John, 226
Schiefflein, Jonathan, 42, 43
Schifflein, Jacob, 43
Schill, Adolph, 116
Schilling, Frederick, 89
Schindler, Teresa, 363
Schlach, Frederic August (Lieut.) 47
Schlach, Leonard, 46
Schlatter, Michael, 23
Schlegelmilch, Christian, 340
Schleiermacher, Faithful, 152
Schlesingers, the, 334
Schlessinger, Ferdinand, 327
Schloectmeyer, Prof. Hugo F., 178
Schloss, Emmanuel, 333
Schloss, Seligman, 333
Schlosser, Ensign, 37
Schlosser, Peter J., 181
Schmedding, Jan, 203
Schmeman, Karl, 320
Schmid, Emanuel, 244
Schmid, Frederick (Pastor), 54, 89, 90, 91, 244
Schmidt, Anton Joseph, 188
Schmidt, Carl Eugene, 194, 312
Schmidt, Conrad, 83
Schmidt, C. K., 313
Schmidt, George, 78
Schmidt, Herbert William, 172
Schmidt, Louis Ernest, 234
Schmidt, Thomas, 49
Schmidt, Traugott, 304, 318
Schmidt, Walter K., 313
Schmitt, 327
Schmittdiel, John, 69

Schmittdiel, John S., 319
Schmorrenberger, Jacob, 39
Schnable, 78
Schnack, Peter, 76
Schnacker, Rudolph, 309
Schneckenburger, Joseph, 316
Schneider, Family, 70
Schneider, Francis Lee, 171
Schneider, Frederick, 112
Schneider, Matthias (Brother Gelinas), 189
Schnol, John J., 77
Schober, F. A., 310
Schoenemsgruber, John George,185
Schoenfield, 88
Scholl, John William, 162
Scholz, Ignatius, 219
Schontz, Homer Leroy, 233
Schott, Franz, 272
Schotterbeck, Julius O., 164
Schraeder, Fred, 80
Schrembs, Right Rev. Joseph, 239
Schremser, Emil, 227
Schriver, Frederick, 113
Schroeder, Edward, 272
Schroeder, George, 96
Schubert, George P., 173
Schuetz, Johann Adam, 184
Schulenberg, Charles, 310
Schull, Aaron G., 162
Schull, Charles A., 162
Schulte, Casper, 272, 316, 320
Schultz, Louis F., 225
Schumacher, 19
Schumacher, Nicholas, 96
Schunck, Peter, 43
Schuneman, 21
Schunk, 88
Schuppe, August, 320
Schurz, Carl, 88, 291
Schwab, John Heinrich, 246
Schwab, Leopold (Brother Alfred), 188
Schwarthout, Antony S., 91
Schwartz, (Pastor), 56
Schwartz, Jerome B., 324, 325
Schwartz, John E., 68, 104, 347
Schwartz, Rudolph, 219
Schwartz, William, 184
Scolla, Otto Rev., 241, 242
Scrimger, James, 104
Sebring, Rudolph, 82

Sederick, John, 94
Sedgeman, Theodore, 45
See, Gottfried, 86
Seefreid Family, (?) 70
Seegmiller, William A., 357
Seek, Conrad, 69
Seeker, Robert Rex, 173
Seelig, 19
Seib, Christian, 185
Seideff, 69
Seiffert, Rev. F. A., 364
Seiman, Henry, 97
Seitz, Fred, 69
Seitz, George F., 69
Seitz, John H., 69
Seligman, Jacob, 332, 333
Selkrig, Rev. James, 249
Sellings, the, 334
Semec, John, 356
Semmons, Cornelius, 91
Senninger, Nicholas, 310
Senter, M. D., 272
Sewall, Henry, 157
Seyffardt, William, 320
Shaler, Heinrich, 246
Shearer, James, 152
Shimberg, Lillian Ruth, 228
Shoemaker, Michael, 117, 119, 207
Shoemaker, Robert, 119
Showalter, Conrad, 42
Siebert, Jacob, 116
Siebring, Adam, 77
Sievers, Ferdinand, 183, 246, 339
Silver, Jacob, 347
Simon, John Solomon, 185
Simon, Philip, 95
Simon, Sigmund, 320
Simon, Sigmund, 333
Singelinger, Frederick, 169
Singer, Emil, 227
Skillbeck, Jacob, 78
Slinger, John, 74
Sloman, Adolph, 333
Sloman, Mark, 333
Smelzer, Nicholas, 93
Smeltzer, Arnold, 77
Smith, Henry, 77
Smith, Jacob, 78
Smulders, Rev. Egidius, 190
Snyder, G. W., 320
Sokey, Albert, 173
Soloman, Archibald, 308

INDEX

Solomons, Ezekiel, 43
Sommers, Jacob Sr., 85
Sonntag, William Louis, 217
Sorter, George, 103
Spackman, John, 104
Spalding, Volney M., 158
Spanggenburg, Bishop, 26
Speckhardt, Gottlieb, 254
Speich, Michael F., 176
Speicht, 69
Speil, Rudolph, 227
Spenkenberl, Rachel, 83
Spier, Frederick, 287
Spies, August, 253, 325
Spies, Augustus, 325
Spitzley, Henry, 288
Spottiswoode, Gov., 26
Spranger, Francis Xavier, 270
Sprann, Henry, 80
Stable, Fred, 320
Stadler, Anton, 69
Stahl, August (Brother Azedan) 189
Stahl, Jacob, 320
Stahl, Joseph, 325
Stammler, George Frankeier, 173
Stauber, Jacob, 316
Stauch, George Jacob, 85
Steck, George and Catherine, 76
Steeger, Edward, 272
Steffens, Albert (Brother Concordius), 188
Steiger, Andrew, 25
Stein, Carl, 25
Stein, Karl, 226
Steinback, John, 52, 68
Steinbrook, Samuel, 281
Steiner, Sergeant, 37, 80
Steiner, Royal Stewart, 172
Steinhauser, Philip, 181
Steininger, John W., 80
Steinmetz, Family, 69
Stephens, D. S., 181
Stern, Solomon, 356
Steuben, Baron, 42
Stevens, Alviso B., 165
Stevens, Harrison Albert, 228
Stevens, Marcus, 308
Stichler, George, 83
Stoepel, William C., 254
Stoll, Florence Amelia, 171
Strang, Gabriel, 342

Strang, James L., 341, 342
Streit, John, 68
Strelow, Albert, 316
Stricker, David, 70
Striker, Daniel, 279, 320
Stroh, Bernhardt, 310
Stroh, Julius, 319
Strohwaer, John, 78
Stronach, Joseph, 362
Strong, Philip G., 96
Struber, Ludwig, 309
Stubbs, Michael, 347
Stuch, J. F., 277
Stulle, Andreas, 195
Stumpenhausen, Henry, 91
Stutte, A., 224
Sunderland, Edson R., 164
Suppen, Solomon, 311
Sutter, Brother, 329
Swartz, Delbert, 172
Swegles, John Jr., 76, 347
Sweitzer, Martin, 74
Swensberg, Conrad G., 316
Syke, Peter, 142
Tenwinkle, Henry, 363
Terchners, the, 334
Terhorst, Gerhardt, 241
Thies, Wilbur Herman, 171
Thomas, Calvin, 158
Thoman, Frederick, 343
Thompson, Edward Hughes, 57
Thuener, Heinrich, 272
Thurtell, Henry, 170
Tietsort, August, 105
Timken, Henry, 317
Tisen, 19
Toll, Isaac De Graff, 108
Traut, Jacob, 83
Treigehen, William, 47
Tripp, Johannes, 80
Troester, John, 104
Troxler, Jacob, 51
Tunnecliffe, Dr. Joseph Sr., 263
Twachtman, John, 217
Uhl, Edwin F., 278
Ulman, John J., 105
Ulrich, Peter, 76
Unterkercher, George, 309
Uppleger, 88
Valentiner, Dr. W. R., 217
Van Armin, John, 105, 276
Van de Vanter, Eugene, 108

INDEX

Van de Walle, Jacob, 19
Van Gresen, John, 95
Van Steenberg, Cecile, 171
Van Tyne, Claude H., 163
Van Wagener, Ethel Philips, 171
Vedder, Prof. Herman Klock, 170
Veit, 25
Vertin, Right Rev. John, 240
Victorinus, Brother Imbert, 188
Vidior, Henry, 69
Virgil, Brother Herbert, 188
Viscoszky, Rev. Andrew, 95
Visgar, Jacobus, 44
Voelker, Paul Frederick, 234
Vogt, Joseph, 188
Vogt, William (Brother Besas Adolph), 189
Voigt, Edward W., 312
Voigt, Carl G. A., 315
Voigtlander, Walter, 225
Volkening, George L., 86
Volz, Christian, 183
Volz, Emil Conrad, 171
von Kocherthal, Joshua, 21
von Kraut, Max (Lt.), 113
von Platen, Godfrey, 316
von Schlegel, Arthur, 317
von Schon, Hans August Evald Conrad, 284
von Suchtelin, Franz Herman Hendrick, 171
von Tungeln, George Henry, 171
Vosburg, Bernard, 114
Voss, Ernest Carl Johannes, 231
Vrooman, Tunis, 77
Wachall, Martin, 116
Waechterhauser, Joseph, 70
Waechterhauser, Louis, 78
Wack, Pastor Caspar, 24
Wagener, Max, 170
Wagener, William, 362
Wagner, Anna, 91
Wagner, Edward, 219
Wagner, Frank Casper, 166
Wagner, J., 70
Wagner, Ralph B., 173
Wald, Adolph Nicholas, 173
Waldo, Jonathan, 28
Waldorf, Frederick, 355
Waldseemueller, Martin, 17
Walker, Edward L., 157
Waltensperger, Charles, 216

Walthausen, F. W., 272
Wampler, Joseph, 281
Wappenhans, Charles Frederick Robert, 210
Ward, Eber Brock, 87
Warthin, Aldred S., 162
Wass, George, 173
Wasserman, Casimir (Brother Hermenegild), 188
Watson, James C., 155
Watt, William Henry, 166
Waustinberg, Frederick, 130
Webber, Jacob, 115
Weber, George, 69
Weber, Henry, 304-309
Weber, Joseph F., 176
Weber, William C., 254
Wedemeyer, William W., 257
Wedthoff, Albert, 95
Weed, Charles K., 156
Wehner, Herman, 221
Weidner, Paul, 320
Weigand, 21
Weikamp, George B., 241
Weil, Charles L., 170
Weimer, Albert Carl, 172
Weimer, George E., 275
Weinert, Albert, 219
Weinman, Adolph Alexander, 218-219
Weirich, Peter, 363
Weiss, Gross, 74
Weiss, J. P., 310
Weissenhagen, John P., 179
Weitzel, Col. Godfrey, 202, 282
Weitzel, John, 69
Weld, Wm. F., 318
Welde, Carl, 224
Weller, Ferdinand, 78
Weller, Frederick, 291, 295
Weller, Joseph, 85
Weltz, Robert, 85
Welz, George, 121
Welz, Jacob, 121
Welz,, Philip, 121
Welz, Philip, 311
Welz, Dr. Walter, 168
Welz, Wilhelmina, 121
Wendt, Wylie Brodbeck, 170
Weninger, Francis Xavier, 142
Wentz, E. L., 93
Wentz, John, 75

INDEX

Wermers, Bernard J., 242
Wernar, Kiester, 95
Wertmuller, 19
Wesener, Hugo, 113
Weskowski, Ludwig, 86
Westrick, 88
Weyerhauser, Frederick, 312
Wheeler, Orlando B., 154
White, Alfred Holmes, 166
White, Andrew D., 155
Whitney, Allen S., 161
Whitney, Charles, 45
Wiethoff, Wilhelm, 298
Wilczewski, Rev., Joseph, 179
Wildman, C. D., 311
Williams, Arthur S., 181
Williams, Eugene, 337
Wiltberger, Percy Barnet, 171
Winterstein, Hermansan, John Christ, 183
Winegar, William, 115
Winkle, 88
Winkler, John Frederick, 184
Winkler, Max, 161
Winterhalter, Albert Gustavus, 207
Winterhalter, Michael, 70, 95, 108
Wirt, David, 249
Wise, Rabbi Isaac, 252
Witmer, Jacob, 188
Witner, Lorenz (Brother Elisian), 188
Wittenmeyer, John, 108
Wittlock, Ernest, 170
Wolf, Jacob, 116
Wolf, John, 86
Wollenwebber, Matthias, 120

Wonderlich, Nicholas, 87
Wood, James C., 157
Worpenberg, George, 178
Wramplemeier, Theodore John, 105
Wright, Frederick Eugene, 324
Wuertzner, Joseph, 310
Wunsch, Henry, 320
Wunsch, William Frederick, 234
Yax, John, 52
Yax or Yachs, Michael, 20-52
Yax, Pierre, 52
Yacks, Simon, 52
Yax, Peter, 68-85
Yeiser, Engelhardt, 25
Yeiter, Frederick, 96
Yerkes, Joseph, 75
Yerkes, William Purdy, 279
Yunck, Wilhelm, 225
Zanier, Augustus, 113
Zanelius, John George, 43
Zedler, Prof. John, 181, 233
Zeigler, John C., 308
Zeigler, Rev. Paul, 249
Zeisberger, 84
Zenger, John Peter, 23
Zermer, 88
Ziegle, Christ, 309
Zimmerman, Eugene, 305
Zimmerman, John F., 320
Zinzendorff, 24
Zirndorff, Heinrich Rabbi, 251
Zoellner, Frank, 112
Zolly, Felix (Lt.), 113
Zucker, Adolph Edward, 295
Zunderman, John, 116
Ziwet, Albert, 162

Other Heritage Books by Don Heinrich Tolzmann:

Amana: William Rufus Perkins' and Barthinius L. Wick's History of the Amana Society, or Community of True Inspiration

Americana Germanica: Paul Ben Baginsky's Bibliography of German Works Relating to America, 1493–1800

Biography of Baron Von Steuben, the Army of the American Revolution and Its Organizer: Rudolf Cronau's Biography of Baron von Steuben

CD: German-American Biographical Index (Midwest Families)

CD: Germans, Volume 2

CD: The German Colonial Era (four volumes)

Cincinnati's German Heritage

Covington's German Heritage

Custer: Frederick Whittaker's Complete Life of General George A. Custer, Major General of Volunteers, Brevet Major General U.S. Army and Lieutenant-Colonel Seventh U.S. Cavalry

Dayton's German Heritage: Karl Karstaedt's Golden Jubilee History of the German Pioneer Society of Dayton, Ohio

Early German-American Newspapers: Daniel Miller's History

German Americans in the Revolution

German Immigration to America: The First Wave

German Pioneer Life and Domestic Customs

German Pioneer Lifestyle

German Pioneers in Early California: Erwin G. Gudde's History

German-American Achievements: 400 Years of Contributions to America

German-Americana: A Bibliography

Germany and America, 1450–1700

Kentucky's German Pioneers: H. A. Rattermann's History

Lives and Exploits of the Daring Frank and Jesse James: Thaddeus Thorndike's Graphic and Realistic Description of Their Many Deeds of Unparalleled Daring in the Robbing of Banks and Railroad Trains

Louisiana's German Heritage: Louis Voss' Introductory History

Maryland's German Heritage: Daniel Wunderlich Nead's History

Memories of the Battle of New Ulm: Personal Accounts of the Sioux Uprising. L. A. Fritsche's History of Brown County, Minnesota (1916)

Michigan's German Heritage: John Andrew Russell's History of the German Influence in the Making of Michigan

Ohio's German Heritage

Outbreak and Massacre by the Dakota Indians in Minnesota in 1862: Marion P. Satterlee's Minute Account of the Outbreak, with Exact Locations, Names of All Victims, Prisoners at Camp Release, Refugees at Fort Ridgely, etc. Complete List of Indians Killed in Battle and Those Hung, and Those Pardoned at Rock Island, Iowa

The German Element in Virginia: Herrmann Schuricht's History

The German Immigrant in America

The Pennsylvania Germans: James Owen Knauss, Jr.'s Social History

The Pennsylvania Germans: Jesse Leonard Rosenberger's Sketch of Their History and Life